Unemployment and the state in Britain

MANCHESTER
1824
Manchester University Press

For my Mum and Dad,
and in memory of my grandparents

Unemployment and the state in Britain

The means test and protest in 1930s south Wales and north-east England

Stephanie Ward

Manchester University Press
Manchester and New York
distributed in the United States exclusively by Palgrave Macmillan

Published by Manchester University Press
Oxford Road, Manchester M13 9NR, UK
and Room 400, 175 Fifth Avenue, New York, NY 10010, USA
www.manchesteruniversitypress.co.uk

Distributed in the United States exclusively by
Palgrave Macmillan, 175 Fifth Avenue, New York,
NY 10010, USA

Distributed in Canada exclusively by
UBC Press, University of British Columbia, 2029 West Mall,
Vancouver, BC, Canada V6T 1Z2

British Library Cataloguing-in-Publication Data
A catalogue record for this book is available from the British Library

Library of Congress Cataloging-in-Publication Data applied for

ISBN 978 0 7190 86809 hardback

First published 2013

Typeset
by SPi Publisher Services, Pondicherry, India
Printed in Great Britain
by TJ International Ltd, Padstow

Contents

Figures and tables

Figures

Tables

Acknowledgements

This study began as a PhD which would not have been possible without a very gratefully received ESRC studentship. I was also very thankful for smaller grants from the Labour History Society and the Glamorgan County History Trust.

My first thanks must go to Steve Thompson who was a superb supervisor and an excellent source of encouragement and intellectual stimulation. The study owes much to him and to Neil Evans. Neil helped me unearth primary material and frame arguments in addition to helping in so many other ways. I owe both Steve and Neil a great debt. At Aberystwyth University, I was fortunate to work with a fantastic group of colleagues and friends. Paul O'Leary, Angela V. John, Phillipp Schofield, Martyn Powell, Awen Dafydd, Richard Coopey, Roger Price and Richard Rathbone deserve particular mention. As examiners, Malcolm Chase and Sian Nicholas provided excellent feedback, which has certainly helped shape the final piece.

Since moving to Cardiff University, I have found myself in the privileged position of working alongside some brilliant and supportive colleagues. While it doesn't seem fair to single some out, I really should pay particular thanks to Bill Jones, Tracey Loughran and Kevin Passmore. Thank you also to Ian Dennis for drawing my maps.

While completing my research, Matt Perry was a great source of advice and with Matthias Reiss organised some perfectly timed conferences on unemployment. Matt also put me in touch with Stuart Howard who arranged for me to have access to see the files of the Durham Miners' Association. Seeing those files really strengthened this study, and I am grateful to the National Union of Mineworkers for granting me access.

Archivists and librarians in Wales and England have helped immensely. My thanks extend to the staff at the National Library of Wales (especially Ewan, Jayne and Rhydian), the South Wales Coalfield Collection, the South Wales Miners' Library, Glamorgan Archives, Durham Record Office, the Labour History Archives, Tyne and Wear Archive Services and the National Archives. I would also like to thank the superb staff at Manchester University Press.

The support of friends and family has been invaluable, and it is impossible to thank everyone. Although fearful of leaving someone out, I want the following people to know how much their support has meant. Thank you Tracey Cooper, Owen Collins, Eleanor Mithan, Vicki Price, Elspeth Harris, Clare Aldridge, Laura Routley, Sylvia Lechner, Tuncay Kardas, Zara Grey, Rhiannon Thomas and Leah Kirkaldie. Phillip and Josephine Eggerton, Doreen Morris, and Dave and Joyce Summers have shown kindness and constant encouragement throughout.

My brother Chris and his wife Jo are perhaps unaware of how much they help and support me. They deserve more than a mention here. Living with someone who is writing a book isn't always easy, but Matthew Eggerton takes this all in his stride. I'm forever grateful our paths crossed and for the love, support and humour he brings every day. Thank you.

My Mum and Dad are the kindest and most generous of people, and they have gone far beyond parental duty in the support that they have given. I don't know what I would have done without them. As a small token of my gratitude, I dedicate this book to them, with love and respect, and to the memory of my grandparents whose stories helped inspire this project.

Abbreviations

CLC	Central Labour College
DMA	Durham Miners' Association
DMOR	Durham Area Miners' Office, Redhills
DRO	Durham Record Office
GAC	Glamorgan Archives, Cardiff
GRO	Gwent Record Office
ILO	International Labour Office
ILP	Independent Labour Party
LHASC	Labour History Archive and Study Centre
MFGB	Miners' Federation of Great Britain
NAC	National Administrative Council (National Unemployed Workers' Movement)
NAW	Northumberland Archives, Woodhorn
NMMCA	Northumberland Miners' Mutual Confident Association
NUWCM	National Unemployed Workers' Committee Movement
NUWM	National Unemployed Workers' Movement
PAC	Public Assistance Committee
SWCC	South Wales Coalfield Collection
SWMF	South Wales Miners' Federation
SWMIU	South Wales Miners' Industrial Union
SWML	South Wales Miners' Library
TNA	The National Archives
TUC	Trades Union Congress
TWAS	Tyne and Wear Archive Services
UAB	Unemployment Assistance Board

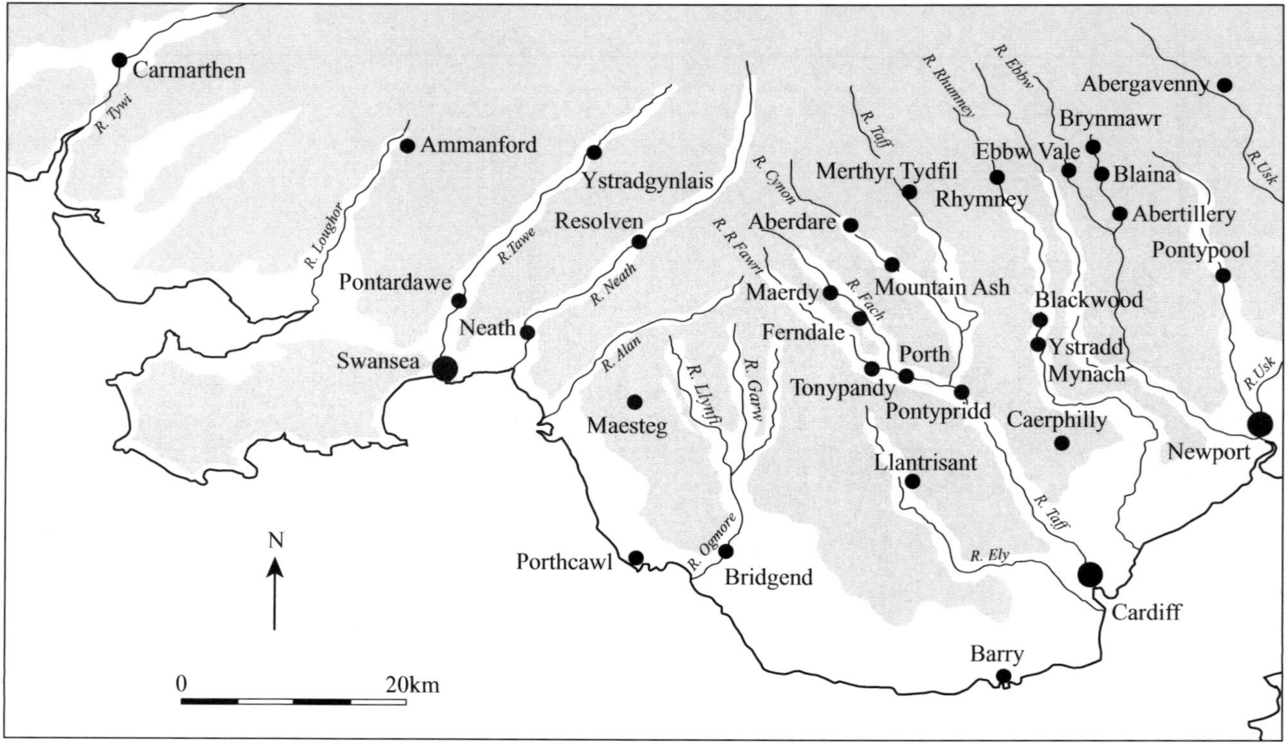

Map of south Wales

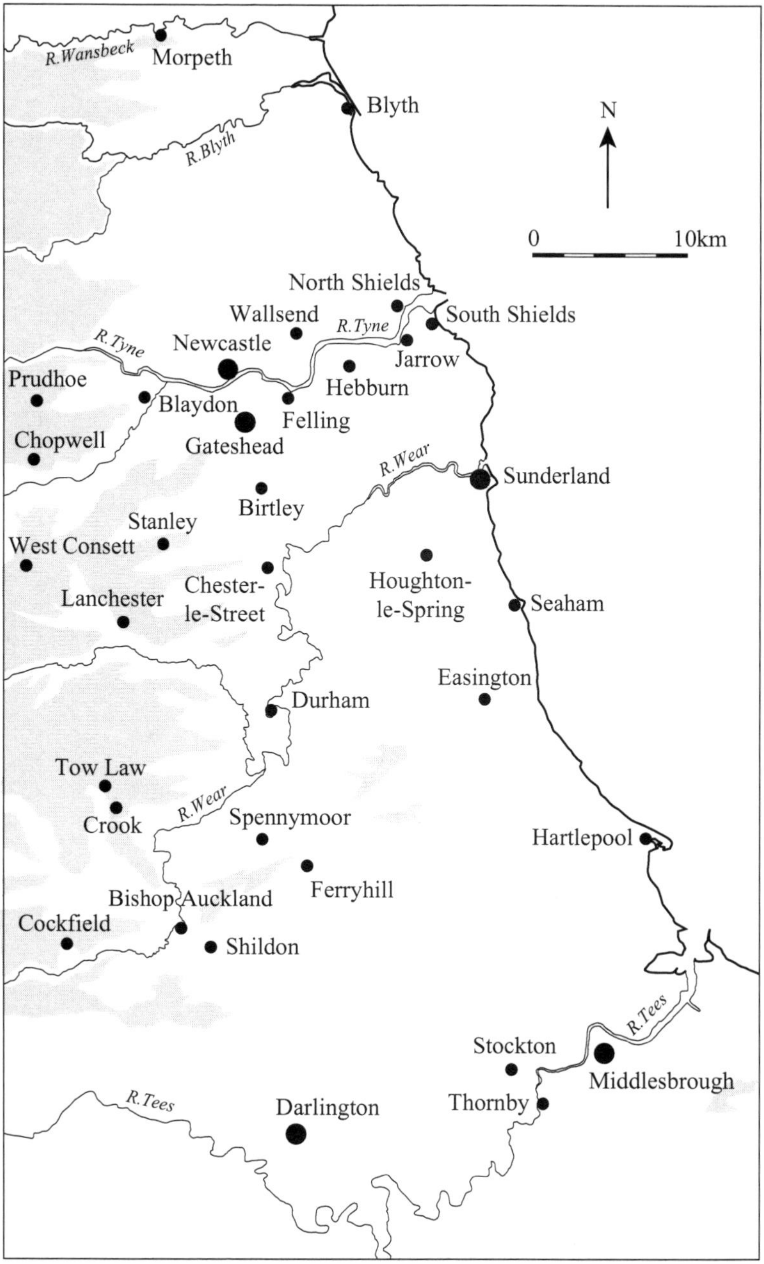

Map of north-east England

Introduction

The Means Test lives in memory,
A scar upon their soul.
The land they'd fought for heroes to live in
Had put them on the Dole.[1]

In the closing weeks of 2011, the head of the International Monetary Fund Christine Lagarde warned in a speech at Washington D.C. that the world economy risked 'sliding into a 1930s-style slump'.[2] This was not the first time comparisons to the Great Depression had been drawn upon since the recession of the early twenty-first century began in 2007. The 1930s – while providing an economic yardstick for politicians, economists and journalists – also revealed its still powerful cultural imagery as a time of hardship, poverty and want. As in the 1980s, the idea of a return to the 1930s has been something to dread even if the decade is now beyond the living memory of most. Revisionist historians may have revealed that living conditions and income improved for the majority, yet the popular image of the 'devil's decade' persists. The purpose of this book is to explore one aspect of the decade which helped create this image and memory of the 1930s.

If the depression of the 1930s cast its shadow over the history of interwar Britain, then it was the means test that was often the focus of public and private debates about it. The use of a household means test for the long-term unemployed was the most debated aspect of social policy with opposition to the measure from across the political spectrum. Protest against the means test was responsible for the largest examples of collective action in the period; some argued that such a scale of opposition had not been seen since the days of Chartism.[3] Contemporaries believed the test attacked the bonds of working-class families, forced girls into prostitution and starved mothers and their children. Such a perception of the means test and its place in working-class literature secured its legacy in popular memories and political culture as a potent symbol of government failure, hardship and suffering.[4] This image lingered long after the 1930s. It influenced debates about the post-war welfare programme, and even in the twenty-first century, the memory of the means test still has the ability to inform political debate.[5] In many respects, the means test has become as representative of the worst effects of the interwar depression as the powerful imagery of soup kitchens, dole queues and men standing idle on street corners. However, although no serious study of the depression would fail to mention the means test, as yet, a detailed investigation of its impact and the response of the unemployed has not been undertaken. This study attempts to redress this balance by comparing the impact of the means test in two regions most affected by the economic crisis, south Wales and the north-east of England.

No study of the interwar years can begin without reference to the largely polarised historiographical viewpoints of the period and the idea of the myth of the 1930s. As Juliet Gardiner noted in her 'intimate history', 'the thirties is a statement as well as a decade.'[6] The attempt to question the 'myth' of the 1930s as a period of extreme politics and unrelenting hardship owes much to the revisionist history *The Slump* by John Stevenson and Chris Cook. Although not the first to question the characterisation of the decade, *The Slump* stands out as furthering debates about how historians should approach this period. Stevenson and Cook argued that the view of the 1930s as a period of mass unemployment and radical politics was largely invented by politicians and writers from the Left to help celebrate the creation of the welfare state and social democracy of the post-war period.[7] This approach remains popular. Martin Pugh in his 2008 study, tellingly entitled *We Danced All Night*, noted 'the British Left … scored a belated victory in writing the history of the interwar period as one of poverty, failure and reaction.'[8] The idea after the Second World War of 'no return to the 1930s' and of 'guilty men' was indeed politically influential, and revisionist historians were able to point to rising living standards, the growth of the new industries and improvements in health to rebuke the imagery of hunger marches and dole queues. In *Narrating the Thirties*, John Baxendale and Christopher Pawling set out to examine the 1930s as a 'cultural construct' which is 'produced not just from the mentality of a particular era, but within specific patterns of social and cultural relations.'[9] Indeed, James Vernon in his cultural history of hunger maintains 'that remembering that harrowing decade still remains central to the program of British social democracy.'[10]

The rise of mass unemployment in the 1980s and the social policy pursued by the Thatcher governments begin to explain why some historians were so keen to challenge revisionist accounts. Yet, it is not only a desire to further a certain invention of political culture that has led historians to discredit the revisionist thesis. The work of Matt Perry clearly demonstrates that the experience of the 1930s was not erected along with the National Health Service after the Second World War. Perry challenges the 'liberal and conservative consensus' of revisionist accounts and particularly the role of social movements by examining in detail the experience and imagery of the unemployed.[11] While the 'hungry thirties' may in part have been created or invented, the image of an economically depressed period was more than a myth to cement the value of social democracy. There was a cultural significance, both politically and socially, to the view of the 1930s as depressed and one which existed amongst contemporaries beyond writers and social commentators.

The fear of unemployment and poverty was pervasive, and the organisation and protest of the unemployed had important reverberations for the relationship between citizens and the state, the working class and the government. The impact of the depression was largely regional, and this is a crucial point. If we can argue that there are two experiences or images of working-class life in this period, then what perhaps reconciles them, if indeed we need to, is the shadow of economic crisis. As Richard Overy has argued, for many this was a 'morbid age'.[12] Millions of people out of work, mass protests, royal tours of the depressed regions and a depressed economy that lasted well beyond predictions of a temporary cyclical downturn must have influenced outlook and culture even as living standards rose. The experience of the means test in the 1930s and its perception and portrayal did much to fix a particular popular memory of this period which was equally as pervasive as that born from the post-war Left.

This study primarily focuses upon the experience of the unemployed and their relationship with those in positions of authority including the government, local authorities and the police. The nature and administration of the means test provides a fascinating insight in this respect and considerably adds to our understanding of the framing of social policy, the identity and voice of the out of work and the impact of collective action. An analysis of the unemployed in the 1930s contributes to the growing history of unemployment with studies of protest burgeoning in particular.[13] How the identity of working-class men and women was affected by long-term unemployment and how the unemployed could form their own peculiar identity are an integral part of this work.

In November 1931, as part of the National Government's retrenchment, a household means test was introduced for the first time for all long-term unemployed insured, or previously insured, applicants. While a means test had been administered in the 1920s, its scope was limited; a full household means test for the unemployed had previously only been used for poor relief and then public assistance applicants.[14] The controversy surrounding it had much to do with the very nature of a household means test and its administration. Until 1935, Public Assistance Committees (PACs) were given responsibility for administering the means test and determining scales of benefit. Local councillors grappled with their consciences and parties over whether to implement the means test or not, and disparities arose in the payments made in different areas. In the early 1930s, the Ministries of Labour and Health investigated and threatened to remove local authority control for councils across Britain; Durham and Rotherham PACs were eventually replaced by government commissioners. The government's attempts to stop recalcitrant councillors susceptible to local influence by establishing the autonomous Unemployment Assistance Board (UAB) played a key role in the increasingly centralised machinery of welfare. Yet, despite the importance of the relationship between the unemployed and the authorities that this episode reveals, it has formed a minor part of the historiography.[15] How strictly PAC officials implemented the means test could have an effect upon household standards and the response from the unemployed and is therefore vital to an understanding of such issues. Moreover, it helps to demonstrate the importance of local factors to studies of the unemployed suggesting that those out of work did not form a homogeneous group with a shared common experience.

Although the means test dominated many of the social and political debates on unemployment in the 1930s, the historiography has largely not reflected this trend. The means test has principally been discussed as an example of the hardship that the unemployed faced and as a cause of agitation.[16] The latter in particular has drawn much attention, but, in line with the general historiography of the unemployed, it is the activities of the National Unemployed Workers' Movement (NUWM) that most historians have focused upon. The hunger marches and key upsurges of protests associated with the NUWM have become synonymous with the response of the unemployed to the means test. The work of Peter Kingsford, Richard Croucher and, more recently, Richard Flanagan, Matt Perry and Matthias Reiss have demonstrated how the campaign against the means test was adopted by the movement as its chief cause.[17] While these historians have bettered our understanding of the general effects of the means test and how the unemployed were mobilised for action, the response to the test has ultimately been limited to key episodes of action and to the activities of only one movement. The mobilisation of the unemployed for collective action throughout the period and just why the means test provoked such bitterness remain unexplored. As Flanagan has noted, it was the means test more than any other measure that provoked outcry: to focus on the response to the test will allow a greater understanding of how protest was made by a group who have traditionally been characterised as apathetic.[18]

The comparative methodology provides a distinct advantage for the historian of the unemployed and of protest movements. By emphasising the importance of political culture and place, a comparative analysis challenges the assumptions of contemporary sociologists, and later revisionist historians, that the long-term unemployed were a uniform and largely impassive group. The comparative case study of south Wales and the north-east of England allows for a detailed analysis of the influence of political and industrial traditions, as well as wider society, upon both the development of protest movements and how the means test was administered. It will be shown not just how but why the unemployed protested against the means test in certain regions. Comparison prevents crude stereotypes being formed. Moreover, by comparing the two regions assumed particularities in either case can be proven or, conversely, shown to have been a shared experience. As Stefan Berger has argued, 'no other historical method is so adept at testing, modifying and falsifying historical explanation than comparison.... It allows historians to gain a vantage point outside the particular regional or national history, and makes history a less provincial undertaking'.[19]

Explaining levels of radicalism and expressions of protest is not the only value of comparing south Wales and the north-east of England. If studies of the interwar period are to move away from the implicit notion that the unemployed were a homogeneous group, then comparative regional histories are needed to convey how long-term unemployment was experienced in different areas. This study, through the comparative method, suggests that the identity and the experience of the unemployed require much greater attention within the historiography. Such an exploration will begin to demonstrate the nature of the relationship between the government and the working class and the importance of public and private spheres in the framing of social policy and its consequences.

Although very profitable, the comparative method should be utilised cautiously. As Berger has noted, not enough comparative histories are being written, and this is principally because of the pitfalls associated with the methodology.[20] Failure to carry out detailed primary research, a lack of understanding of the historiography or distorted comparisons, most often asymmetrical, can undermine the value of the method. For those who argue that comparison seeks to only promote the exceptionalism of a particular case study (most often a nation), exploring trends across states, 'entangled' or transnational histories, has proved more fruitful.[21] The pitfalls associated with the comparison do not make writing comparative histories an impossibility and can be overcome with care.[22] In particular, it is essential for the comparative historian to carefully define the two, or indeed more, comparators. If like is to be compared with like, it is imperative that a similar area/region/case is identified so that false conclusions are not drawn. The regional comparative historian needs to be mindful that regions form part of wider state and international communities.

Regions are not stable geographical entities, and any boundaries that are designated are artificial.[23] The borders of a region can be determined by administrative boundaries, industry and economics, politics, levels of urbanisation or the presence or certain linguistic, class or ethnic groups. At another level, regions are ideological constructions and identity becomes important in initiating borders. Edward Royle has concluded that 'region historically ... is not a fixed concept but a feeling, a sentimental attachment to territory shared by like-minded people.... It is an imagined community no less than the nation is'.[24] Regions are, therefore, simultaneously economic expressions, a geographical area of a country and a place with which individuals identify culturally. Comparing regions complicates the definition as the borders of the areas being compared are largely determined by the theoretical questions posed as William Sewell has identified.[25] These definitions cannot be separated from wider understandings of a region, and comparative studies perhaps work best when regions are understood as being multidimensional with borders that are fluid and permeable.

South Wales and the north-east of England have often been compared. As two major export regions whose economies were dominated by the extraction and production of coal, iron and steel, parallels have frequently been drawn.[26] This 'basic similarity' has meant that the two regions almost lend themselves to comparison in studies of industrialisation and of mining in particular.[27] However, it is the key difference between the two regions in the levels of militancy and radicalism that has most attracted the attention of comparativists.[28] While striking similarities existed at a basic industrial and economic level, in levels of militancy in the late nineteenth and early twentieth centuries, the regions stood at opposite ends of the spectrum of protest: south Wales gained a reputation for trade union militancy and a propensity to strike that the workforce in the north-east never came close to challenging. While both regions were sympathetic towards dissenting religion, Liberal politics and trade unionism and, by the interwar period, were strongholds for the Labour Party, in south Wales, militancy and radicalism characterised many of these developments. Why such different traditions emerged has much to do with the process of industrialisation and urbanisation, topographical factors, gender and class identities and the culture of both regions.

Martin Daunton, Neil Evans and Stefan Berger have all shown the importance of examining the longer industrial traditions and political culture of a region to explain the nature of the labour movement and patterns of militancy within a comparative study.[29] Such an analysis contributes to a wider critique of the 'radical miner' and demonstrates that structural factors and social conditions are essential to explaining the emergence of radicalism within a population.[30] Proponents of resource mobilisation theory in studies of unemployed protests have equally shown the importance of a consideration of industrial factors and political culture.[31]

Although, as Neil Evans has noted, different patterns in industrialisation 'cannot explain all differences, such as they were, between south Wales and the north-east of England', they do help to explain a number of key factors.[32] Indeed, the process of industrialisation and the formation of the working class were fundamental to the nature of working relations, settlement patterns, community development and the political culture of a region.[33] Broad parallels can be drawn in the process of industrialisation in south Wales and the north-east, but significantly the timing and pace of industrialisation were quite different. Principally, a much longer tradition of industry existed in the north-east, and it 'was the pioneer of the coal trade, and of industrial society in Britain'.[34] When major industrial expansion began in the later eighteenth century, a foundation of industry already existed from as far back as the seventeenth century which could be developed.[35] In south Wales, by contrast, industry had only existed from the late eighteenth century, the coalfield was only really a recognisable entity from the 1870s, and it continued to expand at a rapid rate right up until the First World War.[36] These differences are shown quite clearly in the population levels in Glamorgan and Durham; while Durham's sharpest decennial increase in population occurred between 1861 and 1871, it was not until at least after 1881, and particularly after 1901, that the same steep increase materialised in Glamorgan and Monmouthshire.[37]

In the north-east, the longer tradition of industry led to a greater connection with forms of labour organisation more closely related to agricultural than industrial practices including the yearly bond and the provision of company housing. Coal owners adopted a more paternalistic role, and even when the management of a mine passed into the hands of capitalists, paternalistic practices continued throughout the expansion of the coal industry.[38] These peculiarities in the Durham and Northumberland coalfields were compounded by the structure of work which favoured the cavilling system and a three-shift work pattern.[39] By choosing lots to determine a workplace, the cavilling system prevented victimisation and gave the miners greater autonomy. Hewers chose their workmate for a stall (known as marras), and they often came from the same family creating a clear generational career path. All boys would enter the pit as haulage workers, progressing to the position of putting at around sixteen to eighteen years and then finally to hewer.[40] The independence and autonomy of the miners meant that grievances were often resolved within the workforce which limited antagonism between employers and employees.

The later formation of the coalfield in south Wales left the industry in much of the region largely free from the constraints of agricultural practices and paternalism.[41] Colliery owners and their companies influenced coalfield society for over a century. This situation was exaggerated by the formation of large combines.[42] Indeed, the authors of the 1917 *Commission of the Enquiry into Industrial Unrest* argued that 'this tendency towards monopoly has aroused considerable alarm in the minds of miners, and many regard the combine movement as being directed towards their industrial subjugation'.[43] The owners were often detached from their workforce, and salaried managers were responsible for 'dealing with labour and restraining wage costs on a day to day basis'.[44] Work practices in south Wales because of the longwall mining system were far more individualistic, and there was no generational employment progression. Each hewer had greater responsibility for his workplace and earnings, but lacked the independence of the north-eastern miner. In south Wales, miners came into far greater contact with managers on a daily basis to negotiate both their place of work and their pay than in the north-east.[45] Antagonism between the workforce and employers was, therefore, much more probable: this was to have important consequences for levels of militancy and the political culture that it encouraged.

In south Wales, the different tenure patterns meant the influence of companies did not extend beyond the workplace into communities.[46]

The coal seams lay underneath the huge valleys which dominated the landscape and gave south Wales a unique topography (see Map of south Wales), the effects of which remain a matter of debate amongst historians and sociologists alike.[47] The pattern of settlement created a market where speculative housing made economic sense.[48] In comparison to most other industrial areas, the respectable worker in south Wales aimed to purchase their own home once married.[49]

While the effect of home ownership has traditionally been thought to have had a stabilising effect on the working class, Steven Thompson has revealed how this was not always the case. He concludes, 'the political militancy of trade unionists, and trade union leaders, in south Wales might have been at odds with the political conservatism of home-owners and it is possible that these two very different political attitudes coexisted within Welsh communities'.[50] In the north-east, the company ownership of houses was thought to have a stabilising effect, and this assertion has yet to be disputed.[51] However, settlement patterns were also important for other reasons. While many historians may have emphasised the isolation of one valley from the other,[52] within each valley communication was much easier than in the more fragmented settlement pattern in most of Durham and Northumberland.[53] The valleys provided an important arena for protest during the years before the First World War and especially in the 1930s. During the anti-means test demonstrations, the protestors were able to march up and down valleys to express opposition in a way that was not possible outside the Tyneside area in the north-east. Housing along the Tyne was in many ways more similar to patterns in south Wales than the rest of the region. Homes were rarely provided by companies, and workers would either rent or enter into a building club scheme.[54] The topography and industry of the Tyne led to a pattern of development where one industrial settlement merged into another with similar consequences.

The geology of the coal seams and the topography of the north-east region meant that, aside from settlement along the Tyne, 'the settlement pattern was generally one of dispersed self-contained villages'.[55] The importance of this point is often overlooked by historians despite the consequences of such topography. Although urban in character, pit villages in Durham and Northumberland remained somewhat isolated and surrounded by an essentially rural agricultural landscape which played an important part in community life.[56] The isolation of villages from each other hindered communication that could have allowed for more unified labour and protest movements.

The similarities between the two regions were more apparent in social structure. In the pit villages of south Wales and the north-east, the working class dominated. The middle class only made up a small proportion of the population, and teachers, doctors and shopkeepers primarily existed to serve the working class. The Methodist minister R. J. Barker commented of the Rhondda Valleys, 'the Rhondda is narrower than a one-class community, it is almost entirely a one-trade community: even the teachers are in the main sons and daughters of Rhondda miners'.[57] In the north-east, this was also true of larger towns. Unlike the major urban centres in south Wales, Newcastle remained much more part of the wider industrial landscape even though it had a stronger middle-class presence than the neighbouring towns.[58] The domination of the working class meant that the overwhelming majority of the population were therefore reliant on the fortunes of one or two of the staple industries. Eli Ginzberg believed that such a settlement had 'contributed greatly to solidifying the community'.[59] It also had negative repercussions, and when adversity such as a strike or industrial depression struck, an entire village could be affected.

Where mines, steel and iron foundries, and docklands dominated, job opportunities for women were limited. Women's marginal position as formal wage earners was compounded by an ideology of domesticity: a married woman's place was viewed as being in the home, focused upon caring for her husband and family.[60] Girls usually undertook some employment until marriage, such as domestic service, but often remained in the home assisting mothers with domestic duties.[61] Once married, women were expected to end paid work and concentrate upon domestic chores and raising a family. As Sue Bruley has asserted, 'there was a high degree of sexual segregation, and gender boundaries were rigidly enforced' within coalfield communities.[62] Women spent most, but not all, of their time within the home or socialising with other women, and men at work or socialising with other men.[63] Although women until the inter-war period had little power within the public political world, they should not be thought of as entirely powerless, and, as Valerie Gordon Hall has demonstrated, there 'was no uniform category of "woman"'.[64] Rosemary Jones's conclusions of the south Wales coalfield can be applied also to the north-east of England: 'it needs to be emphasised … that although most women exercised no formal power within the "public" arena, this did not preclude participation within wider neighbourhood affairs. Despite the constraints of "separate spheres," there was considerable scope for female agency, both in shaping their own lives and those of immediate family and neighbors'.[65]

The construction of masculinity for working-class men in south Wales and the north-east within this highly masculine culture was achieved through the progression of key stages within the life cycle. The first step towards manhood was to leave school and secure work in order to gain the fundamental independence that underlined masculine identity. Valerie Gordon Hall's view of 'an exaggerated masculine identity' was 'based upon the ability to earn a household wage and cope, without fear, with a dangerous and onerous job'.[66] In the next stage in the life cycle, young men were expected to take their independence a step further and act as a provider for their own family by marrying and having children. It was, according to John Tosh, from the late nineteenth century that becoming the family's breadwinner became 'the goal of the better paid worker'.[67] In both regions, masculinity was displayed through hard work/labour, physical strength and becoming the head of a family.[68] Inevitably, periods of strike or unemployment could affect the ability of a man to display and construct his own masculine identity.

The segregation of the sexes demonstrates the importance of defining communities in both regions as being multidimensional. In south Wales and the north-east, community was symbolic and embodied an individual's attachment to a place and membership to a number of interlinked networks operative within that given locality. Anthony Cohen has shown the importance of seeing community as an ideological construction; 'the quintessential referent of community is that its members make, or believe they make, a similar sense of things either generally or with respect to specific and significant interests, and further, that they think that that sense may differ from one made elsewhere'.[69] Networks existed between men within a workplace, men who socialised together outside of work, women who lived close to each other, nuclear and extended families, streets and entire villages.[70] No network was exclusive and membership frequently crossed over.

The strength of community in uniting or unifying people was dependent upon a number of shared common factors. If work and family were central to working-class culture and community, so too was religion until at least the First World War. Further parallels can be drawn between the two regions in the popular appeal of Nonconformity, but there were again important caveats. In the north-east, while many community leaders of the nineteenth century emerged from the Primitive Methodists, historians have suggested that faith was not as central to the workers in the north-east as it was in south Wales. The primary importance of religion appears to have been the social code it created and the leadership it provided when the more formal organisation of the workforce began.[71] In south Wales, the power of Nonconformity was only gradually displaced by the growth of socialism. The significance of the initial religious fervour and the religious revival of 1904–05 lay not in its lasting impact but in what it indicated. The revival was symptomatic of the infancy of the communities, 'a frontier sport ... expressive of the bewilderment people felt in this period'.[72]

In working-class, mono-industrial villages with a culture dominated by a particular occupation and gender which had shared social values (i.e. religious, political, moral), community cohesion was much greater.[73] Such communities existed within south Wales and the north-east, and central to the lives of the majority was the ability to work and the importance of family.[74] Historians and sociologists have long considered whether such characteristics had a wider or exaggerated significance within the coalfields and if there was a separateness of mining communities from wider society which encouraged strike action.[75] Although generalisations can be made for accepted or shared values within communities in south Wales and the north-east, a consideration of such factors in fact undermines Kerr and Siegel's hypothesis that in mining communities there existed an 'homogenous, undifferentiated' isolated mass.[76] It is difficult to sustain an argument that the miners were separated from wider trends in British culture. As Church and Outram have demonstrated, while some aspects of the isolated mass thesis help explain strike levels, 'massed isolation appears to have "facilitated" strike activity ... but did not ensure such activity'. As the comparison here suggests, Church and Outram's careful attention to employer relations and isolation from management begins to explain differences within British coalfields, as does the nature of industrial relations.[77] Structural and external forces must be further considered.

The longevity of industry in the north-east brought with it a longer tradition of trade unionism than anywhere else in Britain.[78] In Durham and Northumberland, attempts had been made to organise the miners since the beginning of nineteenth century, and an earlier tradition of organisation along Tyneside was drawn upon in this period.[79] The most important miners' unions emerged in the 1860s with the formation of the Northumberland Miners' Mutual Confident Association (NMMCA) in 1864 and Durham Miners' Association (DMA) in 1869. After an initial collapse, there was no further attempt to establish a coalfield or regional trade union. Likewise, shipbuilders, maritime engineers and steel and iron workers were not organised regionally and were represented by numerous trade unions; there was not even a county-wide organisation for their occupation.[80] The north-east working class was, nonetheless, extremely well organised, and the DMA was amongst the first trade unions to appoint full-time paid officials.[81]

Although diverse, one feature that united many of the trade unions was a policy of conciliation and an objection to strikes. The NMMCA pursued a policy of no strike action, and Austrin and Beynon have noted that during the formative years of the DMA 'in relating to the employers ... the overwhelming concern was an accommodating one, stressing conciliation and arbitration and opposing strike action'.[82] Likewise, the Boilermakers and Iron Shipbuilders Society adopted a policy of aversion to industrial action and 'the union on many occasion stopped strikes'.[83] Although there was an obvious need to pursue such a policy so that unions could win the recognition of employers, for certain unions a preference for conciliation and good relations between the union and management had an enduring relevance.[84] Union leaders, often Primitive Methodists with a repugnance for strike action, were not looked to for leadership for an immediate battle but rather as a long-term presence of support.[85] In both legal and political matters, unions offered assistance and backing; the DMA had an appointed legal representative from its early days, and by 1874 the miners in the north-east were returning parliamentary candidates.[86]

An aversion towards militancy persisted into the twentieth century, and one of the main reasons for the DMA's reluctance to join the Miners' Federation of Great Britain (MFGB) was 'the distaste of the North-East leadership for the seeming militancy of the national union'.[87] Also important was the 'regional and elitist' attitudes of the DMA and the NMMCA which favoured separatism from nationwide unions to maintain regional privileges.[88] It was not until 1907 that both unions joined the MFGB, and even after affiliation to the Labour Party, it is apparent that many remained Liberals at heart. There was certainly no desire for a more radical agenda from Labour leaders.[89] Although David Douglass has written quite scathingly of the policy of 'arbitration and conciliation', there is little evidence to suggest that the miners in the north-east ever seriously challenged the leadership of the DMA or the NMMCA.[90] Radicalism was confined to a minority, and importantly it was mainly in those areas where newer pits were sunk and where a longer tradition of industrialism and organisation did not exist, as Valerie Gordon Hall has demonstrated in Northumberland.[91]

Dick Geary has raised the important point that in Britain conflict in the mining industries often occurred because mine owners were sensitive to wage levels as they made up such a large proportion of total costs.[92] In the north-east, the hangover of paternalistic practices and the cavil and marra system prevented many more strikes occurring because of the labour relations this gave rise to. In practice, the need for industrial action and for union intervention was largely removed, and so the NMMCA's and DMA's desire for limited strike action was borne out. This situation, and the emergence of the trade unions as a response to the organisation of the mine owners, had a profound effect on the labour movement throughout the north-east region: it did not create a situation where radical politics emerged in such an explosive fashion as in south Wales.

In south Wales, structural factors in the production of coal created a situation where antagonism between management and miners was more probable. Up until the First World War, wages generally accounted for 70% of production costs and were therefore 'a matter of crucial concern for all coalowners'.[93] The industry's overwhelming reliance on an overseas market compounded the situation.[94] By the late 1880s as an economic depression affected the minimum level of wages, the practice of a sliding scale adopted in the 1870s became deeply unpopular. John Williams has concluded that the 'resultant antagonism between owners and men was not the product of the personal characteristics on either side ... it was embedded in the economic realities which made labour-cost the most important consideration for everybody and thus continually underlined the inherent conflict of interest between owners and miners'.[95]

The image of militancy, because of the volume of industrial conflict, was not therefore an inherent characteristic of mineworkers as Geary and Williams have shown. Neither, in the case of south Wales, was it what Ramsay MacDonald saw as the 'racial temperament of the Welsh'.[96] Rather, the number of strikes and stoppages was, in part at least, the consequence of the structural nature of an industry based on an overseas market and of the desire of the coal owners to keep costs down.[97] The coal owner David Evans demonstrated how the constant negotiations over pay and for working in 'abnormal' places in particular led to 'friction' between managers and workers.[98] The higher accident rate in south Wales than elsewhere in Britain accentuated the sense of bitterness over wages as Julie Light has noted.[99] Without a tradition of organisation, antagonism between employers and workers was not readily resolved. What exacerbated the situation was the continuing expansion of industry and settlements.

It was not until 1898 that the South Wales Miners' Federation (SWMF) finally emerged. The union was established not as a response to the organisation of the employers, as in the north-east, but after militant action over the sliding scale.[100] The SWMF became one of the most 'progressive' unions within the MFGB with which it affiliated soon after the latter's inception. The union covered the whole of the coalfield in south Wales. It was only the miners who were organised across the region, and other occupations outside the coalfield lacked this level of unity between their movements.[101] However, given the domination of the coal mining industry in the region, focusing on the events of this occupational group can say much for south Wales as a whole. As Neil Evans has noted, 'the south Wales miners had surged ahead as the undisputed leading force in the Welsh working class after the formation of the Fed [SWMF] in 1898'.[102]

The level of organisation had important consequences for strike action as the entire coalfield could come out on strike. It also gave the SWMF an important place within society. Between its formation and the start of the First World War, the percentage of miners who belonged to the union fluctuated between 47 and 87%, but eventually 'membership of the Fed became a condition for membership of the community'.[103] Union leaders were initially drawn from the ranks of the Nonconformists, a perhaps unsurprising parallel with the DMA given the importance of religion in both areas. However, in south Wales the links with religion and the labour movement were not to last as in the north-east.[104]

Hywel Francis has stressed how the position of the SWMF within communities and the autonomy of lodges 'encouraged in its turn an independent or even a rather "anarcho-syndicalist" rank and file outlook'.[105] Radicalism, if present, could not be suppressed so easily by leaders; as Leighton James has argued, it was the unity of the miners and solidarity that was emphasised in the discourses of the union and not subversion to leadership.[106] While the first great miners' leader the Lib-Lab Mabon may have favoured conciliation, the rank and file gradually began to be much more influential in negotiations as the battle for Mabon's Day, a miners' monthly holiday, indicates.[107]

Industrial unrest in 1910–11, and the Cambrian Combine dispute in particular, revealed the bitterness in relations between employers and workers.[108] In 1915, G. R. Carter reflecting on the events of these years wrote that 'the miners of South Wales have an inherent objection to every form of coercion' and 'stubborn resistance ... to employers, police and military forces'.[109] While syndicalism may have been restricted to a minority, the Cambrian Combine dispute and the syndicalist tone of *The Miners' Next Step*, published in 1912, were reflective of wider social change and did mark a move towards a more radical socialism.[110] As Geary has noted, 'at the same time as the *Miners' Next Step* appeared in South Wales and the "Fed" established deep roots in the valleys, Liberalism remained strong in the coalfields of Durham and Northumberland'.[111] Why radical and socialist politics gained such popularity in the region at an earlier stage than in the north-east is again largely attributable to the rapid development of communities in south Wales.[112]

In explaining the rise of the Labour Party within the coalfields, Duncan Tanner believed that 'the age and structure of coalfield communities may also have been influential. Inhabitants of newer settlements, younger families with different housing and social needs and fewer established community political norms, were more easily converted to Labour's political creed'.[113] Tanner's argument about Labour politics can be applied to the rise of syndicalism and socialist politics more broadly; in south Wales, the continuous rate of development up until the First World War created the right conditions for such ideas to advance.[114] Contemporary commentators, while disputing the overall impact, agreed that the rapid formation of settlements and communities in south Wales was pivotal to the advancement of socialist politics.[115] The emergence of radicalism from within younger settlements was not peculiar to south Wales. The militants in the north-east, where they did exist and gain ground, came mainly from the youngest part of the coalfields where the lack of an industrial and organisational tradition also created the right conditions for socialist ideas to spread.[116] In south Wales, these factors were undoubtedly exaggerated within a region that was experiencing rapid growth across much of its geographical stretch.

Education also played an important role in the growth of socialist ideas. The contrast between the educational opportunities and development of the working class in south Wales and the north-east was stark. While the Central Labour College (CLC, formed in 1909) operated throughout south Wales and was closely linked to the SWMF, the NMMCA sponsored just one place at Ruskin College and one place at the CLC, and the DMA only four places at the CLC.[117] In the north-east, the coal owners had had a much greater influence over the provision of education from the mid-nineteenth century, and Durham University had a closer relationship with the miners than any university or college in south Wales.[118] In south Wales, the Workers' Educational Association and CLC were largely responsible for fostering an internationalist outlook amongst the working class in the region and, more broadly, for the emergence of more radical politics.[119]

In the north-east, the longer industrial tradition and longevity of the settlements in much of the region prevented the development of a political culture which was sympathetic to syndicalist, and initially socialist, politics. The powerful authority held by the DMA leadership, which was influenced by these factors, prevented more radical ideologies, when they did emerge, from gaining widespread sympathy.[120] The investigators of the *Commission of Enquiry into Industrial Unrest* concluded that in the north-east 'the relations of employers and employed have on the whole been, and continue to be good'. Here, unlike in south Wales, it was argued that the trade unions had assisted in formulating this relationship.[121]

That older settlements with a longer tradition of industry were less volatile is demonstrated by the relative quiescence shown by steel and iron workers in comparison to the miners in south Wales.[122] Although temporal factors were fundamental, in evaluating the success of the spread of these new ideas, the topography of both regions must again be considered. The organisation of districts on valley principles must have allowed ideas to spread more easily than in the isolated settlements of the Durham or Northumberland coalfields.[123] To this end, the closer settlement patterns along the Tyne also allowed for the easier dispersion of radical ideas, and here too, as in the most radical parts of both regions, there was a higher proportion of young males.[124] Although sharing much in common with the rest of the region, these factors were significant enough to make the Tyne more susceptible to radicalism than elsewhere. However, the Tyne, like much of the north-eastern region, had a longer tradition of industry, settlement and organisation. Therefore, what made an atmosphere more receptive of radical ideologies in south Wales were favourable temporal and topographical factors coupled with the nature of work practices which created greater antagonism between employers and employees. The internationalist outlook and strongly Marxist world-view that had been fostered amongst the miners in south Wales was not lost with the upheavals of the First World War and was later demonstrated in the popularity of Communism in the 1920s and 1930s.

When the depression hit south Wales and the north-east, its effects were equally devastating, and together they were hailed as examples of the worst affected regions and were both earmarked for particular funding.[125] However, again key differences emerged in the response to mass unemployment. While in south Wales the unemployed marched in tens, and even hundreds, of thousands, in the north-east such a display of protest was far less common. Yet, in the 1930s it was in the north-east, and not south Wales, that government commissioners replaced Labour councillors who refused to implement the means test. The tradition of industrial militancy in both regions only partially accounts for these differences. Theories of strike action and levels of occupational militancy can only offer a partial explanation of protest movements of the unemployed in the 1930s. The resources the unemployed could draw upon were often distinct from those associated with the workplace and do not account for the involvement of other members of the community beyond the miners.[126] By comparing the administration, the effects and the response to the means test, a greater understanding can be obtained not only of the experience of unemployment but also of the reasons why militancy was more apparent in south Wales and why it was the authorities in the north-east which were replaced. An examination of the social conditions and the experience of unemployment in the interwar period will also add significant nuances to the historiography of both regions. Regional histories in both cases, despite the richer historiography of south Wales, have tended to focus on the principal trade unions.[127]

For the purpose of this comparison, the regions of south Wales and the north-east of England have been loosely identified, at one level, by the administrative boundaries of the major historic counties. The area primarily focused upon within this broader definition follows the boundaries of south Wales and the north-east of England as laid out in the Special Areas Act, 1934. The Act was designed to give special funding and attention to what were considered the most depressed areas of England, Scotland and Wales. The areas denoted as being in need of special attention, while not encompassing all of the worst affected localities, do serve as a good indication of where unemployment was most prolonged and therefore where the highest proportion of means-tested applicants lived.

South Wales is defined broadly as including the industrialised parts of the historic counties of Monmouthshire, Glamorganshire and Carmarthenshire. This area includes the south Wales coalfield and the coastal towns that supported the mining, iron and steel industries. Within the three counties, the industrial valleys from Swansea across to Monmouthshire form the major focus of the analysis as this was where unemployment was at its highest and most prolonged. Wyndham Portal in his investigation into the industrial conditions in south Wales concluded that the worst affected part of the region was 'from the Eastern Valley of Monmouthshire to and including Port Talbot on the East, bounded on the North by the Breconshire boundary, and excluding Cardiff, Penarth, Barry, Llantwit Major and Porthcawl on the seaboard in the South'.[128] The towns and villages within this vicinity were affected to a much greater extent than the area to the west of Port Talbot or along the coastal fringe. Both quantitative and qualitative evidences therefore indicate that in south Wales long-term unemployment was a much more prevalent feature in the industrial valleys and the towns and villages on the northern outcrop of the coalfield. It is these areas that will form the focus of the study but, not exclusively so, and where necessary, a wider definition of the region will be employed.

The north-east region of England is understood in a broader sense as the historic counties of Durham and Northumberland where heavy industry was most prevalent. This area largely encompassed the coal mining and shipbuilding districts and was identified in *An Industrial Survey of the North East Coast Area* as 'roughly triangular in shape, and is contained within lines drawn from the mouth of the Coquet to Hartlepool, thence to Woodland in S.W. Durham, and thence back to the mouth of the Coquet'.[129] Within this region, the area that forms the main focus is based upon the findings of Captain D. Euan Wallace for the *Investigations into the Industrial Conditions in Certain Depressed Areas*. Wallace decided that the most depressed part of the region was 'Tyneside and the County of Durham'. Teesside was not included because of the establishment of chemical works and continuation of iron and steel production and the area above Tyneside because it was 'by comparison ... prosperous'.[130]

In the north-east, prolonged unemployment existed largely in pockets rather than in a distinct part of the region as in south Wales. Three definite areas can be identified from Wallace's survey where unemployment was at its most severe and the number of means-tested applicants was at its highest. The south-western part of County Durham formed one particularly affected part, Sunderland and Blyth and their surrounding districts another, and along the river Tyne the majority of the towns on both the north and south banks faced protracted unemployment for much of the period. These areas form a rough triangular shape from Blyth down to Hartlepool, across to Cockfield and back to Blyth, and are the main focus of the analysis.

The definition of south Wales and the north-east of England as regions which are multilayered is employed throughout so that the working-class experience of mass unemployment can be gauged on a local and a regional level. The book begins with an overview of the depression in interwar Britain, demonstrating the significance and place of mass unemployment in contemporary politics and culture. The administration, effects and response to the means test are explored in Part II, during the PACs administration of the means test from 1931–34 and, in Part III, during the control of the autonomous UAB from 1935 until the end of the test in 1941. Chapters 2, 5 and 6 outline how the means test was administered and the role of local government in this process. In particular, the relationship between councillors and MPs and their unemployed constituents is considered, including an examination of how pressure could be exerted on local political figures. It was the concern of the effects of the means test, both perceived and real, that prompted councillors and MPs to speak out. Such issues are explored in chapters 3, 5 and 6 which outline the major arguments placed against household means testing in both regions and the case made against the measure. The nature of protest against these effects and the ability of the unemployed to enter the public sphere and make their voices heard are addressed in chapters 4, 5 and 6 which explore the changing leadership of the unemployed and expressions of protest. Finally, the conclusion assesses the major effects of the means test throughout the period and proposes why two regions with such strong similarities could respond so differently. In this chapter, a broader assessment of the means test is also given to suggest why the means test provoked such outcry, and not the many other hardships the unemployed faced, and why it became so entrenched in public consciousness as a legacy of the 1930s.

Notes

1 Mary Louise Walker de Medici, 'A Land for Heroes?', in Keith Armstrong and Huw Beynon (eds), *Hello Are You Working? Memories of the Thirties in the North East of England* (Newcastle, 1977), p. 71.

2 *The Guardian*, 16 December 2011.

3 *Daily Herald*, 23 January 1935, p. 9.

4 For example,Walter Brierley, *Means-Test Man* (London, 1935); Walter Greenwood, *Love on the Dole* (London, 1935); Gwyn Jones, *Times Like These* (London, 1936); Lewis Jones, *We Live* (London, 1939); Max Cohen, *I Was One of the Unemployed* (London, 1945); Gwyn Thomas, *Sorrow for Thy Sons* (London, 1986); Alex Ferguson, *The Pineapple King of Jarrow and Other Stories* (North Shields, 2004).

5 When Gordon Brown introduced a means test for pensions, connections were immediately made with the situation in the 1930s in the media. Rupert Jones, 'The Budget: Means-Test Fear Hangs over Pension Top-up', *The Guardian*, 20 April 2002; William Keegan, 'Brown's Pensions for Good Sense', *The Observer*, 9 April 2006.

6 Gardiner's volume is revealing of the continued popular as well as historical appeal of the 1930s. Juliet Gardiner, *The Thirties: An Intimate History* (London, 2010), p. xiii.

7 John Stevenson and Chris Cook, *Britain in the Depression: Society and Politics 1929–39* (London, 1994), pp. 10–11.

8 Martin Pugh, *We Danced All Night: A Social History of Britain Between the Wars* (London, 2008), p. vii.

9 John Baxendale and Chris Pawling, *Narrating the Thirties: A Decade in the Making, 1930 to the Present* (London, 1996), pp. 2–3.

10 James Vernon, *Hunger: A Modern History* (Cambridge, MA, 2007), pp. 257, 271.

11 Matt Perry, *Bread and Work: The Experience of Unemployment, 1918–1939* (London, 2000), pp. 23–33. See also Alan Howkins and John Saville, 'The Nineteen Thirties: A Revisionist History', *Socialist Register*, 16 (1979), pp. 89–100.

12 Richard Overy, *The Morbid Age: Britain and the Crisis of Civilization, 1919–1939* (London, 2009), pp. 364–6.

13 See the special issue on unemployed protests, *Labour History Review*, 73:1 (2008), and Matthias Reiss and Matt Perry (eds), *Unemployment and Protest: New Perspectives on Two Centuries of Contention* (Oxford, 2011).

14 Alan Deacon and Jonathan Bradshaw, *Reserved for the Poor: The Means Test in British Social Policy* (Oxford, 1983), pp. 15–16.

15 The classic accounts are Frederic M. Miller, 'The Unemployment Policy of the National Government, 1931–1936', *The Historical Journal*, 19:2 (1976), pp. 453–76; Frederic Miller, 'The British Unemployment Assistance Crisis of 1935', *Journal of Contemporary History*, 14 (1979), pp. 329–52; Deacon and Bradshaw, *Reserved for the Poor*, pp. 5–29; W. R. Garside, *British Unemployment 1919–1939: A Study in Public Policy* (Cambridge, 1990), pp. 66–81. The work of Anne Digby has begun to demonstrate the importance of regional comparisons, but not within the context of the experience of unemployment. Anne Digby, 'Changing Welfare Cultures in Region and State', *Twentieth Century British History*, 17:3 (2006), pp. 297–322.

16 See above and, John Stevenson, 'The Making of Unemployment Policy, 1931–1935', in Michael Bentley and John Stevenson (eds), *High and Low Politics in Modern Britain* (Oxford, 1983), pp. 182–213; Richard Flanagan, *'Parish-Fed Bastards': A History of the Politics of the Unemployed in Britain, 1884–1939* (London, 1991), pp. 181–96; John Burnett, *Idle Hands: The Experience of Unemployment, 1790–1990* (London, 1984), pp. 258–64; Stevenson and Cook, *Britain in the Depression*, pp. 168–216; Neil Evans, '"South Wales Has Been Roused as Never Before": Marching Against the Means Test, 1934–36', in David W. Howell and Kenneth O. Morgan (eds), *Crime, Protest and Police in Modern British Society: Essays in Memory of David J. V. Jones* (Cardiff, 1999), pp. 176–206; Perry, *Bread and Work*, pp. 106–24.

17 Peter Kingsford, *The Hunger Marchers in Britain 1920–1939* (London, 1982), pp. 134–65; Richard Croucher, *We Refuse to Starve in Silence: A History of the National Unemployed Workers' Movement, 1920–46* (London, 1987), pp. 119–44; Flanagan, *'Parish-Fed Bastards'*, pp. 181–96; Perry,

Bread and Work, pp. 106–13; Matthias Reiss, 'Not All Were Apathetic: National Hunger Marches as Political Rituals in Interwar Britain', in Jörg Neuheiser and Michael Schaich (eds), *Political Rituals in Great Britain 1700–2000* (Augsburg, 2006), pp. 93–121.

18 Flanagan, *'Parish-Fed Bastards'*, p. 181. *Marienthal* is the classic study which concludes that long-term unemployment resulted in apathy. Marie Jahoda, Paul F. Lazarsfeld and Hans Zeisel, *Marienthal: The Sociography of an Unemployed Community* (English edition, London, 1972). For a more recent discussion of these issues see Ross McKibbin, *The Ideologies of Class: Social Relations in Britain, 1880–1950* (Oxford, 1991), pp. 228–58; Matthias Reiss and Matt Perry, 'Beyond Marienthal: Understanding Movements of the Unemployed', in Reiss and Perry, *Unemployment and Protest*, pp. 3–7.

19 Stefan Berger, 'Comparative History', in Stefan Berger, Heiko Feldner and Kevin Passmore (eds), *Writing History: Theory and Practice* (London, 2003), p. 165. The best account of the value of comparative histories remains Marc Bloch, 'Toward a Comparative History of European Societies', in Frederic C. Lane and Jelle C. Riemersma (eds), *Enterprise and Secular Change: Readings in Economic History* (London, 1953), pp. 494–521.

20 Berger, 'Comparative History', pp. 161–2; Stefan Berger, 'Introduction', in Stefan Berger, Andy Croll and Norman LaPorte (eds), *Towards a Comparative History of Coalfield Societies* (London, 2005), p. 3.

21 For example, George M. Fredrickson, 'Exceptionalism to Variability: Recent Developments in Cross-National Comparative History', *The Journal of American History*, 82:2 (1995), pp. 587–604.

22 Within this study, primary sources are extensively utilised, extended research visits have been completed for both regions, and the comparators are given equal value. It should be noted that it was not possible to compare similar sources in every case.

23 Stefan Berger, 'Working-Class Culture and the Labour Movement in the South Wales and the Ruhr Coalfield, 1850–2000: A Comparison', *Llafur*, 8:2 (2001), p. 7; Edward Royle, 'Introduction: Regions and Identities', in Edward Royle (ed.), *Issues of Regional Identity: In Honour of John Marshall* (Manchester, 1998), pp. 1–4.

24 Royle, 'Introduction: Regions and Identities', p. 4; see also, J. K. Walton, 'Review of *North East England, 1850–1914*, Graeme J. Milne', Institute of Historical Research (Review no. 579), http://www.history.ac.uk/reviews/paper/ walton2.html, date accessed 8 November 2007, p. 1.

25 William H. Sewell, 'Marc Bloch and the Logic of Comparative History', *History and Theory*, 6 (1967), p. 213.

26 Neil Evans, 'Two Paths to Economic Development: Wales and the North-East of England', in Pat Hudson (ed.), *Regions and Industries: A Perspective on the Industrial Revolution in Britain* (Cambridge, 1989), p. 203.

27 *Ibid.*, p. 203.

28 M. J. Daunton, 'Miners' Houses: South Wales and the Great Northern Coalfield, 1880–1914', *International Review of Social History*, 25:2 (1980), pp. 143–75; M. J. Daunton, 'Down the Pit: Work in the Great Northern and South Wales Coalfields, 1870–1914', *Economic History Review*, 34:4 (1981), pp. 578–97; Neil Evans, 'Patterns of Protest and Regional Labour Implantation in South Wales and the North-East of England, 1780–1950', Regional Implantation of the Labour Movement in Britain and the Netherlands, Papers Presented to the Seventh British-Dutch Conference on Labour History, Groningen, *Tijdschrift voor sociale geschiedenis*, no. 2/3 (1992), pp. 212–30; Lewis Mates, 'Durham and South Wales Miners and the Spanish Civil War', *Twentieth Century British History*, 17:3 (2006), pp. 373–95.

29 Daunton, 'Miners' Houses', pp. 143–4; Evans, 'Patterns of Protest', pp. 212–30; Berger, 'Working-Class Culture and the Labour Movement', pp. 5–40.

30 John Williams, 'The Myth of Miners' Solidarity', in John Williams, *Was Wales Industrialised? Essays in Modern Welsh History* (Llandysul, 1995), pp. 310–23; Chris Williams, '"The Hope of the British Proletariat": The South Wales Miners, 1910–1947', in Alan Campbell, Nina Fishman and David Howell (eds), *Miners, Unions and Politics 1910–47* (Aldershot, 1996), pp. 121–41; Dick Geary, 'The Myth of the Radical Miner', in Berger, Croll and LaPorte, *Towards a Comparative of History Coalfield Societies*, pp. 43–59.

31 Paul Bagguley, *From Protest to Acquiescence? Political Movements of the Unemployed* (London, 1991), p. 47; Andrew Richards, 'Mobilizing the Powerless: Collective Protest Action of the Unemployed in the Interwar Period', Working Paper 175, Juan March Institute (2002), p. 21.

32 Evans, 'Patterns of Protest', pp. 228–9.

33 Political culture is here understood as encapsulating industrial relations, trade unionism, party politics and the labour movement. Berger, 'Working-Class Culture and the Labour Movement', pp. 5, 8–11.

34 Evans, 'Two Paths to Economic Development', pp. 204–11.

35 For major studies of these factors, see, Arthur Smailes, 'Population Changes in the Colliery Districts of Northumberland and Durham', *The Geographical Journal*, 91:3 (1938), pp. 220–9; Norman McCord, *North East England: An Economic and Social History* (London, 1979), pp. 25, 41, 112, 140–1; D. J. Rowe, 'The Population of Nineteenth Century Tyneside', in Norman McCord (ed.), *Essays in Tyneside Labour History* (Newcastle, 1977), pp. 1–16; J. F. Clarke, 'Workers in the Tyneside Shipyards', in McCord, *Essays in Tyneside Labour History*, pp. 109–28; and Evans, 'Two Paths to Economic Development', pp. 204–7, 211–15.

36 Neil Evans, 'As Rich as California...': Opening and Closing the Frontier: Wales 1780–1870', in Gareth Elwyn Jones and Dai Smith (eds), *The People of Wales* (Llandysul, 1999), p. 133; John Williams, '1890–1930: The Rise and Decline of the Welsh Economy', in Williams, *Was Wales Industrialised?*, pp. 37–55.

37 See Appendix 1.1–1.3.

38 Note that in some instances in the more remote parts of the north-eastern coalfield, employers had no option but to provide houses as there was no housing market. The yearly bond was only officially abolished in Northumberland in 1844 and in Durham in 1872, after an Act of Parliament. Daunton, 'Miners' Houses', pp. 164–6; Huw Beynon and Terry Austrin, *Masters and Servants: Class and Patronage in the Making of a Labour Organisation: The Durham Miners and the English Political Tradition* (London, 1994), pp. 23, 29–33.

39 This factor, however, was determined by geology and not the longevity of industry. Daunton, 'Down the Pit', p. 582.

40 For a discussion of the cavil and marra system and the importance of it, see Daunton, 'Down the Pit', pp. 585–9; Beynon and Austrin, *Masters and Servants*, pp. 149–53; and Valerie Gordon Hall, 'The Anatomy of Changing Consciousness: The Miners of Northumberland, 1898–1914', *Labour History Review*, 66:2 (2001), p. 167.

41 Neil Evans, 'As Rich as California...', p. 131; Alun Burge, 'Exorcising Demonologies? Coal Companies and Colliery Communities in South Wales', *Llafur*, 9:4 (2007), pp. 101–9.

42 For example, the Powell Duffryn and Ocean Coal Companies became synonymous with coal producing in south Wales, and both were established in the 1860s. Trevor Boyns, 'Growth in the Coal Industry: The Cases of Powell Duffryn and the Ocean Coal Company, 1864–1913', in Colin Baber and L. J. Williams (eds), *Modern South Wales: Essays in Economic History* (Cardiff, 1986), pp. 156–69.

43 *Reports of the Commission of Enquiry into Industrial Unrest: No. 7 Division, Wales and Monmouthshire* (Cmd 8668), 1917–18, xv, p.103.

44 John Williams, 'The Coalowners', in Williams, *Was Wales Industrialised?*, p. 108.

45 Daunton, 'Down the Pit', pp. 584–91; David Evans, *Labour Strife in the South Wales Coalfield 1910–1911: A Historical and Critical Record of the Mid-Rhondda, Aberdare Valley and Other Strikes* (Cardiff, 1911), pp. 215–16.

46 Daunton, 'Miners' Houses', pp. 174–5.

47 David Gilbert argues that the importance of the unique settlement 'goes well beyond providing a dramatic backcloth to the industrial and political dramas in the region's history. The physical form of the valleys was a controlling factor in the development of a distinctive urban form and society'. David Gilbert, *Class, Community and Collective Action: Social Change in Two British Coalfields, 1850–1926* (Oxford, 1992), p. 54.

48 Daunton, 'Miners' Houses', p. 166.

49 Steven Thompson, '"Conservative Bloom on Socialism's Compost Heap": Working-Class Home Ownership in South Wales, c. 1890–1939', in R. R. Davies and Geraint H. Jenkins (eds), *From Medieval to Modern Wales: Historical Essays in Honour of Kenneth O. Morgan and Ralph A. Griffiths* (Cardiff, 2004), pp. 246–63.

50 *Ibid.*, p. 261.

51 The practice ended for Northumberland miners in 1873. Daunton, 'Miners' Houses', p. 161; Gilbert, *Class, Community and Collective Action*, p. 67. Although the extent to which it occurred has now been questioned, some argued that companies could evict tenants for militant activity. Ned Cowen, *Of Mining Life and Aal Its Ways* (Place of publication unknown, 1973), p. 3.

52 Evans, 'Patterns of Protest and Regional Labour Implantation', p. 222.

53 See map of north-east England.

54 R. Grace, 'Tyneside Housing in the Nineteenth Century', in McCord, *Essays in Tyneside Labour History*, pp. 178–93; E. Allen *et al.*, *The North-East Engineers' Strikes of 1871: The Nine Hours' League* (Newcastle-upon-Tyne, 1971), p. 15; Kit Pearce, 'Newcastle's Tyneside Flats 1850–1900: By-Law Housing or Cultural Phenomenon?', in Bill Lancaster (ed.), *Working Class Housing on Tyneside 1850–1939* (Whitley Bay, 1994), pp. 39–85.

55 Daunton, 'Miners' Houses', p. 167.

56 Such settlement was only apparent in south Wales in villages at the very top of the valleys or western and anthracite districts of the coalfield. Thomas Sharp, *A Derelict Area: A Study of the South-West Durham Coalfield* (London, 1935), pp. 17–20; Beynon and Austrin, *Masters and Servants*, pp. 108–16.

57 Reginald J. Barker, *Christ in the Valley of Unemployment* (Suffolk, 1936), p. 14.

58 Craig Armstrong has argued that Newcastle had the largest middle class in the north-east. Craig Armstrong, 'A Northern Community at War, 1939–1945: "Tyneside Can Take It!"', *Northern History*, 44:1 (2007), p. 135; M. J. Daunton, *Coal Metropolis: Cardiff 1870–1914* (Leicester, 1977), p. 54.

59 Eli Ginzberg, *A World Without Work* (New Jersey, 1991 edition; first published as *Grass on the Slag Heaps*, 1942), p. 5.

60 June Purvis, *Women's History: Britain, 1850–1945. An Introduction* (London, 1995), pp. 53–5.

61 Valerie Gordon Hall, 'Contrasting Female Identities: Women in Coal Mining Communities in Northumberland, England, 1900–1939', *Journal of Women's History*, 13:2 (2001), pp. 109–10.

62 Sue Bruley, 'Women', in John McIlroy, Alan Campbell and Keith Gildart (eds), *Industrial Politics and the 1926 Mining Lockout: The Struggle for Dignity* (Cardiff, 2004), p. 231.

63 *Ibid.*, p. 231; Dot Jones, 'Counting the Cost of Coal: Women's Lives in the Rhondda 1881–1911', in Angela V. John (ed.), *Our Mothers' Land: Chapters in Welsh Women's History 1830–1939* (Cardiff, 1991), p. 112; Rosemary Crook, '"Tidy Women": Women in the Rhondda Between the Wars', *Oral History*, 10:2 (1982), pp. 40–6.

64 Hall, 'Contrasting Female Identities', p. 108.

65 Rosemary Jones, 'Sociability, Solidarity, and Social Exclusion: Women's Activism in the South Wales Coalfield, ca. 1830–1939', in Jaclyn J. Gier

and Laurie Mercier (eds), *Mining Women: Gender in the Development of a Global Industry, 1670 to 2005* (Hampshire, 2006), p. 97.

66 Hall, 'Contrasting Female Identities', p. 109.

67 John Tosh, 'Masculinities in an Industrializing Society: Britain, 1800–1914', *Journal of British Studies*, 44 (2005), p. 332.

68 Bruley, 'Women', p. 232.

69 Anthony P. Cohen, *The Symbolic Construction of Community* (London, 1985), p. 16.

70 Craig Armstrong has employed a similar understanding of community in his work. Armstrong, 'A Northern Community at War', p. 137.

71 Robert Moore, *Pit-Men, Preachers and Politics: The Effects of Methodism in a Durham Mining Community* (Cambridge, 1974), p. 139; T. P. MacDermott, 'Irish Workers on Tyneside in the 19th Century', in McCord, *Essays in Tyneside Labour History*, p. 163; Beynon and Austrin, *Masters and Servants*, p. 49.

72 Bill Jones, 'Banqueting at a Moveable Feast: Wales 1870–1914', in Jones and Smith, *The People of Wales*, p. 169; Dai Smith, *Aneurin Bevan and the World of South Wales* (Cardiff, 1993), pp. 54–5; Chris Williams, *Democratic Rhondda: Politics and Society, 1885–1951* (Cardiff, 1996), p. 20.

73 Bill Williamson, *Class, Culture and Community: A Biographical Study of Social Change in Mining* (London, 1982), pp. 5–9.

74 Ginzberg, *A World Without Work*, p. 86.

75 The work of Kerr and Siegel is most important in this respect. Clark Kerr and Abraham Siegel, 'The Interindustry Propensity to Strike – An International Comparison', in E. W. Evans and S. W. Creigh (eds), *Industrial Conflict in Britain* (London, 1977), pp. 233–53.

76 *Ibid.*, pp. 235–6.

77 Roy Church and Quentin Outram, *Strikes and Solidarity: Coalfield Conflict in Britain 1889–1966* (Cambridge, 1998), pp. 152–3, 264–5.

78 J. L. Hammond and Barbara Hammond, *The Skilled Labourer, 1760–1832* (London, 1920), pp. 12–13; J. F. Clarke, 'Engineering Workers on Tyneside', in McCord, *Essays in Tyneside Labour History*, pp. 88–91.

79 Allen *et al.*, *The North-East Engineers' Strikes of 1871*, p. 58; Robert Colls, '"Oh Happy English Children!": Coal, Class and Education in the North-East', *Past and Present*, 73 (1976), p. 84.

80 Clarke, 'Engineering Workers on Tyneside', pp. 88–91.

81 David Douglass, *Pit Life in County Durham: Rank and File Movements and Workers' Control*, History Workshop Pamphlets, No. 6 (1972), p. 81.

82 Allen *et al.*, *The North-East Engineers' Strikes of 1871*, p. 83; Beynon and Austrin, *Masters and Servants*, p. 66.

83 Clarke, 'Workers in the Tyneside Shipyards', p. 115.

84 McCord, *North East England*, p. 198.

85 Beynon and Austrin, *Masters and Servants*, p. 77.

86 *Ibid.*, p. 104; W. R. Garside, *The Durham Miners, 1919–1960* (London, 1971), p. 319.
87 Evans, 'Patterns of Protest and Regional Labour Implantation', p. 220.
88 Norman McCord, 'The Regional Identity of North-East England in the Nineteenth and Twentieth Centuries', in Royle, *Issues of Regional Identity*, p. 110; Hall, 'The Anatomy of a Changing Consciousness', p. 167.
89 Barry Naylor has asserted that 'it is worth stressing that the DMA commitment to Labour was instrumental, as far as many of its leaders were concerned, rather than ideological'. Barry E. Naylor, 'Ramsay MacDonald and Seaham Labour Politics', *North-East Labour History Bulletin*, 15 (1981), p. 15; Lewis Mates, 'A "Most Fruitful Period"? The North East District Communist Party and the Popular Front, 1935–9', *North East History*, 35 (2004), pp. 85–6.
90 Douglass, *Pit Life in County Durham*, pp. 81–2; Hall, 'The Anatomy of Changing Consciousness', pp. 175–6.
91 Naylor, 'Ramsay MacDonald and Seaham Labour Politics', pp. 7–11; Hall, 'The Anatomy of Changing Consciousness', pp. 173, 178–9.
92 Geary, 'The Myth of the Radical Miner', p. 57.
93 Williams, 'The Coalowners', pp. 111–12.
94 *Ibid.*, p. 111.
95 *Ibid.*, p. 112.
96 J. Ramsay MacDonald, *Syndicalism: A Critical Examination* (London, 1912), p. 43. The image of militancy and radicalism as the 'racial characteristics of the Welsh' was one John Williams disputed in his article on the Tonypandy riots of 1910. John Williams, 'The Road to Tonypandy', in Williams, *Was Wales Industrialised?*, p. 219.
97 Williams, 'The Road to Tonypandy', p. 219; Berger, 'Working-Class Culture and the Labour Movement', p. 28.
98 Evans, *Labour Strife in the South Wales Coalfield*, pp. 214–16.
99 Between 1901 and 1910, the death rate in south Wales was on average 1.78 per 1,000 workers in comparison to 1.08 in Durham and Northumberland. *Reports of the Commission of Enquiry into Industrial Unrest: No. 7 Division*, p. 87; Julie Light, 'The 1917 Commission of Enquiry into Industrial Unrest – A Welsh Report', *Welsh History Review*, 21:4 (2003), p. 707.
100 Attempts to organise the coal owners in south Wales had failed throughout the later nineteenth century. Evans, *The Miners of South Wales*, pp. 161–7.
101 Daunton, *Coal Metropolis*, p. 181. For a greater discussion of the labour movement in Cardiff see, Neil Evans, 'Cardiff's Labour Tradition', *Llafur*, 4:2 (1985), pp. 77–90.
102 Evans, 'Cardiff's Labour Tradition', p. 79.
103 Chris Williams, *Capitalism, Community and Conflict: The South Wales Coalfield, 1898–1947* (Cardiff, 1998), pp. 88–9; Berger, 'Working-Class Culture and the Labour Movement', p. 25.

104 Richard Lewis, 'Political Culture and Ideology, 1900–1918', in Duncan Tanner, Chris Williams and Deian Hopkin (eds), *The Labour Party in Wales 1900–2000* (Cardiff, 2000), pp. 91–3.

105 Hywel Francis, *Miners Against Fascism: Wales and the Spanish Civil War* (London, 1984), p. 33.

106 Leighton James, 'Trade Union Development in the Ruhr and South Wales, 1890–1914', in Berger, Croll and LaPorte, *Towards a Comparative History of Coalfield Societies*, p. 259.

107 Williams, 'The Hope of the British Proletariat', p. 124; Andy Croll, 'Mabon's Day: The Rise and Fall of a Lib-Lab Holiday in the South Wales Coalfield, 1888–1898', *Labour History Review*, 72:1 (2007), pp. 63–4.

108 David Smith, 'Tonypandy 1910: Definitions of Community', *Past and Present*, 87 (1980), p. 176.

109 G. R. Carter, 'The Coal Strike in South Wales', *The Economic Journal*, 25:99 (1915), p. 454.

110 David Egan has rightly noted of the authors that 'the tag "industrial unionist" suits them better than "syndicalist"'. David Egan, '"A Cult of Their Own": Syndicalism and *The Miners' Next Step*', in Campbell, Fishman and Howell, *Miners, Unions and Politics*, p. 25; Smith, 'Tonypandy 1910: Definitions of Community', pp. 158–84.

111 Geary, 'The Myth of the Radical Miner', p. 47.

112 Duncan Tanner, 'The Labour Party and Electoral Politics in the Coalfield', in Campbell, Fishman and Howell, *Miners, Unions and Politics*, p. 61.

113 *Ibid*., p. 77.

114 Many historians have used a 'frontier' analogy to describe south Wales during this period, and David Egan has noted that contemporaries made a comparison with the American West. Egan, '"A Cult of Their Own"', p. 16; Smith, *Aneurin Bevan*, pp. 54–5; Williams, 'The Coalowners', p. 115.

115 Carter, 'The Coal Strike in South Wales', p. 455; *Reports of the Commission of Enquiry into Industrial Unrest: No. 7 Division*, pp. 12–18.

116 Naylor, 'Ramsay MacDonald and Seaham Labour Politics', pp. 8–9; Hall, 'The Anatomy of Changing Consciousness', p. 178.

117 Smith, *Aneurin Bevan*, p. 201; Hall, 'The Anatomy of Changing Consciousness', p. 176; Garside, *The Durham Miners*, p. 298.

118 *Reports of the Commission of Enquiry into Industrial Unrest: No. 7 Division*, p. 100. See also Colls, '"Oh Happy English Children"', pp. 75–99, and the two rejoinders to this piece, A. J. Heesom and Brendan Duffy, 'Debate: Coal, Class and Education in the North-East', *Past and Present*, 90 (1981), pp. 136–41.

119 Richard Lewis, *Leaders and Teachers: Adult Education and the Challenge of Labour in South Wales, 1906–1940* (Cardiff, 1993), chapters one and two.

120 Mates, 'Durham and South Wales Miner', p. 376.

121 *Reports of the Commission of Enquiry into Industrial Unrest: No. 1 Division, North-Eastern Area* (Cmd 8662), 1917–18, xv, pp. 9–10.

122 This was, however, in contrast to an earlier tumultuous period. Williams, 'The Hope of the British Proletariat', p. 133.

123 Chris Williams has noted the importance of geography to the nature of lodge politics. *Ibid.*, p. 130–1.

124 Henry A. Mess, 'The Social Survey of Tyneside: An English Regional Survey', *The American Journal of Sociology*, 33:3 (1927), p. 425. Craig Armstrong has also shown how a strong sense of community existed along the Tyne and not just in villages and towns. Armstrong, 'A Northern Community at War', pp. 135–6.

125 Hilda Jennings, *Brynmawr: A Study of a Distressed Area* (London, 1934); Thomas Sharp, *A Derelict Area: A Study of the South-West Durham Coalfield* (London, 1935); John Newsom, *Out of the Pit: A Challenge to the Comfortable* (Oxford, 1936); *Men Without Work: A Report Made to the Pilgrim Trust* (Cambridge, 1938); A. J. Lush, *The Young Adult in South Wales* (Cardiff, 1941); Eli Ginzberg, *Grass on the Slag Heaps* (New York, 1942).

126 Church and Outram, *Strikes and Solidarity*, pp. 260–8.

127 The exceptions are Trevor Herbert and Gareth Elwyn Jones (eds), *Wales Between the Wars* (Cardiff, 1988); Steven Thompson, *Unemployment, Poverty and Health in Interwar South Wales* (Cardiff, 2006). Key examples of this work for south Wales include: Hywel Francis and Dai Smith, *The Fed: A History of the South Wales Miners in the Twentieth Century* (Cardiff, 1998); Francis, *Miners Against Fascism*; Smith, *Aneurin Bevan and the World of South Wales*; Williams, *Capitalism, Community and Conflict.* Key examples for the north-east of England include: Garside, *The Durham Miners*; Martin Bulmer, *Mining and Social Change: Durham County in the Twentieth Century* (London, 1978); McCord, *North East England*; Beynon and Austrin, *Masters and Servants.*

128 Ministry of Labour, *Reports of Investigations into the Industrial Conditions in Certain Depressed Areas, III: South Wales and Monmouthshire* (Cmd 4728), 1933–4, xiii, pp. 440–1.

129 *An Industrial Survey of the North East Coast Area* (London, 1932), p. 1.

130 Ministry of Labour, *Reports of Investigations into the Industrial Conditions in Certain Depressed Areas, II: Durham and Tyneside* (Cmd 4728), 1933–4, xiii, pp. 381–2.

Part I
Overview

and 'after 1874 it did not in any year fall below 2 per cent'.[5] It was to take the unprecedented demands of the war effort along with conscription to see the virtual eradication of unemployment during the First World War. Indeed, in some areas, underemployment became an issue, and the ranks of the workforce swelled with women taking posts where men could not. While the large workforce was recognised as a necessity for a successful war effort, ministers were cautious about the transition to peacetime when demobilised men and women would flood the labour market. Works such as Keynes's *The Economic Consequences of the Peace* (1920) helped stimulate debate and serve as a warning to what was an issue fraught with the complications of finance as well as public opinion.[6] The *Commission of Enquiry into Industrial Unrest* highlighted how the desire for good industrial relations stimulated debate as much as economic reasoning.[7]

Peacetime arrangements for the labour market were an incredibly politically sensitive area. Figures such as Christopher Addison, the Minister for Reconstruction, argued it was essential that the government provided some form of temporary limited out-of-work donation for all unemployed people including women. Addison felt that given an estimated 10 million people remained excluded from the national insurance scheme, even after the extension of 1916, it was pivotal that cover be given for men, women and dependent children as unemployment may be caused by a 'temporary shortage of raw materials, dislocation and defective organisation, &c'.[8] Support was found within the government for such a scheme, and from the announcement of armistice, an out-of-work donation could be claimed for a period of six months. The following year, reflective of the optimism of the government, the national insurance scheme was extended to cover practically all workers, entitling some 12 million to unemployment benefit.[9] Married men were given preference in the new scheme which, Marjorie Levine-Clark has argued, was placed within 'a cultural framework which reasserted a breadwinner model of masculinity as a means to return to "normal", to distance British society from the public and private traumas of war'.[10]

In the initial months after the end of war, many staple industries witnessed a boom period. While production and output levels may not have surpassed the pre-war pinnacle, the demand for raw materials was high enough to see the absorption of many workers back into the labour market. As an indication of the initial boom, in south Wales and the north-east of England, the number of employed coal miners reached its zenith in 1921.[11] Of course, this picture of prosperity was uneven. The jubilation of the end of the war did little to ease the bitter reality of a life dependent upon the state and the care of others for injured men. Women who had desired continued employment found the gentle nudge and then angry push back into the home a difficult prospect. In the early months of 1919, it was clear that the promise of work for all was not being fulfilled. Demobilised men felt angry that wartime rhetoric of a better future was left unrealised as industries struggled to readjust. The years immediately after the war are viewed by historians as representing 'the high tide of working-class unrest'.[12] The wave of race rioting in the first half of 1919 was an ugly demonstration of the tensions which existed within British society. A common spark in the riots in many of Britain's seaports was competition for work from demobilised men.[13] While local relations with immigrant and ethnic minority populations need careful consideration, the patterns of rioting revealed the areas most affected by post-war economic problems.[14]

The economic dislocation of the immediate post-war years was reflected in the outburst of social and industrial action. A series of smaller stoppages took place throughout 1919 including the strike of 3,000 men in the Rhondda Valleys on New Year's Day over unemployment thought to have been caused by rapid demobilisation.[15] Industrial relations in the mining industry were eased by the temporary boom and the findings of the Sankey Commission; the recommendation of the nationalisation of the coal mining industry was much favoured by the workforce. More serious strike action occurred within the shipbuilding industries, and iron, steel and engineering trades most affected after armistice. In the autumn, a strike amongst 50,000 moulders within the iron industry lasted over three months and affected trade and employment within engineering also.[16] To add to the picture of unrest, strikes also broke out amongst cotton and railway workers as well as the police; industrial relations were particularly bitter in Clydeside and Belfast.[17]

The developing unrest was indicative of the upheaval in industry and the tension between employers trying to reduce costs and workers fearful for unemployment and a lowering of living standards. For those unable to find employment, frustration at the lack of opportunities after returning from war led men and women to take to the streets. Just a month after the armistice was announced, a demonstration of an estimated 30,000 against unemployment was organised by twenty-six trade union branches along the Tyne. Richard Croucher sees this action as reflecting 'a widespread feeling among both industrial workers and servicemen that a "land fit for heroes" was precisely what was required after the enormous sacrifice of war'.[18] From 1919, the level of unemployment began to be described as a 'gravc' problem: from 1920, economists began to point towards a 'crisis' which threatened both economic recovery as well as political stability. The year 1920 was pinpointed as the beginning of the post-war depression which, temporary improvements through cyclical fluctuations aside, lasted until 1938. Unemployment was viewed as an unprecedented situation without parallel in pre-war depressions. To many, it was one of the most pressing concerns of the government. The American economist Herbert Feis warned in 1921 that in Britain 'unemployment has risen to the dimensions of a calamity' and felt that 'English [sic] labor will fight before it will accept a reduction of its standard of living to the pre-war standard'. Feis concluded that 'since the question of wage reduction is such a thorny one, and the question of unemployment is so acute, the present government will find its march back to the gold standard no easy one'.[19] Feis was writing at the beginning of a national coal strike in 1921 and predicted further action. Indeed, while the unemployed and ex-servicemen were taking to the streets more readily, in 1921 it was events in the coal industry which diverted the attention of the press and the government.

After the First World War, the labour movement found itself in a stronger and more confident position with increased trade union membership and growth within the Labour Party, which was now winning both parliamentary seats and taking control of local governments.[20] The war had had both a radicalising affect and acted as a catalyst for the continued development of socialist politics and working-class militancy. Both south Wales and the north-east of England emerged as strongholds for the Labour Party and as regions within which trade unionism was an essential feature of industrial and community life.[21] There were key differences in the naturc of these experiences, and militancy had grown to characterise the union in south Wales. Even during the upheaval of the First World War, the SWMF made the decision to strike as it was believed that coal owners were exploiting an opportunity to make profits.[22] David Egan has described the strike as representing 'a new highpoint in militancy'.[23] Yet, it was not only the working class in south Wales which exhibited the power of collective action: the working class on Tyneside revealed their growing separateness from more general regional trends through the aforementioned unemployed protests. Indeed, in the north-east, while consensus may have characterised industrial relations in the pre-war era, the response of the coal owners in negotiations over pay during the return of industry to private ownership led to calls for strike action. Although the DMA was initially wary of such action, W. R. Garside has pointed out that 'relations between the Durham miners' and the coal owners' Associations rapidly deteriorated immediately prior to the start of the lock-out'.[24]

The coal lockout of 1921 lasted for four months and saw the defeat of the miners and the trade unions. The resultant lower wages within south Wales and the north-east exacerbated the increasingly hostile relationship between employers and employees; the consequences of this would, ultimately, be played out in 1926. Problems within the mining industry only continued as markets were evermore affected by the global disruption to trade. Other industries also felt the effects of this, most notably, shipbuilding, iron and steel production and textile manufacturing. The disruption of the labour market impacted not only working hours and wage levels but also what can be termed the psychology of workers threatened by unemployment. Feis was not the only economist to argue that further strike action would likely transpire. J. Morgan Rees believed that 'a very revolutionary period of trade disputes and suffering' in Europe was imminent without governments taking steps to intervene.[25] G. D. H. Cole saw the increase in militancy during the Great War as a consequence of the removal of the fear of unemployment, a situation that Andrew Thorpe has argued continued in the post-war boom which strengthened the unions. Cole believed that although in the short term the out of work would feel angry enough to protest and demonstrate, ultimately he recognised that unemployment was demoralising and would greatly affect self-respect.[26] While the worst years of the depression were to come, in the early 1920s Britain was already affected by the increasingly regional patterns of unemployment.[27] The social consequences of unemployment were becoming more manifest with Britain facing stubbornly high levels of unemployment when compared internationally.

Unemployment rose steadily from the spring of 1920 reaching 6.1% by December and then more rapidly to 23.1% by June 1921.[28] Rees noted in his international overview of post-war unemployment that 1921 and early 1922 represented the worst period of the slump with the crisis beginning in Japan, affecting next America and then spreading to much of Europe and the British dominions. Thereafter, improvements, outside of central Europe, began to be witnessed although the recovery was uneven. In Britain, however, the improvements were less marked with unemployment still standing at over 14% at the end of 1922 'when France, Belgium and the United States had thoroughly recovered'.[29] The severity of the unemployment situation, even after numbers began to decline, led to a series of international investigations and conferences on how to tackle and remedy the situation. The International Labour Office (ILO) hoped its pooling of information on unemployment insurance would allow states 'to profit by each other's experiences'.[30] These reports fitted into the wider agenda of the ILO from the Washington Conference of 1919 to try and regulate labour internationally. Its 1922 report demonstrated how unemployment insurance was becoming an intrinsic feature of state labour policy, not only to mitigate suffering but to help reduce social unrest and raise awareness of problems within the labour market; 'thanks to public insurance, the misery of the unemployed is no longer only manifested by collective demonstrations, to which, when abandoned to their [the unemployed] fate, they are necessarily driven... . In short, unemployment insurance reveals, in part at least, the cost of unemployment to society'.[31] It was these principles that formed the basis of the British unemployment insurance scheme, although not all ambitions were met.

Following the collapse of the post-war boom, demonstrations amongst the unemployed gradually increased. Sporadic outbursts of protest became more organised affairs as the out of work established committees and movements to formulate plans of action. These early organisations formed the basis for what was to be a movement with a longevity which surpassed all expectations of its leaders and sceptical observers. London was certainly the centre of activity, and in 1921, the National Unemployed Workers' Committee Movement (NUWCM) was formed there to coordinate the activities of the unemployed throughout the country. Under the leadership of Wal Hannington, the NUWCM was to be 'central to British history between the wars'.[32] While unemployment insurance had been extended in 1920, the number of those who were exhausting their right to benefit was increasing. Combined with the fear of losing work, ex-servicemen and other unemployed workers angrily took to the streets to demand fair maintenance from the government. In Cardiff, in late 1921, a deputation of the unemployed met with the Board of Guardians, and concessions were granted. A spokesman for the deputation had argued that homelessness was increasing and 'we find the present scale insufficient... . We have been experiencing hunger and suffering too long'.[33] Across the country, large demonstrations were staged and unemployed workers from Birmingham took the dramatic step of marching to the capital in August 1922. The action of the unemployed in Birmingham, and subsequent calls in the *Daily Herald* for further activity, led to the NUWCM organising its first national hunger march to London in the autumn of 1922.[34] Contingents of shipyard workers from the Tyne and miners from south Wales both participated.[35]

The events of the early 1920s in many ways set the pattern of the relationship between the state and the unemployed, regardless of which party was in power. The hunger marchers were refused a meeting with the government and the King, but saw a victory in raising awareness of their plight. The unemployment policy of the government was equally telling, as, throughout the interwar period, it remained overwhelmingly dictated by a desire to appease social unrest and, simultaneously, to reduce public expenditure.[36] Alan Deacon has argued that concessions made in this period show that while the actual threat posed by the upheaval can be debated, 'there is no doubt as to the sense of fear and even panic which pervades the Cabinet and departmental papers'.[37] The *Daily Mirror*, for example, questioned whether the 1922 hunger march was 'secretly inspired from Moscow'.[38] However, the end of the boom period also created a climate where the government needed to begin to make economies as it was borrowing up to £30 million to cover spending on unemployment benefits.[39] In 1921, the genuinely seeking work test was first applied to extended benefits, and the first means test was introduced in the following year. The tests affected those who had exhausted their statutory right to insurance benefits and were receiving what were called uncovenanted, extended and then transitional benefits. Despite the furore that was later to surround both of these tests, in the early 1920s the focus of the cuts on women and single men living at home helped to ensure they roused little opposition.[40] In south Wales and the north-east, the tests had little impact upon the working class. This situation was aided by the fact that Local Employment Committees in both regions were noted for their generosity in administering the tests.[41] The control the Labour Party now had on councils was undoubtedly assisting the situation.[42]

In 1924, the first Labour government was elected to power under the leadership of Ramsay MacDonald whose own constituency was in Aberavon in south Wales. Labour fared best in the older industrial regions, and the close relationship between the party and the unions was proving to be fruitful.[43] In south Wales and the north-east of England, the Labour Party continued its hegemonic rise. The domination of the south Wales coalfield was particularly spectacular, with Labour forming a stronghold which was to last until the end of the twentieth century.[44] Labour showed itself to have become the party of choice for the working class in both regions, and this was reflective of the wider political ideology enhancing the rights of workers. However, the growth of the Left was not only manifested in votes for Labour; the South Wales Socialist Society played an important part in the negotiations to found the Communist Party of Great

Britain.[45] Although support for the party was drawn from a minority within the region, it was to become an important political force amongst radical militants and especially so as industrial relations continued to worsen.

The Labour government lasted only eleven months in power and fell amidst controversy surrounding the fabricated Zinoviev letter published in the *Daily Mail*. While the election of a Labour government emboldened hope for a transformation of industrial organisation, Cabinet members were cautious in introducing reforms focusing instead on proving Labour's ability to govern. The party remained committed to nationalisation within certain key industries, as laid out in the Sankey Commission, but did not take steps to implement this policy.[46] When a Conservative government returned to power, the future of the coalfields dominated debates on industrial policy, overshadowing political and social discussions about the unemployed. A national stoppage by the Triple Alliance in 1925 was only prevented by government intervention on the much celebrated Red Friday. In May 1926, the continued failure to reach agreement over pay and working hours led the Trades Union Congress (TUC) to call a General Strike. 'The nine days that shook Britain' have been viewed by historians as a pivotal moment in industrial relations and trade union militancy. However, within the coalfields, it was the continued lockout for seven months after the collapse of the General Strike which provided the battleground for a community struggle which was to have lasting repercussions well beyond 1926.

The events of the lockout in south Wales and the north-east of England have rightly been characterised as having a fundamental impact upon society both during and after the dispute.[47] In south Wales and the north-east, the mining communities held out for longer than anywhere else in the country; the strength of the labour movement in each was revealed, as was the solidarity of the communities.[48] Hester Barron and Sue Bruley's impressive studies of Durham and south Wales reveal most pertinently how community solidarity was forged to allow the miners to maintain the fight for much longer than elsewhere.[49] In both regions, the labour movement and political culture were cohesive in 1926. The power of the trade unions allowed for collective action, and entire communities were mobilised for the cause of the lockout. The parallels between the two regions in 1926 were stronger than at any other moment, and both displayed high levels of militancy.[50] Indeed, Hester Barron has raised the important point that 'while the Welsh and Scottish unions also had considerable success in building collectivist response to the lockout ... their dominance over the hearts and minds of their constituents was neither greater nor less than that forged by the DMA'.[51]

The exceptionality of the situation caused by the strike allowed more radical ideas to spread. In the north-east, Communist Party membership, for the interwar period, peaked in 1926.[52] Boards of Guardians also displayed a certain level of militancy. Solidarity with the miners was shown in Chester-le-Street in the north-east and Bedwellty in south Wales where the Boards of Guardians were taken over by central government officials for making excessive payments.[53] Furthermore, the repercussions of the defeat of the miners upon the labour movement and the wider effect upon communities in both regions were monumental. The major mining unions were weakened as membership declined and union activists were blacklisted and victimised. Beynon and Austrin have emphasised how the Durham miners were 'demoralised and disorganised'.[54] Similarly in south Wales, McIlroy has described the response as 'cruel' and not least because of the growth of a revival company union, the South Wales Miners' Industrial Union (SWMIU).[55] However, after the defeat of the miners, the similarities between the two coalfields were not to last, and attitudes towards militant action and the presence of radicalism varied considerably.[56]

The labour movement was considerably destabilised at the end of lockout, and the unions needed to rebuild and regain confidence in their leadership. In south Wales, the problems the SWMF faced were intensified by the presence of the SWMIU; membership declined much more drastically than it did for the DMA.[57] Francis and Smith have noted that although the impact of the company union was limited, 'its removal came to be seen as the essential prerequisite of the re-establishment of Federation hegemony'.[58] The SWMIU remained until 1938 and its formation and perseverance revealed that after 1926 the power of the SWMF within the region was challenged.[59] In Durham and Northumberland, disillusionment appears to have been a greater problem for the labour movement than alternative leadership: company unionism did not make massive inroads into either county, and union membership was much more stable.[60] Dickie Beavis recalled how

> The men were very demoralised during the 1930s. They had stood together in 1926 and held out for almost a year but they had to go back to longer hours, and huge debts. The older men would never again trust anyone. It was as if they lost faith. And from then onwards Durham became politically dormant. Creeping paralysis I've called it![61]

The events of 1926 mark an important turning point in the history of interwar Britain, and especially the histories of south Wales and the north-east of England. Dickie Beavis's comments reveal the longevity of the ideological, and even perhaps psychological, consequences of the defeat and the ramifications for trade unionism and industrial action.[62] Of equal, and perhaps even greater, importance, the strike was a turning point both historically and in the eyes of the working class because it signalled the start of a rapid increase in unemployment which was to become protracted. Ferdynand Zweig in his enlightening study into coal mining communities after the Second World War noted that for miners 'the coal strike is vividly impressed on their minds, like an event which happened only yesterday. To any troublesome problem you may bring up, the first statement you will hear will be: "You know that we had a General Strike in 1926, and all the worst troubles in coal-mining started then."'[63] The situation within the coal mining regions deteriorated quickly, and many pits did not reopen.

The government needed to adopt a serious strategy for the 'depressed' areas but simultaneously maintain its commitment to managing the financial crisis. While Conservative ministers refrained from placing blame for the situation at the hands of the miners, there was certainly an implicit suggestion that the lockout had worsened conditions for all industries. When meeting with a deputation from the General Council of the TUC in December 1928, the Minister of Labour explained that the government's underestimate of the worsening industrial situation was because of the unforeseen 'impoverishment of the country' caused by the 'long stoppage' in 1926.[64] Such meetings allowed the government to publicise that dialogue with organisations like the TUC was the accepted mode of communication, not protest marches, and permitted the government to continue to introduce cuts at a time when public awareness of the plight of the unemployed was increasing.[65]

The TUC deputation was prompted by concern about the effects of the restrictions introduced under the 1927 Unemployment Insurance Act which was based upon findings from the Blanesburgh Report. Published in January 1927, the Blanesburgh Report recommended the application of the genuinely seeking work test to all cases, reductions in benefit levels and the removal of the means test.[66] The position of those workers whose benefit had been continuously extended when the eligibility to receive it was exhausted was of particular concern to the government. It recognised that such a large number of people could not be turned over to the poor law because of the outcry that this would cause. In working-class communities, stigma was still attached to receiving poor law assistance as it was a symbol of destitution and the loss of respectability. The introduction of the genuinely seeking work test reflected the view that while maintenance would continue for the long-term unemployed, benefits were neither unlimited nor a form of charity and would only be paid to the deserving. Aside from the continued financial support of the government, the only other major action to alleviate unemployment was the establishment of the Industrial Transference Board in 1928. The Board offered financial assistance to encourage workers to move to more prosperous areas. The scheme was deeply unpopular, and the implication that older industrial regions were permanently derelict roused much bitterness. The success of the policy was limited, and many of those who did migrate through the Board returned home.[67] The policy towards the unemployed was underpinned by the government's belief that high unemployment was a consequence of a temporary downturn in the market *and* personal failing. Amongst the latter were the workshy, those who failed to move to more prosperous areas and strikers who had exhausted family resources. While protest against unemployment had been rumbling since the early 1920s, the application of a test for benefit in regions where work was becoming evermore sparse led to anger and did not pass unheeded as in previous years.

The failure of the lockout may have left the labour movement with reservations about future possibilities of industrial action, but it did not remove the strength of feeling in favour of collective action entirely. This was certainly the case in the coalfields in south Wales and Scotland. In 1927, a hunger march was organised from south Wales to London to express opposition to the unemployment situation, the Blanesburgh Report and the Act that it had inspired. The march went ahead despite aversion shown to the event by the SWMF, the TUC and the MFGB: the independent spirit and radical nature of the labour movement in south Wales was once more confirmed.[68] Wal Hannington, who led the march, believed that 'the tremendous agitational value of the march cannot be denied even by our strongest opponents. It awakened not only the people in the towns where we stayed, but it carried the message of the poverty stricken areas into the smallest village and hamlet through which we passed.'[69] The march also demonstrated the increasing importance of the Communist Party and the NUWCM in the region. Although the initial impetus for the march had come from the miners, it was the NUWCM who helped to organise the march.[70] Three hundred miners marched to London and it was clear that in south Wales some were not prepared to sit down and accept their fate even when the trade unions were offering little leadership for action.[71]

The Rhondda Communist Party felt that 'the miners of South Wales rouse[d] the whole country by organising an Unemployed Miners'

March to London'.[72] Indeed, Richard Croucher has argued that the 'the miners' march ... had unforeseen consequences on an international level'; the number of unemployed movements in other countries did increase following Hannington's vision at the July 1928 Congress of the Communist International of what could be achieved through such unemployed action.[73] From the late 1920s, it was clear that the NUWCM and the Communist Party were to have an important role in leading the growing body of unemployed men and women across Britain more broadly as the 1929 hunger march showed.[74] However, that said, aside from sporadic outbursts of action, outside of south Wales only in Scotland did such a similar display of marching and demonstrating take place.[75] For example, although during the General Strike the working class in the north-east may have displayed a degree of militancy, it was clear that after the lockout there was a return to an aversion to collective action.[76] As Anthony Mason has demonstrated the 'high tide of radicalisation ... did not last, or if it did, then the Labour Party, which already had a virtual monopoly in the area's mining constituencies, was the chief beneficiary'.[77] The NUWCM made few inroads into the region in this period, and the DMA and Labour Party remained the major source of leadership; membership of the Communist Party had already considerably declined by 1927.[78]

While the government wrangled over the cost of maintaining the unemployed and the NUW(C)M, trade unions and political parties struggled to provide a voice for the workless, the situation in the older industrial regions continued to deteriorate. Many of these regions had, to varying degrees, faced financial difficulties since the first crisis of 1920. The eating away of savings and accumulation of debts in the General Strike and lockout only added to existing privations in some areas. The 1925 investigation *Has Poverty Diminished?*, for example, revealed the hardship present in Stanley, County Durham, which was thought to have been representative of the wider coalfield.[79] In regions like south Wales and the north-east which had enjoyed relative prosperity in the pre-war and wartime period, those facing unemployment were often unused to longer periods without work. This was a factor picked up upon in the case of Stanley in Bowley and Hogg's report; Stanley which in 1913 had a 'favourable position' was by 1923 'worse off than in Bolton, Northampton or Warrington'. They concluded that 'the general reduction of poverty, evidenced in the industrial towns, has not taken place in the coal districts'.[80] Similar conclusions were found in the lengthy investigative reports run in *The Times* in March and September of 1928.

The reports on south Wales and the north-east of England offered readers of *The Times* a vivid portrayal of the effects of economic collapse and publicised the position of two regions which had fallen from grace.[81] A sense of hopelessness and impending doom pervaded all columns, and the description of the 'social disaster' in south Wales was especially bleak.[82] The reader was reminded that the miners in both regions were used to higher wages and 'past prosperity', symbolised in Durham in the weekly Sunday roast dinner.[83] As such, the author was keen to note that miners were no longer 'wild and thoughtless' although the isolation of the communities was emphasised. This was seen to have impacted upon the world view of the miner giving rise to a sense of abandonment, one which readers could help to challenge through practical support. Indeed, it was not only the miners who suffered, and the hardship faced by wives and young adults was also demonstrated. Perhaps one of the most interesting aspects of the conclusions drawn, in light of the later analysis of this book, is the difference which was believed to have existed in the mentality of the miners: 'economically, the present situation in the northern coalfield scarcely differs from that of South Wales. But there the whole environment is startling, the people unusual, the formation of the land curious, and coal forces itself perpetually on the mind. Here that is not so: the same blow has fallen on a country and a people less out of the common.'[84] The militancy of south Wales in comparison to the stoicism of the north-eastern miner alludes to both the *Enquiry into Industrial Unrest* and later studies of the regions. In Durham, it is noted that the miner 'know[s] the meaning of self-help', and this aspect is praised above a politically militant response. In offering a practical solution to the deep-seated problems, expanding the work of the Lord Mayor's Fund and training centres is suggested, but widespread transference and emigration are seen as the essential remedies.[85]

While an editorial accompanying the final report in *The Times* argued that the focus on the two regions should not detract from the 'misfortunes of miners in the other depressed areas', south Wales and the north-east were becoming exemplars or bywords for industrial stagnation.[86] In November 1928, the National Council of Social Services established the Coalfields Distress Emergency Committee and decided to focus its efforts on stimulating 're-creative activities in the South Wales and Durham Coalfields'. Grants were obtained from the Carnegie Trust to provide music, education and drama. One letter received by the National Council of Music sent onto the Committee urged, 'send us something; this place is a cemetery'.[87]

The Wall Street crash in October 1929 served to exacerbate an already grave financial and unemployment record in many parts of Britain. Sally Alexander's comments of the early 1920s have a resonance for the decade as a whole: 'the presence in London in the 1920s of demobbed soldiers disillusioned, depressed by unemployment and humiliated by the Poor Law, undermines the image of the "careless twenties."'[88] By the end of the 1920s, debates about unemployment were no longer confined to the ILO or left-wing movements. Concern for the fate of the unemployed combined with the belief Britain was on the brink of financial collapse made unemployment one of the most pressing governmental issues for the second Labour government.

When the Labour government formed, registered unemployment stood at 1.1 million, by January 1930, this figure had reached 1.5 million, and by the end of the year, it stood at approximately 2.7 million.[89] It was clear that something drastic needed to be done, and the government became caught between making economies and maintaining its socialist principles.[90] Under growing criticism, it did finally abolish the genuinely seeking work clause which during its application had disallowed 3 million people from the right to obtain benefit.[91] In recognition that cuts needed to be made, it appointed a commission in December 1930 under the chair of Judge Holman Gregory to enquire into the unemployment insurance scheme. Meanwhile, further economies were made under the 1931 Anomalies Act which saw many seasonal and part-time workers and married women ousted from the insurance scheme.[92] The interim report on unemployment insurance came at a crucial moment for the government. In July, the May Committee on National Expenditure indicated a budget deficit of £120 million and recommended that cuts of £96 million were needed, including a 20% cut in unemployment benefit.[93]

In the face of growing public outcry from all sides, the Labour government remained divided over how best to achieve economies. In late August, nine members of the Cabinet continued to disagree with the cuts in unemployment benefit proposed by MacDonald and the Chancellor of the Exchequer, Philip Snowden. Crucially, the TUC also made clear its opposition to the programme of retrenchment. With only eleven Cabinet members supportive of cuts to unemployment, it became the issue that was to topple the government.[94] Ramsay MacDonald, Prime Minister and member for the Seaham constituency, offered the government's resignation to the King on 23 August 1931. On the subsequent day, the National Government was formed under the premiership of MacDonald as the King and the opposition realised 'that the cuts might be less controversial if introduced by a "socialist" Prime Minister'.[95] In October, a general election was called and the National Government won a huge majority in what seemed to be public endorsement of the needs for cuts. A total of 470 Conservative MPs were returned in a parliament of 615. Tarnishing his legacy, MacDonald in a 'great betrayal' became Prime Minister, a position he would hold until 1935. The Labour Party was heavily defeated, and only forty-six MPs were returned.[96]

In south Wales, Labour MPs maintained their stronghold, and a majority for the party was returned in the region with the Conservatives struggling to even find candidates.[97] Indeed, Lewis Mates has noted that 'in the 1931 general election debacle, South Wales remained so loyal that the Labour vote actually increased'.[98] In the north-east, however, the picture was quite different: only two of the seven miners' candidates that were chosen were elected.[99] The defeat of the Labour Party in the north-east has been explained as the consequence of Conservatives and Liberals joining forces to oust Labour candidates and the figure of MacDonald standing for the National Government in the Seaham constituency. Beynon and Austrin have argued that these factors and 'the area's Liberal tradition help to explain a lot about 1931'. They maintained that although the conversion to Labour was complete, there was not a 'development of vibrant constituency politics'.[100] The longer political and industrial traditions of the region clearly influenced the nature of contemporary politics despite the very pressing recent events.

In south Wales, the unity of the labour movement and the militancy of it, largely as a consequence of economic factors and the relative infancy of the communities, ensured that the Labour Party maintained its majority in the region. The SWMF also continued to be an important force for many. However, it was clear that the situation was beginning to change. Although no one could seriously doubt the power and support of the SWMF and the Labour Party amongst the working class in south Wales, the membership of the Communist Party and the NUWM did increase in numbers during the late 1920s. The affiliation to both must be seen as part of the tradition of rank-and-file militancy and as a somewhat intermittent alternative, not entirely separate, form of leadership. Stefan Berger has noted how 'the Communist Party in south Wales ... remained part and parcel of a more unified working-class culture' than his comparator, the Ruhr. The party appealed, Berger has concluded, 'because they were popular champions of working-class interests in the workplaces and neighbourhoods of south Wales'.[101] Chris Williams has expressed similar sentiments, noting that 'the development of "revolutionary" strategies such as syndicalism and communism took place within the context of a more generalised and hegemonic labourism'.[102] The increase in membership of the Communist Party also conveyed the continued power of the rank and file and the influence of a workers' education that encouraged an international outlook. The unemployed had already shown in 1927 that they were not prepared to accept their position without challenge. When leadership for action was not provided by the trade union or the Labour Party, it was sought elsewhere.

In the north-east, the labour movement did not appear to show the unity that was displayed in south Wales. By 1931, Labour Party domination in the constituencies was lost, and the effects of the strike appear to have had a 'greater and longer lasting psychological impact'.[103] However, the continued majorities of the Labour Party on local councils and the persistent support for the trade unions in the north-east suggest that the labour movement was resilient. Although sympathy for the Communist Party did exist in the north-east, it did not pose a significant challenge to the unions nor did it provide an alternative source of leadership.[104] The longer tradition of industry and organisation coupled with a relationship built upon consensus with employers continued to prevent a significant militant or radical attitude forming.[105] Loyalty to the DMA and other trade unions therefore remained strong.[106]

While the events of 1926 had long-lasting repercussions, and local factors remained paramount, following the Wall Street crash it was the economic crisis and mass unemployment that shaped more than anything else the activities of the labour movement and the nature of political culture. Unemployment emerged as the central issue for individual representatives' advice and collective action. Economists may have viewed unemployment as a crisis in the 1920s, but the real catastrophe was to emerge in the 1930s, a decade in which unemployment dominated as a social and economic issue. As unemployment levels soared to 2.4 million in 1932, politicians, economists and the Left stood almost awestruck by the apparent human waste caused by capitalism's collapse. Indeed, Richard Overy has argued that while a narrative of civilisation's decline had become 'intellectually fashionable' in the 1920s, it was the slump of the 1930s that really gave characterisation of the period as the 'morbid age'.[107]

It was not only the level of unemployment that was significant. As W. R. Garside has noted, the 'key characteristic' of unemployment in the 1930s was its duration.[108] Long-term unemployment on such a wide scale was unprecedented and lay at the heart of the direst social conditions experienced in those areas reliant on only one or two industries. It was this regional nature of the depression which is also crucial for understanding the impact of the slump. While optimistic historians like Martin Pugh have argued that the depression was not the only feature of the 1930s, the point remains that mass unemployment provided the backdrop for the most depressed regions amongst the working class.[109] It dictated the very quality of life and lifestyles from minor household judgements over the replacement of broken crockery to major decisions of marriage and residence. Key milestones in the life cycle were disrupted, and the pervasive influence of the slump on the outlook of those living in poverty-stricken regions was inescapable regardless of the continuation of cultural and leisure pursuits and the conclusion that Britain remained politically stable. Matt Perry has made the case very clearly that the experience of prosperity or poverty in interwar Britain was very much dependent upon who you were.[110] This was, of course, in part determined by where you lived. The cases of south Wales and the north-east with the reliance on the fortunes of coal, shipbuilding (in the north-east) and iron and steel (to a lesser extent) highlight the significance of place.

Richard Overy's compelling thesis of the collapse of civilisation as first an intellectual and then wider public preoccupation emerged, he argued, following the First World War after decades of seemingly unending progress.[111] South Wales and the north-east exemplify this position. As J. B. Priestley deplored of the plight of Gateshead, 'the town owes its existence, on this scale, to Britain's famous industrial prosperity, to which the town itself in turn contributed. The prosperity itself is now behind us, like the Victorian age with which it is so closely associated, and now we may ask what are the signs and marks of it left in Gateshead?'[112] While south Wales and the north-east drew in migrants searching for work in their hundreds of thousands and wealthy industrialists in the nineteenth century, it was only charities, curious journalists and government officials who were making the journey in the 1930s. Where once men and women had flocked in search of high wages, in the years of the depression they escaped in their hundreds of thousands. In south Wales, 292,353 people left the region between 1921 and 1935 and in the north-east 265,000.[113] Government-assisted transference was only partly responsible for the relocation to more prosperous regions; the majority left of their own accord. Unemployed migrants were drawn to the midlands and the south-east of England where the new 'light' industries offered the prospect of relative affluence or at least the hope of work. Until the later 1930s, there was very little investment into the older industrial regions. As a consequence, transference was viewed as the only option for those living in south Wales and north-east England and the unemployed in the industrial belt of west Scotland and west Cumberland. Together, these four regions were officially recognised as depressed areas under the 1934 Special Areas Act which created commissioners with powers to invest to restructure the economy.[114] Although undoubtedly the most depressed regions, Liverpool and parts of Lancashire were equally deprived.[115]

The long-term unemployed were not a homogenous undifferentiated mass, and the probability of being out of work was affected by location, level of skill and age.[116] Social investigators noted how unemployment was far more likely to occur for those people in the depressed regions, lower-skilled workers and those aged over forty-five years.[117] Such factors determined the effects of unemployment, and the experience of being out of work differed widely amongst the millions of insured workers; a skilled unemployed man from a depressed area was to have a starkly different experience to an unemployed labourer from London. Within south Wales and the north-east of England, while age was still an important factor in being out of work, unemployment was often indiscriminate amongst those it affected: skilled workers were just as likely to find themselves unemployed as labourers. G. D. H. and M. I. Cole shrewdly observed, 'the strangest social fact of the post-war period is that destitution has stalked out from its lurking places in the slums and spread its contagion over the homes of respectable people – even over whole towns and once-flourishing villages in the depressed areas'.[118] The experience of unemployment for those it affected and the rest of the household was therefore in part determined by what stage the individual was in the life cycle, their position within the home and their status within the workplace. As Ross McKibbin has noted, 'they were not the "unemployed" but working men and women out of work. How they coped with unemployment ... was largely determined by the working culture in which they were raised; not by the consequences of unemployment itself'.[119]

The regional nature of the depression shaped wider attitudes towards and of the unemployed: in the south-east, images of the workshy and idle could easily proliferate while, within the depressed areas, the unemployed lamented the ignorance of their plight. The belief of a 'forgotten region' was fundamental to the protest patterns which emerged. However, it was not only orderly lines of marchers or the headline grabbing riots of the unemployed which attracted wider public attention. The work of early sociologists, social investigations and studies of the experience of unemployment continued.[120] Added to the ranks of sociologists were well-meaning novelists and intellectuals as well as political activists and the government. Whether to raise awareness, suggest reforms or pass judgement, those who ventured to worlds without work (to paraphrase E. W. Bakke's study) became crucial in influencing popular representations of the unemployed.[121] Pioneering documentary makers of the Grierson school used ground-breaking film techniques to combine social commentary with startling images to reveal communities without work and glimmers of hope through charity and self-help. *To-Day We Live* and *Eastern Valley* stand as two of the best examples of the social realist documentaries of the period and were funded by the National Council of Social Services. The conditions of life in south Wales are bleakly portrayed, and the contrast of rural Cirencester in *To-Day We Live* conveyed most poignantly Ruby Grierson's efforts to capture capitalism's decline.[122] The work of charities in both sent home the clear message that self-help and practical support were a more hopeful and meaningful alternative to political radicalism.

The works of volunteers, charities and the settlement movements became an important part of public discourses on unemployment. Indeed, the National Council of Social Services encouraged the viewpoint that unemployment offered an extended period of leisure which could be spent profitably. In doing so, they sought to redefine what unemployment meant.[123] The work of charities provided a much needed lifeline for some, and educational courses in particular were seen as a marvellous opportunity. For others, the summer camps of groups of Oxford students, the craft classes and agricultural schemes of the Quakers were an opium intended to pacify and distract from a bitterness at the lack of work. Despite popular perceptions of the workshy, and there were of course cases of dole abuse, the majority of the unemployed desired work more than anything else. By far the biggest impact upon the mindset of the unemployed was the loss of relationships, structure and sense of fulfilment that work brought. The wife of an unemployed man from the Rhondda stated, 'his life was his work ... and though he has given up all hope of working no alternative will take its place'.[124] Without work, a sense of uncertainty pervaded; there was no set time to rise in the morning, no clear structure to the day and no set time to return home.[125] Concern about the psychological impact of the loss of work went beyond the charities attempting to find a remedy to bitterness through self-help.

In the debates about the impact of unemployment in the 1930s, the question of whether the unemployed became bitter and revolutionary or apathetic and listless was central and has remained a matter of debate. Paul Lazarsfeld, Hans Zeisel and Marie Jahoda's classic study of Marienthal concluded that the psychological state of an unemployed person passed through a series of degenerative stages concluding in 'resignation'.[126] Historians have since questioned such an interpretation, and Ross McKibbin has noted that

> there was never any reason to doubt that the lives of most men and women were in some sense work-centred. Nor is it surprising, therefore, that the lack of work could cause dismay and even despair. But it is hard to go beyond that. We cannot convincingly argue that the unemployed disintegrated, that their mental faculties withered, that they lost interest in work, that they became apolitical, or that there was some sort of progressive decline. What is surprising, rather, is how little any of these things happened.[127]

Whether or not the majority of unemployed did become apathetic, it was clear that identity and mindset were affected in some way. How such effects were manifested was highly dependent upon the individual. For example, Mr H. Vickerstaff, from Durham, when speaking at a conference on unemployment felt that 'the inevitable and deadly result of unemployment is apathy. This is general'.[128] John Evans, an unemployed miner from the Rhondda Valleys, felt mixed emotion at being unemployed: 'one moment I feel I could almost lick a man's boots for a favour: another time I feel I could bash him in the face'.[129] While it may be difficult to argue that long-term unemployment resulted in a certain psychological state for all of the unemployed, it cannot be doubted that the loss of income, the increase in uncertainty for the future and the lack of structure to life did weigh heavily on the minds of men and women. Again, it must be emphasised that this was because so many of those facing long-term unemployment were unprepared for such an eventuality.

Although social investigators mainly focused their attention on the unemployed man, the wives and children of the unemployed were equally affected by an out-of-work breadwinner.[130] The promises of the Labour Party to reform welfare for women and children within this social climate saw Labour maintain its appeal within certain areas even after the apparent 'betrayal' of Ramsay MacDonald.[131] The work of Labour at a local level and arguments for work and investment made inside the House of Commons also helped to rebuild the party.[132] For the labour movement more broadly, unemployment took centre stage. With so many unemployed members, trade unions struggled to recapture their lost positions. Within such a precarious labour market, strikes and the campaign for hours of work and pay continued, particularly from the later 1930s. In south Wales, the stay-in strikes from 1935 were emblematic of the SWMF's dual loyalties to workers as well as the unemployed.

As this case demonstrated, unemployment was not the only issue. For trade unions across Britain, the Spanish Civil War saw attention diverted along with negotiations for working members once rearmament spurred the economy from 1936. However, in regions like south Wales and the north-east where unemployment figures remained high right into the war years, unemployment was a key issue throughout. The attempts to lobby the government, offer practical advice on the complex benefits system, raise funds and offer leadership for protest filled up the pages of minute books and reports of trade unions, cooperatives and the Labour Party.

The widespread deprivation of the depressed regions made unemployment an issue that the National Government simply could not ignore despite the pressing nature of international events.[133] The insistence of the cyclical nature of the economy and a classical approach to the handling of the economic crisis saw the government committed to a narrow range of policies. Throughout the 1930s, the government faced a barrage of questions about the unemployed in the House of Commons; numerous requests for deputations from unemployed marchers, church leaders, medical experts and trade unions; and public criticism in the seemingly endless pamphlets, tracts and monographs dedicated to the subject. While Britain did not face the threat of political extremism or a revolution, Home Office files indicate that the government was nonetheless deeply concerned about the collective action of the unemployed. This apparent threat combined with criticism for living conditions made unemployment a major issue alongside other international and domestic issues.

In south Wales and the north-east of England, the depression was clearly the defining feature of the 1930s. The loss of population and the plight of those who remained were to a large extent shaped by the industrial and economic backdrop. This is not to deny or downplay improvements which did exist. Rather, it is to acknowledge the human cost through the social effects of mass unemployment and the repercussions of this beyond both regions. Unemployment was an important governmental issue throughout the interwar period and became at certain moments the most pressing concern. How successive governments responded to the unemployed is revealing of the relationship between marginal groups and the state as well as the government and the working class. The impact of social policy and the protest movements established to help the unemployed find a voice in the public arena were to have a legacy beyond the crisis of the interwar period which preoccupied not only the intellectuals and novelists of the 1920s and 1930s.

Notes

1 G. D. H. Cole, *Out of Work: An Introduction to the Study of Unemployment* (London, 1923), p. 8.

2 Matt Perry, *Bread and Work: The Experience of Unemployment, 1918–1939* (London, 2000), pp. 2–3.

3 Alan Deacon, 'Systems of Interwar Unemployment Relief', in Sean Glynn and Alan Booth (eds), *The Road to Full Employment* (London, 1987), p. 34.

4 Tracts against the evils of unemployment appeared from the early nineteenth century, and by the industrial depressions of the 1880s and 1890s, the unemployed were seen as one of the most pressing industrial issues. London School of Economics Digitised Pamphlets, Fred Hammil, *Out of Work: The Problem of the Unemployed* (Newcastle, 1894); Arthur J. Martin, *The Remedy for Unemployment* (London, 1895); James Keir Hardie, *The Unemployed* (London, 1895).

5 William Beveridge, *Full Employment in a Free Society* (London, 1944), pp. 42–3.

6 John Maynard Keynes, *The Economic Consequences of the Peace* (London, 1920).

7 *Reports of the Commission of Enquiry into Industrial Unrest: No. 1 Division, North-Eastern Area* (Cmd 8662), 1917–18, xv, pp. 10–12.

8 The National Archives, London (hereafter, TNA), CAB/24/67 Cabinet Memorandum. Demobilisation and Unemployment Memorandum by the Minister of Reconstruction, 19 October 1918.

9 The measures were introduced under the Unemployment Insurance Act, 1920. Teachers, nurses, agricultural workers and domestic servants remained excluded. Percy Cohen, *The British System of Unemployment Insurance* (London, 1932), p. 116.

10 Marjorie Levine-Clark, 'The Politics of Preference: Masculinity, Marital Status and Unemployment Relief in Post-First World War Britain', *Cultural and Social History*, 7:2 (2010), p. 235.

11 John Williams, *Digest of Welsh Historical Statistics Volume I* (Pontypool, 1985), pp. 126, 128.

12 Perry, *Bread and Work*, p. 38; Martin Pugh, *We Danced All Night: A Social History of Britain Between the Wars* (London, 2009), p. 86.

13 Jacqueline Jenkinson, *Black 1919: Riot, Racism and Resistance in Imperial Britain* (Liverpool, 2009), pp. 38–66.

14 Race rioting broke out in Barry, Cardiff, Glasgow, Hull, Salford, South Shields, Liverpool, London and Newport. *Ibid.*, p. 1. For a global perspective, see Neil Evans, 'Across the Universe: Racial Violence and the Post-War Crisis in Imperial Britain, 1919–25', in Diane Frost (ed.), *Ethnic Labour and British Imperial Trade: A History of Ethnic Seafarers in the UK* (London, 1995), pp. 59–88.

15 *The Times*, 2 January 1919, p. 3.

16 *Ibid.*, 27 October 1919, p. 2 and 24 December 1919, p. 10; R. B. Crewdson, *Our Unemployment Problem* (London, 1923), p. 26.

17 J. A. Dowie, '1919–20 Is in Need of Attention', *Economic History Review*, 28:3 (1975), p. 429.

18 Richard Croucher, *We Refuse to Starve in Silence: A History of the National Unemployed Workers' Movement, 1920–46* (London, 1987), pp. 23–4.

19 Herbert Feis, 'The Industrial Situation in Great Britain: From the Armistice to the Beginning of 1921', *The American Economic Review*, 11:2 (1921), pp. 265–6.

20 In 1921, trade union membership for the Durham Miners' Association stood at 151,029 and for the South Wales Miners' Federation 197,668, some 73% of the workforce. W. R. Garside, *The Durham Miners, 1919–1960* (London, 1971), p. 96; Chris Williams, *Capitalism, Community and Conflict: The South Wales Coalfield, 1898–1947* (Cardiff, 1998), p. 89.

21 Graham Turner, 'The Stronghold of Labour', in Martin Bulmer (ed.), *Mining and Social Change: Durham County in the Twentieth Century* (London, 1978), p. 124; Chris Williams, 'Labour and the Challenge of Local Government, 1919–1939', in Duncan Tanner, Chris Williams and Deian Hopkin (eds), *The Labour Party in Wales 1900–2000* (Cardiff, 2000), p. 141.

22 G. R. Carter, 'The Coal Strike in South Wales', *The Economic Journal*, 25:99 (1915), pp. 453–65; Hywel Francis and Dai Smith, *The Fed: A History of the South Wales Miners in the Twentieth Century* (Cardiff, 1998), pp. 26–7.

23 David Egan, '"A Cult of Their Own": Syndicalism and *The Miners' Next Step*', in Alan Campbell, Nina Fishman and David Howell (eds), *Miners, Unions and Politics 1910–47* (Aldershot, 1996), p. 29.

24 Garside, *The Durham Miners*, pp. 141, 155.

25 Feis, 'The Industrial Situation in Great Britain', pp. 266–7; J. Morgan Rees, *Unemployment as an International Problem* (London, 1926), p. 42.

26 Cole, *Out of Work*, pp. 10–11; Andrew Thorpe, 'The Industrial Meaning of "Gradualism": The Labour Party and Industry, 1918–1931', *The Journal of British Studies*, 35:1 (1996), p. 85.

27 W. R. Garside, *British Unemployment 1919–1939: A Study in Public Policy* (Cambridge, 1990), pp. 9–11.

28 Rees, *Unemployment as an International Problem*, p. 71.

29 *Ibid.*, p. 115.

30 International Labour Office, *Unemployment Enquiry: Remedies for Unemployment* (Geneva, 1922), p. 3.

31 *Ibid.*, pp. 5–16.

32 Croucher, *We Refuse to Starve in Silence*, p. 11.

33 Wal Hannington, *Unemployed Struggles 1919–1936: My Life and Struggles Amongst the Unemployed* (London, 1977 edition; first published, London, 1936), p. 39.

34 *Ibid.*, pp. 28–80.

35 Peter Kingsford, *The Hunger Marchers in Britain 1920–1939* (London, 1982), p. 33.
36 Perry, *Bread and Work*, p. 40.
37 Deacon, 'Systems of Interwar Unemployment Relief', p. 34.
38 *Daily Mirror*, 25 November 1922, p. 2.
39 Cohen, *The British System of Social Insurance*, p. 121.
40 Alan Deacon, *In Search of the Scrounger: The Administration of Unemployment Insurance in Britain 1920–1931* (London, 1976), pp. 54–5. See also, G. D. H. and M. I. Cole, *The Condition of Britain* (London, 1937), p. 195; Keith Laybourn, *The Evolution of British Social Policy and the Welfare State* (Keele, 1995), p. 189.
41 Deacon, *In Search of the Scrounger*, p. 55.
42 This was shown in the case of Poplar where George Lansbury and other council members were prosecuted for providing illegally generous payments. Pugh, *We Danced All Night*, pp. 78–9.
43 Andrew Taylor, 'Deadweight or Bedrock? The Mineworkers and Labour', in Matthew Worley (ed.), *Foundations of the British Labour Party: Identities, Cultures and Perspectives, 1900–39* (Aldershot, 2009), p. 60.
44 Chris Williams, 'Introduction', in Tanner, Williams and Hopkin, *The Labour Party in Wales 1900–2000*, pp. 1–2.
45 Andrew Thorpe, *The British Communist Party and Moscow, 1920–43* (Manchester, 2000), p. 27.
46 Thorpe, 'The Industrial Meaning of "Gradualism"', pp. 86–95.
47 The historiography for the Durham is not, however, as rich as Hester Barron has noted. John McIlroy, Alan Campbell and Keith Gildart, 'Introduction: 1926 and All That', in John McIlroy, Alan Campbell and Keith Gildart (eds), *Industrial Politics and the 1926 Mining Lockout: The Struggle for Dignity* (Cardiff, 2004), p. 1; Hester Barron, *The 1926 Miners' Lockout: Meanings of Community in the Durham Coalfield* (Oxford, 2010), pp. 12–13.
48 Huw Beynon and Terry Austrin, *Masters and Servants: Class and Patronage in the Making of a Labour Organisation: The Durham Miners and the English Political Tradition* (London, 1994), pp. 243–6.
49 Barron, *The 1926 Miners' Lockout*; Sue Bruley, *The Men and Women of 1926: A Gender and Social History of the General Strike and Lockout in South Wales* (Cardiff, 2010).
50 David Gilbert, *Class, Community and Collective Action: Social Change in Two British Coalfields, 1850–1926* (Oxford, 1992), p. 53.
51 Barron, *The 1926 Miners' Lockout*, p. 263.
52 Lewis Mates, 'A "Most Fruitful Period"? The North East District Communist Party and the Popular Front, 1935–9', *North East History*, 35 (2004), p. 57.
53 Sian Rhiannon Williams, 'The Bedwellty Board of Guardians and the Default Act of 1927', *Llafur*, 2:4 (1979), pp. 65–77; Anne Digby, 'Changing Welfare Cultures in Region and State', *Twentieth Century British History*, 17:3 (2006), pp. 303, 305–12.

54 Beynon and Austrin, *Masters and Servants*, p. 329.

55 McIlroy, 'South Wales', in McIlroy, Campbell and Gildart, *Industrial Politics and the 1926 Mining Lockout*, p. 153.

56 Lewis Mates, 'Durham and South Wales Miners and the Spanish Civil War', *Twentieth Century British History*, 17:3 (2006), pp. 377–8.

57 See Appendix 1.4–1.5.

58 Francis and Smith, *The Fed*, p. 113.

59 Hywel Francis, *Miners Against Fascism: Wales and the Spanish Civil War* (London, 1984), p. 42.

60 Hester Barron has argued that 'it could be argued that the collectivist culture seen in Durham in 1926 exceeded that of South Wales, as it maintained a lower proportion of blacklegs throughout'. Austrin and Beynon, *Masters and Servants*, pp. 336–7; Barron, *The 1926 Miners' Lockout*, p. 263.

61 Dickie Beavis, 'Never Again', in Keith Armstrong and Huw Beynon (eds), *Hello, Are You Working? Memories of the Thirties in the North East of England* (Newcastle, 1977), pp. 22–3.

62 Taylor, 'Deadweight or Bedrock', p. 69.

63 F. Zweig, *Men in the Pits* (London, 1949), p. 10.

64 London School of Economics Digitized Pamphlet HD7/236, *Administering Unemployment Insurance: Report of Trades Union Congress Deputation to the Minister of Labour* (TUC General Council, London, 1929), p. 11.

65 See, for example, the series of special investigations into the coalfields in south Wales and the north-east of England in *The Times* in 1928. *The Times*, 28 March – 2 April, 10–13 September 1928.

66 *First Report of the Royal Commission on Unemployment Insurance* (Cmd 3872), 1930–31, xvii, pp. 900–1.

67 A total of 190,000 men and women migrated through the transference scheme between 1928 and 1937. Of these, around 55,600 returned home between 1930 and 1937. *Royal Commission on the Distribution of the Industrial Population* (Cmd 6153), (HMSO, 1940), p. 150.

68 A. J. Cook, general secretary of the MFGB, marched with the miners and addressed crowds in London, but the march did not have the official endorsement of any of the mining unions. Wal Hannington, *The March of the Miners: How We Smashed the Opposition* (London, 1927), pp. 7–10; Kingsford, *The Hunger Marchers*, pp. 82–7.

69 Hannington, *The March of the Miners*, p. 33.

70 Croucher, *We Refuse to Starve in Silence*, p. 88.

71 The union did, however, support its unemployed members, and the executive committee took an interest in their needs throughout the 1920s. South Wales Coalfield Collection, Swansea University (hereafter, SWCC), South Wales Miners' Federation Executive Council Minutes, 26 March 1926 and 27 January 1928.

72 Jack Jones and Arthur Horner led the marchers. National Library of Wales (hereafter, NLW), Idris Cox Collection, Item No. 44, Rhondda Communist

Party, *South Wales in the March of History: A Message to YOU from the Communist Party* (Tonypandy, 1937), pp. 8–9.

73 Croucher, *We Refuse to Starve in Silence*, p. 90.

74 The name of the movement changed in 1929 to the National Unemployed Workers' Movement (NUWM).

75 Kingsford, *The Hunger Marchers*, pp. 86–7.

76 Mates, 'Durham and South Wales Miners', p. 378.

77 Anthony Mason, 'The General Strike in the North East', *Occasional Papers in Economic and Social History*, No. 3 (Hull, 1970), p. 102.

78 Mates, 'A "Most Fruitful Period"', p. 57. Branches of the NUWCM were active in Stanley and Chester-le-Street. Durham Record Office (hereafter, DRO), UD/CS 203, Chester-le-Street Urban District Council: Correspondence with Chester-le-Street Unemployment Association, 1925.

79 The investigation focused upon the five towns of Reading, Northampton, Warrington, Bolton and Stanley. It aimed to assess whether any improvements had been made since the original inquiry published in 1915. A. L. Bowley and Margaret H. Hogg, *Has Poverty Diminished? A Sequel to 'Livelihood and Poverty'* (London, 1925), pp. 167–200.

80 *Ibid.*, p. 23.

81 In south Wales, the number of miners had declined from 240,000 to 170,000. In Durham and Northumberland, the corresponding figures were from 240,000 to 172,000. *The Times*, 28 March 1928, p. 17, and 10 September 1928, p. 13.

82 *Ibid.*, 28 March 1928, p. 17.

83 *Ibid.*, 28 March 1928, p. 17, and 11 September 1928, p. 15.

84 *Ibid*, 10 September 1928, p. 13.

85 *Ibid.*, 28 March–2 April, 10–13 September 1928.

86 *Ibid.*, 13 September 1928, p. 13.

87 NLW, Papers of Dr Thomas Jones CH, Collection Class C, Vol. 14, Items No. 1, 3, 9 and 20.

88 Sally Alexander, 'Men's Fears and Women's Work: Responses to Unemployment in London Between the Wars', *Gender & History*, 12:2 (2000), p. 402.

89 Andrew Thorpe, *A History of the British Labour Party* (London, 1997), p. 69.

90 Garside, *British Unemployment*, p. 58.

91 Deacon, *In Search of the Scrounger*, pp. 38–9; Perry, *Bread and Work*, p. 43.

92 Cohen, *The British System of Social Insurance*, p. 142.

93 *Report of the Committee on National Expenditure* (Cmd 3920), 1930–31, xvi.

94 Philip Williamson, *National Crisis and National Government: British Politics, the Economy and Empire, 1926–1932* (Cambridge, 1992), pp. 312–17, 339.

95 Thorpe, *A History of the British Labour Party*, p. 76.

96 Williamson, *National Crisis and National Government*, pp. 456, 480–1.

97 *Daily Herald*, 14 October 1931, p. 2.

98 Mates, 'Durham and South Wales Miners', p. 376.

99 Garside, *The Durham Miners,* p. 341.
100 Beynon and Austrin, *Masters and Servants*, pp. 340–1.
101 Stefan Berger, 'Working-Class Culture and the Labour Movement in the South Wales and the Ruhr Coalfield, 1850–2000: A Comparison', *Llafur*, 8:2 (2001), p. 30.
102 Chris Williams, '"The Hope of the British Proletariat": The South Wales Miners, 1910–1947', in Campbell, Fishman and Howell, *Miners, Unions and Politics 1910–47*, p. 140.
103 Mates, 'A "Most Fruitful Period"', p. 379.
104 Communist Party support only existed in pockets. North Tyneside Community Development Project, *North Shields: Working Class Politics and Housing 1900–1977* (Newcastle-Upon-Tyne, 1978), p. 26.
105 Stuart Macintyre has stressed the importance of relatively late industrialisation to the nature of community and militancy amongst the populations in Maerdy and Lumphinnans. Stuart Macintyre, *Little Moscows: Communism and Working-Class Militancy in Inter-war Britain* (London, 1980), pp. 177–80.
106 Neil Evans, 'Patterns of Protest and Regional Labour Implantation in South Wales and the North-East of England, 1780–1950', Regional Implantation of the Labour Movement in Britain and the Netherlands, Papers Presented to the Seventh British-Dutch Conference on Labour History, Groningen, *Tijdschrift voor sociale geschiedenis*, 2/3 (1992), p. 227.
107 Richard Overy, *The Morbid Age: Britain and the Crisis of Civilization, 1919–1939* (London, 2009), pp. 50–69.
108 Garside, *British Unemployment*, p. 15.
109 Pugh argues that even the 'social impact' of heavy regional unemployment 'was mitigated by extensive migrations of people'. Pugh, *We Danced All Night*, pp. 97–9; John Stevenson and Chris Cook, *Britain in the Depression: Society and Politics 1929–39* (London, 1994), pp. 10–14.
110 Perry, *Bread and Work*, p. 26.
111 Overy, *The Morbid Age*, p. 10.
112 J. B. Priestley, *English Journey* (London, 1968 edition; first published, 1941), p. 303.
113 *Report of the Labour Party's Commission of Enquiry into the Distressed Areas: South Wales* (London, 1937), p. 3; *Report of the Labour Party's Commission of Enquiry into the Distressed Areas: Durham and the North-East Coast* (London, 1937), p. 5.
114 The commissioners' ability to stimulate the economy within the depressed regions was seriously impaired by their restrained budget of only £2 million. The creation of trading estates at Team Valley outside Gateshead; Treforest, near Pontypridd in south Wales; and Hillington near Glasgow was one of the most positive achievements. *Royal Commission on the Distribution of the Industrial Population*, p. 128.
115 Lee S. Greene, 'State Policy in the British Depressed Areas: An Experiment in Regionalism', *Social Forces*, 18:3 (1940), p. 338.

116 Garside, *British Unemployment*, pp. 14–15.
117 E. Wight Bakke, *The Unemployed Man: A Social Study* (London, 1935), p. 49.
118 Cole, *The Condition of Britain*, pp. 187–9.
119 Ross McKibbin, *Classes and Cultures: England 1918–1951* (Oxford, 1998), p. 161.
120 *An Industrial Survey of the North East Coast Area* (London, 1932); *The Industrial Position of the North-East Coast of England* (London, 1935); *The Second Industrial Survey of South Wales*, Vol. 3 (Cardiff, 1937).
121 Perry, *Bread or Work*, pp. 30–1.
122 *To-Day We Live*, Ralph Bond and Ruby Grierson, dirs (Strand Film Company, 1937) [documentary film]; *Eastern Valley*, Paul Rotha and Donald Alexander, dirs (Strand Film Company, 1937) [documentary film]; Gwenno Ffrancon, 'Documenting the Depression in South Wales: *Today We Live* and *Eastern Valley*', *Welsh History Review*, 22:1 (2004), pp. 103–25.
123 Richard Flanagan, *'Parish-Fed Bastards': A History of the Politics of the Unemployed in Britain, 1884–1939* (London, 1991), pp. 209–10.
124 *Men Without Work: A Report Made to the Pilgrim Trust* (Cambridge, 1938), p. 68.
125 Perry, *Bread and Work*, p. 63.
126 Marie Jahoda, Paul F. Lazarfeld and Hans Zeisel, *Marienthal: The Sociography of an Unemployed Community* (English edition, London, 1972), p. 53. Other social surveys also agreed with this viewpoint, for example, Bakke, *The Unemployed Man*, pp. 65–7.
127 Ross McKibbin, *The Ideologies of Class: Social Relations in Britain, 1880–1950* (Oxford, 1991), p. 253.
128 Papers of Dr Thomas Jones CH, 'Unemployment from the Point of View of the Unemployed. A Paper Read by Mr H. Vickerstaff, an Unemployed Miner', at the BARS Conference at Durham 22 September 1934, p. 5/2.
129 John Evans, 'Time to Spare', in Felix Greene (ed.), *Time to Spare: What Unemployment Means by Eleven Unemployed* (London, 1935), p. 95.
130 Much less work was completed on unemployed women. Alexander, 'Men's Fears and Women's Work', pp. 409–10.
131 For a wider discussion of the position of women within the Labour Party, see June Hannam, 'Women and Labour Politics', in Worley, *Foundations of the British Labour Party*, pp. 171–91.
132 For example, the Labour Party carried out its own investigations into the 'distressed areas' in 1937.
133 The National Government remained in power throughout the 1930s although under different Prime Ministers.

Part II

1931–34

2

Defiance and disobedience: local government, the unemployed and Whitehall

> Councillor J. Williams: What's the use of sending a protest to the Ministry?
> Alderman B. J. Williams: To show them that we are alive. (Laughter).
> Merthyr Public Assistance Committee Meeting, December 1931.[1]

> Suffering could be alleviated and hardships mitigated, but this would not be sufficiently spectacular for the Labour Party, and so, because they will not deal with those cases where abuses are rampant, thousands of innocents are to suffer. It is senseless stupidity and will surely recoil upon them. Obviously, the open defiance of Durham Public Assistance Committee, if permitted, would simply mean the end of Parliamentary Government.
> William McKeag, Liberal MP Durham City, 1932.[2]

When the National Government formed in the autumn of 1931, its primary aim was to reduce the budget deficit of £120 million. The retrenchment of public expenditure was endorsed by many in the public, and the role of the press in running stories of dole abuse undoubtedly influenced public opinion. Reports in national and regional newspapers argued economies were not only financially necessary but would prevent the workshy from claiming the hard-earned funds of taxpayers.[3] The maintenance of the unemployed was one of the largest areas of government expenditure, and by May 1931, 410,000 people were receiving transitional payments, at a cost of £30 million, from the ranks of the now over 2 million unemployed.[4]

The need for economies in the maintenance of the unemployed was highlighted in two key enquiries, the Royal Commission on Unemployment Insurance and the Committee on National Expenditure. In an effort to sway public opinion, the Committee on National Expenditure deliberately exaggerated the extent of cuts that needed to be made so that any reductions would not appear as drastic.[5] G. D. H. and M. I. Cole commented that 'in the face of a threat to skin the unemployed alive, a subsequent decision merely to beat them black and blue would, it was hoped, be mistaken for clemency'.[6] Through a series of Orders in Council, the National Economy Act introduced reductions in public spending that would amount to total savings of an estimated £70 million in 1932. Economies were focused on the five areas of education, national health insurance, policing, road maintenance and unemployment insurance. The latter was earmarked for the largest savings of £26 million with the principal changes reserved for the long-term unemployed. Although this figure was substantially lower than the Committee on National Expenditure's recommendation and a cut of 10% in benefits, not the 20–30% suggested, was less dramatic, the effect of these economies upon the unemployed was considerable.[7]

From 12 November 1931, for the first time every unemployed person who had received twenty-six weeks insurance benefit had to prove their need through a public assistance-style means test. This included, most controversially, the income of other household members.[8] Two classes of unemployed applicants were created between those who received flat-rate insurance payments and those who received means-tested transitional benefit.[9] This division was cultural as well as bureaucratic. The means test investigations were to be carried out by the Public Assistance Committees which had been created under the Local Government Act, 1929, following the abolition of the Boards of Guardians.[10] The PACs were viewed as the successors to the poor law guardians and carried the taint of destitution and loss of respectability. Although the increased number of jobless may have demonstrated that unemployment was an economic problem and not the consequence of personal failure, few of the unemployed wished to be associated with the poor law.

The Cabinet recognised the impact, to some extent at least, of the connotations of treating the long-term unemployed like public assistance cases. Just four days before the means test was established, Ramsay MacDonald commented 'I certainly do not like this Order' and wrote to the Ministry of Labour stressing that 'the treatment [of transitional applicants] should be more generous than if they were Poor Law cases'.[11] MacDonald was concerned that local authorities may investigate cases in the workhouses and argued that 'we must be careful on this point, as it is one of those violations of sentiment which can be used with the most dire results against us'.[12] The Cabinet was justifiably concerned about the public reception to the drastic changes to the unemployment insurance system, and the connection between the poor law and the respectable working class was continuously raised in the House of Commons and provoked wider protest.[13]

From the outset, it was apparent that the introduction of a means test for the long-term unemployed, many of whom were unused to the position, was to be controversial. While the government predicted some disquiet, there was little discussion of the cooperation of elected officials responsible for administering the test. It was this very aspect that was to lie at the heart of later decisions to centralise the welfare state. During the early years of the means test, councillors and PAC officials grappled with their consciences over whether to act illegally and ignore the legislation or whether to follow government procedure and perhaps alienate their electorate. Examining these debates within south Wales and the north-east, two areas with high unemployment and Labour-controlled councils, and the government's response says much about the attitude towards the unemployed as well as the complexity of the relationship between Whitehall and the local government.

At the end of November 1931, 796,392 people in Britain, some 38.5% of all insured unemployed claimants, were to receive means-tested transitional payments.[14] Unemployment in Britain had reached just under a quarter of the insured population, with the long-term unemployed concentrated in the older industrial regions.[15] In Durham and Glamorgan, the average number of unemployed had reached nearly 40% with some towns recording over 70% unemployment.[16] In the north-east, an estimated 40,000 people were to be tested for benefit in Durham, and in south Wales, Glamorgan PAC also had the responsibility for nearly 40,000 cases and Monmouth PAC for 11,000.[17] These figures increased weekly and officials at Durham PAC noted that to the initial number of transitional applicants 'must be added the weekly additional quota of persons who have drawn 156 days Benefit'.[18] The task placed before local authorities was considerable especially as the government expected means test investigations to begin on 12 November, and thereafter monthly, and new determinations to be made within two months.[19] The cost of financing transitional payments was borne by the Exchequer, and payments continued to be made at Employment Exchanges, where applicants had to register as unemployed. All other administrative duties, including determining scales of relief, were undertaken by the PACs, with the responsibility for the investigations given to the guardians' committees, a subdivision of the PACs.

In the means test investigation, all resources available to an applicant were assessed including any earnings, pensions, savings and investments and the income of other household members.[20] In those households where it was deemed that enough resources existed, transitional benefit could be lowered or even stopped. In effect, transitional applicants could be forced to become reliant upon other family members. The power given to the guardians' committees for carrying out these investigations was to have important repercussions once the means test began operation. The guardians' committees, a body often overlooked in histories of welfare and local government, had much greater contact with the local populace and lobbied PACs over issues affecting their area of jurisdiction.[21] Given the relative autonomy local authorities were entrusted with, economies were stressed throughout the Explanatory Memorandum: 'the Minister ... need scarcely emphasise ... the need for economy in public administration, for in this matter, as in the whole administration of the scheme, he relies with confidence upon the sense of duty and public responsibility of each Authority'.[22] It was predicted that the introduction of the means test would bring economies of some £10 million in 1932.[23]

In establishing the means test, local councillors faced not only an administrative challenge and, in many respects, social and cultural aspects caused far greater concern. Councillors across Britain struggled to determine the best course of action throughout the early years of the means test, and for some this appeared to have genuinely caused great anguish. Labour Party councillors were placed in an extremely awkward position in particular.[24] If councillors decided simply to ignore the means test, they were well aware that their powers could be taken away by the government. Ministry of Labour officials were known to have been less generous than local councillors, and a precedent for superseding authorities had already occurred in, most infamously, Poplar in London and Bedwellty and Chester-le-Street in the 1920s.[25] However, if the means test was implemented, local officials were concerned that this would make them directly responsible for lowering benefits, worsening the position of the unemployed, and it may also have suggested that they agreed with what the government was doing. The quandary was made all the more difficult as in this period 'the gulf between recipient and provider was bridged'.[26] Anne Digby has made the point that many of the PAC and guardians' committee officials were of a similar background to those who were facing the means test.[27] Officials could therefore be potentially means-testing friends and neighbours. Placed in this position, Labour councillors attempted to find a middle road or to adopt what Chris Williams has termed 'a more "pragmatic" approach'.[28] In the early months of the means test, few councils or councillors refused outright to operate the measure although many opted for a more generous interpretation. In pursuing this policy, Labour councillors were adhering to official party line sanctioned at a meeting of Labour-controlled councils on 5 February 1932. While opposed to the means test, Labour representatives were urged to use their discretion and administer the test as they could 'do much to lessen the hardships of the unemployed'.[29]

In both south Wales and the north-east of England, steps were taken to establish the machinery of the means test and to set scales of relief in the weeks after the Order in Council created the new scheme. Establishing uniformity and cooperation in the administration and treating applicants like public assistance cases were stressed. Given the magnitude of the task, Durham PAC wrote to the Minister of Labour to request a three-month transitional period.[30] However, despite this outward show of implementing the means test, councillors and MPs in both regions promised that a generous assessment would take place. Rose Davies – the first female member, alderwoman and chair of Glamorgan County Council – noted that 'we hope to manage the Means Test in the most humane way possible'.[31] Such promises did not allay all fears. In Porthcawl, for example, the unemployed were left trying to retrieve their papers from the town dock after they had been thrown there following a raid, by an unknown individual, on the Labour Exchange the previous evening.[32] In the north-east, similar expressions were made; 'in a reference to applying to the Public Assistance Committee for transitional benefit, Mr Ritson [Labour MP, Durham] said it was well for them in Durham County, where they had their own people as members of the Committee'.[33] Mr J. W. Chambers, clerk of Durham PAC, believed that the industrial situation was so bad within the county that he expected 95% of applicants to get a full rate of benefit.[34] Even in these early months, it was evident that councillors were unsure about how far the discretionary element and a commitment to generous payments should be taken. In Durham, a conference of PAC members and representatives of relief subcommittees was held to discuss the 'varying methods adopted throughout their area in the administration of the Order in Council'. Interestingly, the first item on the agenda was a vote on whether the means test should in fact be implemented. The meeting 'unanimously decided to do so', but it was clear that some favoured a more generous administration than others.[35]

When the means test began operation, it was soon evident that the guardians' committees were even less committed to establishing the uniformity officially urged by PACs. In south Wales, from the outset many guardians' committees showed little willingness to treat transitional applicants in the same way as public assistance cases. Indeed, the decision was taken by some guardians' committees not to carry out means test investigations in applicants' homes as the Order stipulated. Instead, Labour Exchanges and other premises were used, and the long-term unemployed were allowed to take along a trade union representative or even their wives to the amusement of some officials.[36] The *Western Mail* picked up upon the situation, reporting 'that in South Wales as a whole and in the mining districts in areas of Glamorgan in particular no serious attempt is being made to observe the rule relating to family income and resources at all ... transitional benefit is being treated as though it is something to which the applicant is entitled under the Insurance Act'.[37]

By not investigating the income of other household members, officials were avoiding an intrusive scrutiny of family income and thereby preventing reductions in allowances being made. How far guardians' committees were ignoring family income became much clearer when the UAB began its work in late 1934. Members of the Board argued that there had been a 'maladministration' in south Wales regarding the resources of household members in particular.[38] In both regions, the main issue over the implementation of the means test was the consideration of resources available to applicants; Labour-dominated authorities were unprepared to see the long-term unemployed lowered to the status of public assistance cases. Many of the long-term unemployed had previously paid into the insurance scheme for long periods, and local officials were well aware of this fact. Cultural signifiers of respectability and upstanding within communities meant officials on guardians' committees were not going to radically alter their view of a group with whom they had previously had little contact.

In the north-east of England, some guardians' committees and councils were quite open about their disagreement with implementing a means test, highlighting the strength of feeling against the measure. Middlesbrough PAC made clear its displeasure from the outset.[39] Gateshead PAC decided at a meeting on 21 October 1931, to refuse to implement the means test. However, when the matter was taken before the council, a majority voted against the PAC's decision. Councillor Ryan resigned from the 'Socialist Group' of the council over the issue.[40] Blyth guardians' committee made a similar initial protest against the means test, and some members refused outright to implement it.[41] The matter eventually appeared before Northumberland PAC, and officials at Blyth were urged to comply.[42] In Gateshead and Blyth, as elsewhere, the approach was taken that it was better that local officials implement the measure rather than government personnel. After these initial disagreements over whether to implement the means test, it was decided, albeit unofficially, that, as in south Wales, applicants would not face a full public assistance-style examination. In particular, ex-servicemen's pensions and disability allowances, a notable area of contention, and earnings from sons or daughters were disregarded.[43] R. B. Hindmarsh, the public assistance officer for Durham PAC, noted in a confidential report to the committee that in 'matters which are to be dealt with on their own merits, there is a marked variance in the procedure of different committees'. Hindmarsh observed that 'disability and other pensions are ignored entirely in some districts, whilst in others a proportion of the pension is taken into account. Similarly as to the Earnings of Adult Children, in one Relief District a specified amount is allowed to a son working.... In an adjoining Relief District the earnings of sons are entirely ignored as household income, and in another adjoining District a son is regarded as a lodger'.[44] Hindmarsh recommended that the Ministry of Labour be asked for an extension of time 'for dealing with these cases'.[45] Yet, despite the efforts of many councillors who urged cooperation, it was clear that in the north-east and south Wales there were great disparities between the official line of PACs and the actual practice of the guardians' committees. Across Britain, variations began to emerge in the level of payments the long-term unemployed received: benefits were increasingly dependent on the politics and attitudes of local councillors.

Although many PACs and guardians' committees used the discretionary element to provide generous payments, not all local authorities interpreted the legislation in this way even within the depressed areas. In South Shields, the PAC was noted to have been one of the strictest in the region, and it awarded just 10s. for a single person living in lodgings in comparison to the 18s. that could be claimed from Gateshead PAC.[46] Similarly, Newcastle PAC was also noted for its rigidity in adhering to the Order in Council.[47] The differences were much greater for men than women, even within generous authorities.[48] By January 1932, just two months into the operation of the means test, the disparities in transitional payments between different PACs were clear as table 2.1 indicates.

The variations in payments awarded in different areas were quite stark; opposition to the principal of means testing only partly accounts for decisions made by local authorities to reduce or disallow the benefit of so few transitional applicants. The fact that transitional payments were a charge upon the Exchequer led many contemporaries, and subsequently many historians, to conclude that councils were paying the highest rate of benefit as it had 'no financial interest in the decision'.[49] Such accusations formed one of the main criticisms of the Majority Report in the final

Table 2.1 Table to show determinations of transitional payments November 1931–January 1932

	Total for Great Britain	*Glamorgan PAC*	*Durham PAC*	*Newcastle PAC*
	12 Nov 1931–23 Jan 1932[a]	12 Nov 1931–30 Jan 1932[b]	12 Nov 1931–22 Jan 1932[c]	12 Nov 1931–15 Dec 1931[d]
Determinations for transitional applicants in %				
Full	49.2	89.1	89.2	42.5
Reduced	35	5.6	8.4	33.8
Disallowed	15.7	5.3	2.4	23.7

Sources: [a]*Ministry of Labour Gazette*, February 1932, p. 46; [b]*Western Mail*, 13 February 1932, p. 9; [c]Report of the Public Assistance Officer on Unemployment Insurance, p. 61A; [d]*Newcastle Journal*, 17 December 1931, p. 9

publication of the Royal Commission on Unemployment Insurance. However, given the stringent economic position of many local authorities, such arguments failed to appreciate the very real financial incentive for sanctioning full or partial payments. Some applicants who were disallowed any payments preferred to face the humiliation of public assistance rather than financially rely on working family members. This led to a dramatic increase in public assistance applications across the country. As early as January 1932, the public assistance officer for Durham PAC drew attention 'to the increasing numbers of persons who have been refused unemployment benefit and have been compelled to apply for public assistance'.[50] This matter was raised in parliament by J. J. Lawson (Labour MP, Chester-le-Street) who stated that 'as a result of the operation of the Means Test it was not denied that nearly 150,000 persons had been pushed back on the Poor Law, and local authorities were now beginning to kick'.[51] Similarly, in south Wales, the *Porth Gazette* questioned why more people were applying for public assistance and concluded that it was 'to one thing only, as far as we can see. To the tightening up of the Dole and the Means Test. In other words we are just taking people off the dole and putting them on the parish'.[52]

Public assistance was funded by local ratepayers, and in the early 1930s the cost of assistance was already running high.[53] The increased number of applicants applying for assistance on account of being disallowed transitional payments further strained the budget of the PACs. Committees could only finance the extra applicants for relief by increasing local rates: effectively, local authorities were being left with the burden of maintaining the unemployed. At the annual meeting of the TUC held at Newcastle in September 1932, Peter Lee, president of the MFGB and general secretary of the DMA, commented that 11,819 people in Durham had to be maintained by the PAC after being disallowed benefit. He argued that the means test should be abolished because the burden had been shifted from a national to a local charge.[54] The decision to generously administer the means test was, therefore, based upon this financial incentive as well as personal opposition, Labour policy and the undoubted influence of the growing protests of the unemployed. Local authorities, for their part, expressed their own opposition to the measure throughout the early months of the means test.[55]

The decision of local councillors to use their discretionary powers to the full featured regularly in the regional press, and soon national newspapers began to monitor the situation.[56] In an editorial of the *Manchester Guardian* in January 1932, the discrepancies in payments between Lancashire on the one hand and Glamorgan and Durham on the other were used to signify the untenable position of the system. The editorial criticised the government stating that the 'immense amount of local friction, the widespread feeling that local administrators have been made the whipping-boys for Whitehall, the sporadic disturbances of the peace are all signs of an ill-thought-out piece of Government policy.'[57] The National Government was unprepared to see the continuation of these perceived abuses in the system and began to investigate the situation.

Given the publicity of the low numbers financially affected by the means test, PACs in south Wales and the north-east of England were perhaps an obvious target for Ministry of Labour officials. Glamorgan PAC was one of the first local authorities that were asked by the Ministry of Labour for assurance that transitional applicants would be treated on the same merit as cases for public assistance.[58] The Ministry of Labour reminded Glamorgan officials that unless they complied, guardians' committee members could be replaced.[59] The use of such a strong ultimatum from the first contact with Glamorgan is perhaps reflective of the region's reputation for militancy. Yet, while councillors and MPs were vocal in their opposition to the means test, the outcome of the investigation was an agreement that guardians' committees would be instructed 'to consider each application on its merits' and not to simply ignore the legislation.[60] Although many may not have agreed in principle, or morally, councillors felt it was better that they and not government officials administered the test.

While Henry Betterton, the Minister of Labour, had served Glamorgan with an ultimatum, he reported to the Prime Minister in late March 1932 that 'in Durham I am not going so far at this stage'.[61] The Ministry of Labour instead wrote to the secretary of Durham PAC that:

> while in reviewing the general administration of the Order by your Council the Minister fully appreciates the effects of the severe and prolonged trade depression in the County of Durham, the practice in the treatment of individual cases ... is a matter of grave concern to him ... the Minister is unable to believe that the amounts determined are, in fact, related to the needs of the applicant.[62]

Without facing the threat of losing its administrative powers, Durham PAC was, unlike its counterparts in Glamorgan, far more prepared to speak out against intervention.

After considering the Ministry of Labour's letter, Durham PAC members decided first that the finance subcommittee should investigate and produce a report.[63] In the next meeting of the PAC, the finance subcommittee reported that 'we recommend that the Minister of Labour be informed, that speaking generally, the Committee deny the assertions made by him but that as they are not conversant with the details of the cases set out in ... his letter they have referred the same to the Guardians Committees concerned for full investigation'.[64] The report was adopted and the motion passed.[65] It was not until the June meeting of Durham PAC that the matter was raised again, and at this stage it was clear that members were not prepared to accept either the accusations made by the Ministry of Labour or the full requirements of the means test legislation. The guardians' committees, after consideration, decided that they would 'adhere to our previous determinations', and they argued that certain features of the legislation made an 'unreasonable requirement' upon transitional applicants. The defence for taking this action was the committees' 'local knowledge and the present local conditions' and that they had 'in the absence of definite guidance from the Minister of Labour' worked 'to the best of our ability'.[66] The lack of guidance resulting in an inability to make payments in line with the Order was also commented upon by Gateshead PAC.[67] While Durham councillors were not yet refusing to implement the means test, they adopted a course of action in these months that would see their eventual replacement by government administrators.

By the summer of 1932, the Ministry of Labour had also written to Monmouth, Sunderland, Lanchester, Swansea, Merthyr and Middlesbrough PACs. In March 1932, Swansea had received its first communication and, like Glamorgan PAC, it agreed to reconsider certain cases and referred the matter to the guardians' committees.[68] Sunderland

PAC was also accused of treating transitional applicants differently from public assistance cases, and it was felt that 'the difference is especially marked in the treatment of family income'.[69] The PAC agreed to refer the matter back to the guardians' committees, and this appears to have been the last time communication from the Ministry of Labour was received.[70] A similar situation occurred in Lanchester and Monmouth PACs, and, there too, the Ministry does not appear to have communicated further after an initial warning.[71] In Middlesbrough, the situation was not resolved until October when the council voted against the PAC's resolution to refuse to administer the means test.[72] The desire to maintain the status of applicants and a level of benefit that was deemed acceptable, as well as keeping public assistance costs down, was leading PAC officials to commit what was in essence fraud; they continued to do so even after they were warned by the Ministry of Labour. In south Wales, despite the assurances given by PACs that cases would be reinvestigated, the Ministry of Labour remained concerned that this was not happening in practice. In July 1932, Glamorgan PAC received further communication from the Ministry of Labour, and in August Swansea PAC was informed that its officials were going to be replaced.[73]

The commitment of Labour-dominated PACs to their unemployed constituents is revealed when their actions are compared with PAC members in councils where Labour did not have such a strong foothold. Newcastle PAC maintained a position of strictly adhering to the regulations despite the outcry that this caused. In March 1932, Sir Robert Aske (Liberal MP, Newcastle East) commented in the local newspaper that he 'had been unable to find any other areas where such a mean standard was taken'. Aske believed 'this inequality of Newcastle relative to other areas is more severely felt, because of the serious depression in the shipbuilding trade.... For this reason one would think that the administration should be on the most generous lines possible'.[74] A large demonstration was held to protest against the PAC, and a deputation declared 'we intend to have this means test abolished, and there will be no peace in Newcastle and no peace in England until it is abolished'.[75] The perceived harshness of the administration even drew the attention of religious bodies, and in April the clergy of Newcastle sent a letter of protest to the PAC complaining that mothers were suffering from undernourishment. The document, which became known as 'the clergy manifesto', caused outcry in the committee and drew national attention.[76]

The clerk of the PAC questioned the evidence upon which the manifesto was based and stated that the clergy should have approached the committee with the particulars of individual cases. The response from the clerk shows how differently councillors could perceive the means testing of the long-term unemployed:

> I think it only right to say, lest the impression should get abroad that the administration is unsatisfactory, that in the opinion of the officers of the Ministry of Health, who deal with matters relating to transitional payments, this Committee stands amongst the three first in England for efficiency in carrying out the administration of the Order in Council. It will, I think, be satisfaction to this Committee to know that those best able to judge, hold such an opinion and appreciate the high standard attained by the Committee in carrying out the extraordinarily difficult task which has been entrusted to them by H. M. Government.[77]

Such a sentiment was not shared by all members of the city council, and councillor W. Thompson responded by saying, 'I have no sense of pride in knowing that we are one of three committees who have won the government's approval'.[78] A heated discussion followed; councillor Oates moved that the committee should refuse to administer the test and councillor Lowery that the committee should meet the Minister of Health. After failure to reach an agreement on either resolution, and despite protestations from councillor King that they were deserting the poor, Oates and Lowery both resigned from their positions rather than continue to administer the means test.[79] For councillors, the means test became a central issue of debate, rousing as it did heated feelings amongst those who saw their duty towards the unemployed first and to make economies second.

The variations of the administration between, and indeed within, different regions provoked outcry across Britain that this was leading to the unfair treatment of the unemployed in certain cases.[80] While Labour-dominated Glamorgan PAC disallowed 1.8% of transitional applicants between 25 January 1932 and 3 September 1932, the 'politically divided' Lancashire PAC disallowed as many as 33.3%.[81] Herbert Samuel, leader of the Liberal Party, wrote to the Prime Minister outlining his concern for the unemployed in Lancashire and not least because he felt the strict administration affected those who were 'usually among the most respectable in their neighbourhoods'. Samuel argued that the actions of the PAC were 'undoubtedly giving rise to much discontent, and, I suggest, legitimate discontent'.[82] Samuel was right to be concerned about the reverberations of the administration of the means test, and the protest against the measure throughout Britain intensified in the autumn of 1932. Serious rioting occurred in Birkenhead and Belfast, and there was another national hunger march in

October. As more men and women took to the streets, PACs across the country denounced the means test with some refusing to administer it at all.

The scale of opposition in September and October 1932 caused alarm within the cabinet and led to a relaxation of certain rules under the Transitional Payments (Determinations of Need) Act. The Act lowered the amount of income that could be taken into account from pensions, compensations and investments and emphasised that an applicant could not be forced to sell or mortgage his or her home.[83] Before the introduction of the new legislation, MacDonald's secretary warned Henry Betterton that 'the Prime Minister says he feels perfectly certain that this is going to be one of the most difficult corners that you will have to get round during this winter, and there might be a serious breakaway on our side unless something was done'.[84] While historians have suggested a 'tacit' understanding was reached by the government and PACs through the concessions in the Act, this was not necessarily the case. Far from allowing a lenient administration of the means test, the Ministry of Labour continued its investigation with PACs feeling the full force of government administration.[85]

The contradictions and tensions in the National Government's policy of reform (to defuse political tension) and retrenchment reflected the ambiguity that surrounded its position regarding the long-term unemployed. On the one hand, the numbers of jobless made them a body to be feared, but, on the other, reports of dole abuse also made them a group connected with illegality, fraud and idleness. While reforms attempted to pacify the unemployed, the commitment remained to eradicating abuses. Undergoing a means test examination was often characterised as a patriotic 'duty' to help the economy. When Ramsay MacDonald wrote to the Morpeth Labour MP, Ebenezer Edwards, before the economy cuts were made, he stressed the necessity of 'some amount of common sacrifice' which 'spread the burden ... equally throughout the community'.[86] If benefits were paid unlawfully, everyone was seen to suffer and the unemployed were asked to carefully consider the fact that they were living off the hard-won earnings of others. Indeed, the *Western Mail* observed that 'transitional benefit is paid wholly out of the funds provided by the taxpayer, and the latter is entitled to insist that it shall be paid only where distress is proved to exist'.[87]

The demonisation of the unemployed in the public mind contributed to the struggle local authorities faced in their decision over whether or not to administer a full household means test. Officials who had been elected into their position also had to consider their future prospects within the county or locality over their handling of the means test: both ratepayers and the unemployed needed to be appeased. In Durham PAC, such tensions reached the fore in late 1932 as officials were caught between their desire to administer the test in a manner they deemed acceptable and to maintain their position on the council. As the only two authorities whose administration was replaced by Ministry of Labour officials, Durham and Rotherham PACs have often been used as exemplars of local authority defiance.[88] The case of Durham highlights how councillors felt gradually pushed to adopting the radical stance of refusing to administer the means test. Throughout these months, the national press closely followed events.

In July 1932, the Ministry of Labour wrote to Durham PAC with an ultimatum: either uniformity be secured and full household income be considered, or the means test administration would be undertaken by Ministry officials.[89] The PAC was given just ten days to respond to the Minister with its course of action, and in August a special meeting was convened for this purpose. The Minister had pointed out that excessive payments were continuing and gave examples of cases where full determinations were made despite the existence of investments of £810.[90] The Minister deemed it unacceptable that transitional applicants and public assistance cases continued to be treated differently.[91] The response to the letter and a report prepared by Harold Jevons, clerk to the county council, and R. B. Hindmarsh split the PAC. Councillor Gilliland moved and councillor Hurst seconded that the Ministry of Labour be asked if a deputation could be received. Councillors Kelly and Wallace proposed the amendment that the council refuse to treat transitional and public assistance applicants in the same way. Further disagreement came from councillors Murray and Benfold who stated that the committee should agree to re-examine all cases. Even within a largely Labour-dominated PAC, reaching a decision with regards to the means test was marred with complications. The final decision was for a deputation to meet with the Ministry of Labour to discuss the situation.[92]

On 6 September 1932, a deputation consisting of George Bloomfield (chair), J. M. Cape (vice-chair) and councillors Jevons and Hindmarsh met, to their annoyance, not with the Minister of Labour but with secretaries to the Ministers of Labour and Health. In outlining its case, the deputation chose to emphasise councillors' expertise of local conditions, which made them the best administrators of welfare and explained the discrepancies in payments. Given the severity of the depression in Durham, the 'only fault' of the long-term unemployed was 'that they cannot obtain work although they are keenly desirous of work of any character'.[93] While councillors understood why family income was considered for public assistance claims, they were 'of the opinion that the same drastic action should not be taken when dealing with transitional cases'.[94] They were not only concerned about the long-term unemployed, and they felt that all family members could be affected by a household means test:

> Does the Minister desire us to believe that young men who are anxious to make their way in the world should devote their surplus income to the upkeep of their father's home and so jeopardise their own chance of getting together a home of their own, or that fathers should be obliged to keep sons of adult age who cannot secure work to the detriment of younger children.[95]

The deputation concluded that if the government insisted on treating transitional applicants like able-bodied paupers, then several councillors 'have definitely declared ... they will not take part in the work'.[96]

While the Prime Minister himself may have expressed anxiety over the position of the long-term unemployed, Sir Francis Floud, from the Ministry of Labour, was keen to reinforce the official line that the government was under no obligation to make payments to the unemployed after 156 days as the long-term jobless 'had ceased to have any contractual rights to benefit'. Therefore, transitional applicants should be tested strictly along the same lines as public assistance cases as they did not have the same right to benefit as workers within the insurance scheme. Floud made it clear that Durham PAC must show 'a definite expression of willingness' to comply with the Order and that it was the responsibility of the county council to ensure guardians' committees were implementing the means test.[97] For the government, the greatest concession was that any maintenance continued for the long-term unemployed at all. It was not prepared to accept any arguments of the social status of claimants or the dire economic circumstances preventing a return to work. However, the government would only supersede an authority when an unequivocal statement of its refusal to administer the means test was given. Within the tense atmosphere of late 1932, the government wanted to make a stand against uncooperative PACs. This demonstrated the government's commitment to economies and to taxpayers; further concessions to the unemployed were only made following unrest.

The deputation to the Ministry of Labour took place just weeks before Rotherham PAC was informed its administration of transitional payments was suspended. As in south Wales and Durham, there had been extensive communication between the Ministry of Labour and Rotherham Council. When Rotherham finally declared that they would not operate the means test in line with the Order, it became the first PAC to lose its powers.[98] The debates within Durham took place as events in Rotherham unfolded.

A special meeting of Durham PAC was convened on 12 September to discuss the deputation's visit and decide how to respond. The decision over whether to continue to administer the means test nearly divided the committee, but, in the end, the vote against was won by twenty-nine to twenty-one.[99] The action of PAC members was met with much criticism from within and outside of the county council. To many, the actions of Labour were seen as opportunistic propaganda, as the cartoon from the *Northern Despatch* in Figure 2.1 indicates.

William McKeag described the actions of the PAC as 'a cruel and flagrant sacrifice of the people on the altar of cheap popularity'. McKeag felt that if the government were to appoint commissioners, the means test investigation would be tightened: 'I can only see more suffering ahead for the people of Durham and all because of the pig-headedness of the Labour Council. The unemployed men and women of Durham County and their families are to be put on the rack to provide political propaganda for the Labour Party'.[100]

As the protests of the unemployed escalated in other parts of the country, an emergency meeting of Durham County Council was held on 11 October to discuss the PAC's decision. The meeting lasted for over two

Gentleman, catching sight of himself in shop window: Good heavens, what an ass I look!

Figure 2.1 *Northern Despatch*, 14 September 1932, p. 4

hours, and there was a heated debate between those who supported the PAC and those who believed applicants would be in a better position if the PAC continued to assess cases. On the side of the moderates, Conservative MP Col. Headlam (Barnard Castle) argued that 'it is our duty as the elected representatives of this county to do our utmost to mitigate suffering, and we can do this best by looking after the people's interests ourselves'. Clearly, it was not only the traditional supporters of the unemployed who could take such a stand. Peter Lee outlined the case against the means test, and at the end of his speech, in which he deplored the Order being carried out to the letter, he was applauded. The views of Lee were supported by the majority of the council, and a resolution was sent to the Ministry stating that the council would no longer administer the means test.[101] On the same day, Glamorgan and Merthyr PACs were told that their administrations were to end, and Newport Council also declared its opposition to the means test. The government, the *Daily Herald* reported, was seriously considering placing the means test under the control of commissioners across the country.[102]

The National Government was left with little choice but to take over the administration of Durham PAC, and, on 1 December 1932, three Ministry of Labour commissioners began to administer the means test. By 28 January 1933, the commissioners had reviewed the determinations of 74,514 cases; 70% were granted full payments, 23.5% received a reduced payment and 6.5% (some 4,878 people) were disallowed. Before the commissioners were appointed, the corresponding figures were 92%, 7% and 1%, respectively.[103] The strict administration and level of cuts generated widespread protest within the county. The commissioners argued that the increased number being disallowed was 'not because of undue severity or rigidity in our administration, but because of those defects and laxities which existed before we took over'.[104] After a year in their post, the commissioners concluded that 'Durham County Council never made any serious attempt to carry out their statutory duties'.[105]

The final decision by Durham County Council not to administer the means test should be seen first and foremost as an ad hoc response to an unexpected turn of events, and next as a reflection of a mixture of Labour Party propaganda and genuine sympathy towards the unemployed. Anne Digby has argued that 'although the term "poplarism" has passed into the English language as being synonymous with generous relief, it was not the London borough of Poplar, but administrators in County Durham that mounted the most prolonged interwar challenge to centrally determined welfare policies'.[106] Within the county, a precedent from 1926 existed for defying government relief policy, and the increased body of unemployed must have prompted further non-cooperation. However, it must be recognised that in the initial months of operating the means test, the PAC officials did show a willingness to cooperate, and outright defiance was not apparent or a policy pursued by councillors. What changed the situation was the failure to reach agreement on the status of transitional applicants, as MacDonald had feared.

Throughout the first year of the means test, PAC officials were consistent in their argument that a separation must be maintained between 'poor law' relief and those who were unemployed because of the depression. It was only when they were forced to either comply or refuse to do so that councillors declared quite firmly against; many felt unable to treat the long-term unemployed in a way that they could not agree with on principle. It must be remembered that those who worked on guardians' committees had to investigate the circumstances of their neighbours or people they used to work with. It was this issue that commissioners saw as key to explaining why the means test had not been properly implemented: PAC officials, they argued, 'endeavoured to combine the dual functions of municipal councillor and investigating officer.... We did not feel that the possession of local knowledge by elected municipal councillors outweighed the objections to employing them in their own or neighbouring areas'.[107] The commissioners' comments also reveal that it was not just the proximity of the councillors to the unemployed population that caused concern. Party policy and personal sympathies in this situation could not be easily divorced, and councillors were concerned for their elected position.

Across the country, the Labour Party was keen to stress its efforts to soften the strict letter of the rules governing the means test and especially during electoral campaigns. In the Glamorgan County Council elections in 1934, the campaign posters for the Labour candidate Tom Davies carried the slogan 'Labour has secured the Maximum Advantage for the Out-of-Work: Remember this on Polling Day'.[108] Davies reminded the voters that 'Despite the iniquities of the Means Tests, perpetuated by the National Government, the Labour members have continued to administer Transitional Payments in the most generous spirit possible'.[109] In County Durham, where the Labour Party had fared so badly in the general election, locally the party wanted to maintain its majority by adopting a popular approach. Beynon and Austrin have argued that as the means test was a National Government policy, if it were implemented by Ministry of Labour commissioners, the local population would see what the policies of the newly elected National Government MPs meant.[110] By adopting the radical measure of refusing to administer the means test, councillors and the Labour Party were able to free themselves from criticisms of worsening the position of the unemployed and could stand united in opposition to a measure implemented by the National Government. Criticism of the means test therefore became directed at Whitehall and not local authorities. Indeed, Labour Party members on Durham Council were praised for their efforts, and protest was much less apparent here. In Durham, a combination of personal, moral, financial and political factors combined to create a situation where the means test was eventually viewed to be unacceptable and councillors risked worsening the position of the unemployed as a consequence. The quite radical decision to refuse to administer the means test was somewhat surprising given the political tradition of the region, and it begs the question why councillors did not do the same in south Wales.

In south Wales, certain PACs were threatened with the removal of administrative powers after continuous refusal to implement the means test properly. As in the north-east, the tension between party and local loyalty and sympathy with the plight of the unemployed were evident, and, after events in Durham unfolded, it was clear that the government was more than prepared to replace local administrations. Both Swansea and Merthyr were informed by the Ministry of Labour that their powers to administer the means test were going to be taken over after constant failures to implement it properly. Merthyr PAC had received such notification in March 1932, and in October of that year, the Ministry of Labour secretary with responsibility for the means test, W. Eady, visited the committee. Eady asked officials to administer the means test 'apart from sympathy or sentiment'.[111] Here, as in Durham, Eady underlined the need for economies regardless of the personal relationship councillors could have with the unemployed. Despite assurances that the test would be properly implemented, in May 1933 the Ministry informed Merthyr PAC that it was to be replaced. Again, the failure to test transitional applicants as public assistance applicants was the main stimulus for intervention.[112]

Merthyr Borough Council decided to send a deputation to visit the Ministry of Labour, and the mayor, councillor Hugh Isaac Williams, and Enoch Morrell, the town clerk, travelled to London almost immediately. They later reported how they met with Eady 'whose attitude towards them was that of "an irate schoolmaster dealing with a truant pupil"'.[113] However, unlike in Durham, councillors at Merthyr were extremely anxious to avoid being taken over. Both the mayor and Morrell met with

George Hall (Labour MP, Aberdare) and George Lansbury, who had taken a lead role in the actions of Poplar Council in 1921, to ask for advice. With the help of Hall, although he was not their MP, they decided that a special committee should be formed to administer the test properly.[114] This was put before the county council and gained a majority in favour. After another meeting with the Ministry of Labour, it was agreed that the PAC would not be taken over.[115] Events in Swansea PAC followed a similar course of action. In early January 1933, the PAC was informed that its powers were going to be given to commissioners after it failed to comply despite assurances made from March 1932. PAC members also decided to visit the Ministry of Labour after hearing that they would be replaced in August. The Minister of Labour conceded on this occasion but argued in future it would be given little choice when generous payments continued to be made.[116] However, again PAC officials were adamant that commissioners would not be appointed, and they took the step of asking 'all members of the Town Council to assist in administering the Means Test'.[117]

Glamorgan PAC, despite ongoing scrutiny from the Ministries of Labour and Health in 1932 and 1933, including a visit from Ministry officials, also managed to avoid seeing its administration replaced.[118] Councillors in Glamorgan believed that they had managed to dupe the Ministry by giving the impression that cuts were being imposed. Councillor W. J. Edwards argued that 'Glamorganshire were playing for time. They had been confronted by many cases in the past few weeks which they were asked to cut down. The County was gaining time by imposing small reductions, knowing that these costs would have to be reconsidered in a few months time'.[119] Such comments were made even more forcefully once the PAC's administration ended.[120] However, given the strictness of the Ministry of Labour in other areas where a similar position was taken, government leniency appears curious. Clearly, other factors were also relevant.

When the UAB began its work, Thomas Jones, the parliamentary secretary and member of the UAB, asked for a special report to be carried out in south Wales as he was concerned about the reception that the tightening up of the means test would have in the region.[121] In the early 1930s, by not directly threatening PAC officials with removal, the government was attempting to avoid public outcry and widespread opposition. Glamorgan County covered a large swathe of the south Wales region including the central valleys which were well known for working-class militancy and political radicalism. Protest marches and demonstrations had occurred with some regularity since the introduction of the means test. It was also an area where the Communist Party was gaining ground. The *Merthyr Express* noted in an editorial in late 1932 that it expected in the forthcoming council elections that the Communist Party in Penydarren would use arguments against the means test as 'a popular war cry which would win many votes for their candidate.'[122] While it would be speculative to suggest that Glamorgan PAC was allowed to implement the means test generously to avoid the area becoming a stronghold for the Communist Party, the desire to avoid widespread unrest in the region must be taken into account. The National Government was keen to avoid giving cause to further outcry following the wave of, often violent, protest in late 1932 across Britain. Without being faced with the imminent threat of a loss of powers, Glamorgan PAC was never forced to agree or disagree with the means test and was able to pursue a more pragmatic line.

By late 1933, PACs across south Wales had been forced into adopting a means test examination which, although still generous, was more in keeping with the rules set out in the Order in Council. The decision by councillors in the region to implement a more lenient form of the means test was met with disapproval locally; taking this course of action did mean that arguments against the means test could be levelled directly to local authorities. At a meeting of the unemployed at Tillery Institute, Abertillery, in April 1932, 'a resolution protesting against the Means Test and "the hypocrisy of the Labour Party in claiming to operate the Means Test 'humanely'," was moved by Mr Reg Jones (Pontypool)'.[123] This meeting included delegates of the surrounding area thought to represent 13,987 people.[124] Labour councillors were criticised directly for the effects of their administration of the means test on the local population; this could lead to other political parties, principally the Communist Party, gaining support. Davies and Morley have shown how in Yorkshire such factors were also played out:

> Although the NUWM itself won little electoral support, its campaigning over the means test brought the issue to the fore, and consequently Labour in opposition was able to win many voters over. Only in Sheffield did it prove to be unhelpful to the party, where Labour control of the PAC worked against its popularity, while conversely the Labour-controlled PAC in Rotherham gathered support by its open defiance of the means test.[125]

By implementing the means test, councillors risked personal criticism and electoral failure. In south Wales, the increasing strength of the NUWM and Communist Party saw councillors keen at public meetings to reveal their generosity and express the anguish they faced in deciding whether or not to administer the means test. After receiving a letter of protest from the NUWM at a meeting of Aberdare Urban District Council, councillor Morgan Richards declared:

> I am sure we all agree that no-one has protested more strongly against the means test than members of this Council. But we are continuing to sit on the committee to try to do our best to help the rank and file unemployed who have come before us. If some of us refused to sit on this committee the people would suffer. At any time our organisations will tell us to finish serving on the Means Test Committee I, personally, would be very glad to get out. It is a personal sacrifice on the part of those who sit on this committee, as we consider there has never been anything so degrading as this Means Test.[126]

In the early years of the means test in the 1930s, the National Government struggled to find a balance between placating taxpayers, the Conservative Party and the potentially dangerous 'army' of unemployed workers. The rhetoric of the patriotic duty of the unemployed to pull together to do their bit, as they had in wartime, and the generosity of the state to provide transitional payments says much about government attitudes towards the unemployed. The economic depression was a battle to be fought and won by citizens who contributed to growth and did not rely on the state. At a time of dire financial crisis, economies were given preference over alleviating the perceived social and monetary impact of the means test. Concessions came only after widespread unrest amongst the unemployed.

In some respects, these debates were played out at a local level. In south Wales and the north-east of England, appeasing rate payers, fulfilling party policy (although in this case overwhelmingly Labour) and conciliating the increasingly disgruntled unemployed proved an equal if not greater challenge. Councillors and local officials were unable to avoid the anger of unemployed men and women and their families. Moreover, they could witness at first hand the consequences of poverty and hardship and the burden of the means test. The decision to generously administer the test was made within this context, and, as the cases of Durham and Glamorgan PACs reveal, the refusal to implement it was not straightforward. The actions of the Ministers of Health and Labour in attempting to restrict local authorities fit into a broader picture of the gradual centralisation of welfare within this period. While J. A. Chandler argues for the importance of Poplar in the 1920s, it is apparent that the decisions of PACs and county councils in the early 1930s greatly contributed to this process.[127]

It was the respectability of the working class that first troubled the Cabinet and Prime Minister. Yet, ministers and Ramsay MacDonald were to face criticisms for a plethora of other effects the means test caused. Alongside maintaining constituents and financial concerns, this helped ensure that protest was kept alive. While variations in the means test continued to exist in 1933, it can be concluded that by this time the majority of transitional applicants were being assessed largely in line with the Order.[128] It was to take the introduction of the UAB in 1935 to ensure that there was a completely standardised system.

The decisions PACs adopted in the early 1930s had wide repercussions and could determine the response to the means test and the character of local protest. Many of the arguments put against the means test by councillors reflected a genuine concern for their constituents and also testify to the belief that the means test was causing people to suffer unnecessarily. The arguments against the effects of the means test and opposition towards it increased from its implementation. When councillors met for monthly PAC meetings, they were not only considering correspondence from the Ministry of Labour but also against their actions. The National Government may have remained resolute that the means test was necessary, but it could not ignore entirely the criticism that it was worsening the position of the unemployed. Politics did not only take place in a tripartite relationship between Whitehall, local councillors and the unemployed. Other factors – the wider labour movement, the social consequences of the means test and the response generated against the measure – shaped council decisions, and these require further consideration.

Notes

1 *Merthyr Express*, 12 December 1931, p. 12.

2 *Durham County Advertiser and Durham Chronicle*, 16 September 1932, p. 9.

3 In August 1931, at the height of calls for economies to be made, *The Times* printed a series of reports of cases of 'dole abuse'. *The Times*, 13 August 1931, p. 6, 14 August 1931, p. 12, 20 August 1931, p. 11, 21 August 1931, p. 7, and 27 August 1931, p. 12. See also, *Evening Chronicle*, 13 November 1931, p. 1; and *Western Mail*, 20 October 1931, p. 8, 24 October 1931, p. 8. Matt Perry has noted that such reports 'peaked at times of "economy" campaigns.' Matt Perry, *Bread and Work: The Experience of Unemployment, 1918–1939* (London, 2000), p. 59.

4 Transitional payments were previously called 'uncovenanted' or 'extended' benefits and were received by those no longer eligible for insurance benefits.

First Report of the Royal Commission on Unemployment Insurance (Cmd 3872), 1930–31, xvii, p. 911.

5 Alan Deacon, 'Systems of Interwar Unemployment Relief', in Sean Glynn and Alan Booth (eds), *The Road to Full Employment* (London, 1987), p. 36.

6 G. D. H. and M. I. Cole, *The Condition of Britain* (London, 1937), p. 206.

7 *Memorandum on the Measures Proposed by His Majesty's Government to Secure Reductions in National Expenditure* (Cmd 3952), 1930–31, xviii, pp. 372–82; *National Economy Bill, 1931*, 1930–31, iii, p. 457.

8 *Unemployment Insurance (National Economy) (No. 2) Order, 1931. Transitional Payments Explanatory Memorandum* (non-parl), HMSO, 1931, p. 1.

9 W. R. Garside, *British Unemployment 1919–1939: A Study in Public Policy* (Cambridge, 1990), pp. 64–5.

10 Two-thirds of the PAC membership was composed of councillors from the county or borough council who had been democratically elected to their position. The rest of the committee was made up of co-opted members. G. Grant McKenzie, *County Council Guide England and Wales, Excluding London* (Labour Publications Department London, 1937), p. 24.

11 TNA, PRO 30/69/442, Correspondence between Ramsay MacDonald and Mr Usher, 3 October 1931.

12 *Ibid*.

13 *Hansard*, HC (series 5) vol. 257, cols 280–5 (29 September 1931), vol. 259, col. 989 (19 November 1931), vol. 260 cols 551–68 (26 November 1931).

14 *The Ministry of Labour Gazette*, December 1931, p. 455.

15 *Local Unemployment Index*, October 1931.

16 In Jarrow, 77% of insured workers were unemployed and in Ferndale 75%. *Ibid*.

17 The number of transitional applicants for the north-eastern parliamentary division (which included a larger area than the counties of Durham and Northumberland) was 196,668. The corresponding figure for Wales was 79,529. *Hansard*, HC (series 5) vol. 259, cols 981–2, 987 (18 and 19 November 1931); *South Shields Daily Gazette*, 20 November 1931, p. 1; *Western Mail*, 8 December 1931, p. 5.

18 DRO, Durham County Council Public Assistance Committee Minutes (hereafter, Durham PAC Minutes), 29 October 1931, p. 322.

19 This period could only be extended by the Minister of Health. *Transitional Payments Explanatory Memorandum*, pp. 6–7.

20 *Ibid*., pp. 1–8; Irvine Herbert Dearnley, *The 'Needs Test' for Unemployment Insurance Transitional Payments and Public Assistance* (London, 1931), pp. 9, 13–15, 19–25.

21 For example, on 24 September 1931, the Auckland area guardians' committee appealed to Durham PAC for a cancellation of relief arrears where it was deemed that they could not be paid. Durham PAC Minutes, 24 September 1931, p. 272.

22 *Transitional Payments Explanatory Memorandum*, p. 8.

23 *Memorandum on the Measures Proposed by His Majesty's Government to Secure Reductions in National Expenditure*, p. 381.
24 Alan Deacon and Jonathan Bradshaw, *Reserved for the Poor: The Means Test in British Social Policy* (Oxford, 1983), p. 16.
25 J. A. Chandler has argued that 'the long-term implications of the battles waged in the first instance by Poplar Borough Council from 1919 to 1925 were to have major significance for the relationship between local and central government.' J. A. Chandler, *Explaining Local Government: Local Government in Britain Since 1800* (Manchester, 2007), p. 135.
26 Anne Digby, 'Changing Welfare Cultures in Region and State', *Twentieth Century British History*, 17:3 (2006), p. 311.
27 *Ibid.*, p. 311.
28 Chris Williams, 'Labour and the Challenge of Local Government, 1919–1939', in Duncan Tanner, Chris Williams and Deian Hopkin (eds), *The Labour Party in Wales 1900–2000* (Cardiff, 2000), p. 155.
29 Labour Party, *Smashing the Unemployed! The Meanness of the Means Test* (London, 1932), p. 11.
30 Glamorgan Archives, Cardiff (hereafter, GAC), Glamorgan County Council Public Assistance Committee Minutes (hereafter, Glamorgan PAC Minutes), 25 November 1931, p. 282; Durham PAC Minutes, 29 October 1931, pp. 294–327, and 26 November 1931, p. 332.
31 *Aberdare Leader*, 14 November 1931, p. 2.
32 *Daily Herald*, 14 November 1931, p. 9.
33 *Durham County Advertiser and Durham Chronicle*, 9 October 1931, p. 2.
34 *Evening Chronicle*, 24 November 1931, p. 10.
35 'Minutes of conference held to discuss transitional payments, 11 December 1931', Durham PAC Minutes, 28 January 1932, pp. 16–17.
36 At a meeting with SWMF representatives at Merthyr PAC, councillor S. O. Davies remarked to laughter that wives could attend investigations at the council 'because she is "ex-officio" every time.' *Aberdare Leader*, 14 November 1931, p. 2; *Western Mail*, 14 November 1931, p. 5; *Merthyr Express*, 12 December 1931, p. 12.
37 *Western Mail*, 24 February 1932, p. 4.
38 TNA, AST 12/16, Unemployment Assistance Board Minutes, 9 October 1934, p. 52, 25 October 1934, p. 96.
39 Kate Nicholas, *The Social Effects of Unemployment on Teesside, 1919–39* (Manchester, 1986), p. 169.
40 *Evening Chronicle*, 13 November 1931, p. 7.
41 *The Newcastle Journal*, 21 November 1931, p. 3.
42 *Evening Chronicle*, 2 December 1931, p. 1.
43 *Ibid.*, 24 November 1931, p.10, 7 December 1931, p. 4.
44 *Report of the Public Assistance Officer on Unemployment Insurance (National Economy) (No. 2) Order, 1931*, 22 January 1932, Durham PAC Minutes, 28 January 1932, pp. 61B–61C.

45 *Ibid*., p. 61C.
46 *South Shields Daily Gazette*, 24 November 1931, p. 4.
47 Tyne and Wear Archive Services (hereafter, TWAS), Newcastle, Newcastle Public Assistance Committee Minutes (hereafter, Newcastle PAC Minutes), 2 May 1932, pp. 75–8.
48 *Manchester Guardian*, 8 April 1932, p. 4.
49 *Royal Commission on Unemployment Insurance Final Report* (Cmd 4185), 1931–32, xiii, p. 541. For example, Garside, *British Unemployment*, p. 68.
50 Durham PAC Minutes, 28 January 1932, p. 34.
51 *Durham County Advertiser and Durham Chronicle*, 15 April 1932, p. 13.
52 *Porth Gazette*, 14 May 1932, p. 5.
53 R. Smith, 'The Reform of Local Government Finance, 1928–37: A Study of South Wales', *Welsh History Review*, 21:1 (2002), pp. 152–3.
54 *The Times*, 2 September 1932, p. 6; *Evening Chronicle*, 2 September 1932, p. 4.
55 *Aberdare Leader*, 19 December 1931, p. 3. Gwent Record Office (hereafter, GRO), Cwmbran, Monmouthshire County Council Public Assistance Committee Minutes (hereafter, Monmouthshire PAC Minutes), 3 February 1932, pp. 489–90.
56 *Manchester Guardian*, 1 January 1932, p. 2.
57 *Ibid*., 14 January 1932, p. 8.
58 'Report of the "Needs" Test Sub-Committee', Glamorgan PAC minutes, 12 February 1932, p. 377.
59 PRO 30/69/442, Correspondence, Henry Betterton to Ramsay MacDonald, 30 March 1932.
60 'Report of the "Needs" Test Sub-Committee', Glamorgan PAC Minutes, 1 April 1932, p. 435.
61 PRO 30/69/442, Henry Betterton to Ramsay MacDonald, 30 March 1932.
62 PRO 30/69/442, Correspondence, W. Eady to the Clerk of Durham County Council, 29 March 1932.
63 Durham PAC Minutes, 31 March 1932, pp. 133–4.
64 *Ibid*., 28 April 1932, p. 167.
65 *Ibid*., 28 April 1932, p. 168.
66 *Ibid*., 30 June 1932, pp. 242–5.
67 *The Newcastle Journal*, 7 December 1931, p. 9.
68 *The Times*, 3 January 1933, p. 10.
69 TWAS, SDB/A39/1/2, County Borough of Sunderland Public Assistance Committee Minutes, 4 May 1932, p. 7.
70 There is no further record of contact from the Ministry of Labour in the PAC minutes.
71 *The Newcastle Journal*, 13 May 1932, p. 12; Monmouthshire PAC Minutes, 5 April 1932, pp. 2–3; *South Wales Weekly Argus*, 16 April 1932, p. 4.
72 *The Times*, 6 August 1932, p. 10, 12 October 1932, p. 14.

73 'Report of the "Needs" Test Sub-Committee', Glamorgan PAC Minutes, 23 July 1932, p. 115; *The Times*, 3 January 1933, p. 10.
74 *Evening Chronicle*, 8 March 1932, p.1.
75 *Ibid.*
76 Newcastle PAC Minutes, 2 May 1932, pp. 75–6; *The Newcastle Journal*, 3 May 1932, p.7; *Manchester Guardian*, 18 April 1932, p. 4.
77 Newcastle PAC Minutes, 2 May 1932, pp. 75–6.
78 *The Newcastle Journal*, 3 May 1932, p. 7.
79 *Ibid.*, 3 May 1932, p. 7; *Evening Chronicle*, 14 April 1932, p. 16.
80 Sam Davies and Bob Morley, 'The Reactions of Municipal Voters in Yorkshire to the Second Labour Government, 1929–32', in Matthew Worley (ed.), *Labour's Grass Roots: Essays on the Activities of Local Labour Parties and Members, 1918–45* (Aldershot, 2005), p. 138.
81 *Final Report of the Royal Commission*, p. 463; Digby, 'Changing Welfare Cultures in Region and State', p. 312.
82 PRO 30/69/442, Correspondence and report, Herbert Samuel to Ramsay MacDonald, 3 June 1932.
83 It was estimated that the Act would see the cost of transitional payments to increase by £1 million. *Transitional Payments (Determination of Need) Bill*, 1931–32, iii, pp. 607–9; *Transitional Payments (Determination of Need) Memorandum on Proposed Financial Resolution* (Cmd 4190), 1931–32, xiv, p. 1009.
84 PRO 30/69/442, Correspondence, 'PR' to Sir Henry Betterton, 14 October 1932.
85 Garside, *British Unemployment*, p. 69; Perry, *Bread and Work*, p. 44; Chandler, *Explaining Local Government*, pp. 152–3.
86 DRO, D/X 1063/41, Correspondence, Ramsay MacDonald to E. Edwards, 25 August 1931.
87 *Western Mail*, 14 March 1932, p. 8.
88 Garside, *British Unemployment*, p. 69.
89 'Special Meeting of the PAC held at Shire Hall, Durham', Durham PAC Minutes, 31 August 1932, pp. 299–304.
90 It should be noted that the investments only provided the couple with a total income of £1 4s. 4d, which was lowered to 9s. 5d after outgoings. Such cases could, however, be sensationalised.
91 'Special Meeting of the PAC held at Shire Hall, Durham', 31 August 1932, pp. 299–304.
92 *Ibid.*, pp. 304–9.
93 'Report of the Deputation from Durham PAC to the Ministry of Labour 6 September 1932', Durham PAC Minutes, 12 September 1932, p. 313.
94 *Ibid.*, pp. 310–13.
95 *Ibid.*, p. 313.
96 *Ibid.*, p. 312.

97 *Ibid.*, pp. 313–14.
98 *Hansard*, HC (series 5) vol. 269, cols 5–9 (18 October 1932).
99 'Special Meeting of the Public Assistance Committee', Durham PAC Minutes, 12 September 1932, p. 315.
100 *Durham County Advertiser and Durham Chronicle*, 16 September 1932, p. 9.
101 *Ibid.*, 14 October 1932, pp. 9, 16.
102 *Daily Herald*, 12 October 1932, p. 11.
103 *Report to the Minister of Labour by the Commissioners Appointed to Administer Transitional Payments in the County of Durham* (Cmd 4339), 1932–33, xv, p. 1036.
104 *Ibid.*, p. 1036.
105 *Ibid.*, p. 1044.
106 Digby, 'Changing Welfare Cultures in Region and State', p. 305.
107 *Report to the Minister of Labour by the Commissioners Appointed to Administer Transitional Payments in the County of Durham*, p. 1044.
108 Aberdare Library, W. W. Price Collection, LG5/4/33, Handbill for Glamorgan County Council Elections, 1934.
109 W. W. Price Collection, LG5/4/31, Election Handbill for Tom Davies for the Glamorgan County Council Elections, March 1934.
110 Huw Beynon and Terry Austrin, *Masters and Servants: Class and Patronage in the Making of a Labour Organisation: The Durham Miners and the English Political Tradition* (London, 1994), p. 347.
111 *Merthyr Express*, 15 October 1932, p. 12.
112 *Ibid.*, 27 May 1932, p. 12.
113 *Ibid.*
114 *Ibid.*
115 *Ibid.*, 17 June 1932, p. 13.
116 *The Times*, 3 January 1933, p. 10.
117 A 'revisory committee' was created which was composed of six Labour members and five independents to oversee the means test. *South Wales Evening Post*, 17 January 1933, p. 8, 31 January 1933, p. 5.
118 'Report of the "Needs" Test Sub-Committee', Glamorgan PAC Minutes, 11 March 1933, p. 431, 24 June 1933, p. 122, 30 June 1933, p. 128 and 30 September 1933, p. 291.
119 *Aberdare Leader*, 15 October 1932, p. 8.
120 *Ibid.*, 12 January 1935, p. 7.
121 Unemployment Assistance Board Minutes, 9 October 1934, p. 53.
122 *Merthyr Express*, 22 October 1932, p. 13.
123 *South Wales Weekly Argus*, 30 April 1932, p. 5.
124 *Ibid.*
125 Davies and Morley, 'The Reactions of Municipal Voters in Yorkshire to the Second Labour Government', p. 142.

126 *Aberdare Leader*, 13 January 1933, p. 6.
127 Chandler, *Explaining Local Government*, pp. 152–3.
128 Ian Gazeley has gone as far as to argue, 'although some PACs were more generous than others, there is no real evidence that the means test was administered more leniently after the first few months of operation'. Ian Gazeley, *Poverty in Britain, 1900–1965* (London, 2003), p. 127.

3

Accusations, image and experience: the effects of the means test, 1931–34

> When the Means Test started, it became impossible. The P.A.C. reduced the man's allowance from 29s. 3d. to 11s. 3d. I shall never forget his despair when he came before the committee. 'I have struggled all my life to get out of the slums', he said; 'now we must get back to them'.
>
> Public Assistance Committee Official, Newcastle.[1]

> Well, this time next week the Means Test investigator would have been and gone. That agony-day once a month, he dreaded it, more for Jane's sake than his own; it almost killed her every time. And he was so helpless, had to see her suffer and couldn't say anything comforting. And his was a pointless, hopeless existence. He suffered one way, she another.
>
> Walter Brierley, *Means-Test Man* (1935).[2]

While considerations of local finances and political advantage undoubtedly influenced the decision to generously administer the means test for some officials, the actions of councillors must also be seen as a response to the social conditions of their constituents. Councillors witnessed first-hand the appalling effects of long-term unemployment both on the individual and their families and recognised the great difference a few extra pennies could make to the weekly budget. Moreover, local officials were sensitive of cultural hierarchies in working-class communities.[3] Within the depressed regions, many of those facing the means test were considered to be from the respectable working class – a group who expected state maintenance through insurance benefits. The means test, once it began operation, accentuated many of the worst effects of long-term unemployment for this group. Families shared the impact of a household means test, which was not limited to the purse. Like unemployment, the most damaging effects were psychological, as the above opening lines of Walter Brierley's semi-autobiographical novel indicate. The means test became a disruptive, intrusive and unwelcome feature of unemployed households.

Discussions of the means test have often focused upon its general effects across the 1930s. However, the differences in the implementation of the test by the PACs demonstrate how important place and local politics were to the nature of the examination transitional applicants underwent. Whether a means test was strictly implemented or not shaped the impact on the unemployed. This point is crucial. In areas where the means test was administered leniently, the unemployed would have had a different experience from those places where the PAC was much stricter. Although certain effects of the means test were more or less universal, others only emerged when a more rigorous household examination was applied.

While it may be difficult to ascertain the precise effects of the means test in different areas, given the great variation that existed between guardians' committees, a clearer distinction needs to be made between the PAC and the Unemployment Assistance Board with its centralised and standardised administration of the test. Paul Bagguley has demonstrated the importance of the different administrations of the test for the patterns of protest that emerged.[4] Such an analysis should also be applied to a discussion of the effects of the means test. The distinction between the first phase of the means test, 1931–34, and the second phase, 1935–41, clarifies the importance of legislative changes, considerably enhances understanding of protest movements and demonstrates why the means test remained politically important after the Second World War.

So much of our understanding of the means test is drawn from social investigations, many of which dedicated a chapter or large sections to the issue. It must be borne in mind how, for contemporaries, publicising the impact of the measure also had a political dimension. Claims that the means test caused families to separate, led to a drain of youth from the depressed areas and caused young children to starve, were highly emotive and created a negative image of the measure. Such assertions could be used to generate opposition not only against the means test but also the National Government. The representation of the means test within south Wales and the north-east influenced patterns of protest and notions of identity amongst the unemployed. Within Britain, it ultimately helped shape the legacy of the 1930s.

Long-term unemployment disrupted all aspects of life for the working class, and its effects reached far beyond a change in financial circumstances for the unemployed and their families. The prominent place of male breadwinners within contemporary accounts of long-term unemployment should not obscure from the fact that the economic and psychological challenge of unemployment stretched much further. The work of Keith Laybourn, Sally Alexander and others has highlighted the experience of female unemployment.[5] Even in industrial areas with low rates of female economic activity, long-term unemployment was still a damaging and disruptive experience for women. Young women coming of age, like young men, found the 'normal' life course disrupted when the jobless outnumbered those in work. For the wives of the unemployed, their experience was not confined to managing the weekly budget. The wider social climate and conditions are essential to understanding the impact of the long-term unemployment on working-class families. In some respects, certain aspects of the experience of unemployment were, and are, universal across regions, countries and even time periods. However, in order to fully appreciate the impact of unemployment on lives and lifestyles in south Wales and the north-east, an understanding of the nature of mass unemployment in areas with a narrow industrial base is needed. The protracted unemployment of a male breadwinner and the grinding poverty of working-class communities as a consequence reveal the strongest parallels between the two regions in a comparative analysis.

Work was at the very centre of working-class culture in south Wales and the north-east of England. The ability to work was an essential part of the route to adulthood and independence; it gave life its structure, helped forge friendship networks and was essential for an individual's standing within communities that judged the workshy as harshly as the government.[6] Furthermore, Ross McKibbin has highlighted the importance not just of the act of working but viewed that workplace 'culture' was equally important: 'for many men this culture as inextricable from work proper, and it was the culture which gave working life its meaning and satisfaction'.[7] While there was often little difference in the financial circumstances of the short- and long-term unemployed, a distinction was apparent in their relative status. A prolonged period without work left men facing endlessly free hours, with feelings of alienation and isolation even in areas with a high number of unemployed.[8] H. Vickerstaff, an unemployed miner from Spennymoor, Durham, commented:

> Where once each one's troubles, joys and cares were shared, there are so many in the same plight today that each one has enough suffering of his own without caring for others. That fellowship, that was once the mainspring of our lives, is being destroyed. And truly, lack of fellowship is death.[9]

The effects of the loss of the comradeship of work upon the individual gradually dawned as unemployment persisted. The Communist writer and intellectual Allen Hutt argued that 'it is necessary to spend some time in the townships of the Welsh valleys to realise what the mental torture of prolonged unemployment means to active men. The boredom of life becomes insupportable'.[10] Skilled workers, in some respects, felt the effects of long-term unemployment much more acutely than labourers or casual workers.[11] They had enjoyed a better wage, living standard and higher status within their community. Former skilled workers 'mostly surprised and ashamed at the spectacle of their own calamity' found it harder to adapt to a lower level of living.[12]

Unemployment prevented men from occupying their normal spaces as they became distanced from the workplace and social activities that required spending money. Gradually, men were forced to spend more time in the private space of the home.[13] While some men resented being thrown into the domestic sphere, many more felt that they were intruding into their wife's space. However, the presence of fathers and husbands within the home did not just represent a physical change since without an income a man was no longer in principle the head of household. For some men, this loss of status made them unable, or unwilling, to assert their authority. E. Wight Bakke, following his social investigation, noted that 'practically every man who had a family showed evidence of the blow his self-confidence had suffered from the fact that the traditional head of family was not able to perform his normal function'.[14] Traditional patterns in the life cycle within south Wales and the north-east of England were, therefore, gradually being undermined, highlighting how unemployment affected the entire household.

Long-term unemployment was associated much more so than short-term unemployment with destitution. As household items wore out or broke, they became much more difficult to replace. Hilda Jennings stated in her study of Brynmawr in south Wales that 'prolonged unemployment results in the exhaustion of savings and family resources, so that it becomes difficult to do more than lead a hand to mouth existence'.[15] It was the wives of the unemployed who were given the onerous task of balancing the household budget which gradually became more meagre. In oral testimonies, women were often praised and pitied by their husbands and sons for their sacrifices during the depression. The unemployed miner John Evans from the Rhondda Valleys commented that 'it's upon the wives of the unemployed that the real burden falls. It means they have to scrounge round for the cheapest food and for anything in the shape of clothes'.[16] Placed in a position of having less money with which to feed the same family, many women decided to sacrifice their own welfare for the sake of their husbands and children.

Social surveys revealed how women physically suffered the most within an unemployed household as it was they who would deny themselves food so that their husband and children could eat. In *Working-Class Wives*, Margery Spring Rice found that in the face of inadequate scales of relief women were skipping meals, or eating very little, in order to stretch provisions to feed the rest of their families.[17] The Pilgrim Trust likewise reported how 'all of us agreed that in most unemployed families the parents, and in particular the wives, bore the burden of want, and in many instances were literally starving themselves in order to feed and clothe the children reasonably well'.[18] Such a situation was not specific to the years of the depression, and traditionally within industrial communities, women would feed other members first.[19] However, as Steve Thompson has noted in the case of south Wales, 'there was a cultural ideal that the earning capacity of the family needed to be maintained and that this was best achieved by maximising the food consumption of the (usually male) breadwinner(s). This assumed a greater relevance during the interwar period'.[20] Women shared the mental strain of the loss of status, in addition to their struggle to keep children fed and the morale of husbands maintained.

When the National Government announced its economic cuts in 1931, one of the few remaining certainties in the lives of the unemployed was the collection of weekly unemployment benefit payments. Although such payments had been subject to cuts and qualifications, the receipt of benefit had become widely accepted and free from any stigma. The introduction of a means test removed this certainty, and the status of the long-term unemployed was immediately lowered. The decision to test the unemployed for their benefit was initially objected to on the grounds that it was unlawful to test those men and women in a scheme to which they may have contributed for over a decade.[21] Unemployment had demoralised workers by taking away the ability to earn a wage: the transitional benefit scheme accentuated such feelings by making benefit conditional and not a right. In some instances, transitional benefit was even referred to as a 'charity' payment.[22] The means test's connection to the poor law amplified the lowering of status of transitional applicants.

The connection to the poor law provoked outrage because it damaged the carefully constructed sense of working-class respectability. Application for public assistance suggested failure, destitution and an inability to support one's family. Paul Johnson has argued that 'pauperdom was the ultimate disgrace. It represented a complete loss of independence, respectability and community status and esteem, and it was worth avoiding almost regardless of cost'.[23] Working-class men and women would have prided themselves on their ability to avoid applying for public assistance, and even in a situation of mass unemployment, it was very much the last resort. Bakke noted in his study of south Wales that 'the feeling among the workers still exists that there is a stigma attached to being in receipt of Poor Law relief'.[24] Similarly, Carr-Saunders argued as late as 1936 that 'the poor law is still regarded with aversion'.[25] Indeed, one of the major reasons why the government introduced transitional payments was to avoid turning the unemployed over to the poor law. However, it was the level of public outcry that any connection with the poor law would bring that most concerned the Cabinet, rather than the loss of workers' status. On 13 October, Sir Herbert Samuel (Home Secretary) wrote to the Prime Minister expressing his concern about how the new act would be received in this respect.[26] While PACs in south Wales and the north-east took steps to prevent such an association, the link with destitution remained.

It was not only the loss of status that affected applicants. The household means test also had practical implications once it began operation despite the best efforts of some PAC officials. Just three months after the means test started, the General Council of the TUC met with the Minister of Labour to express their concerns about some of its major effects. The General Council demanded the abolition of the 'vicious and inequitable means test' because it was 'bound to result in the penalisation of decent people ... whose only crime is that they are unemployed'.[27] While the complaints vocalised by the TUC could be dismissed as propaganda for the labour movement's cause, such sentiment was also being expressed within both regions.

One of the major grievances against the operation of the means test was the actual investigation into means, which weighed heavily upon the minds of all transitional applicants (whether male or female, young or old) and their families. Wal Hannington, the Communist leader of the NUWM, observed that 'the old adage that "the Englishman's home is his castle" was blown sky-high by the Means Test. The privacy of his family life was violated, and he even became liable to the indignity of being followed and spied upon by Means Test investigators in all his public movements'.[28] Although many applicants in south Wales and the north-east of England may have avoided a strict examination into their financial position, any form of investigation was likely to have been viewed as an insult.[29] An unemployed miner from the Rhondda felt that 'to men who had worked in the only industry they had known (mining) for anything from fifteen to fifty years, this was a new experience, of the most humiliating and degrading kind'. Transitional applicants gradually began to feel that they were 'being spied upon' and were at risk of being caught out.[30] These visits must have been especially frustrating for the many unemployed whose circumstances did not alter from one week to the next.[31]

The means test investigator became a hated figure within working-class communities, and in many respects they evolved to become an archetypal image of the 1930s. Walter Brierley's writings on the experience of the means test are one of the most poignant examples in literature of the struggles that families could face. Brierley, an unemployed colliery banksman from Derbyshire, first began writing while facing protracted unemployment. The *Means-Test Man*, his first novel, was published in 1935 and exposed most pertinently the psychological impact of the visits of the means test investigators.[32] Matt Perry believes that 'of all the indignities which the unemployed shouldered in the interwar period, the means test "inquisition" was the most despised'.[33] This image of the means test investigator, and the humiliation the unemployed faced, while existing in the earlier 1930s, was strengthened during the second phase of means testing under the UAB officials.[34] However, such an image did exist in this earlier period and especially in County Durham where the commissioners were known to have been stricter in their examination. Unemployed miner H. Vickerstaff pronounced that the means test investigator:

> is the Big Bad Wolf who blows your house down whether it be built of straw, sticks or bricks. The monthly visitations, the prying into the most private affairs, and the continued espionage over every halfpenny of his income is an unnecessary insult to the man. The days of expectation of these officials, and the waiting in for them for a whole day, has a harassing effect upon the mind of an unemployed man.[35]

For those unemployed who were still fortunate enough to hold any assets, the investigations reduced their allowances. Fears that applicants would be required to sell their more expensive possessions and spend all of their savings were rife before the means test began.[36] While in some areas 'applicants for transitional payments have been exposed to the full rigour of the Poor Law', the requirement to be completely destitute before payments were awarded was generally not made in south Wales and the north-east.[37] The image of the unemployed being made to sell dressers and pianos was a popular, and maybe to an extent invented, memory of the 1930s.[38] However, while most investigators did not go this far, the inclusion of savings within a means test examination still roused criticism.

Given the economic climate that had prevailed in the two regions, it was highly likely that the majority of transitional applicants did not have large savings.[39] Yet, the press still argued that the means test caused thrift to be penalised amongst the unemployed soon after its implementation.[40] Even within south Wales, where the PACs were renowned for the generosity, the local press condemned the means test for forcing the unemployed to spend their hard-earned savings.[41] The condemnation of the means test for penalising thrift was often the main objection of councillors to the measure. At a meeting of Houghton-le-Spring Urban District Council, J. A. Hall raised the motion, which was carried, to support Gainsborough Urban District Council which was urging the abolition of the means test on the grounds that 'the Means Test is penalising thrift ... I know of a case where a man saved a little bit of money and purchased a house. He has now been unemployed for 12 months and is penalised to the extent of 8s. per week because he owns the house'.[42]

It had long been an objective of social policy to encourage working-class thrift, and the 'better class' of worker invested money to ensure his family's financial independence. Many of the working class had become accustomed to saving for periods of sickness through friendly societies, trade unions and personal saving schemes or the purchase of pawnable goods.[43] Money was also likely to have been put by for items such as shoes and clothes. This money symbolised more than a precaution against exceptional circumstances and was another signifier of respectability. Eschewing extravagances and alcohol, the respectable worker was prepared to meet financial challenges as they arose without having recourse to the poor law.[44] The apparent penalisation of the more respectable members of the working class was viewed with abhorrence as it suggested that the means test favoured less respectable unemployed applicants.

In June 1932, Herbert Samuel, as part of his complaint about the operation of the means test, raised the question of the penalisation of thrift with Ramsay MacDonald. Samuel used the example of Lancashire, where the means test was strictly administered, and questioned the fairness of making people who 'are usually among the respected in their neighbourhoods' spend all of their savings before being eligible for benefit.[45] Henry Betterton was careful, upon the advice of MacDonald, to reply to Samuel before the matter was raised in Cabinet. Although lamenting that those without savings simply received 'maintenance from the community without much question', Betterton felt that the plight of the taxpayer also needed consideration and, once more, the patriotic duty of the unemployed was emphasised. Taxpayers had likewise 'had to raid their small savings in recent months' in part to 'meet taxes, required among other things to assist the unemployed'.[46] In a climate of national emergency, arguments about respectability fell on deaf ears. Indeed, the very existence of such savings was regularly used to justify the existence of a means test, and in this case to avoid 'bitter resentment'.[47]

The commissioners appointed in County Durham reported after their first year cases of applicants receiving maintenance despite investments of as much as £1,990.[48] Stories appeared in the local press throughout the early 1930s that the unemployed were receiving transitional payments despite large savings. One particularly striking case appeared in the correspondence column of the *Durham County Advertiser*. The letter, signed 'HONESTY', declared that a friend of the author had overheard a conversation on a bus between two unemployed men who had deceived PAC inspectors about the extent of their earnings. One of the men apparently claimed that with the interest gained on the 'few hundred pounds' he and his wife had in the Building Society, 'we can both settle down and make the dole a pension for life'.[49] Such reports, almost certainly fabricated, helped ensure that the government was able to justify calling upon the unemployed to do their 'duty' for their country by living off their own savings.

Arguments of patriotism could, however, also be used against the National Government; the inclusion of army pensions in a means test assessment was a particular source of grievance amongst the unemployed. Again, the lack of definite advice on this issue had led to disparities in its implementation. Opposition on this point was especially strong in Durham where the British Legion protested against war pensions being used to support the unemployed.[50] Less than two decades after the First World War, it is clear to see why men injured in service, or the widows of servicemen, would be unwilling to use this money to support periods of unemployment. The British Legion protested against the use of the means test to the Royal Commission when it was gathering evidence for its final report. William Asbury and Clara Rackham found that many ex-servicemen had had their pensions taken into account in a means test examination and 'this had resulted in reducing their standard of living and their physical condition'.[51] Concerns that the means test was causing a reduction in living standards were not confined to the cases of ex-servicemen.

The assessment of need calculated the bare minimum that an unemployed person required. While all income within a household was assessed, outgoings were generally limited to insurance payments and expenses for earning members. The resultant transitional benefit did not include a consideration of fuel costs, lighting, food, medical expenses nor provision for the replacement of vital items such as clothes and shoes. Many unemployed argued that the transitional benefit was consequently not enough to survive upon, a point since made by historians of the unemployed.[52] In Beales and Lambert's 1934 study *Memoirs of the Unemployed*, an unemployed miner from the Rhondda Valleys commented that 'it was very difficult for us to adapt ourselves to the new payment of transitional benefit, or rather the 2s. 9d. cut, with growing family, needs growing, household goods, bedclothes, underwear, clothes, more shoes needed'.[53] Although spending on luxury items may have decreased, for essential items there was little practical difference in the amount of money needed for a household. The struggle to balance the household budget for wives of the unemployed become an almost impossible task as the weekly income subsided. Inevitably, many homes where the head of household was receiving transitional payments witnessed a lowering of standards.

After the first year of means-tested transitional benefits, the authors of the *Minority Report of the Royal Commission on Unemployment Insurance* concluded that 'reductions in, and disallowances of, benefit have caused a great increase in pauperism and vagrancy'.[54] The reduction of household standards was felt acutely by those unemployed who had struggled to maintain an acceptable level of living. Even after many years of unemployment, a projection of the image of respectability remained vitally important for personal standing within communities. While poverty and unemployment were connected, it cannot be argued that in either south Wales or the north-east of England there was a definite deterioration of standards in the outward *appearances* of households. Fenner Brockway noted during his visit to south Wales that 'again and again I have found during this enquiry that it is in the homes which are seemingly above destitution level that the greatest privation is suffered'.[55] The upkeep of a home and the appearance of their families remained important despite a lower weekly income. The Pilgrim Trust reported in their investigation there was 'in Crook and in the Rhondda on the whole high standards of household management with a real feeling of traditional culture in the best homes'. In Crook, 'there was a determination not to give way to unemployment', and a similar picture was painted for south Wales: 'in a typical Welsh household of the best type when one of us called late in the afternoon, tea was on a spotlessly clean white tablecloth'.[56] Other social investigations revealed a similar picture.

Hilda Jennings concluded that within Brynmawr 'pride in personal appearance seems little affected by prolonged unemployment'. Jennings stated that when all efforts had failed to maintain what was regarded as an outwardly respectable appearance, unemployed families would remain at home on a Sunday 'rather than show their shabbiness'.[57] In Durham, John Newsom found that the unemployed who had long attempted to maintain their household struggled to adapt. Newsom stated that when a man's clothes became too worn, he 'shuns the society of his fellows. The world becomes an alien and hateful place, he imagines that people are looking at him, despising him, laughing at him ... I know a man who tells me that going into a shop makes him sweat with fear'.[58] The consequences of reduced benefits were not only cultural, and debates raged over the physical condition of the unemployed.

The claim that the means test undermined the health and welfare of an applicant and his or her family reveals the importance of contemporary perceptions. Whether the means test caused ill health was contentious as this factor more than any other was strongly, and perhaps inextricably, linked to the general effects of long-term unemployment. While a conclusion on the physical effects of the means test cannot be reached for these reasons, the belief certainly existed amongst some medical professionals, social investigators and politicians that there was a correlation between the means test and poor health. E. W. Bakke commented that men receiving transitional benefit were in a physically worse state than 'men on ordinary benefit [who] were of a distinctly better physique'.[59] A PAC officer for Newcastle informed Fenner Brockway that in the north-east 'the under-nourishment of unemployment, particularly since the Means Test was introduced, is increasing illness'.[60] The NUWM took the accusations against the means test much further. In 1932, they argued that the means test was a 'weapon of mass murder' causing 'stark poverty, misery and starvation to enter thousands of working class homes in Great Britain'.[61] Clearly, the impression existed that the means test was responsible for affecting all aspects of an unemployed person's life, and such arguments were to be a powerful weapon in opposition to the measure.

While the loss of respectability and arguments about the lowering of household standards and physical state were applicable to all transitional applicants, others were more dependent upon age and status. In many respects, the effects of the means test appeared far more profound for older men than for men in their early twenties. The older unemployed man would have worked for many more years and would have been far more accustomed to the status and stability that this brought. With the arrival of mass unemployment, men aged over 40 years across the industrial regions were more likely to experience long-term unemployment as employers favoured younger men who were cheaper and fitter. Many men spoke of feeling too old at forty although a working life could have continued until around the age of fifty-five.[62] Priestley singled out older men for particular attention in *English Journey*: 'I saw again the older men who, though they knew they were idle and useless through no fault of their own, felt defeated and somewhat tainted. Their self-respect was shredding away. Their very manhood was going ... I saw these older men as a series of personal tragedies'.[63]

The loss of status that the means test brought was felt intensely by the older unemployed man who was aware that the dole represented his financial future and was most likely to have children old enough to be considered in a means test examination. While the loss of function as breadwinner was a situation that had existed prior to the means test, the household investigation further injured the masculinity of the jobless man. A councillor from Newcastle noted how 'it is humiliating for a father to make him dependent upon his son or daughter, instead of recognising his own right to benefit'.[64] How could a sense of masculinity be asserted when a father's son or daughter was supporting him?

One of the most controversial charges against household means testing was that it caused families to split. Deacon and Bradshaw have noted that 'the enduring image of the means test in the 1930s was a young couple who were told that their savings would now have to go towards the maintenance of one of their parents, [and] the family which was told to live off the pension paid to a war veteran'.[65] It was customary for working-class families to support one another financially during periods of unemployment, but the legal requirement to do this under the means test was objected to on the grounds of principle. Indeed, since the First World War the insurance scheme had evolved to favour the male breadwinner, responsible for maintaining his family.[66] While family responsibility was, as M. A. Crowther has noted, an important part of the welfare scheme until 1948, it was largely associated with the poor law.[67] For transitional applicants, it led to a situation where the general level of the household was lowered when other household income was calculated.[68] All household members were liable to face an examination, including those who were not close relatives, such as uncles, and even lodgers who were not related at all.[69] In a situation where the transitional applicant was the only unemployed person in the household, others who were earning were compelled to wholly support him or her when benefit was disallowed. It is clear to see why this situation could cause resentment within a culture where an individual's capacity to support themselves was a matter of pride. Under such circumstances, critics of the means test argued that families were choosing to split in order to avoid the income of earning members being taken into account. Either the individual still in employment would leave, or the unemployed applicant would take up new lodgings.[70]

Whether families did actually divide was highly contentious as in some instances sons and daughters simply pretended to get an alternative address, what Deacon and Bradshaw have termed 'collusive desertion'.[71] In *The Road to Wigan Pier*, George Orwell observed that 'I have seen cases of the evasion of the Means Test, but I should say that in the industrial towns, where there is still a certain amount of communal life and everyone had neighbours who know him, it is much harder than it would be in London'.[72] The government could not ignore the accusation of splitting families, and in November 1932, Edward Hilton Young, the Minister of Health, wrote to Ramsay MacDonald to quell his fears in this regard. Young had asked Ministry of Health officials across the country to investigate the matter and concluded that 'the reports show that there is very little substance in the allegations which have been made'. He believed that the argument that homes were splitting had largely stemmed from the few cases where this occurred in Lancashire 'on occasion not without encouragement from people anxious to discredit the needs test'.[73] However, evidence emerged throughout the period to counteract such governmental assurances.

In the first phase of means testing, it is unlikely that many families separated in south Wales, as one of the biggest criticisms pledged against the PACs in the region was that they failed to take family income into account. However, in both regions, there is evidence that some men would refuse to disclose how much their daughters were earning for fear of being made dependent upon them. One unemployed man from Durham refused to disclose his daughter's teaching salary 'as he stated that he has nothing to do with her earnings and that she only contributes a small amount towards her keep'.[74] Such evidence demonstrates how the means test undermined gendered sensibilities. In the north-east, evidence of families splitting generally came after the commissioners were established. They ensured that a rigorous assessment was carried out and family income included. It was not only fathers who were affected. One unemployed man observed that in Spennymoor a caravan town slowly grew up where unemployed sons went to live so that other family members would not have to support them.[75]

Even if families did not split, the means test still detrimentally affected household members. Life in general became strained and all family members were likely to have experienced deterioration in circumstances, whether monetary or social. M. A. Crowther has argued that the test generally 'penalized the stable families which had remained together'. She concluded that 'for many families where housing was in short supply and wages were low, the claims of an elderly relative or unemployed member of the household could mean a fall from a modest subsistence to a grinding struggle'.[76] It was the wives and mothers of the unemployed who were often left to manage meagre unemployment payments and keep harmony within the family home.

Far less is known about the psychological effects of the means test and long-term unemployment on the wives and mothers of the unemployed than on the unemployed themselves.[77] While unemployment took away the ability of a man to perform his wage-earning duties, for women routine chores continued in the same way despite the reduced budget. The torture of the struggle to provide for the family was evident. Fenner Brockway described how he found it 'almost impossible' to listen to the wife of an unemployed man in south Wales describe her ordeal.[78] In 1932, a special report was prepared for the National Conference of Labour Women on the effects of the means test upon wives of applicants. It found that 'the effect of wage reductions ... the cuts in unemployment pay, and the cutting down of relief work, though bearing directly on the man, are ultimately shouldered by the wife ... The burden she has to bear is greater than can be measured in terms of the money actually saved'. The effects of the means test examinations which in some parts of south Wales did not take place in the exchanges were also noted:

> if the unemployed man is summoned for an interview by the Public Assistance Committee, his wife generally has to go with him, because alone he is unable to answer all the questions about the most intimate circumstances of their family life. Inquisitions, in these circumstances, often take on the character of 'third degree', and the women come out of such an ordeal frightened and nervously exhausted.[79]

For the majority of women, the means test impacted negatively upon their already burdensome lives. However, within some households, the breakdown in gender hierarchies went beyond male feelings of emasculation. In a number of cases, men started to help out their wives with the more cumbersome household chores. Mrs E. Vickerstaff, the wife of an unemployed Durham miner, observed that far more women had become involved in politics since mass unemployment. She believed that this was because 'the attitude of the Durham miner towards his wife has changed a good deal of late years. Instead of looking upon her as the drudge of days past, he is willing to help her all he can and let her have as much freedom as possible'.[80] Prior to the depression, it was unlikely that men would have helped out around the house in this way. While David Vincent argued that unemployed husbands often 'saw more of their children, but only rarely more of the stove or the washtub', it is evident that some men were assisting with domestic tasks.[81] For long-term unemployed men, the desire to assist wives with their chores must have originated out of a sense of guilt at no longer being a wage earner and simply just for something to do.[82] Neil Penlington has made the important point that in south Wales for the minority, who did assist in chores, they were often heavier tasks and this did not necessarily undermine domestic hierarchies.[83] Hilda Jennings suggested that wives of the unemployed 'realise the necessity of providing some occupation for their husbands in order to keep them even moderately content'.[84]

Despite women's best efforts to maintain the morale of her household, the children of the unemployed remained the focus of attention for social investigators and the government. Although the health of children was noted to have improved during the interwar years, there was still unease about the social conditions that the children of the unemployed were being raised within. As dependants of the long-term unemployed, children, like women, were believed to have been adversely affected, and social investigators who spoke out against the means test were keen to stress the possible negative impact of the environment in which they lived.[85] Allen Hutt in his social investigation of south Wales expressed much concern over the issue. Although housing and sanitary conditions were awful, 'viler than all these things is the blow that declining capitalism has struck at the children of the working-class in derelict areas'.[86] Hutt catalogued the conditions he discovered on his journey through south Wales and lamented the appalling surroundings children were growing up in. One particularly severe case was found in Dowlais:

> The children of this family all suffer from sores, due to malnutrition; but seven of them share two beds. Only one boy, who is especially delicate, has a bed to himself, at the express instructions of the doctor. These children play in the yard just outside the house, where are the lavatories serving the houses in the row. The mother, when asked why she didn't send them out on the mountain slopes to play in the fresh air and sunshine, replied that she was afraid that they would return with too large an appetite.[87]

While such descriptions may have been politically motivated, they still demonstrate the concern for children and the impression that existed of the awful effects of the depression.

In the north-east, both Priestley and Newsom were apprehensive about children's futures. For Priestley, the 'children are the worst off', and an unemployed man in Newsom's account stated that 'it's the kids I worry about most, growing up in the village and no chance of a job'.[88] Unemployment in the home was viewed as creating an unhealthy atmosphere in which to raise children, especially when the prospects of them securing unemployment themselves appeared so remote. It was again the psychological impact of the depression that most worried investigators. Effectively, a generation of children had never seen their fathers in employment and was becoming accustomed to watching their parents face means test examinations. Vickerstaff commented upon how children were being brought up in an 'atmosphere of unemployment... The presence of unemployment affects them in their conversation, and in their games'. He recalled, 'in playing "Houses" I have heard children carry on long conversations with a make-believe Means-Test man about the conditions in her make-believe house'. Vickerstaff felt that 'these things must obviously have an effect in after-life'.[89] The means test was clearly beginning to have a deep impact upon south Wales and the north-east of England.

In British society, the means test evolved to become part of everyday life and had entered into popular consciousness. *The Labour Woman* even carried a recipe for 'Means Test Pudding' sent in by a housewife from Great Yarmouth.[90] The means test was a regular source of debate in national and local newspapers and took a prominent place in social investigations. In *English Journey*, Priestley conveys how the means test was slowly becoming part of general conversation amongst the working class in the north-east; there was a 'never-ending stream of talk about books, plays, railways, shipbuilding, coal, the Means Test, Russia, Germany, politics, sport, life and death'. He further commented 'our merry laughter rang out whenever the Means Test was mentioned, for it was amusing to find Britannia herself, with her Lion and her Unicorn, in our midst, cross-examining old women to discover if there was any truth in the rumour that their sons had earned a shilling a week ago'.[91] The condemnation the measure received, largely because of the alleged effects, ensured that the issue would remain at the forefront of private and public debate for some years to come.

The terms of the unemployment legislation introduced in 1931 were framed with the intention of lowering public spending and wiping out 'abuse' from the system. The government by not throwing millions over to the poor law believed it had avoided affronting respectability and status. When the means test began operation, it was these very factors that caused the greatest outcry. Those people who had managed to maintain savings, were fortunate enough to have children working, had kept a decent standard within the homes and preserved the family unit, suffered most from the implementation of a household means test. Those families which had prided themselves on an ability to avoid destitution and public assistance were appalled and insulted to find themselves the objects of investigation by PAC officials. It was the connection to the poor law that, above all else, provoked the most alarm during the first phase of means testing in the 1930s.

Even during the height of the depression, social signifiers of respectability remained paramount: cleanliness and outward appearance were maintained, and public assistance and its connotations of destitution were avoided at all costs. The means test affected all members of a household, and the privacy of the family home was lost as investigators examined the financial details of parents, sons, daughters and lodgers. The decision to make children responsible for their unemployed fathers upset the traditional hierarchy of the household. Like many of the effects of the means test, it accentuated the very worst consequences of long-term unemployment. It was argued that in such a situation families were choosing to separate. All of these effects, and claimed effects, were present in both south Wales and the north-east of England. Although administrative differences made certain effects more prominent in some areas than others, overall there was little quantifiable difference in the impact of the means test. In both regions, the means test became central to the lives of the unemployed. Evidence of ill health, families splitting and mental distress pervaded.

The means test was surrounded by an air of negativity and controversy. The denunciation of the measure was not only made by the unemployed; numerous social investigators condemned the impact the means test was having upon the lives of those out of work. The construction of this image was vital both for the protest that was to occur and for the bitter legacy of the test. Public outcry and the revelation of how household means testing affected the unemployed demonstrate why some Labour councillors were prepared to interpret leniently how the test was administered. Their opposition reveals the strength of feeling that existed against the means test. While men standing idle on street corners were one archetypal image of the 1930s, equally important was the image of the unemployed marching from all parts of Britain to London to protest against the government.

Although unemployment and the means test may have affected all aspects of the lives of those who faced the investigation, it did not divorce the working class entirely from their previous identities. John Evans urged 'please do think of us, not as "the unemployed", but as individuals like yourselves. We have the same ambition to get on in the world; we have just the same feelings as you have'.[92] Those struggling with the psychological impact of long-term unemployment and means testing needed to find both motivation and leadership to battle against a test that roused bitterness and anger. As the means test impacted upon unemployed households and working-class communities in a similar way, it was evident that other factors would determine the nature of this response.

Notes

1 A. Fenner Brockway, *Hungry England* (London, 1932), p. 104.
2 Walter Brierley, *Means-Test Man* (London, 1983 edition; first published, 1935), p. 3.
3 The Sheffield Labour Party councillor William Asbury and the former suffragist, factory reformer and Labour Party activist Clara Rackham provided the only dissenting voices to the majority conclusions on the Royal Commission on Unemployment Insurance. 'Minority Report', *Royal Commission on Unemployment Insurance Final Report* (Cmd 4185), 1931–32, xiii, p. 779.
4 Paul Bagguley, *From Protest to Acquiescence? Political Movements of the Unemployed* (London, 1991), pp. 3, 40–4.
5 For example, Sue Bruley, 'A Woman's Right to Work? The Role of Women in the Unemployed Movement Between the Wars', in Sybil Oldfield (ed.), *This Working-Day World: Women's Lives and Culture(s) in Britain 1914–1945* (London, 1994), pp. 40–53; Sally Alexander, 'Men's Fears and Women's Work: Responses to Unemployment in London Between the Wars', *Gender & History*, 12:2 (2000), pp. 401–25; Keith Laybourn, '"Waking up to the Fact that there are any Unemployed": Women, Unemployment and the Domestic Solution in Britain, 1918–1939', *History*, 88:292 (2003), pp. 606–23.
6 G. D. H. and M. I. Cole, *The Condition of Britain* (London, 1937), p. 191; *Men Without Work: A Report Made to the Pilgrim Trust* (Cambridge, 1938), p.68; Alan Deacon and Jonathan Bradshaw, *Reserved for the Poor: The Means Test in British Social Policy* (Oxford, 1983), p. 16; Matt Perry, *Bread and Work: The Experience of Unemployment, 1918–1939* (London, 2000), p. 63.
7 Ross McKibbin, *Classes and Cultures: England 1918–1951* (Oxford, 1998), p. 129.
8 *Ibid.*, p. 154; Chris Williams, *Capitalism, Community and Conflict: The South Wales Coalfield, 1898–1947* (Cardiff, 1998), p. 74.

9 NLW, Papers of Dr Thomas Jones CH, 'Unemployment From the Point of View of the Unemployed. A Paper Read by Mr H. Vickerstaff, an Unemployed Miner', at the BARS Conference, Durham, 22 September 1934, p. 5/3.
10 Allen Hutt, *The Condition of the Working Class in Britain* (London, 1933), p. 45.
11 McKibbin, *Classes and Cultures*, pp. 153–4.
12 Cole, *The Condition of Britain*, p. 191.
13 Perry, *Bread and Work*, p. 64.
14 E. Wight Bakke, *The Unemployed Man: A Social Study* (London, 1935), p. 70.
15 Hilda Jennings, *Brynmawr: A Study of a Distressed Area* (London, 1934), p. 138.
16 John Evans, 'Time to Spare', in Felix Greene (ed.), *Time to Spare: What Unemployment Means by Eleven Unemployed* (London, 1935), p. 90.
17 Margery Spring Rice, *Working-Class Wives: Their Health and Conditions* (London, 1939), pp. 157–61.
18 *Men Without Work*, p. 112.
19 Sue Bruley, 'Women', in John McIlroy, Alan Campbell and Keith Gildart (eds), *Industrial Politics and the 1926 Mining Lockout: The Struggle for Dignity* (Cardiff, 2004), p. 233.
20 Steven Thompson, 'Unemployment, Poverty and Women's Health in Inter-war South Wales', in Pamela Michael and Charles Webster (eds), *Health and Society in Twentieth-Century Wales* (Cardiff, 2006), p. 101.
21 Sid Elias, *Mass Murder: An Exposure of the Means Test* (London, 1932), p. 4.
22 *Rhondda Fach Gazette*, 16 April 1932, p. 5.
23 Paul Johnson, 'Credit and Thrift and the British Working Class, 1870–1939', in Jay Winter (ed.), *The Working Class in Modern British History: Essays in Honour of Henry Pelling* (Cambridge, 1983), p. 159.
24 Bakke, *The Unemployed Man*, p. 146.
25 A. M. Carr-Saunders, 'The Unemployment Assistance Board', *The Political Quarterly*, 7:4 (1936), p. 539.
26 TNA, PRO 30/69/442, Correspondence, Herbert Samuel to the Prime Minister, 13 October 1931.
27 Henry Betterton, the Minister of Labour, was unprepared to accept such criticism at such an early stage and was only willing to investigate individual cases. PRO 30/69/442, Memorandum of Trades Union Congress General Council Deputation to the Minister of Labour on Monday 1st February 1932, on Transitional Benefit and the Means Test; *The Times*, 2 February 1932, p. 7.
28 Wal Hannington, *A Short History of the Unemployed* (London, 1938), p. 63.
29 Investigations did become more thorough as the means test regulations were tightened after intervention from the Ministries of Labour and Health.
30 'Seven Years Without Hard Labour – A Rhondda Miner', in H. L. Beales and R. S. Lambert (eds), *Memoirs of the Unemployed* (London, 1934), pp. 143–4.
31 '"We Would Rather Be Dead" – A Derbyshire Miner's Wife', in Beales and Lambert, *Memoirs of the Unemployed*, p. 219.

32 Although the whole novel is relevant, see in particular Brierley, *Means-Test Man*, pp. 80, 155–6, 204, 228–31, 244–79.

33 Perry, *Bread and Work*, p. 76.

34 The difference can partly be explained by the fact that the UAB was more rigorous and was viewed as a much more alien body within working-class communities.

35 'Unemployment From the Point of View of the Unemployed. A Paper Read by Mr H. Vickerstaff', p. 3.

36 The *Western Mail* interviewed Alderman C. W. Melhuish, Chair of Cardiff PAC, who denied that the unemployed would be made to sell their furniture in order to appease the situation. *Western Mail*, 10 October 1931, p. 14.

37 'Minority Report', p. 778.

38 See the conclusion for a wider discussion of this issue. There are some examples of such instances. In November 1931, the *Daily Herald* reported how at London County Council's PAC concerns were raised by councillors about radios and pianos being taken into account in means test assessments. *Daily Herald*, 26 November 1931, p. 11.

39 While the Ministry of Labour and the commissioners in Durham reported large savings amongst some, such examples made up only a minority of transitional applicants. PRO 30/69/442, 'Examples of individual cases in which Transitional Payments have been determined by Guardians' Committees in the County of Durham', Correspondence between W. Eady and the Clerk of Durham Public Assistance Committee, 29 March 1932; Steven Thompson, *Unemployment, Poverty and Health in Interwar South Wales* (Cardiff, 2006), pp. 52–3.

40 Before the Determinations of Need Act in late 1932, the regulations regarding the assessment of savings and investments were unclear. This led to a situation where some authorities disregarded all savings, while others took all investments into account, including small savings.

41 *Rhondda Fach Gazette*, 16 April 1932, p. 5.

42 *Durham County Advertiser and Durham Chronicle*, 12 February 1932, p. 12.

43 Johnson, 'Credit and Thrift and the British Working Class', pp. 168–70.

44 Avram Taylor, '"More Tick Than Big Ben": Working Class Credit on Tyneside in the Interwar Years', *North East Labour History Bulletin*, 26 (1992), pp. 76–7; David Vincent, *Poor Citizens: The State and the Poor in Twentieth Century Britain* (Harlow, 1991), pp. 92–3; Thompson, *Unemployment, Poverty and Health*, pp. 46–50.

45 PRO 30/69/442 Correspondence between Ramsay MacDonald and Herbert Samuel, 3 June 1932.

46 PRO 30/69/442, Correspondence between Henry Betterton and Ramsay MacDonald, 5 June 1932, report enclosed to Sir Herbert Samuel.

47 *Ibid*. *The Times* examined the impact of the means test in London and using the position there as an example considered that 'it was impossible not to

draw the conclusion from the figures that, in a large number of cases before the operation of the "needs" test, State money was drawn where it was not really needed'. The paper noted twelve 'striking cases' where benefit had been applied for despite adequate household income or savings. *The Times*, 9 March 1932, p. 7.

48 Again it must be emphasised that such investments only existed amongst a minority of cases. *Report of the Minister of Labour by the Commissioners Appointed to Administer Transitional Payments in the County of Durham* (Cmd 4339), 1932–33, xv, pp. 1037–43.

49 *Durham County Advertiser and Durham Chronicle*, 15 January 1932, p. 8.

50 *Ibid.*, 11 December 1931, p. 11, 13 May 1932, p. 13, and 10 June 1932, p. 6.

51 'Minority Report', p. 778. The Transitional Payments (Determinations of Need) Act, 1932, was partly a response to the criticism that the means test was causing unnecessary hardship by taking into account the pensions of ex-servicemen.

52 W. R. Garside, *British Unemployment 1919–1939: A Study in Public Policy* (Cambridge, 1990), p. 26.

53 'Seven Years Without Hard Labour – A Rhondda Miner', p. 142.

54 'Minority Report', p. 780.

55 Brockway, *Hungry England*, p. 160.

56 *Men Without Work*, pp. 74, 114–15.

57 Jennings, *Brynmawr*, pp. 94, 158.

58 John Newsom, *Out of the Pit: A Challenge to the Comfortable* (Oxford, 1936), p. 47.

59 Bakke, *The Unemployed Man*, p. 51.

60 Brockway, *Hungry England*, p. 113.

61 Elias, *Mass Murder*, p. 5.

62 Newsom, *Out of the Pit*, p. 21; Evans, 'Time to Spare', p. 94.

63 J. B. Priestley, *English Journey* (London, 1968 edition; first published, 1934), p. 407.

64 Brockway, *Hungry England*, p. 111.

65 Deacon and Bradshaw, *Reserved for the Poor*, pp. 27–8.

66 Marjorie Levine-Clark, 'The Politics of Preference: Masculinity, Marital Status and Unemployment Relief in Post-First World War Britain', *Cultural and Social History*, 7:2 (2010), pp. 238–9.

67 M. A. Crowther, 'Family Responsibility and State Responsibility in Britain Before the Welfare State', *The Historical Journal*, 25:1 (1982), pp. 132–3.

68 Newsom, *Out of the Pit*, p. 24.

69 Deacon and Bradshaw, *Reserved for the Poor*, p. 17.

70 'Minority Report', p. 778.

71 Deacon and Bradshaw, *Reserved for the Poor*, p. 17.

72 George Orwell, *The Road to Wigan Pier* (London, 2001 edition; first published, 1937), p. 72.

73 PRO 30/69/442, Correspondence between E. Hilton Young and Ramsay MacDonald, 22 November 1932.
74 'Examples of individual cases in which Transitional Payments have been determined by Guardians' Committees in the County of Durham'.
75 'Unemployment From the Point of View of the Unemployed. A Paper Read by Mr H. Vickerstaff', p. 3.
76 Crowther, 'Family Responsibility and State Responsibility', p. 145.
77 Out of the twenty-five oral testimonies collected by Beales and Lambert, only one focuses upon the wife of an unemployed man, and only one other examines the position of a female who is unemployed. Beales and Lambert, *Memoirs of the Unemployed*, pp. 5–6. The experience of female unemployment or single women drew even less attention. Perry, *Bread and Work*, pp. 65–6.
78 Brockway, *Hungry England*, pp. 160–3.
79 Labour History and Archive Study Centre, People's History Museum, Manchester (hereafter, LHASC), *Report of the Thirteenth National Conference of Labour Women held at The Dome, Brighton June 14, 15 and 16, 1932 together with Notes of Private Business Conference held on June 14* (London, 1932), p. 52.
80 NLW, Papers of Dr Thomas Jones CH, 'Unemployment: By an Unemployed Miner's Wife, Read by Mrs E. Vickerstaff', at the BARS Conference, Durham, 22 September 1934, p. 7. The changing role of a wife entering politics while a husband helped out with the chores was also described by Lewis Jones in his novel *We Live*. When Mary was elected as a Communist councillor, her unemployed husband Len began to help out with the housework far more. Lewis Jones, *We Live* (London, 1939), p. 225.
81 Vincent, *Poor Citizens*, p. 95.
82 Brierley, *Means-Test Man*, pp. 98–9.
83 Neil Penlington, 'Masculinity and Domesticity in 1930s South Wales: Did Unemployment Change the Domestic Division of Labour?', *Twentieth Century British History*, 21:3 (2010), pp. 284–9.
84 Jennings, *Brynmawr*, p. 139. The *Western Mail* also urged women to be understanding of their husband's problems and to help in any way that they could. *Western Mail*, 15 September 1931, p. 5.
85 Bakke, *The Unemployed Man*, p. 23.
86 Hutt, *The Condition of the Working Class*, p. 10.
87 *Ibid.*, p. 12.
88 Priestley, *English Journey*, p. 339; Newsom, *Out of the Pit*, p. 21.
89 'Unemployment From the Point of View of the Unemployed. A Paper Read by Mr H. Vickerstaff', p. 3.
90 *The Labour Woman*, 20:1, January 1932, p. 6.
91 Priestley, *English Journey*, pp. 297, 348.
92 Evans, 'Time to Spare', p. 89.

4

Taking a stand: the response of the unemployed 1931–34

> These demonstrations are crude but eloquent testimony that human nature is not yet demoralized to the brute level of being satisfied with mere existence. It is still demanding, through the only voice it is able to find, a chance to live a bit better.
>
> E. Wight Bakke, *The Unemployed Man: A Social Study* (London, 1935).[1]

> I will never forget the historic scene when we marched into Risca as the old day was dying. The thousands upon thousands of working men and women and children lined the mile long streets to greet and cheer their marchers as they tramped past in perfect time, with their bands playing and their banners floating proudly and defiantly in the evening breeze.
>
> Lewis Jones, 1933.[2]

While the marches of the unemployed in 1921–22 could be impressive displays of collective action, it was the demonstrations of the 1930s which really captured the public imagination.[3] Hundreds, thousands and even hundreds of thousands participated in single demonstrations, and a further three national hunger marches in 1932, 1934 and 1936 descended upon the capital. The unemployed marched for work, food, fuel and, above all else, the abolition of the means test. Although the grievances of the unemployed were wide ranging, the objection to the means test provided a focus and framework for action. No other single piece of governmental policy in the interwar period provoked as much ink, miles marched and words of oration as the means test. The objection to the means test cut across hierarchical and social demarcations; the unemployed and employed, men and women, working and middle classes vocalised opposition through street protests and print. Yet, many of these protests were in essence class-based: anger against the ruling elite for neglecting the plight of the unemployed working class was at their core. While gendered divisions remained important, women were also to participate on the public stage of protest along with male members of their class. Studies of protest have overwhelmingly focused upon men, a hangover, perhaps, of the initial marginalisation of women within key organisations such as the NUWM.[4] This is especially true of the part played by the wives of the unemployed; a picture of the experience of working women in protest has begun to emerge.[5] The wives of the unemployed together with women's sections in the labour movement played a fundamental part in marches and demonstrations. In both south Wales and the north-east of England where levels of formal female economic activity were low, women marched in solidarity against the effects of unemployment upon family and community life.

Drawing upon a longer radical tradition, the protests of the earlier 1930s were also important in laying the foundation for the largest examples of collective action in the interwar period. Under the administration of the PACs, marchers had a clear target for their grievances. While PAC officials in Labour strongholds were often sympathetic to the unemployed and their families, the refusal to meet deputations and bow to the demands of demonstrators established a trench between the two groups. The perception that the police used heavy-handed tactics that were sanctioned by local councillors and Whitehall further contributed to this fractious relationship. It was those who marched under the banner of the Communist-affiliated NUWM who were singled out for the excesses of police control and council indifference. The authorities for their part both reviled and feared the organised mass of the unemployed. Outbreaks of violence and rioting left the unemployed, whatever banner they marched behind, risking the characterisation of an unruly and unpatriotic mob for the decision to take to the streets even on peaceful marches. Such representations of the unemployed had wider repercussions for their treatment.

While anti-means test demonstrations sprung up across Britain, protest against the test was never automatic. Certain areas witnessed much greater levels of action with the unemployed in east London, Bristol, Birkenhead, Belfast, Glasgow and south Wales producing some of the most explosive examples of action. As a comparison of protest levels in south Wales and the north-east of England reveals, cultural and political traditions were fundamental to the nature of the response to unemployment and the means test. An absence of collective action was not necessarily reflective of political stability or apathy amongst the unemployed as scholarship from the later twentieth century has shown.[6] The 'resources' available to the unemployed which could be drawn upon, including organisational, financial and cultural (i.e. a historical precedent for marching), were of fundamental importance to the organisation of collective action as resource mobilisation theorists, like Paul Bagguley and Andrew Richards, have revealed.[7] Even in more militant areas like south Wales, the unemployed were not necessarily able to access the same resources for protest as those still in employment. Although the NUWM were an extremely important group in leading the unemployed, it must be remembered that many of the workless continued to turn to the traditional leaders of the working class for support.[8] Leadership and the nature of the labour movement were intrinsic to levels of action and, importantly, the type of protest that emerged.

While the marches and demonstrations were undoubtedly the most powerful display of opposition, they were not the only way protest was expressed. Written forms of protest, meetings and deputations not associated with marches were also an important expression of protest that have often been overlooked in the historiography.[9] These forms of opposition served a vital function in the movement against the means test; an examination of them allows for a greater understanding of the relationship between the unemployed and the wider labour movement and perceptions of protestors and the out of work. Moreover, these alternative forms of opposition let groups not normally associated with the protest of the workless to gain prominence. Indeed, the outpouring of writing against the measure ensured that the test was denounced from all quarters; councillors, politicians, Christian ministers, teachers, academics, trade unionists, working men and women, writers, doctors and social investigators all condemned the use of a household means test. The criticisms of such groups not only highlighted the effects, at least in their opinion, of the means test, they also acted as a form of opposition.

The imagery evoked by Lewis Jones's description of the 1933 Monmouthshire hunger marchers' entry to Risca conveys the importance of ritualism and ceremony that surrounded all forms of protest.[10] The bright banners, the use of music and the strict line formation of marchers, like the ceremonial formalities of passing a written resolution, give greater insight into working-class organisations and the creation of self and public representations of the unemployed. A comparative study allows these nuances of working class organisation to emerge and reveals how national directives played out in local arenas.

While there were important regional variations, patterns or waves of protest can be traced within the United Kingdom which ebbed and flowed with the seasons, becoming a 'rising tide of militancy' at certain moments.[11] In the early 1930s, the first wave of protest broke out after the announcement of benefit cuts in the autumn of 1931 and fairly sustained activity lasted until the spring of the following year. The tens of thousands who turned out to demonstrate in London when parliament was reconvened marked, along with demonstrators elsewhere in the country, a turning point in the protests of the unemployed.[12] Mass action was reported in London, Manchester, Bristol, Wigan, Glasgow, Dundee, parts of south Wales and the north-east.[13] Together, it was indicative of how opposition to the means test provided an organisational banner giving focus to previously disparate and sporadic outbursts of action. An attempt to calculate the number who took to the streets against the means test needs careful consideration given how figures were prone to partisan under-recording or exaggeration. A better indication of the level of action and opposition to the means test is the number of marches and demonstrations that occurred. In this respect alone, it was evident that such levels of action had not been witnessed since the early 1920s; the crucial difference was now the unemployed were much better organised and appeared more determined.

The ambition of the marchers was twofold. First and foremost, it was hoped that through a show of strength and public pressure, the government could be persuaded to abolish the means test. In the interim, energies were focused upon local authorities to encourage officials to refuse to administer the test, and, as in previous decades, local government offices became a key destination for marchers.[14] The discrepancies which emerged in the administration of the means test were in part reflective of the susceptibility of councillors to local pressure. Paul Bagguley has argued that when elected councillors were sympathetic to the unemployed, there existed 'a *realisable collective goal for local protest*'.[15] In addition to these primary ambitions, it was hoped that the spectre of a peaceful demonstration of the respectable working class would help evoke public sympathy and thus increase pressure for reform upon local PACs and the Prime Minister. Here, the press played a crucial role, and to avoid the representation of lawless rioters, the conduct of the marchers was paramount, although never a guarantee of sympathetic treatment.[16] While movements like the NUWM viewed militant (although disciplined) action as essential, the labour movement was often uncertain of the benefits of marching and varied in its response. The different patterns of protest within south Wales and the north-east of England, and within the north-east itself, were reflective of both the policy of the leadership and who the unemployed wished to be led by.

South Wales was alive with protest in the autumn of 1931, and particularly within the industrial valleys. What characterised the protests of these months was the level of action and organisation which had developed since the National Government's benefit cuts.[17] The NUWM continued to offer leadership to the unemployed. Highlighting the significance of the region in unemployed protests, the first action of the NUWM nationally in the autumn of 1931 was to organise 'a march to Bristol from South Wales to press the Trades Union Congress'.[18] Within south Wales, the Councils of Action were fundamental in coordinating protest activity and included representatives from the SWMF lodges, branches of the Independent Labour Party, the Communist Party and the women's co-operative guilds.[19] The Mid-Rhondda Council of Action was important in organising the large demonstrations throughout the two valleys which became a key area of action. The *Daily Worker* reported a march of as many as 6,000 at Porth on 11 October and argued that this was 'the first real massing of workers in a demonstration in the Rhondda Valley since the strike of 1926'.[20] Elsewhere in the region, the *Daily Worker* recorded marches of 1,000 at Maesteg and Swansea, and the mining villages around Caerphilly were similarly active.[21] It was not only unemployed men who were mobilised, and women and children participated in the demonstrations.[22]

In the early months of the means test, the local Labour Party and trade unions also organised demonstrations. The protest at Waun-y-Pound Common at Ebbw Vale in late September is telling of the ritualism and symbolism at the larger protests led by both groups. A protest march headed by jazz bands processed through the town and was followed by a large demonstration at the Common. Councillors, trade unionists, an alderwoman and Labour MPs addressed the 'huge crowd'. The most rousing speech was made by Aneurin Bevan (Labour MP, Ebbw Vale), and he stated that although in the House of Commons 'the unemployed were no longer human beings in the discussions there ... as far as he was concerned these people were still the human beings that he loved'.[23] Marches offered hope for change, and, as Matthias Reiss has argued in the case of the hunger marches, the street protests showed how the unemployed could be 'actors in the public arena'.[24] In south Wales, the labour movement and the NUWM orchestrated marches and demonstrations to allow the unemployed and their families to make their political voices heard.

In the north-east of England, neither the unemployed nor the labour movement appeared to have the same level of determination in the stance adopted against the means test, although there were some notable exceptions. While larger demonstrations did occur, such as the march of 3,000–4,000 to Gateshead Town Hall on 2 October 1931, smaller marches or an absence of action were more common.[25] As in south Wales, Committees of Action, the Labour Party, trade unions and the NUWM played a role in organising the unemployed. However, in the north-east, there was a dearth of regional coordination beyond certain localities. In early October, a demonstration at West Cornforth in south-west Durham showed the potential for protest within the area. A platform of Labour MPs, the women's section of the Labour Party, trade unions and unemployed organisations addressed an audience of around 500 and passed resolutions against the means test.[26] Indeed, marches were less evident despite the positive consequences of action. Blyth council in Northumberland issued a resolution of protest following a deputation of unemployed marchers. Tellingly, when reporting on the march of 500 organised by a Committee of Action, it was noted that 'in every area of the borough mass meetings against the cuts have been held, the like of which have never been witnessed in the town'.[27] Action in Blyth and West Cornforth, however, failed to inspire more widespread militant action in the rest of the coalfields.

Across the region, Tyneside emerged as the area of greatest activity. A number of demonstrations took place in Newcastle including a NUWM march in November 1931 which attracted contingents from North Shields, Byker, Wallsend and Sunderland.[28] Further action within the city came in December with a march from Willington Quay and Wallsend to Moot Hall. On this occasion, PAC officials met with the marchers and passed a resolution urging PACs across the country to petition the government to end the means test.[29] On the same day, the unemployed at Hebburn and Felling demonstrated with the unemployed at Jarrow, and 'a crowd of several thousand' gathered outside of the town hall where a meeting of the guardians' committee was taking place. The committee after meeting with a deputation agreed to pass on their demands to Durham PAC.[30] At the end of the Tyneside industrial belt, North Shields was a more militant area, and the estimated crowd of 2,000 in November who marched to the PAC marked the first stage in a long campaign against the means test.[31]

The strictness of the PAC administration in Newcastle only partly accounts for greater regularity of protest along the Tyne and not least because many of the residents actually came under the jurisdiction of Durham PAC. Moreover, this picture does not account for the scale of protest in south Wales in spite of the known laxity of the administrations of many PACs. Clearly, other factors were important. As the marches and demonstrations noted above indicate, the leadership and organisation of the unemployed were vital for the success of collective action. Indeed, Andrew Richards has argued that 'in terms of forging the unemployed into an organized movement, which functioned over a sustained period of time, the role of external agents was critical'.[32] While the trade unions and the Labour Party were important in coordinating some of the demonstrations, the NUWM emerged as the most active organisation in mobilising the unemployed for protest in both regions. Matthew Worley has recently argued that NUWM had a 'more or less unrivalled position in relation to organizing the unemployed' because 'both the trade unions and the Labour Party remained loath to take on unemployed organization prior to 1932 and, consequently, the [Communist] party and NUWM members often monopolized, and set, the political agenda of the unemployed'.[33] The means test undoubtedly helped the NUWM gain more recruits.[34] Between October 1931, when the means test was announced, and the end of the year, the NUWM was gaining an average of 2,239 new recruits a week throughout Britain.[35] This period likewise saw a rise in Communist Party membership. The *Manchester Guardian* reported a rise in numbers of 145% on Tyneside and 135% in south Wales in 1932. Nearly half of all members were unemployed.[36] The success of the marches in the first months of the means test was therefore, in part at least, related to the success of the NUWM within the regions.

When considering the position of the NUWM in south Wales and the north-east of England, it must be borne in mind that as a movement of the unemployed, the membership was much more fluid than other working-class organisations. Many simply passed through the ranks which made calculating members difficult, and many more participated in demonstrations without necessarily being paid up members.[37] Reports from the branches to the movement's official paper *The Unemployed Special* provide the best indication of those areas with an active NUWM membership.[38] In the north-east, branches at Sunderland, Gateshead, South Shields, Birtley, Ferryhill, Blyth and Houghton-le-Spring were most energetic. In contrast to south Wales, there also existed a number of active women's branches at Sunderland, Middlesbrough and Gateshead. The Tyneside women's section (which covered much of the area) was praised for its work.[39] The efforts of these branches, however, did not necessarily translate into collective action. The Communist Party was concerned by the low numbers participating in collective action in the region. *The Party Organiser* lamented that while 'all facts show that there is tremendous feeling against the Means Test', the Communist

Party had 'failed to develop any real mass demonstrations of the unemployed'.[40] As Lewis Mates has stated, 'in strong contrast to South Wales, there was very little Communist permeation in the DMA' and the Durham coalfield.[41] In the absence of a stronger presence from the NUWM or Communist Party, the trade unions and the Labour Party remained the major source of leadership.

The NUWM in south Wales reported that twenty-eight branches existed by June 1932, and the number of marches recorded in the first few months suggests that the NUWM was active across much of the region.[42] By 1933, it was claimed there were eleven branches alone within the Monmouthshire district of the movement.[43] The influence of the NUWM was also notable in the anthracite part of the western coalfield, despite the lower levels of unemployment. Across the region, branches in the Rhondda Valleys, Aberdare, Llanelli and Merthyr were most active.[44] The strength of local support for the Communist Party was reflected in Wal Hannington's decision to contest the seat at the 1934 by-election in Merthyr.[45] In the initial movement against the means test, the unemployed in south Wales were far better organised for the purposes of collective action.

While south Wales may have been better organised, in both regions after the initial surge in activity, protest only rumbled on into the summer months.[46] Nevertheless, Richard Croucher has argued that continuation of protest at all during a usually quieter time of year revealed the 'depth of feeling against the Means Test'.[47] In County Durham, during the May Day demonstrations, Labour MPs and ex-Labour MPs spoke out against the means test and its effects and praised the efforts of Labour councillors.[48] A month later at the annual demonstration of the women's sections of the Durham Labour Party, a reported 20,000 marched and gathered to hear speeches. Mrs Corner, a leader of the Labour women's section in Durham, denounced 'the hated means test which was placing their men-folk on the same basis as the recipients of poor relief'.[49] The annual march of Durham Labour women was one of the biggest within the country.[50] Although the number of women participating in demonstrations as a whole was lower in Durham, the march highlighted women's agency against the test and the vibrancy of Labour women's organisation. Indeed, Labour women's protest was not confined to annual marches. For example, the Sunderland women's section of the Labour Party joined a demonstration against the means test on 21 May 1932 and planned to drape their banner as a mark of respect to the death of Marion Phillips.[51]

Protests such as these revealed both the strength of feeling against the means test and the power of the unemployed in the region to participate in street protests when mobilised for action. On the same Saturday as the Labour women gathered in Durham City, in Washington, seventeen sections of the British Legion marched to show their opposition to the means test.[52] However, important as these demonstrations were, such displays of protest were not repeated with any regularity or frequency in County Durham, and many were an established part of the labour movement calendar. Labour movement leaders lamented the lack of action. At a May Day demonstration at Rowlands Gill, the chair James McNestry from Chopwell saw the small attendance as giving the impression that 'everybody was satisfied'. He believed that despite the appalling conditions in the area, 'people were more prepared to go to Redcar races' than demonstrate.[53] Such concerns were repeated at an Independent Labour Party (ILP) meeting in Blaydon in July 1932. Fenner Brockway, the invited speaker, addressed the audience on the 'bewilderment' of the working class who has lost faith in the labour movement.[54] The disparities that had developed between Tyneside and the rest of the north-east region, and with south Wales especially, were to become most evident in the autumn of 1932 when the number taking to the streets nationally dramatically increased once more. In these protests, more militant organisations were to play a vital role.

Across Britain, the number of people marching and demonstrating escalated in the autumn months of 1932. Violence was to characterise the protests of the unemployed in these months, with serious rioting in Birkenhead and Belfast. In Birkenhead, pitched battles between the unemployed and the police occurred for a week from 13 September. In Belfast in early October, five people died in a rare example of non-sectarian violence.[55] While not all protests descended into clashes with the police in these months, feelings were undoubtedly heated and especially with a further NUWM national hunger march on the horizon.

In early September, the NUWM, including the movement's leader Wal Hannington, organised marches and demonstrations to coincide with the annual meeting of the TUC in Newcastle. Mass anti-means test demonstrations were planned along Tyneside, and the occasion attracted NUWM members from across the region. On 6 September, contingents from Sunderland, Hartlepool and Middlesbrough, numbering some 1,000, converged on Newcastle, and men, women and children marched alongside each other. The anxiety of the local authorities at such a high number of marchers was reflected in the strong police presence of over 200 police and plain clothes officers. Despite passing a resolution against the means test, the TUC refused to meet a deputation after Walter Citrine advised that the march was held under the auspices of the NUWM. This decision was challenged in the meeting by Mr Evans from the SWMF who wished to note that 'every miner in South Wales was in full sympathy with the unemployed and certainly the South Wales miners were in favour of receiving the deputation.' The only presence of the deputation in the end were two Communists who reportedly managed to enter the meeting and even appeared in an official photograph.[56]

The NUWM continued to organise public demonstrations along the Tyne throughout the following months. This was a crucial period given the crisis point being reached within Durham PAC and the well-publicised strictness of Newcastle PAC. Early October witnessed high levels of sometimes quite violent activity. On the same day as the rioting occurred in Belfast, violence also broke out in North Shields. Marchers were determined to make their voices heard, despite a prior warning that it was not North Shields council's policy to meet a deputation accompanied by a demonstration.[57] On 5 October, a crowd of 'thousands of people' gathered outside the PAC offices. The demonstrators had processed through the streets carrying banners bearing the slogans 'Down with the Means Test' and 'Down with Police Tyranny'.[58] Frustration between the police and marchers gradually increased. The shouts of 'come on lads, get at them' by the Communist Michael Harrison were thought to have sparked missile throwing from the protestors which ended in a police baton charge. In the violence that ensued, shop windows were broken and smaller battles took place on the streets in the surrounding areas. The violence resulted in the arrest of four men and drew national press attention.[59]

The aftermath of the demonstration in North Shields matched the experience elsewhere. Although the unemployed asserted their right to protest, those taking to the streets were viewed with suspicion by the press and the police and especially as the NUWM or Communist Party were involved. The charge read against the men at North Shields Police Court the following day reveals most pertinently the attitude of the police to the marchers:

> Together with divers other evilly-disposed persons, to the number of ten and more, unlawfully and riotously did assemble and gather together to disturb the public peace, and then unlawfully, riotously, routously and tumultuously did make great noise, riot, tumult and disturbance to the great terror and disturbance of His Majesty's subjects ... did assault, beat, wound and ill treat one [PC] Dennis Wood, against the peace of his Sovereign Lord the King his crown and dignity.[60]

The police were reported to have been 'very tolerant and patient' although, to local outrage, the four men who appeared in court were 'heavily bandaged'; mass assemblies were held throughout the area to express sympathy with the defendants.[61] The following week in South Shields, a mass meeting passed the resolution that 'we pledge our whole-hearted support to the North Shields unemployed in their fight for the abolition of the Means Test ... We emphatically condemn the repeated baton charges of the police ... and demand the release of all unemployed workers who have been arrested'.[62] Outcry against the men's treatment was not restricted to the region, and the Labour Party conference at Leicester passed an emergency resolution against the actions of the police.[63] During the course of the trial, thousands reportedly gathered outside to protest, and extra police enforcements were brought in. The strength of the feeling against the test was apparent, and continuing his own protest, the charged Michael Harrison shouted 'Down With the Means Test!' as he left the court. The eight men finally charged received sentences between four and twelve months.[64] The arrests did little to dampen the fight against the means test by the NUWM despite the imprisonment of some of the leadership.[65]

The local protests along Tyneside and within south Wales were important in maintaining pressure upon councils at a time when the Ministry of Labour was investigating the conduct of PACs. They formed part of a national campaign by the NUWM against the means test which included a fourth hunger march that in many ways overshadowed events within the regions. The relationship between the authorities and unemployed demonstrators had hardened in these months, as the violent outbursts of local protest provoked by the strength of feeling against the means test and the nervous, or predisposed, actions of police conveyed. When the first contingents of the hunger march took to the road in September 1932, they were closely monitored and policed from the outset in what was to be the most violent of all marches on the capital.[66] The purpose of this demonstration was to present a petition against the means test which had been signed by over one million people. This was the first hunger march of the three that would be organised against the means test in the 1930s. The grievances of those marching within the regions were largely confined to the local political arena. By participating in a national march to the seat of government in London, it was hoped that the abolition of the means test could be achieved. Moreover, Mathias Reiss has argued that the marches gave the unemployed 'the publicity they sought and needed to become a factor in national politics'.[67]

Eighty marchers left Newcastle on 2 October 1932 and were joined along the way by others from Darlington, Middlesbrough and Hartlepool. Together, these marchers made up the north-east contingent, and it numbered in total 150 people by the time it reached London.[68] Police and MI5 intelligence noted of the north-east contingent that 'reports of their conduct have been extremely good'.[69] This discipline was an important feature of the march as it ensured that those participating could not be dismissed as 'an unruly mob'.[70] Not all contingents received the praise of the north-eastern marchers in this instance. In the course of the march to London, a violent clash occurred between the Lancashire contingent and the police at Stratford-upon-Avon.[71] Further clashes broke out once the marchers entered London. The prospective power held in the presence of so many marchers passing through towns and villages across the country, and strict orders from Whitehall to monitor and control contingents, left police forces at best jittery and at worst liable to resort to their most heavy-handed tactics. For those marching, it appeared as if the police needed scant evidence to embrace the baton despite the noted good conduct of the majority.[72] Like others, the south Wales contingent clashed with the police, but in this instance it was before the marchers had even properly set off. What makes the episode so unusual is that while the marchers decried the actions of the police, the latter downplayed the episode entirely.

Conflict occurred after the Tonypandy contingent (from the Rhondda Valleys) ignored the request that they go straight to their lodgings in Cardiff, on the first part of their journey to London. Instead, the marchers dismounted their train at Llandaff station, in a suburb of Cardiff, where they were met by a police presence. Arthur Griffiths, one of the south Wales contingent leaders, later claimed that the marchers 'were set upon by our kind "cop" people in blue ... They wanted to smash us up'.[73] The Chief Constable of Cardiff City Police, James Wilson, however, stated that when told they could not march through the city, the contingent 'sauntered in a lethargic manner through unimportant suburban streets'. Wilson claimed that even when the marchers proceeded through 'two working class districts ... they excited no enthusiasm and they themselves did not appear enthusiastic'. He concluded, 'the Police did not observe any misbehaviour or intemperance on the part of individual marchers'.[74]

The disparity that arose in the statements of the marchers and the police was perhaps unsurprising as it was common for both parties to exaggerate or downplay events. However, the comments also suggested something of the nature of relations between the unemployed, the police and the government. The Chief Constable was trying to demonstrate his force's command of the situation. His comments on the conduct of the marchers reveal that, in this instance, they were not viewed as a threat but rather as apathetic and listless. What is most telling of the relationship between the police and the unemployed was Wilson's point that 'in this City the marchers, for some reason best known to themselves, adopted a friendly attitude towards the Police'.[75] While relations may have been peaceable on this occasion, Wilson was clearly suspicious of the unemployed marchers and expected them to behave in an unacceptable manner. The marchers, for their part, complied with the police in Cardiff after the incident to ensure that they were allowed to continue on their course to London. When Arthur Griffiths spoke out against the conduct of the police, he echoed the sentiment made by many other NUWM members after their experiences on their route to London.[76] The strained relationship between the unemployed who felt they had a right to demonstrate and the police who feared social unrest was only to continue.

In total, thirteen contingents and around 1,500 people participated in the 1932 hunger march. Once assembled within London, the marchers continued to clash with the police, and the public were urged not to turn out to see the protestors.[77] The prized petition was seized by the police, and a deputation from the NUWM was not permitted to meet with anyone from the Cabinet.[78] Moreover, soon after the march, many of the leaders were imprisoned including Wal Hannington, Sid Elias and Tom Mann. The march did help lead to some minor concessions from the government, and it did undoubtedly succeed in demonstrating how the unemployed could be successfully mobilised and the political power this gave to the workless.[79]

In both south Wales and the north-east, despite the imprisonment of key national leaders, the NUWM and the unemployed continued to demonstrate. Just a few weeks after the end of the hunger march, the NUWM was mobilising the unemployed in south Wales in the fight against the means test. Once again, the Rhondda Valleys became an important area of protest, and the south Wales branch of the NUWM was 'supposed to be existent and deliberating at Tonypandy'.[80] Indeed, Arthur Horner and Lewis Jones, both well-known and active Communist Party members, resided in the Rhondda Valleys and were involved in the protests of the unemployed.[81] Horner was even arrested for seven months for his involvement in preventing an eviction at Maerdy which, from 1926, had been branded a 'Little Moscow'.[82] As events at North Shields and during the hunger march demonstrated, the relations between the unemployed and the police were often acrimonious. In the Rhondda Valleys, the situation was fuelled by the police's concern at the militancy of the unemployed and the connection to Communist politics as was evident at a march on 17 November 1932. On this day, around 300 of the unemployed led by the NUWM attempted a march to the guardians' committee offices at Pentre. The police were claimed to have 'paraded' the valleys, and meetings were broken up at Treorchy, Maerdy, Trealaw, Tonypandy and Ton Pentre. As the committee was unable to meet the demands made, the crowd passed a resolution urging protest to be carried out throughout the county. The police, clearly nervous at the presence of the NUWM members who sang the Internationale to end the meeting, broke up many of the gatherings. The conservative *Western Mail*, sharing the authorities' suspicion, reported the story under the headline 'PROCESSION BROKEN UP: RHONDDA "REDS" AND THEIR DEMANDS'.[83]

By 1933, south Wales and Scotland, as in previous years, were thought to have been the strongest areas for the NUWM.[84] The Labour Party and the SWMF also continued to be an important voice for the unemployed in south Wales, but they were not always as active in organising street protests.[85] In the north-east of England, a comparable level of activity throughout the region most affected by the means test was not evident. As the pattern of protest in October of 1932 indicated, street protests remained largely confined to the Tyne. Sunderland was the exception to the general trend, but, aside from here, while the NUWM organised meetings throughout the region, the unemployed did not readily take to the streets.[86] Throughout the first year of the means test, despite the strength of feeling against the measure displayed at the PAC meetings, the unemployed rarely took to the streets in opposition. It was to take the imposition of the commissioners in Durham PAC in December 1932 to ignite a broader protest movement against the means test. The course of these events is quite telling of protest in the Durham coalfield.

The stricter administration of the means test by the commissioners roused much resentment amongst the unemployed within the north-east, and it caused the labour movement to take a stronger stand. In early 1933, the Labour Party, the DMA and the NUWM organised marches and demonstrations in the county; this was the first time that the unemployed had been organised on such a scale for protests specifically against the means test. The first large march took place at the end of January and was noted to have been 'carefully-organised and much-advertised'.[87] The local press argued that the march embodied a united front of the unemployed, councillors, Communist and Labour party members, cooperative movements and ex-servicemen.[88] However, it was the NUWM that was most strongly represented, and around sixty NUWM members from the Tyneside branch travelled to Durham. *The Unemployed Leader* noted the 'sterling' role played by the women who marched.[89] Although it was predicted that 20,000 people were to march, the 'official' figure reported in the press was only 2,000. While not disputing the number who marched, *The Unemployed Leader* argued that 15,000 demonstrated in the city.[90] The marchers represented a broad geographical area; contingents were present from Gateshead, Chester-le-Street, Lanchester, Sunderland, South Shields, Jarrow, Houghton-le-Spring, South Bank, Ferryhill, Coxhoe, Bowburn, Blaydon and Birtley. Both men and women were represented. There was still no evidence of participation from the south-western part of the coalfield.[91]

The commissioners refused to meet with a deputation, although they agreed to investigate individual cases. Despite marching through different routes in the city, the presence of the police outside council buildings prevented the passage of the marchers at a number of streets. Following a final mass meeting to collect funds for the bus journey home, the marchers left the city at around midnight.[92] The *Newcastle Journal* concluded that 'it is doubtful if anyone is any better off for all the trouble undertaken and bother and inconvenience occasioned to the powers-that-be'.[93] For some, the march represented a propaganda manoeuvre on the part of the Communist Party. The night after the march, Durham MP William McKeag, a known critic of the actions of Labour councillors, advised a meeting of his constituents that 'I would also urge you not to be persuaded into joining the hunger marchers and similar demonstrations. They do not help matters at all. They accomplish nothing except bring additional misery and suffering upon those who take part in them, and, moreover, they are usually organised for the glorification of a few individuals'.[94] The *Northern Echo* also felt that 'the virtual ignoring of Monday's demonstration is a further indication that from now onwards no quarter will be given to proposals emanating from Communist sources'. The paper encouraged its readers to instead associate themselves with the marches and meetings that were organised by the DMA.[95]

The DMA marches in these months were part of the TUC's call to action in early 1933. This was one of the few occasions where the TUC attempted to organise and endorse collective action. In October 1932, as protests increased across the country, the General Council of the TUC had a lengthy debate about organising unemployed demonstrations to protest against the means test and the government's unemployment policy.[96] The decision to coordinate a procession and 'National Demonstration' at

Hyde Park of trade unions, the Labour Party and co-operative movement was sanctioned by the National Joint Council in November. The demonstration was to coincide with the opening of parliament, and 'mass meetings or Conferences, in the principal provincial centres' were encouraged.[97] On Sunday 5 February 1933, the march and demonstration to Hyde Park drew a crowd of a reported 100,000 and an estimated further 250,000 spectators. The *Daily Mirror* billed the success of the march as 'the most spectacular labour demonstrations ever seen in this country'.[98] The unity of these demonstrations and the numerical strength, based on the *Daily Mirror* figures, reveals the power of the TUC in rousing the working class to protest. In later February, the TUC even organised a film showing of the Hyde Park demonstration.[99]

On three Saturdays on the 4 and 11 February and 4 March 1933, the DMA organised mass demonstrations throughout County Durham.[100] On the first Saturday, 'mass meetings were held at nearly a dozen centres in the county'. Resolutions were passed at all calling for the abolition of the means test, and the crowds were addressed by MPs, councillors, Labour Party members and miners' agents. Addressing a crowd at Seaham, Joshua Ritson, the former Labour MP for Durham, argued that 'by such meetings as these Mr MacDonald will find that Durham is not dead'. He condemned the Prime Minister as a 'political coward'.[101] Such scenes were repeated on the second day of demonstration on 11 February. As in the previous marches, villages and towns were represented that had not previously been noted for their protest. At Stanley, a crowd of 600 attended the demonstrations, and at Ferryhill 500 men and women were present. A further 600–700 met in Consett to listen to councillors from Spennymoor, Sherburn Hill and Newcastle. The purpose of these meetings was to demand an end to the means test; at Houghton-le-Spring, councillor W. Lumley (Ryhope) called for the TUC to call a 48-hour stoppage against the test. Again, the Labour Party and the DMA dominated the leadership and speakers at the demonstration. The only noted presence of the NUWM was at a meeting at Ferryhill where the interruptions of William Todd, chair of a NUWM branch and 'well-known Communist', caused the meeting to end and the police were threatened to have been called.[102] Further demonstrations were organised on the following Monday in Sunderland as part of this wave of action.[103]

The month of protest culminated on 4 March when the Durham County Federation of Divisional Labour Parties convened a meeting at Redhills, the Miners' Hall, in Durham City. A further resolution against the means test and Ramsay MacDonald was passed. Again the NUWM presence was limited to heckling speakers for greater action.[104] The three days of protest finally confirmed the leadership of the unemployed and the unity amongst the labour movement within Durham. At all meetings, Labour MPs, or ex-Labour MPs, Labour councillors and miners' agents spoke to the crowds. It was clear; if the Durham unemployed were going to march on any scale, it was not the NUWM or the Communist Party who were going to lead them: outside the Tyne, the influence of the more radical and militant movements of the unemployed was marginal. In much of Durham County, the traditional labour movement remained the most important source of leadership. Indeed, opposition from within the labour movement and the demand for more militant action was marginal. While the protests did little to improve the administration of the means test, they did draw the attention of the national press, and the resolutions against the Prime Minister would have helped maintain public opposition to the measure. MacDonald may have kept his Seaham seat, but the Labour Party gradually distanced itself from him in order to regain party votes and maintain the loyalty of its existing membership.

The NUWM, although a small influence in the county, continued to attempt to organise the unemployed. In April 1933, a sequel to the January march took place, and this time the marchers were far more determined to meet with the commissioners. In the weeks leading up to the march, the Ferryhill branch of the NUWM attempted to rouse the unemployed to action in the neighbouring villages of Chilton, Shildon and Spennymoor.[105] The demonstration and march on 10 April attracted an estimated 600–1,200 people from all over County Durham.[106] However, at this march a much broader movement against the means test was evident, in spirit at least. The Chopwell Lodge of the DMA later claimed that the march '*had the financial and moral support* of many DMA lodge[s], Women's Co-Op Guilds, Branches of Unemployed Workers, Local Labour Parties, Communist Parties, together with the whole Hearted support of the great mass of the unemployed worker[s] in Durham County'.[107] In some ways, the events of January were repeated; the commissioners refused to meet a deputation, and a strong police presence prevented entrance to the council. However, the day did not end as peacefully and instead evolved into a 'fierce struggle' between the marchers and the police; the *Manchester Guardian* and *The Times* closely followed events.[108] The march was later depicted as a riot under NUWM leadership and, once more, illustrates how the unemployed could be portrayed as subversives by the authorities.

The ritualistic dimension of the Durham march was particularly theatrical and suggests that the demonstrators planned to battle with the police. At the trial of the protestors, a police sergeant described a 'curious ceremonial' where a march leader 'had a horse-shoe in his hand and he placed it upon the ground. He then picked it up and kissed it several times, apparently performing some kind of ceremony. Then he called to the mob, "Come on lads, do not be afraid," and the attack began.'[109] The charge took place to the sound of a band playing the Dead March, and police claimed to have been assaulted with 'sticks, poles, and missiles'.[110] *The Times* reported that the protestors 'were out for blood'.[111] The police responded with a baton charge, and in the violence that ensued, shop and bus windows were broken, a car was smashed and 'a perambulator was overturned, throwing the child into the street'.[112] Although Alice Robinson, the mother of the child in the pram, claimed the baby was not thrown into the road, she suffered a terrifying ordeal nonetheless. It was the first time Robinson had been out with her eleven-day-old baby, and she claimed 'there was a rush of Marchers towards me, followed by the police. All the Marchers had sticks, but I did not see any of the Marchers use them, because I was knocked down flat on my back ... My perambulator was dragged out of my grasp and overturned ... Whilst I was on the ground I was kicked in the stomach and back of my legs'.[113] Lena Ridley, Robinson's friend, also noted how she was hurt and 'received kicks on my leg and in my back from the marchers'.[114] An estimated twenty to thirty demonstrators and four police officers required medical attention. Eleven men were arrested including the leaders of the march; the majority were granted bail on the condition that they would not participate in NUWM demonstrations. At their trial, the men, despite the seizure of weapons including sticks weighted with lead and studded with nails, claimed they had been forced forward by the weight of the crowd and that the police attacked them.[115]

The aftermath of the protest lingered for some time, and many shopkeepers attempted to claim compensation for the damage that had been done to their businesses under the Riot Damages Act, 1886.[116] Alice Jevons and the father of Lena Ridley also wrote to the council requesting compensation, but both were refused.[117] While it was the marchers who were noted to have caused the damage within the area, many decried the actions of the police. Members of Ryhope Lodge wrote to the council to ask 'that in the event of any further Demonstrations the members of the Durham County Council will do all that they can to prevent any recurrence of such treatment towards those who are only seeking to retain such a standard in Life as will enable them to make the necessary provision for wives and children'.[118] Complaints were also received from some of the more militant DMA lodges at Harraton, Chopwell and Follonsby; the Jarrow branch of the NUWM, who bemoaned that their drum had been taken by the police; and a mass meeting of NUWM members at Teesside.[119] The scale of the violence and the general antipathy towards the NUWM go some way to explaining why this was to be the last large example of a march or demonstration in Durham during the first phase of means testing.

In much of County Durham, the workless continued to look to the DMA and the Labour Party for leadership. It was their three days of action that generated the most backing and interest from the unemployed. The nature of the DMA protests was considerably different from typical NUWM action. Although they were primarily held against the means test and the commissioners in particular, none involved marches to government buildings or to the commissioners' offices. Instead, marches or 'mass meetings' were held in civic centres with speeches given by Labour Party members and DMA officials. The commissioners' publicised refusal to only meet with 'official' bodies in prearranged deputations was heeded and must have quenched the desire for protest amongst the unemployed.[120] When the DMA organised no further protests, large-scale action in the streets effectively ended. The two larger marches which did involve the NUWM saw lower numbers of the unemployed on the streets than in other examples of protest in the region despite the fact it was not a local march.[121] It was men and women from the more militant villages of the Durham coalfield, Tyneside and outside of the region who were involved. The unemployed from some of the worst affected parts of County Durham preferred to only associate with activity organised by the trade unions or the Labour Party. However, by the summer of 1933, even along the Tyne, the unemployed had quietened.[122]

In 1933, it was not only the TUC and trade unions which attempted to orchestrate the unemployed for action. The NUWM embarked on a series of regional marches throughout Britain.[123] One such march in south Wales organised by a local branch of the NUWM formed an important part of the campaigning activities in the region. The 'Monmouthshire Hunger March' took place in late August 1933. It was structured along the same principles as a national hunger march; preparations and arrangements were made months in advance, discipline was emphasised and a military theme in the style of the procession was again evoked.[124] The purpose of the march, in a similar vein to the 1932 hunger march, was to get Monmouthshire County Council to meet with a deputation and to present a petition which was signed by over 17,000 people. Ten demands were to be put before the council, the second of which was 'that the PAC shall refuse to operate the "Means Test" by granting full benefit to all claimants, and on no account to take any notice of any other income that the unemployed or their relatives may have'. In a commemorative pamphlet, the Monmouthshire Marchers' Council concluded that 'at least one-third of the County population were affected by the March Agitation'. Even local businesses and chapels became involved, offering food, cigarettes, accommodation and moral support.[125] As with all NUWM marches, the language of class struggle was employed throughout. Lewis Jones – the regional organiser of the NUWM and one of the march leaders – argued that 'the mighty response to the March was a preliminary warning to all enemies of the working class that the Men of Monmouthshire are no longer going to meekly submit to the intolerable conditions which they suffer'.[126] The march highlighted how well organised the unemployed were in the region and their treatment by a Labour-dominated council when they marched under the banner of the NUWM.

On 29 August, the first march contingent left Brynmawr and travelled down the Monmouthshire Valley to Crumlin gathering other contingents, including women's, along the route. After refreshments and a rest at Crumlin, the now 400 marchers began the journey towards Risca where they were scheduled to spend the night. Between Crumlin and Cwmcarn, it was estimated that 50,000 people lined the streets.[127] By the time the marchers reached Newport, the following day, it was reported that they now numbered some 1,000.[128] The course of the march shows the importance of the valleys as an arena and passage of protest, as the map below indicates.

Once in Newport, a strong police presence greeted the marchers. A deputation consisting of R. Jones (Pontypool), R. Hanson (Garndiffaith) and Jack Jones (Abertillery) met with the council, but they were not given a sympathetic hearing. Few of the marchers' demands were met, and buses home were only provided after Lewis Jones organised a sit-in on council steps.[129] However, the marchers were successful in raising awareness of their plight, drawing wide press coverage, and the need to organise for action.

The NUWM believed that the Monmouthshire hunger march 'revolutionised the character of the workers' struggle in the County' and noted that three new branches of the movement had, as a consequence, been established.[130] In the pamphlet created by the movement to honour the

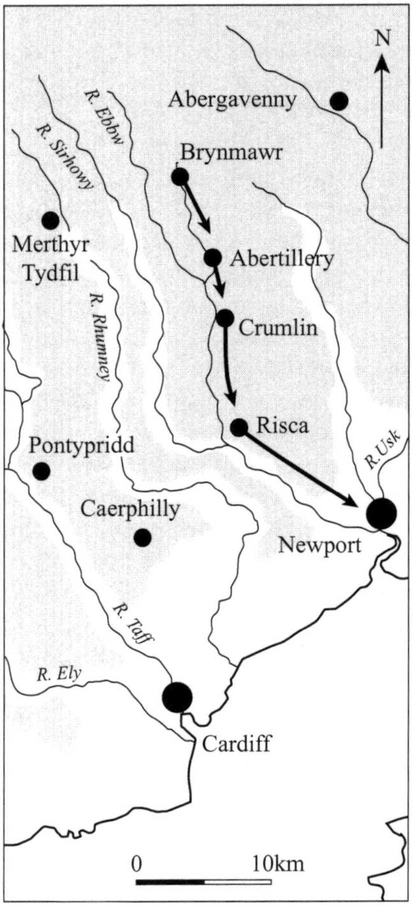

Figure 4.1 Map of the route of the Monmouthshire Hunger March, 1933

hunger march, repeated references were made to the 'spirit of the Chartists', hoping to continue the radical tradition within the county in the fight against the means test, unemployment benefit cuts and the National Government.[131] In calling upon the supposed 'radical tradition', the NUWM were enhancing the increasingly popular imagery of the out of work in the area. The iconography of militancy and radicalism was powerful within the industrial valleys of south Wales and was used not only as a battling call for those who led the unemployed but also as a weapon against the out of work.

Charismatic Communist Party leaders became vocal proponents of the rights of the unemployed, and especially prominent in this respect were Lewis Jones; Arthur Horner; Trevor Williams (Aberdare); Arthur Eyles (Merthyr-Dowlais), although later a Fascist; and Jack Jones.[132] The public profile of these leaders allowed the local authorities and the government to dismiss the marches and demonstrations of the unemployed as the actions of Communists, regardless of the motivations of the protestors. Such treatment was in tune with the values of the conservative local and national press which frequently portrayed the demonstrations in an unsympathetic light. *The Times* report of an unemployed protest in London encapsulates this sentiment most clearly. On 15 December 1931, over 2,000 unemployed from across London marched to County Hall to protest against the means test. Although the march, 'for the most part, was quite orderly', *The Times* emphasised that 'the majority of the marchers were irresponsible youths'. The paper suggested that violence was only prevented as 'the police throughout were extremely tactful in their handling of the long and straggling procession, and no doubt the drizzling rain dampened the ardour of the ringleaders'.[133] The *Western Mail*, in reference to the activities of the party and the NUWM in south Wales, declared that 'it is high time those people who are crying out upon the alleged injustices of the means test came to a realisation of the fact that their own case is hopelessly prejudiced by their own conduct'.[134] Such a dismissal of activity and popular support for a clampdown on radical politics also gave the police grounds to break up the marches of the unemployed.[135] The polarisation of opinion between the right to march and the desire to stop processions could lead to clashes and disturbances as the larger marches at North Shields, Durham and the Rhondda Valleys showed. Such scenes were repeated with particular acrimony in the Ogmore Valley in October 1933.

On 9 October 1933, around 200 unemployed men and women from Maesteg set out on a march to the PAC offices at Bridgend. Before the marchers, who were considered to be partaking in a 'peaceful march', could reach the destination, they were prevented by the Glamorgan Constabulary who used both reinforcements and, quite extraordinarily, an aeroplane to monitor the marchers.[136] The use of a plane at an unemployed demonstration was unprecedented and roused outcry.[137] At the monthly meeting of Aberdare Urban District Council, D. H. Jones declared that 'for the first time in the History of the British working class movement ... an aeroplane was used in conjunction with the police to keep observation on a demonstration of the unemployed'. It was decided that the area's

MP, George Hall, would be asked to raise the matter in parliament.[138] Bridgend Central Marchers' Council took the step of writing to the Home Office 'to protest against the unwarranted and unconstitutional action of the Glamorgan Constabulary, under the direction of Col. [sic] Lindsay in using mass police formation, [and] an aeroplane'.[139]

The Home Office were able to assume even before an investigation had taken place that 'the CCs [Chief Constable's] justification would presumably be the common law duty of the constable to take action to prevent a breach of the peace where he has good ground to anticipate [what] is about to occur'.[140] The supposition that the unemployed would have acted unlawfully was reinforced by reports from both Captain Lindsay, Chief Constable of the Glamorgan Constabulary, and the Ministry of Health. Lindsay was acting upon MI5 intelligence reports that Jack Jones had moved to Maesteg for the purpose of increasing support for the Communist Party. Lindsay claimed that he therefore prevented the march because of its illegality and size and noted that Jones was to be arrested for his communist speeches.[141] The association of the Communist Party with the unemployed worked to reinforce the government's perception of those protesting in the streets. The Ministry of Health's much quoted comments on the events are reflective of more general attitudes: 'one rather hopes this may give the movement a wholesome check, for marches long and short are becoming all too common'.[142] Based upon its evidence, the Home Office concluded that 'it is clear that the march was deliberate intimidation and propaganda', and they decided not to pursue the complaint.[143]

Police heavy-handedness during demonstrations of the unemployed was not uncommon in Britain in the interwar period, and in south Wales, the figure of Captain Lindsay served only to antagonise the situation.[144] The connection drawn by Lindsay between the Communist Party and the jobless ensured that the unemployed who protested were treated as potential criminals.[145] Will Paynter later reflected that 'it can be said without malice that the Glamorganshire police at that time were being recruited more for their brawn than their brains ... The chief constable by background and inclination favoured strong arm methods'.[146] While a fraught relationship between the police and the working class in south Wales was apparent from an earlier period, and during the 1926 lockout especially, the numbers taking to the streets and the response of the authorities only exacerbated matters. For Lewis Jones, the marches in late 1933 made it 'clear that the authorities were prepared to use extreme measures to prevent the unemployed demonstrating for better conditions'.[147]

The unemployed were treated much more favourably when they marched behind the banners of the trade unions or the Labour Party.[148] This prejudice was also apparent in government at all levels. Although Labour councillors may have expressed sympathy with the unemployed, such sentiment was often not extended when their leaders were drawn from the ranks of the NUWM. At the Monmouthshire hunger march, for example, the council agreed to only meet briefly with a deputation of three despite the apparent popularity of the march within the region. Similarly, at the December 1931 meeting of Merthyr PAC, the deputation of the SWMF led by Noah Ablett, a known militant miners' agent, was given a more sympathetic hearing than the NUWM representative Arthur Ayles.[149] In some respects, it is clear to see why the authorities monitored the movement so closely. It was often areas with an active local NUWM branch that produced the most marches as the cases of south Wales and the north-east demonstrate.[150] What was also crucial was the NUWM had the power to organise nationally and could even draw in the support of some sections of the wider labour movement as shown in the 1934 hunger march.

It was not only the abolition of the means test that generated the fifth national hunger march to London in February 1934; the new Unemployment Bill which proposed widespread reform to the administration of the means test had provoked outcry since its inception. Francis and Smith have argued that, aside from the 1936 march, 'the march of February 1934 proved to be the largest, most representative and best organised to leave South Wales'.[151] On this occasion, the wives of the unemployed were represented in a separate contingent headed by Mrs Pearce, a representative of women's organisations in south Wales. This was one of two women's contingents, the other representing working women originated from the north-west of England. For the women of south Wales, the march strengthened their political voice which could often be marginalised within the male-dominated labour movement, despite their prevalence in street protests. Dora Cox, active in Communist Party along with her husband Idris Cox, recalled how the women marching in red berets in front of 200 men from south Wales had a 'very big effect' on the crowds they marched past.[152]

The end of the 'class against class' policy of the Communist Party and the beginning of the 'popular front' strategy undoubtedly helped strengthen support for this march from across the labour movement. In south Wales, the SWMF donated funds and, in a more surprising move, so did individual lodges of the DMA.[153] Labour Party MPs spoke out against the means test and the new Unemployment Bill on platforms alongside the NUWM and Communist Party members. Aneurin Bevan and ILP MPs James Maxton and John McGovern addressed crowds with Ellen Wilkinson who was to be elected as Jarrow's most celebrated MP the following year.[154] Despite the wider support for this march, the police and MI5 still kept close watch over the marchers. This was particularly true of Lewis Jones who led the Welsh contingent.[155] Clearly, it was not only the politics of the leaders of the unemployed that could affect the response of their protest; also vital was the expression of opposition.

Marches and demonstrations were a form of protest that sought and drew public attention; people lined the streets to watch marchers process, the police and the media monitored the actions of the marchers and a response was warranted from the targeted group or organisation. What most influenced the public reaction to a march or demonstration was its form and the behaviour of those involved. The Monmouthshire Marchers' Council believed 'if the March succeeded in its object without a clash with the police, then we would have been able to rally the workers for greater activities and so to have taken the Leadership of the workers out of the hands of the Labour Party'.[156] The descent into violence could have the damaging repercussion of blighting the reputation of all those who took to the streets. Ellen Wilkinson shrewdly observed of the hunger marches that 'the comfortable had dismissed these efforts as "Communist demonstrations", as though that accounted for everything'.[157] Within such a climate, other forms of opposition were often utilised. Deputations, letters, petitions and meetings were not only an alternative method of protest, they also acted as a complementary form of action or even, for some groups, the main outlet of opposition. What made this expression appealing was the 'respectable' connotations of this protest in comparison to demonstrating in the street.

Organising meetings, the act of passing and sending resolutions and arranging deputations all reflect positive action which did not have more radical connotations. Examining such action exposes how groups that were perhaps not associated with the agitation of the unemployed could involve themselves in protest. The TUC, for example, rarely advocated marching against the means test and instead favoured the passing of resolutions and organising deputations.[158] Indeed, Wal Hannington wrote how 'many resolutions ... to compel the Government to withdraw the Means Test, were passed in the Trade Union branches' as the TUC leaders were opposed to 'militant action along with the unemployed'.[159] Meetings, resolutions and petitions were not as radical a method of protesting as marches, and this helps to explain the affiliation to this method of opposition by trade unions, the Labour Party, religious bodies and other groups like the British Legion. An examination of forms of protest other than marches and demonstrations therefore reveals a much broader level of discontent from groups who appeared uninvolved and areas which on the surface seemed quiescent. Although not as dramatic as the large marches, they still drew press attention. These alternative expressions of protest are especially important in ascertaining a picture of discontent in the case of the north-east of England.

Given the lower number of marches and demonstrations within much of the north-east, it might be concluded that the means test roused little discontent within the region. However, a consideration of the resolutions that were passed by trade unions and other organisations in Durham and Northumberland reveals that opposition against the means test was strong. From the implementation of the means test, PACs and councils received numerous written protests from groups whose involvement in street demonstrations was less common. For example, the Tyne and Blyth District Committee of the Shipconstructors' and Shipwrights' Association appear to have only placed their opposition to the means test through letters.[160] In January 1932, Durham PAC received resolutions and letters of protest from the County Borough of Dewsbury, Eldon Lane and District Branch of the British Legion, Tyne and Blyth District Committee of the Shipconstructors' and Shipwrights' Association, the Jarrow Labour Party and Trades Council and the Jarrow branch of the NUWM.[161] While many of these protests came from areas already noted for their agitation against the means test, they still reveal a much broader level of discontent. In the case of the DMA, however, a better picture can be ascertained of protest against the means test within other parts of the region.

The marches organised by the DMA in 1933 were in part a reaction to calls from members for direct action. Peter Lee commented that the union hoped that the marches of 1933 would 'meet the wishes of our people who desire to attend and enter their protest against the action of the Government towards our unemployed, and the carrying out of the Order dealing with the Means Test'.[162] Throughout the first phase of means testing in the 1930s, individual DMA lodges passed resolutions and wrote to PACs and the executive council of the DMA, and in line with TUC policy, passed resolutions against the means test which were sent to the National Government.[163] At the annual meeting of the executive council in 1931, 'a resolution was carried condemning the action of the Government in instituting the Means Test for the unemployed, and it was decided to send a letter on the subject to Members of Parliament'.[164] The following month, the executive committee passed another resolution which 'strongly protest[ed] against the action of the Government in introducing a "Means Test"'. The council felt that 'in our opinion it is causing undue hardship to honest working men and women'. The resolution was forwarded to the government.[165] While the DMA may not have been as involved in street protests as other organisations, the means test was nonetheless an important issue for the union.

It was not only individual trade unions who protested against the test, and a degree of unity was apparent in some instances. In February 1932, Newcastle PAC considered a resolution sent to them by a meeting of trade union representatives of the Walker district on Tyneside. The tone of the resolution conveys the disgust that many of the trade unions felt at the prospect of their members being means-tested: 'we, the workers' representatives of this District, strongly protest against the operation of the Means Test, which they claim to be the most inhumane and callous ever inflicted upon the workers of a country which claims to be civilised'.[166] The *Manchester Guardian* picked up upon a protest in Wallsend on Tyneside of 2,000 people who signed a 'declaration of allegiance to the Wallsend-on-Tyne Labour and Trades Council' in its fight against the means test.[167] In Newcastle, the trade unions were so opposed to the means test they formed the Newcastle Means Test Abolition Committee which was composed of 'Trade Union representatives and kindred organisations'. The Committee spurred the PAC into holding special meetings to discuss the means test. The existence of such an organisation shows the commitment of the trade unions against a household means test which is perhaps not reflected elsewhere. The concerted action and organisation of protest through the Committee and the acceptance of a deputation on more than one occasion show how effective these other methods of protest could be in transmitting opposition to the authorities.[168]

It was not only in the case of trade unions that a clearer pattern of protest emerges when resolutions and meetings are considered. Another group that mainly expressed their opposition through means other than marches was the British Legion, whose disabled members could also be marginalised from the more prominent displays of protest. The main objection of the British Legion to the means test was the use of ex-servicemen's pensions in an assessment. Opposition was especially vocal in the north-east of England. In addition to marching, the British Legion held meetings and sent letters and resolutions to PACs, councils and the government.[169] The British Legion often received a sympathetic reception within the press, and their protest was not demonised in a way that much of the unemployed opposition could be. However, while the protest of the British Legion may have been more evident in the north-east of England, utilising resolutions and meetings as a way of expressing protest was not confined to the region.

In south Wales, the nonconformist chapels were especially vocal in opposing the means test even though they did not demonstrate with the unemployed in the streets. During centenary celebrations of the Monmouthshire English and Welsh Association, which was attended by Baptist chapels from across the county, a resolution was passed against the test. Rev. Melville Evans of Oakdale Baptist Church, Blackwood, believed that because of the means test, 'family life was undermined, home life unsettled, morals disturbed'. He moved that 'while recognising the need to make economy ... the association protests against the burdens placed on those who are unfortunately deprived of opportunity of earning a livelihood'.[170] At the Welsh Congregationalist Conference at East Glamorgan in 1933, a resolution was passed against 'this cruel Means Test'. It was argued that a household investigation was 'un-Godly' and created 'enmity and dissatisfaction in the family'. In a letter to the local paper highlighting the resolution, it was urged for 'all churches and chapels and other organisations throughout the valleys' to make 'a united stand to get this Means Test removed. Then men and women can once again call their souls their own'.[171] The actions of church groups in 1932 within Newcastle in publicly opposing the test sparked much controversy locally, and the matter was raised in the House of Commons.[172]

Resolutions and meetings served an important function in keeping the means test in the public arena and building up opposition that allowed the larger marches to emerge. Moreover, they kept a constant level of opposition against the National Government. Indeed, in South Shields councillor Noble argued that 'the more resolutions the government was bombarded with the better'.[173] Resolutions formed an important part of the networks between local branches and dialogue with national leadership. Wansbeck Divisional Labour Party in Northumberland determined whether to pass resolutions in the context of decisions made by the executive committee of the Labour Party. While it passed a joint resolution from Newburn and District Labour Party and Pegswood Miners' Lodge against the means test, it did not respond positively to demands from Gateshead Labour Party and Trades Council and, later, Newbiggin Labour Party that the Labour Party should further consider its position on the means test.[174] Demands for more militant action also came from south Wales. At the half yearly conference of the Aberdare Divisional Labour Party in

October 1932, a resolution was passed against the means test which called 'upon the Labour Party and the TUC to organise a national campaign demanding its abolition'.[175] In the absence of national leadership from the TUC and the Labour Party, both of whom urged caution, it was left to individual local branches to maintain the fight against the means test.[176]

As part of a cycle of protest, petitions served a valuable function in directly engaging with a local population; as well as the meetings that were held in the area to collect signatures, homes needed to be visited and residents lobbied. Petitions demonstrated the volume of opposition to the measure that could not necessarily be revealed through a march, and targets for the number of signatures were set. The labour movement in both regions utilised petitions, and in a sequence of protest, they could precede larger marches.[177] In March 1932 at a mass meeting organised by the Ferndale Lodge, it was 'resolved that we organise for the immediate abolition of the Means Test, this meeting agrees to assist the Committee to interview all the inhabitants of Ferndale and Blaenllechau to ask for their signatures'. It was agreed that the petition should be sent to other lodges in the area.[178] At the local district meeting of the SWMF, although it transpired that only the Ferndale Lodge was interested in the petition, it was later presented to the House of Commons by Lieut-Col. D. Watts-Morgan (Labour MP, Rhondda East).[179]

The petition contained 10,000 signatures from the Ferndale area, showing the strength of feeling against the means test.[180] When Watts-Morgan presented the petition, he stressed that the means test 'is proving destructive to family life, driving sons and daughters from the homes of their parents, and disturbing those familial relationships which have been the characteristics of Welsh Christian households for generations in the past'. The petition ended with the plea that the means test be abolished as it was 'devastating in its effects upon the lives and well-being of the British people'.[181] A petition organised by the Blyth branch of the NUWM in October 1932 further highlighted the importance of interaction with the local population. The 2,000 signatures were collected by canvassing against the means test door to door.[182] The petition of 50,000 signatures across Tyneside in March 1932 should similarly have roused the local population.[183]

While the NUWM may have been one of the most prominent organisers of the unemployed, it too utilised meetings, resolutions and petitions as a method of expressing opposition and generating support for marches. Moreover, the movement produced pamphlets denouncing the means test which encouraged public debate. Sid Elias, in the provocatively titled

Mass Murder: An Exposure of the Means Test, claimed that the test 'has caused stark poverty, misery and starvation to enter thousands of *working class* homes'.[184] On a local level, the NUWM sent numerous resolutions to PACs and councils in addition to organising deputations. For example, on 14 November 1931, the NUWM sent a resolution to Aberdare Urban District Council which stated, 'we, members of the Aberdare Branch of the National Unemployed Workers' Movement, herewith record our strongest protest against the present National Government in its support and operation of the most callous and brutal method hitherto conceived, to suppress, humiliate, and starve the working masses of the country'.[185] While the language in the resolution was passionate, and even exaggerated, the council supported the resolution stating that 'this meeting ... strongly protests against the savage attack made by the Government on the unemployed workers of the country'.[186] The NUWM was treated in this instance much more favourably than when street protests were held. This type of action should, as in other cases, also be seen as a mechanism by which large support could be generated.

The Monmouthshire hunger march in late August 1933 was the culmination of a much longer stretch of opposition against Monmouthshire PAC by the NUWM in the region. The action here demonstrates the function of different forms of protest. In the previous year, the NUWM began to coordinate action; in April 1932, a conference representing 13,987 unemployed workers was held against the means test in Abertillery. Richard Legge, secretary of the Brynmawr branch, presided over the meeting, and Reg Jones, Pontypool branch, passed a resolution against the Labour Party's administration of the means test.[187] The following July, when preparations for the hunger march were well underway, Richard Legge wrote to Monmouthshire County Council asking for a deputation to be met. The PAC members replied to Legge that they did not feel 'that any useful purpose would be served by your attendance, in view of the ... observations of your demands'. In particular, the PAC argued that it was better that they administrate the means test rather than government commissioners.[188] The NUWM continued to organise opposition against the means test, including a petition, which was eventually expressed through the hunger march.[189]

In the north-east of England, the NUWM also used both meetings and resolutions to supplement the marches that were held. For example, in the autumn of 1932, the NUWM organised an open-air meeting with councillor Stanley Holmes of Tynemouth PAC. A crowd of 'several hundred' turned out to listen to Holmes, but it was noted that 'it was utterly impossible to hear the speaker, and the piercing shrieks and cat calls of women, many with children in their arms, increased the din'.[190] The incident shows how the unemployed could still be demonised even when participating in meetings. Without the presence of more 'respectable' bodies, protests made within a public space could still be dismissed as unruly. It is, therefore, difficult to suggest how successful this form of protest was. Short-term goals in many instances remained unfulfilled and demands unmet. However, grievances within written expressions of protest were not always as easily ignored as those placed by the deputation of a march. The striking aspect of written resolutions is the response they often generated, and protestors were able to enter into correspondence with PACs. While, more often than not, the unemployed were informed that their requests would not be fulfilled, their protest was still discussed and debated within monthly meetings. This effectively kept the means test alive in political debates and in the public arena and, like the larger marches, was another example of how the unemployed were able to be political actors.

There was little regional and local variation in the levels of written protests and meetings between and within south Wales and the north-east of England. Trade unions, political parties and unemployed organisations utilised these expressions of protest in both. The greatest contrast was the significance of other forms of protest. In the north-east, and areas outside the Tyne especially, protests against the means test centred around organising meetings and passing resolutions. A consideration of the methods of opposition conveys the level of discontent that existed against the means test within the region, and further, it demonstrates how these trade unions remained an important organiser of the unemployed. In south Wales, conversely, the unemployed utilised expressions of protest other than marches to maintain a constant barrage of criticism against the National Government and local authorities. The diverse methods of expressing protests in these first years of the means test helped to create a wide movement of opposition against the measure that would be displayed most spectacularly when the government attempted to centralise its administration.

From the moment a household means test was suggested as a requirement for transitional payments, the unemployed mobilised to protest against it. Even before the Order in Council had fully passed through parliament and the specifics of the legislation were known, opposition was organised.[191] Once the test began operation under the administrative control of the PACs, and the effects were felt in homes unused to investigations into personal circumstances, the movement against the measure gathered momentum. While the means test may have increased privation and negatively impacted upon the mental well-being of the unemployed and their dependants, it also roused anger and determination to see its abolition. Across south Wales and the north-east of England, hundreds of thousands of men, women and children marched in the street demonstrating their ability to take a stand in the face of adversity. Feeling against the means test was strong in both regions, and marches, meetings, deputations, petitions and resolutions were organised to express opposition. Viewed individually, the pattern of protests suggests that the unemployed in south Wales and the north-east took a determined stand against the National Government. However, when the movement against the means test is compared, stark differences in the nature and form of protest emerge. The unemployed in south Wales marched in the street much more readily than in the north-east of England where street demonstrations were largely confined to the Tyneside industrial belt.

If miners 'above all ... formed the mainstay of unemployed protests', then it was the miners from south Wales who dominated activity.[192] Even the wives of the unemployed in south Wales were thought to have been the most militant amongst their sex.[193] The reputation of the unemployed within the region had much justification; from September 1931 until the end of PAC control, hundreds of thousands marched against the means test. Across the area affected most by the test, the unemployed protested in the streets to express opposition. Comparisons were drawn with events in 1926, and it appeared as if, once more, the working class in south Wales would become a byword for radicalism.[194]As Macintyre has noted, the south Wales region, excluding the coastal belt, was alive with activity and not just a few pockets. He concluded that 'by the beginning of the 1930s Maerdy was no longer an area of particular Communist strength and there were other parts of the coalfield – in the neighbouring Aberdare valley, in the western valleys of Monmouthshire, and in the Maesteg valley – where the militants were much stronger'.[195]

In the north-east of England, a return to the patterns of militancy evident during the General Strike and lockout was not apparent. In fact, it was noted of the meetings held at Blyth, one of the most radical areas of the region, 'the like of which have never been witnessed in the town'.[196] In contrast to south Wales, street protests were confined to pockets within the region. The unemployed on Tyneside were particularly active, and as many as 10,000 assembled to protest at an individual demonstration at North Shields. Within the rest of Durham and Northumberland, protest against the means test was largely expressed through forms other than marches and demonstrations. Meetings, resolutions and deputations (not attached to marches) were proactive methods of displaying protest that were favoured over demonstrating in the street. The largest mobilisation of the unemployed in Durham took place during the spring of 1933, and the role of the DMA was critical to the success of the collective action. In the north-east, as in south Wales, the leadership of the unemployed was crucial to the protest that emerged.[197] In both regions, the nature of the labour movement and the political culture of the working class, including previous traditions of industrial action, were instrumental in how protest was expressed. It was these factors that determined who provided leadership for action and who the unemployed looked to for support.[198]

In south Wales in the first years of the means test, it was the Communist Party and the NUWM who emerged as the most active leaders of the unemployed within the region, and they were responsible for many of the larger marches that took place. Although the SWMF and the Labour Party organised demonstrations and passed countless resolutions against the means test, it was the role of the NUWM within the localities that allowed an organised unemployed movement against the means test to be established. In the north-east, conversely, the unemployed continued to largely seek support from the traditional leaders of the working class. The DMA and the Labour Party remained crucial, and both favoured written forms of opposition over demonstrations. Marches were most common where the NUWM was active, and such areas existed mainly along the Tyne, in Sunderland and in Blyth in the north of the region. Even in Chopwell which, like Maerdy, was considered to be a 'Little Moscow', the unemployed were not noted for their protest.[199] While Maerdy's reign as a Little Moscow was checked by the growth of other areas of militancy, Chopwell's decline marked the end of radicalism within the locality.[200] However, the unemployed within the region, by utilising other forms of protest, were still able to express discontent and keep opposition against the means test within the public arena. Moreover, written forms of protest generated far less suspicion from the police and therefore prevented some of the negative coverage of the out of work in the media.

Although the protests of the unemployed may have kept the means test within public, and indeed private, debates, the ultimate goal of the protestors in removing the means test from the statute book was unfulfilled. Indeed, by mid-1933, the National Government began to outline moves to centralise the administration of the means test and tighten control of the regulations. However, these early protests against the means test cannot be dismissed entirely. Whether expressed through spectacular processions in the streets or resolutions debated in councils and parliament, the protest of the unemployed gave the workless a voice and a place within the political arena. Although the unemployed were traditionally marginalised by society and were still feared by conservative elements within the local authorities, the effects of the means test were enough to ensure that it would not be accepted without battle. The protest during the first phase of the means test awakened the labour movement to the cause of the unemployed and laid the foundations for the largest displays of collective action in the interwar period. When the government announced its changes to the unemployment benefit scheme, the unemployed and the labour movement were ready to meet the new challenge as the 1934 NUWM hunger march conveyed.

Notes

1 E. Wight Bakke, *The Unemployed Man: A Social Study* (London, 1935), p. 151.

2 Monmouthshire Marchers' Council, *Monmouthshire Hunger March, of August 1933* (National Unemployed Workers' Movement, Monmouth, 1933), p. 3.

3 In addition to these protests, the march of the miners from south Wales to London should also be considered. Wal Hannington, *The March of the Miners: How We Smashed the Opposition* (London, 1927), pp. 7–10; Wal Hannington, *Unemployed Struggles 1919–1936: My Life and Struggles Amongst the Unemployed* (London, 1977 edition; first published, London, 1936), pp. 28–80.

4 Sue Bruley, 'A Woman's Right to Work? The Role of Women in the Unemployed Movement Between the Wars', in Sybil Oldfield (ed.), *This Working-Day World: Women's Lives and Culture(s) in Britain 1914–1945* (London, 1994), p. 41.

5 *Ibid*., pp. 40–50; Richard Flanagan, *'Parish-Fed Bastards': A History of the Politics of the Unemployed in Britain, 1884–1939* (London, 1991), pp. 192–6.

6 See, for example, Richard Croucher, 'Editorial: The History of Unemployed Movements', Special Issue on the History of Unemployed Movements, *Labour History Review*, 73:1 (2008), pp. 1–17; Matthias Reiss, 'Not All Were Apathetic: National Hunger Marches as Political Rituals in Interwar Britain', in Jörg Neuheiser and Michael Schaich (eds), *Political Rituals in Great Britain 1700–2000* (Augsburg, 2006), pp. 93–118; Matt Perry, *Prisoners of Want: The Experience and Protest of the Unemployed in France, 1921–45* (Aldershot, 2007), pp. 51–174; Matthias Reiss and Matt Perry, 'Beyond Marienthal: Understanding Movements of the Unemployed', in Matthias Reiss and Matt Perry (eds), *Unemployment and Protest: New Perspectives on Two Centuries of Contention* (Oxford, 2011), pp. 1–18.

7 Paul Bagguley, *From Protest to Acquiescence? Political Movements of the Unemployed* (London, 1991), pp. 47–66; Andrew Richards, 'Mobilizing the Powerless: Collective Protest Action of the Unemployed in the Interwar Period', Working Paper 175, Juan March Institute (2002), pp. 8–9, 23–8, 32–44.

8 Richard Croucher, '"Divisions in the Movement": The National Unemployed Workers' Movement and its Rivals in Comparative Perspective', in Geoff Andrews, Nina Fishman and Kevin Morgan (eds), *Opening the Books: Essays on the Social and Cultural History of British Communism* (London, 1995), pp. 23–43.

9 For a wider discussion of this, see, Stephanie Ward, '"The Workers Are in the Mood to Fight the Act": Protest Against the Means Test, 1931–1935', in Reiss and Perry, *Unemployment and Protest*, pp. 245–64.

10 Monmouthshire Marchers' Council, *Monmouthshire Hunger March, of August 1933*, p. 3.

11 The Communist writer Allen Hutt observed a 'rising tide of militancy' in south Wales in late 1931. Allen Hutt, *The Condition of the Working Class in Britain* (London, 1933), p. 51.

12 Hannington, *Unemployed Struggles*, p. 228; Peter Kingsford, *The Hunger Marchers in Britain 1920–1939* (London, 1982), p. 133; Noel Whiteside, 'The Social Consequences of Interwar Unemployment', in Sean Glynn and Alan Booth (eds), *The Road to Full Employment* (London, 1987), p. 25; Matt Perry, *Bread and Work: The Experience of Unemployment, 1918–1939* (London, 2000), p. 106.

13 *The Times*, 3, 7, 16 and 21 December 1931, 15 January, 24 February, 3, 5 and 28 March 1932; *The Daily Worker*, 3 and 6 October 1931.

14 Richard Croucher has noted that a campaign to march on the PACs was also conducted by the NUWM in 1930 against scales of public assistance. Richard Croucher, *We Refuse to Starve in Silence: A History of the National Unemployed Workers' Movement, 1920–46* (London, 1987), p. 112.

15 Bagguley's emphasis. Bagguley, *From Protest to Acquiescence*, p. 95.

16 Reiss, 'Not All Were Apathetic', p. 100.

17 Hywel Francis and Dai Smith, *The Fed: A History of the South Wales Miners in the Twentieth Century* (Cardiff, 1998), pp. 103–4.

18 Will Paynter, *My Generation* (London, 1972), pp. 85–7.

19 Such Councils of Action were created at Merthyr and the Rhondda. *Daily Worker*, 3 October 1931, p. 2 and 13 October 1931, p. 3.

20 *Daily Worker*, 13 October 1931, p. 1.

21 *Ibid.*, 28 September 1931, pp. 1, 7, 1 October 1931, p. 4, 13 October 1931, p. 3.

22 *Free Press and Rhondda Leader*, 3 October 1931, p. 4.

23 *Merthyr Express*, 3 October 1931, p. 17.

24 Reiss, 'Not All Were Apathetic', p. 115.

25 *Daily Worker*, 3 October 1931, p. 2.
26 *Durham County Advertiser and Durham Chronicle*, 9 October 1931, p. 2.
27 *Daily Worker*, 8 October 1931, p. 3.
28 *Ibid.*, 16 November 1931, p. 1.
29 *Newcastle Journal*, 11 December 1931, p. 16.
30 *Ibid.*
31 *Daily Worker*, 27 November 1931, p. 1.
32 Richards, 'Mobilising the Powerless', p. 24.
33 Matthew Worley, 'Left Turn: A Reassessment of the Communist Party of Great Britain in the Third Period, 1928–33', *Twentieth Century British History*, 11:4 (2000), p. 374.
34 Croucher, *We Refuse to Starve in Silence*, p. 121.
35 These figures were calculated by Sam Davies and are based upon the amount of money paid into the membership fund. Sam Davies, 'The Membership of the National Unemployed Workers' Movement, 1923–1938', *Labour History Review*, 57:1 (1992), p. 33.
36 *Manchester Guardian*, 24 May 1932, p. 13.
37 Sam Davies has also noted that membership levels were both exaggerated and under exaggerated. Davies, 'The Membership of the National Unemployed Workers' Movement', pp. 29–32.
38 In November 1932, the paper was renamed *The Unemployed Leader*.
39 SCOLAR, Cardiff University, Microfilm: Papers from the Communist Party of Great Britain Archives: Wal Hannington Papers, CP/IND/HANN/01/07, 'Statement of Branch Debts to Headquarters for the Unemployed Leader' no date; *The Unemployed Special*, No. 2, August 1932, p. 4; *The Unemployed Leader*, No. 7, 1 December 1932, p. 2, No. 8, 16 December 1832, p. 1, No. 9, January 1933, p. 6, No. 11, March 1933, p. 8.
40 *The Party Organiser*, 4, June 1932, pp. 31–2.
41 Lewis Mates, 'Durham and South Wales Miners and the Spanish Civil War', *Twentieth Century British History*, 17:3 (2006), p. 380.
42 Worley, 'Left Turn', p. 375.
43 SWCC, MNA/PP/67/15, W. Eddie Jones Collection, Statement from Monmouthshire District Committee of the NUWM on Character and Aims of the Movement, 1933.
44 'Statement of Branch Debts to Headquarters for the Unemployed Leader' no date; *The Unemployed Special*, No. 1, July 1932, p.7, No. 2, August 1932, pp. 5–7, No. 3, September 1932, pp. 5–7; *The Unemployed Leader*, No. 7, 1 December 1932, p. 1; *The Party Organiser*, 6 September 1932, pp. 12–13; *Aberdare Leader*, 13 January 1933, p. 6; *Merthyr Express*, 15 October 1932, p.12.
45 Hannington polled 3,409 votes, coming fourth narrowly behind the Independent Labour Party candidate. Labour's S. O. Davies comfortably won with 18,645 votes. Wal Hannington Papers, CP/IND/HANN, large scrapbook.

46 One notable exemption was the large demonstration which occurred in Newcastle on 7 March 1932. *Evening Chronicle*, 8 March 1932, p.1.
47 Croucher, *We Refuse to Starve in Silence*, p. 132.
48 *Durham County Advertiser and Durham Chronicle*, 13 May 1932, p. 6.
49 Susan Lawrence, former parliamentary secretary and Labour MP also addressed crowds. *Ibid.*, 10 June 1932, p. 6.
50 LHASC, *Report of the Thirteenth National Conference of Labour Women* (London, 1932), pp. 13–14.
51 TWAS, Colliery Ward, Sunderland, Minutes of the Women's Section of the Labour Party, 17 May 1932.
52 *Durham County Advertiser and Durham Chronicle*, 10 June 1932, p. 6.
53 *Blaydon Courier*, 14 May 1932, p. 8.
54 *Ibid.*, 9 July 1932, p. 8.
55 Interestingly, means test demonstrations also resulted in violent clashes with the police in Sydney, Australia. *Daily Mirror*, 19 September 1932, p. 2 and 20 September 1932, p. 2, 12 October 1932, p. 1 and 13 October 1932, p. 3; *Daily Herald*, 28 October 1932, p. 11; Wal Hannington, *Ten Lean Years: An Examination of the Record of the National Government in the Field of Unemployment* (London, 1940), pp. 55–65, 233–42; A. C. Hepburn, 'The Belfast Riots of 1935', *Social History*, 15:1 (1990), p. 76.
56 *Newcastle Journal*, 7 September 1932, pp. 5, 9; *Evening Chronicle*, 5 September 1932, p. 9, 6 September, pp. 1, 4, 7 September, p. 1 and 8 September, p. 1; *Daily Herald*, 7 September 1932, p. 11; *Northern Despatch*, 1 September 1932, p. 1.
57 *Daily Worker*, 3 October 1932, p. 3.
58 *The Times* estimated 150 people marched but a crowd of 'thousands' gathered, while the *Daily Worker* estimated 3,000 marched. *Evening Chronicle*, 6 October 1932, p. 1 and 13 October 1932, p. 9; *The Times*, 6 October 1932, p. 12 and 14 October 1932, p. 14; *Daily Worker*, 6 October 1932, p. 6.
59 *Evening Chronicle*, 13 October 1932, p. 9; *The Times*, 6 October 1932, p. 12.
60 *Evening Chronicle*, 6 October 1932, p. 1.
61 *Ibid.*, 13 October 1932, p. 9; *Daily Worker*, 7 October 1932, p. 1.
62 *Daily Worker*, 13 October 1932, p. 7.
63 *Northern Despatch*, 6 October 1932, p. 8.
64 *Daily Worker*, 15, 16, 21 October 1932 and 8 November 1932, p. 1.
65 North Tyneside Community Development Project, *North Shields: Working Class Politics and Housing 1900–1977* (Newcastle-upon-Tyne, 1978), p. 31.
66 Croucher, *We Refuse to Starve in Silence*, p. 140.
67 Reiss, 'Not All Were Apathetic', p. 116.
68 The *Daily Worker* put the figure at 80 marchers leaving Newcastle. *Daily Worker*, 3 October 1932, p. 1; TNA, HO 18187 Report on the Hunger Marchers, 11 October 1932 and Unemployed Marchers, Information Received from MI5 on 26 October 1932.

69 HO 18187, Report on the Progress of the Hunger Marchers, 12 October 1932, p. 1.
70 Reiss, 'Not All Were Apathetic', p. 100.
71 Hannington, *Unemployed Struggles*, pp. 243–4.
72 See speeches at Hyde Park referred to below.
73 HO 18187, Transcript of Speeches on the West Plinth at Trafalgar Square 30 October 1932, Arthur Griffiths' speech, p. 7.
74 HO 18187, Correspondence from James A. Wilson, Chief Constable of Cardiff City Police, to Colonel Sir V. G. W. Kell, MI5, 15 October 1932.
75 *Ibid.*
76 Most speakers denounced the actions of the police at Stratford-upon-Avon. Croucher, *We Refuse to Starve in Silence*, p. 140.
77 At the Hyde Park demonstration on 30 October 1932, a resolution was passed which demanded 'a full public enquiry into the attack of the police in Hyde Park on Thursday. We demand the release of the marchers now under arrest together with those already sentenced'. E. G. Llewelyn urged that 'we know to-day that the Police are discovering, that the trouble on Thursday in Hyde Park can be traced to the very provocative acts of the Police, particularly the so-called scum elements that are recruited as special constables into the ranks on such occasions'. HO 18187, Correspondence between the Assistance Commissioner, Special Branch, and the Under Secretary of State, 2 November 1932, Report on Demonstration of Unemployed and the NUWM 30 October 1932, pp. 3, 5; *Daily Herald*, 29 October 1932, p. 2.
78 *Manchester Guardian*, 7 November 1932, p. 16.
79 Kingsford, *The Hunger Marches in Britain*, p. 163; Croucher, *We Refuse to Starve in Silence*, p. 141.
80 HO 18187, Correspondence between Wilson and Kell, 15 October 1932.
81 Lewis Jones was the 'principal NUWM organiser' in south Wales. David Smith, *Lewis Jones* (Cardiff, 1982), p. 17.
82 Stuart Macintyre, *Little Moscows: Communism and Working-Class Militancy in Inter-war Britain* (London, 1980), pp. 32, 40–1; Arthur Horner, *Incorrigible Rebel* (London, 1960), pp. 113–19.
83 *Western Mail*, 18 November 1932, p. 10; *Rhondda Fach Gazette*, 26 November, p. 3.
84 Croucher, *We Refuse to Starve in Silence*, p. 148.
85 SWCC, Cambrian Lodge Minutes, 13 December 1932; *Aberdare Leader*, 22 October 1932, p. 3.
86 For example, in late May 1932, the Sunderland Socialist Party organised a march against the means test, and, on the same day, the NUWM held a parallel demonstration. *Newcastle Journal*, 23 May 1932, p. 10.
87 *Ibid.*, 31 January 1933, p. 7.
88 *Ibid.*, 30 January 1933, p. 12.
89 *The Unemployed Leader*, No. 10, February 1933, p. 8.

90 *Ibid.*; *Newcastle Journal*, 30 January 1933, p. 12 and 31 January 1933, p. 7; *Evening Chronicle*, 30 January 1933, p. 1.
91 *Newcastle Journal*, 31 January 1933, p. 7; *Evening Chronicle*, 30 January 1933, p. 1; *Northern Despatch*, 30 January 1933, p. 5.
92 *Newcastle Journal*, 31 January 1933, p. 7.
93 *Ibid.*
94 *Northern Echo*, 1 February 1933, p. 11.
95 *Ibid.*, 2 February 1933, p. 11.
96 SCOLAR, Microfilm: Archives of the Trades Union Congress: Trades Union Congress General Council Minutes, 26 October 1932.
97 *Ibid.*, 22 November 1932.
98 *Daily Mirror*, 6 February 1933, p. 1; *The Times*, 6 February 1933, pp. 9, 13; *The Labour Woman*, XXI/3, p. 34.
99 Trades Union Congress General Council Minutes, 22 February 1933.
100 DRO, D/DMA/14, Durham Miners' Association Minutes of Committee Meetings, 17 January 1933 and 24 January 1933.
101 *Northern Echo*, 6 February 1933, p. 8.
102 *Ibid.*, 13 February 1933, p. 9.
103 Colliery Ward, Sunderland, Minutes of the Women's Section of the Labour Party, 7 February 1933.
104 On this occasion, a coat was thrown over the NUWM member to prevent them from speaking. *Northern Echo*, 6 March 1933, p. 11; *Manchester Guardian*, 6 March 1933, p. 6.
105 *The Unemployed Leader*, No. 11, March 1933, pp. 2–8.
106 *Newcastle Journal*, 11 April 1933, p. 9; *The Times*, 25 April, p. 16.
107 My own emphasis. DRO, CC/X/8/5, Correspondence, T. Temple, Secretary of the Chopwell Lodge of the DMA, to Harold Jevons, Durham County Council, 1 May 1933.
108 *Newcastle Journal*, 11 April 1933, p. 9; *Manchester Guardian*, 11 April 1933, p. 8, 17 April 1933, p. 14 and 25 April 1933, p. 10; *The Times*, 25 April 1933, p. 16.
109 *Manchester Guardian*, 25 April 1933, p. 10.
110 CC/X/8/5, Inspector-in-Charge's Report of March at Durham, 2 May 1933.
111 *The Times*, 25 April 1933, p. 16.
112 *Newcastle Journal*, 11 April 1933, p. 9; *The Times*, 25 April 1933, p. 16.
113 CC/X/8/5, Correspondence, Alice Robinson to Durham County Council, 20 April 1933.
114 CC/X/8/5, Correspondence, William Ridley to Durham County Council, 22 April 1933.
115 *Newcastle Journal*, 11 April 1933, p. 9; *The Times*, 25 April 1933, p. 16.
116 Such letters were received from Michael McCarton (Irish Linen Warehouse), Northern Assurance Company and Joseph Garbutt (Joseph Garbutt Ltd., chemists). CC/X/8/5, Durham County Council, Standing Joint Committee, Misc. Files, April to September 1933.

117 Robinson asked to be compensated for the pram, which she had only bought the previous week, as she had been forced to buy another one and a pair of shoes. She worried about paying for both prams because 'my husband is expecting coming out of work'. CC/X/8/5, Alice Robinson to Durham County Council, 20 April 1933; William Ridley to Durham County Council, 22 April 1933.
118 CC/X/8/5, Correspondence between Ralph Smith, Secretary of the Ryhope Lodge of the DMA, and Durham County Council, 12 April 1933.
119 CC/X/8/5, Correspondence, William Kay, Secretary of Harraton Lodge, to Harold Jevons 13 April 1933; Correspondence, G. Brown, Jarrow Branch of the NUWM, to Harold Jevons, 15 April 1933; Correspondence, T. Temple, Secretary of the Chopwell Lodge, to Harold Jevons, 1 May 1933; Resolution from Teesside Conference of Workers to Chair of Durham County Council, 6 May 1933; Correspondence, George Harvey, Secretary of the Follonsby Lodge, to Harold Jevons, 8 May 1933.
120 *Report to the Minister of Labour by the Commissioners Appointed to Administer Transitional Payments in the County of Durham* (Cmd 4339), 1932–33, xv, p. 1035.
121 The reporting of events does need consideration.
122 Some demonstrations did continue. Joe Hind later recalled how in June 1933 he went out to the Town Moor in Newcastle and had 'great fun listening to all the speakers ranting and raving about the dole and the Means Test'. Joe Hind, *A Shieldfield Childhood* (Newcastle-upon-Tyne, 1994), p. 49.
123 *Unemployed Leader*, No. 12, April 1933, pp. 1–2.
124 Monmouthshire Marchers' Council, *Monmouthshire Hunger March*, pp. 7–11; Reiss, 'Not All Were Apathetic', p. 99.
125 Monmouthshire Marchers' Council, *Monmouthshire Hunger March*, pp. 2, 7–8.
126 Lewis Jones, 'Foreword', in *ibid.*, p. 3.
127 Monmouthshire Marchers' Council, *Monmouthshire Hunger March*, pp. 9–10.
128 *Ibid.*, p. 11; *The Times*, 31 August 1933, p. 12.
129 Communication between the county council and the Monmouthshire Marchers' Council continued up until the end of 1933. Monmouthshire Marchers' Council, *Monmouthshire Hunger March*, pp. 11–12.
130 *Ibid.*, p. 12.
131 *Ibid.*, pp. 3–16.
132 For example, it was the efforts of Arthur Horner more than the local branch of the Communist Party that earned Maerdy its reputation as a 'Little Moscow'. The *Free Press and Rhondda Leader* saw his increasing popularity in the area as 'a sad reflection on the mentality of our people'. *Free Press and Rhondda Leader*, 8 April 1933, p. 4.
133 *The Times*, 16 December 1931, p. 9.
134 *Western Mail*, 14 March 1932, p. 8.
135 Hannington, *Ten Lean Years*, p. 55.

136 TNA, HO 144/20132, Correspondence, between R. Llewelyn, Secretary of the Bridgend Central Marchers' Committee, and the Home Secretary, 9 October 1933; *Daily Herald*, 10 October 1933, p. 3; *Aberdare Leader*, 14 October 1933, p. 6.

137 HO 144/20132, *Police Review*, 20 October, 1933.

138 *Aberdare Leader*, 14 October 1933, p. 6.

139 Correspondence between R. Llewelyn and the Home Secretary, 9 October 1933.

140 HO 144/20132, Home Office File Minutes, 12 October 1933.

141 HO 144/20132, Correspondence between Lindsay to Trubshaw, 10 October, 1933.

142 HO 144/20132, Ministry of Health to the Home Office.

143 HO 144/20132, Home Office File Minutes, 16 October 1933.

144 For example, in the summer of 1932 particularly violent clashes between the police and unemployed were reported in Bristol. TNA, HO 144/22587, Bristol, Recent Disturbances and the Conduct of the Police, June 1932.

145 Jane Morgan, 'Police and Labour in the Age of Lindsay, 1910–1936', *Llafur*, 5:1 (1988), pp. 15–20.

146 Paynter, *My Generation*, p. 38.

147 NLW, Idris Cox Collection, Item no. 45, Lewis Jones, *From Exchange and Parish to the PAC: For Decency and Destitution* (Central Marchers' Council, Tonypandy, n.d.), p. 7.

148 In the early 1930s, there was little cooperation between the NUWM, the Communist Party and the labour movement as this was the Communist Party's 'class against class' period. This undoubtedly influenced the situation.

149 Arthur Ayles was warned not to use provocative language. *Merthyr Express*, 12 December 1931, p. 12.

150 Richards, 'Mobilising the Powerless', pp. 24–5.

151 Francis and Smith, *The Fed*, p. 251.

152 See the two documentaries, *Dora's Story* (Red Flannel Films, 1993) [documentary film]; *Mam* (Red Flannel Films, 1988) [documentary film].

153 Kingsford, *The Hunger Marchers*, pp. 184–5.

154 TNA, HO 144/19846, 'Report of the Demonstration held in Hyde Park on 25 February by the National Hunger March and Congress Council', Correspondence between the Metropolitan Police and the Home Office, 26 February 1934.

155 Will Paynter recalled that the police far outnumbered the marchers en route. A letter intercepted from Lewis Jones by MI5 claimed that he wrote 'we go into a town and then literally capture it ... doing everything we want to do ... going everywhere we want to go ... ignoring all bans and prohibitions.... It inspires the marchers with added strength and it encourages the workers in those towns where police chiefs have practically abolished working class activity'. Paynter, *My Generation*, p. 95; HO 144/19846, Extracts of Lewis Jones's letters dated 15 February 1934, enclosed in correspondence to the Home Office, dated 20 February 1934.

156 Monmouthshire Marchers' Council, *Monmouthshire Hunger March*, p. 11.
157 Ellen Wilkinson, *The Town That Was Murdered: The Life Story of Jarrow* (London, 1939), p. 198.
158 The great exception was the mass demonstrations organised by the TUC in conjunction with the Labour Party and the Co-Operative Union in Hyde Park in 1933. See also *The Times*, 4 April 1932, 14 and 5 November 1932; TNA, PRO 30/69/442, TUC General Council Deputation to the Minister of Labour, 1 February 1932.
159 Hannington, *Ten Lean Years*, p. 51.
160 DRO, Durham PAC Minutes, 28 January 1932, p. 18; TWAS, Newcastle PAC Minute Book, 1 February 1932, p. 41.
161 Durham PAC Minutes, 28 January 1932, pp. 17–34.
162 *Northern Echo*, 2 February 1933, p. 3.
163 Durham PAC Minutes, 26 November 1931, p. 333.
164 Durham Area Miners' Office, Redhills (hereafter, DMOR), Durham Miners' Association, Minutes of Annual Council Meeting, 5 December 1931, p. 51.
165 DMA, Minutes of Council Meeting, 23 January 1932, p. 56.
166 Newcastle PAC Minutes, 1 February 1932, p. 42.
167 *Manchester Guardian*, 14 March 1933, p. 7.
168 Newcastle PAC Minutes, 7 March 1932, p. 51, 2 May, p. 79 and 3 October 1933, p. 129.
169 Durham PAC Minutes, 21 November 1931, p. 351 and 28 January 1932, p. 18; *Durham County Advertiser and Durham Chronicle*, 11 December 1931, p. 11, 13 May 1932, p. 13 and 9 December 1932, p. 17; *Evening Chronicle*, 20 January 1932, p. 1; *South Shields Gazette*, 21 November 1931, p. 8.
170 *South Wales Weekly Argus*, 21 May 1932, p. 2.
171 *Free Press and Rhondda Leader*, 10 June 1933, p. 6.
172 *Manchester Guardian*, 18 April 1932, p. 4; *Hansard*, HC (series 5) vol. 264, cols 971–2 (21 April 1932); *Hansard*, HC (series 5) vol. 270, col. 1693 (15 November 1932).
173 *South Shields Gazette*, 2 March 1933, p. 1.
174 Northumberland Archives Woodhorn, Ashington (hereafter, NAW), NRO527/A/2, Wansbeck Divisional Labour Party Minutes, 26 March 1932 and 9 April 1932.
175 *Aberdare Leader*, 22 October 1932, p. 3.
176 This was also true of the relationship between individual trade union lodges and regional executive committees. The executive committee of the SWMF, for example, did not develop a definite line with regards to the means test until 1933, and unemployed members were not allowed to vote on all issues before this date.
177 Collecting signatures for a petition was used in the Monmouthshire hunger march in 1933 and, of course, the 1932 national hunger march.
178 SWCC, MNA/NUM/L/33/A/8, SWMF, Minutes of the Ferndale Lodge, 3 March 1932.

179 *Ibid.*, 22 March 1932.
180 *Western Mail*, 14 July 1932, p. 11; *Free Press and Rhondda Leader*, 16 July 1932, p. 1.
181 *Hansard*, HC (series 5) vol. 268, col. 1263 (13 July 1932).
182 *Blyth and Ashington Post*, 17 October 1932, p. 5.
183 *Daily Mirror*, 29 March 1932, p. 4.
184 Elias's emphasis. Sid Elias, *Mass Murder: An Exposure of the Means Test* (London, 1932), p. 5.
185 *Aberdare Leader*, 19 December 1931, p. 3.
186 *Ibid.*
187 *South Wales Weekly Argus*, 30 April 1932, p. 5.
188 SWCC, MNA/PP/67/22, Eddie Jones Collection, Correspondence between Richard Legge and Monmouthshire County Council, 5 August 1933.
189 SWCC, MNA/PP/67/16, Notes on the Demands of the March of the Monmouthshire Workers Upon the Monmouthshire County Council, 30 August 1933, pp. 1–2.
190 *Evening Chronicle*, 5 October 1932, p. 1.
191 DRO, D/DMA (Sam Watson) 45 (Box)/19, Sam Watson Collection, 'Resolution passed by the Executive Committee of the Durham Miners' Association', 9 June 1931.
192 Richards, 'Mobilising the Powerless', p. 21.
193 Bruley, 'Women in the Unemployed Movement', p. 50.
194 *Daily Worker*, 10 October 1931, p. 3, 13 October 1931, p. 1.
195 Macintyre, *Little Moscows*, p. 41.
196 *Daily Worker*, 8 October 1931, p. 3.
197 Richards, 'Mobilising the Powerless', p. 21.
198 Examples of protest without such support were less common, but did exist. For example, the organisation of an unemployed deputation to Easington guardians' committee in December 1931 to demand the abolishment of the means test conveys how the unemployed were able to organise themselves. The crowd of twenty-five vowed to return the following week to continue its protest, but this never materialised. *Durham County Advertiser and Durham Chronicle*, 11 December 1931, p. 2.
199 Aside from resolutions of protest, the events of the unemployed in Chopwell were not noted in the major regional newspapers.
200 By 1933, there were only four Communist Party members in Chopwell. Macintyre, *Little Moscows*, p. 20.

Part III

1935–41

5

The government attempts to take a stand: the establishment of the UAB and mass action

> After the years that I have been in public life I thought I knew something about the arts of misleading the public and that I could detect them immediately I saw them, but I have seen nothing to compare with what has been happening under this new system.... There are friends of mine in my own division, unemployed men, who actually thought that their lot would be made better.
>
> J. J. Lawson, Labour MP, Chester-le-Street.[1]

> South Wales was the centre of the storm. There Communists, Labour men, co-operators, trade unionists, all were now banded together in a single impregnable working-class front, which drew around it the warm support of the small middle-class folk represented by the churches and chapels, the shopkeepers, etc. February 3rd was an historic day for South Wales. There were demonstrations everywhere, no less than 300,000 people attending them; in many places up and down those straggling valleys that day amounted to a general turn-out of the whole population.
>
> Allen Hutt, *The Post-War History of the British Working Class* (London, 1937).[2]

During January 1935, Britain came alive with protest and social unrest on a scale never witnessed before. Individual demonstrations could draw tens of thousands of participants. In many areas, the unemployed were joined on marches by major political parties, trade unions and even middle-class shopkeepers, teachers and business men and women. The hunger marches may have earned a later legendary status in popular memories of the 1930s, but it was these protests which saw the unemployed assume the greatest prominence in the political arena. This was not a matter of mere numbers: the government responded by temporarily suspending certain aspects of its new legislation. Hailed as a victory for the labour movement, these winter marches posed one of the greatest threats to the image of interwar consensus.[3]

The protests of early 1935 have been the focus of much attention in the historiography, principally because of the scale of the demonstrations and the violence they attained in some parts of Britain.[4] Historians such as Garside, Miller, Flannagan and Perry have highlighted how spontaneous action in January and February was provoked by the drastic benefit cuts introduced by the newly formed UABs. Established under Part II of the 1934 Unemployment Act, the primary function of the autonomous UABs was to remove vagaries which had existed in the PACs' administration of means-tested benefit. W. R. Garside and Frederic Miller's analyses remain the best accounts of the chaos surrounding the transition to the new scheme.[5] They argue that heavy reductions were a consequence of the Cabinet's and the central UAB's blind faith in the power of the regulations to bring fair payments and the final rush to get the regulations approved by parliament. Despite reassurances from Lord Rushcliffe, chair of the UAB, of the discretionary powers of investigators and government promises of higher payments, hundreds of thousands of the unemployed saw their benefits reduced following a much more intrusive means test examination.[6] By the end of January, the UAB conceded that the work of officers had 'perhaps' been 'too accurate'.[7] In early February, the government announced a legal standstill of the new regulations.

The reductions in unemployment benefit were indeed intrinsic to the scale of the demonstrations, and especially in occasioning the outcry of middle-class groups. However, events in south Wales and the north-east of England highlight both the significance of protests against the means test in the early 1930s and the gradual build-up to action. The cuts may have provided the final push to protest, but the resentment towards the UABs went much deeper. The continuation of the means test remained a major grievance, although the introduction of compulsory training schemes (labelled 'slave camps') also fuelled much anger. The nature of the new investigations under the stricter UABs meant they became the focus of protestors' attention once the cuts began. Prior to this, the unemployed had continued to march to PACs, local councils and the government in the case of the 1934 national hunger march.

While action in January and February 1935 was in part spontaneous, it also conformed to previous patterns of protest. The industrial valleys of south Wales formed one of the most active areas alongside Scotland and Sheffield. In south Wales, the level of action far outstripped even the NUWM's expectations with Hywel Francis and Dai Smith describing it as 'the greatest volcano of socio-political protest ever experienced in the region'.[8] Like other parts of the country, there was a sense of urgency to the protests. Meetings called by advertisements chalked on the road and word of mouth were held in cinemas, town halls and on waste ground as the unemployed were organised and focused in their appeal to the government. While in the north-east such action was evident, the scale of the response was limited in comparison to south Wales and other parts of Britain. Once more, despite the backdrop of protest in many parts of the country, in Durham and Northumberland, opposition was confined to pockets of activity. This variation in the response to the UAB demonstrates how generalisations about the behaviour of the unemployed can be problematic. A model of how the unemployed responded cannot be applied in either case or, more broadly, to Britain. Marching as a method of protest was never inevitable, and a comparison highlights the importance of the nature of community and culture in how the unemployed were mobilised for action.

The response in south Wales and the north-east provides a fascinating insight into the organisation and leadership of the unemployed and relationship between the working and middle class. The role of the middle class in uniting in opposition saw the protests assume a quite different significance. This impacted upon the perception of protestors and their relationship with the authorities, which was itself transforming. In these months, the very nature of protest and ultimately the relationship between the working class and the government was changing. The UABs by assuming responsibility for all able-bodied unemployed marked one of the first stages in the gradual centralisation of welfare; the dual purpose of the Board was to provide benefits and look after the welfare of the unemployed to ensure they were fit for work.[9] The lessons learnt here, by the working class, politicians and government, were to shape debates about welfare in the post-1945 period.

The 1934 Unemployment Bill was the most debated piece of domestic legislation in the interwar period and took over seven months to pass through parliament. Despite the hope that this Bill would finally remove the unemployment question from British politics, politicians questioned its probable impact and opposed its implementation from the outset. Denounced by MPs from the depressed areas, those from south Wales and the north-east took a prominent role in the debates. MPs expostulated with the Minister of Labour in the House of Commons and condemned the new Act within their constituencies. Aneurin Bevan called the Act a 'studied attack on democracy', and Will John (Labour MP, Rhondda West) when addressing a meeting of the unemployed stated that 'the effects of the Bill when it becomes an Act ... will be to deepen the idea already prevalent in the minds of the unemployed that they are discarded, ostracised and treated as outcasts'.[10]

The Bill attracted much condemnation outside of the House of Commons.[11] The Act became a regular feature of editorials and investigations in the *Manchester Guardian*, and the NUWM and the Labour Party produced pamphlets exposing the latest perceived attack upon the working class.[12] In addition to the production of pamphlets, meetings were held to discuss the terms directly with the unemployed, and councils began to pass and send resolutions to the Cabinet. In January 1934, the Labour Party called on 'workers everywhere' to 'protest against the Unemployment Bill'.[13] From May 1934, *The Unemployed Leader* carried regular articles instructing how mass protests could be organised against the new Act.[14] The long passage of the Act through parliament and the dissemination of knowledge of the scrutinised legislation left transitional applicants well informed and educated of the potential impact for well over a year before the Act was actually implemented. This is a point that has remained overlooked in the historiography.[15] Although the street protests are rightly observed as spontaneous and as part of a movement that escalated as it gained momentum, the foundations of this action lay in this much longer campaign which was being orchestrated in the depressed regions.

In the north-east of England, as early as November 1933, Durham County Council PAC, supported by the county council itself, passed a resolution against the Unemployment Bill following a report from the Special Relief Sub-Committee.[16] The following month, Newcastle City PAC placed its opposition against the Unemployment Act on motion of the Lord Mayor.[17] The DMA also took a decisive line against the means test. In early 1934, the council of the DMA and then its executive committee passed a resolution from North Biddick which stated that 'we believe that these attacks [in the Unemployment Act, 1934] upon our members, both employed and unemployed, are tantamount to the disintegration of our organisation'. The resolution was forwarded to county MPs, the Prime Minister and the Leader of the Opposition.[18] The DMA was clearly taking a firmer stance against the new legislation and agreed 'to co-operate with the County Federation of Divisional Labour Parties by taking part in the protest meetings organised by them in the county'.[19] Labour women were likewise roused to action; at a meeting of the north-eastern section in January 1934, a resolution was passed against the means test and Unemployment Bill.[20]

In south Wales, individual lodges of the SWMF took steps to organise a national conference to discuss the impact of the new Bill in February

1934.[21] However, at this stage, the executive committee of the SWMF continued to distance itself from Communist Party activity, and both speakers for a conference and support for a march organised by the South Wales Marchers' Council were refused.[22] In anticipation of the breadth of opposition that was to come, the Nonconformist chapels made their opposition to the UAB clear early on in south Wales. The Mid-Rhondda Evangelical Council believed that any further 'privation' brought upon the unemployed would be 'incompatible with our interpretation of the New Testament'.[23]

After the passing of the new regulations in parliament, individual MPs and trade union leaders, often in collaboration, focused their energies on explaining the terms of the complex new legislation.[24] Just days before the Act was introduced, the Labour MP for Aberdare, George Hall, who had campaigned throughout the winter months, addressed a meeting at Aberaman. Hall used his platform to stir feelings against an Act that he ardently believed would worsen the position of the unemployed; 'don't think George Hall is justifying the regulations! I don't justify a single one of them ... under these new regulations the longer a man has been out of work, the less sympathy and less financial assistance he is going to get'.[25] While meetings such as these were essential to the formation of the massive protests that occurred, the final impetus for action came from the actual effects of the UAB's administration of transitional payments.

Around 800,000 people came within the scope of the UAB and began from 7 January 1935 to have their circumstances investigated by the newly appointed officials.[26] In south Wales, approximately 100,000 people came within the scope of the UABs and in the north-east approximately 90,000.[27] The establishment of a new administrative machinery ensured that at every level the responsibility for transitional applicants was removed from local influences. The new regulations, administered by these bodies, introduced complex uniform guidelines which encouraged far more invasive investigations into means. Reductions in payments were expected in south Wales and the north-east, and the potential impact was discussed by the central UAB which drafted the regulations.[28] The concerns expressed by the Board reflected not only apprehension about the social effects of lowering benefit levels but also trepidation of the potential political repercussions.[29] Thomas Jones, although wanting to find a way of 'softening the blow in areas such as South Wales', expressed that 'he himself had no sympathy whatever with the lax administration which had produced the present position in South Wales, and he was quite prepared to see South Wales "cleaned up"'.[30] In removing this abuse, however, Jones was 'convinced that there would be a great outburst there as soon as the effect of the Board's scales were known' and requested that a test case to be carried out so the Board had 'ammunition' for dealing with complaints.[31] Board members decided that 'the wisest policy would be to enforce the Regulations strictly' and, telling of the protests against the means test in the north-east, 'leave it to public opinion to come round gradually as it had done in the case of the Durham administration.'[32]

Although reductions in payments were expected, the scale of cuts nonetheless alarmed transitional applicants. Losses were especially pronounced in those regions where the local authorities had generously interpreted the Order in Council. In south Wales, many applicants faced a household means test proper for the first time.[33] As Glamorgan County Council had predicted, 'the Unemployment Assistance Board Regulations are going to appear very much more harsh in Glamorgan – to all those applicants who are not, with their dependants, wholly relying upon the allowances for their maintenance'.[34] In the north-east of England, while the strict administration of the means test under Newcastle PAC and the commissioners in County Durham meant reductions were not as marked, the UAB was still far more rigorous in its assessment than PAC or government officials.[35] This situation was repeated in towns and cities across Britain. With or without drastic reductions, the rigid investigations and bureaucratic machinery were enough to cause discontent.

The new administration meant the establishment of new offices, in some cases officers, and a new system of procedure and appeal. The investigators were no longer susceptible to the influence of local politics and opinion, and they operated in the same manner as any other civil servants (although many may have previously worked for the PACs). The belief 'that the new regulations will be administered coldly and callously' was emphasised at many mass meetings with the effect that means test investigators were seen as the enemy and out to deceive the unemployed.[36] Arthur Sharp, Newcastle district officer, commented:

> in the early days, the new organisation was, perhaps, regarded with some suspicion, and some applicants seemed doubtful whether the new order of things would be to their advantage. Many of the callers during the first few weeks were imbued with a sense of curiosity, and it was obvious that they were more anxious to have a look at the office and the officers than have their assessments explained.[37]

Similarly, the Cardiff district officer, A. Gibb, reflected, 'it is undoubtedly true that in January 1935 the Board and its officers were in this

District regarded with fear and resentment, and one of the most difficult tasks facing officers was to break down this perhaps not unnatural state of mind'.[38] The decreases in benefits that many unemployed faced compounded their fear and distrust of the officers who provided a focus for the unemployed's anger.

A shift in the rhetoric of protest occurred in these months, and press reports on the impact of means testing were no longer confined to transitional applicants or the working class. How the means test affected the *families* of the long-term unemployed was emphasised. Although it had long been a preoccupation of the press and social investigators, in 1935 a direct link was made between the application of the means test and the disruption of family life. The means test was no longer one of the many factors that affected families, where one or more of the members were unemployed, instead it was seen as pivotal to the breakdown of familial relations.

In County Durham, the labour movement believed that the UAB's administration was increasing distress within families. Durham PAC passed a resolution against the Act stating, 'Part II of the Act is totally inadequate ... we strongly protest against its harsh application which is causing untold misery and suffering amongst the families of the unemployed in the County of Durham'.[39] In south Wales, where other household members' income had been ignored, the case was made vehemently. The leaders of the Maes-yr-Haf Quaker settlement in the Rhondda Valleys wrote to the *Manchester Guardian* to highlight the distress of families in south Wales caused by the new regulations.[40] In the regional press, journalists noted in both editorial and news columns how the means test was causing families to split. For example, in the opinion column in the *Rhondda Fach Gazette*, it was argued that 'where the too drastic application of the Means Test is breaking up homes – as we believe it is doing in actual experience – it is certainly going further than any of our legislators ever intended it to go.... It is a nasty weapon and a cruel one.'[41] Furthermore, the *Gazette* predicted that the effects of the UAB would extend beyond the family and 'will make a great difference in an indirect manner.... Everybody is going to feel it; grocers, butchers, bakers, entertainment caterers'.[42] The connection of the impact of the means test to the wider community was an important feature of the denunciation of the UABs.

Businesses and chambers of trade argued that the means test would affect those outside the working class as the spending power of the unemployed became reduced. Many shopkeepers had already suffered from increased rates in the severely depressed areas, and the absence of a disposable income amongst customers heightened the plight of the shopocracy. The test was therefore condemned on behalf of and by those outside the labour movement. The members of the Aberdare and District Chamber of Trade passed a resolution against the means test as it viewed 'with alarm the provisions contained in the new Unemployment Assistance Act. In this district where distress is so prevalent, it is obvious that this Act will prove fatal to family life'.[43] It was the break-up of home life that attracted the condemnation of many groups who had not formerly been as vocal. The churches and chapels were especially concerned over how a stricter application of the means test would affect families. The Mid-Rhondda Evangelical Council passed further resolutions against the test for 'reducing the moral and spiritual life of the whole community'.[44] The churches and chapels in the Aberdare region became particularly disparaging of the Unemployment Act in the pages of the *Aberdare Leader* after George Hall decried their lack of action at a mass meeting in Trecynon.[45] In Merthyr, different denominations united to send a letter of opposition to the *Church Times*, and it formed part of the later debates in the House of Commons.[46]

Working members in the homes of the unemployed also elicited sympathy as practically all of their wages were given over to supporting the family.[47] Parents and those in employment were urged to be tolerant as it was conjectured that tension was causing families to split.[48] It was the greater anxiety about the position of men within the household that caused much concern. How could unemployed members assert their masculinity when they were supported by their relatives? The effects of the means test upon gendered identities were becoming much more apparent. Although this issue was buried in the wider disagreements raised by the UAB administration, it was pivotal to the experience of the unemployed and was raised continually throughout the later 1930s.

The ill effects of the means test hardened attitudes towards the UAB. Although action was anticipated, the sheer magnitude of protest awed even its protagonists. Those MPs, councillors, trade unionists and members of the NUWM, Communist and Labour Parties who had spoken out against the regulations advanced to lead the unemployed. As the effects of the measure were felt or publicised, marches and demonstrations arose in major urban centres throughout Britain. Yet, despite this uproar, regional or local variations remained important. The heightened turbulence of 1935 did not supersede political traditions: organisation and leadership were paramount. In the north-east, regardless of the explosive backdrop, examples of marches and demonstrations were less common, and, as in the early 1930s, the major manifestation of protest was through resolutions passed at mass meetings and petitions. In this instance, however, south Wales was not only militant in comparison to the north-east: no other region in Britain produced the scale of response achieved in south Wales. The industrial valleys of the region became the focus of media attention and hailed as an exemplar by the left-wing press of what could be achieved.

In 1935, the unemployed in south Wales were organised, focused and determined. The abolition of the UABs became a key, if not the only, issue for both industrial and party politics, and support for the unemployed and leadership thrived. In essence, these protests continued the agitation against the means test, and its removal remained at the core of protestor's demands. Neil Evans has noted how calls to end the means test and abolish the UABs 'dominated public and private conversation. It swept through the coalfield with something of a religious revival, though with none of the hysteria'.[49] Although the labour movement in south Wales provided a focus for activity, other prominent organisations within local communities centred their meetings on the issue of the means test and began to participate in the street protests alongside the unemployed. The outstanding feature of the response of the unemployed in south Wales was the scale and level of opposition expressed through the many marches and demonstrations. It was the proliferation of support that imbued the mass mobilisation of the unemployed. Widespread organisation allowed demonstrations and marches to be disciplined affairs without the taint of violence.

On 5 January, the executive committee of the SWMF held a meeting to discuss the Unemployment Act that was addressed by miner MPs. It was decided that a conference 'of all parties interested' should be held on 26 January to determine what action should be taken against the Act. Moreover, MPs and trade unionists were asked to devote all of their time to orchestrating a protest campaign against the UABs.[50] That these plans were made even before the UAB began its work shows how heated feelings were within the region, and it confirmed Thomas Jones's conviction that there would be outcry. The 'all-in' conference became the focus of energies in south Wales and suggests the commitment of the executive committee to organising united action. In 1935, the SWMF no longer waited for the TUC to issue guidelines on the approach to take or for solid evidence of individual cases of hardship. Written means of protest were not enough to satisfy the calls for opposition, and the SWMF began to work closely with other organisations with the notable exclusion of the

NUWM. Although the SWMF executive committee called for united action, they continued to distance themselves from the association of revolutionary overtones of the Communist Party and affiliated movements. The National Administrative Council (NAC) of the NUWM, for its part, issued a circular calling for a presence at the meeting to ensure that the 'reformists ... line of purely formal protests and no mass action' would not be pursued. NUWM members who were a part of the SWMF were urged to attend the meeting.[51] At a local level, in practice, the separation of different political groups became unsupportable.

The Communist Party and the NUWM worked tirelessly to mobilise the unemployed for action throughout January 1935, and their calls for united action were made far more forcefully than any other organisation or party. The NAC from December urged in a series of circulars that 'every branch must immediately mobilise mighty protests in all localities against these cuts.' Members were asked to invite MPs, Labour councillors and trade unions to meetings and to arrange deputations to PACs to demand that they made up losses.[52] Reginald Barker, a Methodist minister in the Rhondda Valleys, argued the introduction of the UAB 'drove many to the side of the Communists' as they 'exploited to the full the situation which arose'.[53] Although obviously committed to the official party line, within localities in south Wales the Communists did appear to have a genuine commitment to leading the unemployed.[54] Certain SWMF lodges worked together with the NUWM, despite official central policy, and developed stronger links with the Communist Party in these months. Maerdy Lodge stands out for its collaboration with the Communist Party, although the relationship between the two was already established.[55]

Maerdy Lodge was certainly one of the more radical elements within the SWMF. At a meeting on 10 January, the lodge members voted, after listening to an explanation of what the new Act would entail from W. H. Mainwaring (Labour MP, Rhondda East), to call for a one-day strike to be held by the miners.[56] The repeated calls for a strike were made throughout the rest of the month by the Cambrian Combine Committee, and it drew the attention of the government who were concerned about the legality of such a move.[57] The increasingly militant attitude of the executive committee of the SWMF was shown in their decision not to dismiss the strike as a possible method of opposition. Events in early 1935 quickly unfolded, and, while efforts were geared towards the all-in conference at the end of the month and strike action, the initiative was taken to make a public stance before these events ensued. The initial protest of mass meetings soon became marches numbering thousands as action was decided upon and the unemployed were mobilised for protest.[58] By the third week of January, individual protests numbered into tens of thousands.

Despite the appalling weather conditions, the unemployed were mobilised for action in villages, towns and valleys with a regularity and persistence that left even the local press and the *Daily Worker* struggling to keep up with the reporting of events. The first march to attract tens of thousands was held, perhaps not unsurprisingly, in the Rhondda Valleys, and it set the tone for further marches. On 20 January, an estimated 50,000–60,000 marched twelve abreast in a four-mile procession down both valleys in the Rhondda and converged on De Winton field in Tonypandy. Five platforms were erected for speakers to address the crowds, and amongst those speaking were Will John, W. H. Mainwaring and Arthur Horner.[59] The march was celebrated in the local press for its size, peacefulness and inclusiveness: these were all themes that were to recur in the media for the larger marches.

The *Free Press and Rhondda Leader* reported that 'people who have lived in the valley all their lives were emphatic that they had never witnessed such a scene of protest and indignation against regulations condemned as inhuman and unjust'.[60] The constancy with which the press reported on the unprecedented numbers attending marches in this way made those involved in the protests conscious of the fact that they were making history.[61] Although the Rhondda Valleys had so often been the focus of protest, in 1935 the number of people taking to the streets was unparalleled. Indeed, the *Daily Worker* professed 'the demonstration in the Rhondda today was the greatest thing in history'.[62] People were no longer marching simply to protest, but to bring about change with a spirit of enthusiasm and unity. The marches were headed by jazz bands, and the colourful banners cut through the grey of the dreary weather. The protest was, in many respects, inclusive. The *Free Press and Rhondda Leader* reported that 'it was not a movement initiated by any particular party, but a united front of local officials, Communists, ministers of religion and business and professional men, with Members of Parliament, magistrates and councillors rubbing shoulders with all members of the population'.[63] This situation was remarkable. That ministers of religion and local business men and women were marching was in itself curious, but that they marched alongside the Communist Party was extraordinary.

The unity evident in the marches was symbolic and yet superficial; public displays of a united front did not reflect a change of long-standing private animosities. However, symbolism was all important in 1935, and the united front displayed in the larger marches demonstrated the importance and power of community in south Wales. Although community was vertically multilayered – and achieved through a variety of horizontal interlinked networks – the members of the community could work together to achieve a public display of unanimity. Community in the Rhondda valleys, and other places in south Wales, embodied more than an attachment to place although this was an essential feature. Community is often defined by ideas of inclusion and exclusion, and the boundaries between such notions became less fluid when the community was in some way threatened. In 1935, when it was perceived that the community in the Rhondda was facing destruction through increased hardship, the population responded to that threat by taking to the streets to make its stance. The Rhondda march also highlighted the importance of the valleys as a spatial arena of protest. The topography of the Rhondda, like other valleys, could be utilised as a path for the route of marches, and it provided a natural course in many parts of south Wales as the demonstrations at the end of January conveyed.

The *Daily Worker* celebrated the demonstration in the Rhondda Valleys as an exemplar of what could be achieved through united front action; it kept referring back to the Rhondda march as a successful example of the current strategy of the Communist Party.[64] Within days, further mass mobilisations in the streets occurred as the protest gathered momentum. On 22 January, 40,000 marched in Merthyr. Two days later, 20,000 marched to Pontypridd and a further 10,000 at marches in Pontypool and Neath the following day. On 27 January, 30,000 people demonstrated in Aberdare, and the following day a further 20,000 congregated at Pontypridd. A total of 15,000 met at Maesteg on 30 January beginning a week's of demonstrations that were to culminate in an estimated 300,000 marching on Sunday 3 February.[65] As Allen Hutt noted when reflecting on the protest of 1935, 'South Wales was the centre of the storm'.[66] This notion was reflected in the national press attention given to the region.[67]

Lewis Jones was able to state with some conviction that 'the workers are in the mood to fight the Act'.[68] In *The Unemployed Leader* Ben Francis opined that 'like an avalanche itself this vast army of angry workers grows day by day, uniting the workers as they've never been united before, and sweeping aside all artificial barriers from its path'.[69] In addition to the marches, resolutions continued to be passed at normal sessions of organisations, and special meetings were also convened to discuss the situation. PACs now distanced from the administrative process were able to freely object to the new Act without facing the threat of governmental sanctions. Councillors were motivated by sympathy for the plight of the unemployed and prompted by demands from the local population. For example, Monmouthshire County Council organised a special meeting to discuss the Unemployment Act after receiving communication from Pontypool and Abersychan Urban District Councils, Pontllanfraith Unemployed Organisation, Garndiffaith Action Committee and Pontypool Joint Action Committee.[70]

Certain groups, while attending marches, still used meetings and the passing of resolutions as a primary method of protest. This was certainly true of churches and chapels which became increasingly vocal once the UABs were established.[71] Similarly, teachers and Trades and Labour Councils identified themselves with protest far more vigorously than in previous years. Of the 450 delegates who attended a conference at Porth to protest against the UAB on 23 January, 250 'attended on behalf of religious organisations ... together with members of the County and District Councils and Chambers of Trades'.[72] Written expressions of opposition and meetings therefore remained an important function of protest, keeping the issue alive and in the public mindset, but could also lead to involvement in marches and demonstrations, a more powerful form of opposition. Although the impetus for the movement against UABs and the means test came from the unemployed and the traditional leaders of the working class, the unity achieved with groups outside of the labour movement gave opposition an edge it may not have otherwise achieved. The 'Aberdaria', the editorial in the *Aberdare Leader*, reflected such a sentiment:

> many people do not disguise their opinion that all this demonstrating is merely 'baying at the moon', but such mammoth demonstrations as those already held in the Rhondda, and those planned for this valley, with representatives of the churches and tradespeople marching side by side with the miners employed and unemployed, are bound to show the Government in no mistakable fashion that the country is roused against the new Act.[73]

Following a week of mass action, the SWMF's all-in conference was held to discuss action against the means test. One thousand six hundred delegates attended the conference, and, aside from the exclusion of the Communist Party and Welsh Nationalists, the delegates represented a united front. A Council of Action was created to decide upon further activities, and the calls made for a one-day strike were to be considered by this body.[74] The *Manchester Guardian* saw this meeting as indicating that 'South Wales is in revolt'.[75] The unwavering commitment of many lodges to a one-day strike against a backdrop of high unemployment and an increasingly competitive labour market showed the absolute dedication of many within the SWMF to the abolition to the UABs.[76] The work of trade union officials meant that the SWMF remained a major source of leadership, despite the growth of the Communist Party and the NUWM.[77] While often working separately, taken together, the three bodies were pivotal to generating the monster demonstrations which occurred at the end of the month. On 28 January, special correspondent of the *Daily Worker*, Bill Francis, marched with the unemployed from Ogmore to Bridgend.[78] Reflecting on the action that had taken place in the last days of January, Francis commented, 'during this weekend the entire working-class movement in Wales were either out on the streets voicing their protest ... or represented at the South Wales Conference of Action'.[79]

Perhaps somewhat surprisingly, given the numbers marching and the anger generated by benefit losses, the mass marches in south Wales largely passed without incident. While the absence of violence is testament to the high level of organisation and determination not to hamper the cause, the reaction of the authorities was also crucial.[80] There was always a strong police presence at the marches, in part a response to Home Office pressure, but also because the Chief Constable of Glamorgan Constabulary, Captain Lindsay, continued to view the unemployed as a subversive group despite the orderliness of their demonstrations.[81] However, unlike in the early 1930s, the police did not battle with the unemployed over planned routes and sites of demonstrations.[82] The presence of many middle-class and religious groups in the larger marches left the police unable to denounce the intended purpose of the marchers. Moreover, the marchers outnumbered the police in their thousands, and the authorities must have feared how quickly events could have escalated if the marchers turned to violence. The police focused much of their attention on meetings organised by the Communist Party. The Glamorgan Constabulary insisted upon placing officers into meetings and disbanding them when they considered speeches to be offensive. Will John wrote to the Home Secretary to complain about such police action.[83]

The marches symbolised the strength of feeling against the means test, and the presence of so many people on the streets was intimidating, even when marches passed without incident. Although the Glamorgan Constabulary may have appeared heavy-handed in their response to the meetings of the unemployed, their actions suggested their momentary weakness. In January and early February, the unemployed of south Wales demanded the attention of the government and dominated press reports of the protests. In other regions, the unemployed were also taking to the streets in their thousands to oppose the UABs. In London, Sheffield and

Glasgow in particular, marches and demonstrations occurred with an increasing regularity and size towards the end of January. Large protests also took place in Lincoln, Taunton, Leicester, Greenock, Manchester, Stoke, Bolton and Blackburn.[84] The *Daily Herald* reported that churches across the country were expressing their opposition and that councillors and MPs were inundated with details of cases of hardship. Councils across Britain met in special meetings to discuss the matter.[85] Wal Hannington felt that 'bitterness was becoming deeper every hour and an almost reckless determination was growing amongst the workers'.[86]

In a month of unprecedented activity on the streets, the unemployed in the north-east of England also organised to march and take a stand. Demonstrations of up to 30,000 were recorded, but in comparison to south Wales, the response of the unemployed in the north-east was sporadic, delayed and uneven. There is little evidence of a sustained regional campaign against the UABs. Following the pattern of previous years, examples of street demonstrations and marches were exceptional and confined to certain areas. The first significant act of street protest took place on 16 January when Ramsay MacDonald visited Newcastle. As MacDonald stepped off the train at Newcastle station, he was greeted by shouts of 'down with the means test', 'Judas' and 'traitor'. The Prime Minister had to be escorted by a police presence to the hall where he made his speech, and outside hundreds gathered to protest against the means test. Although the audience within the hall had been specially selected, cries of 'down with the means test' interrupted MacDonald's speech.[87] The *Northern Echo* praised MacDonald's 'fighting spirit' and noted that the Prime Minister ended his speech to both 'cheers and hissing'.[88] The demonstration at Newcastle reflected how once more the towns along the Tyne river were to form the setting for events and, as in south Wales, the ribbon settlement provided an important arena for protest. However, it was not until the very end of January that action took place even within this more volatile area of the north-east.

On 31 January, two large demonstrations took place at North Shields. In the afternoon, 5,000 unemployed workers marched to the Smith Docks to call the workers to strike, and some of the marchers entered the local church and rang out the bells to draw attention to events. In the evening, a crowd of an estimated 10,000, including the unemployed and employed, assembled outside the town council and were addressed by members of the NUWM and the Communist Party. In demonstrating, the unemployed were ignoring a ban against marching in the town, a possible aftermath of events in the earlier 1930s.[89] Five days later, another large march and demonstration organised by the NUWM took place on Tyneside against the UABs.[90] A comprehensive account of the demonstration from Jim Ancrum, a member of Felling NUWM, was printed in *Heslop's Local Advertiser*. Ancrum detailed how action began in the area on 9 January with 'a splendid mass meeting' of 1,000 in the Imperia Cinema. Once cuts began to take effect, Felling united with Gateshead NUWM and organised a further meeting on 29 January, attracting 1,100, and then a march to the UAB in Gateshead. The editorial of the paper noted 2,000 men and women marched from Felling, and Ancrum stated a demonstration of 15,000 massed outside the UAB offices.[91] This episode conveys quite succinctly the difficulties in ascertaining how many people participated in marches and demonstrations. The *Daily Worker* initially reported that a march numbering 2,000 from Felling united with another 2,000 marchers at Gateshead where they held the demonstration. The paper later published a correction after 'comrades' from Gateshead and Felling wrote to the paper to state it was actually a crowd of 20,000–30,000. At the higher end, this was double Ancrum's calculation.[92] Whether 2,000 or 30,000, the march still shows that along the Tyne the unemployed could be mobilised and were organised for collective action, principally by the NUWM.

Outside the towns and villages along the Tyne, it appears that there was little sustained activity against the UABs during the first month of their operation. Marches and demonstrations tended to be in areas with an active NUWM branch. In Northumberland, in Blyth, on 29 January the NUWM organised an open-air meeting in the marketplace, and a deputation met with the town council which agreed to pass its resolution. A further march of 200, 'including several women with children', took place on the following Tuesday to the UAB offices. Although there was a 'strong body of police', the *Blaydon Courier* reported that it was 'accepted good-humouredly'.[93] Sunderland likewise remained a key area of action within County Durham. The unemployed were noted with some regularity as active in their response to the means test; the *Manchester Guardian* reported how 'great dissatisfaction exists amongst the unemployed' there.[94] The NUWM was foremost in organising these dissatisfied unemployed. Sunderland was possibly the only area in which a united front was achieved.

On 1 February, an 'all-in' conference was held in the co-operative hall in the town which included ten delegates from trade unions. Mr Masheder, a Communist Party member from Sunderland, noted at the Seventeenth Congress meeting how one of the trade union lodges which attended had previously ruled 'that no NUWM, CP, or other literature connected with the militant movement in any way should be read at a lodge meeting'. Masheder explained how this was the first meeting of its type the party had been able to organise, and it showed 'that the workers are not going to let anything stand in the way of united action against the new Unemployment Bill'.[95] At Birtley, the local branch of the NUWM was also active in its campaign against the UABs. The branch organised public meetings to discuss the Act and deputations to meet with the local PAC. In mid-January, it arranged for the signing of 900 pledge cards by the unemployed to resist the compulsory training camps after a mass meeting was held. The popularity of the Birtley branch led its members to try and extend their activities in the surrounding 'unorganised areas' of Chester-le-Street, Washington and Fatfield.[96]

A number of factors can account for the lower number of street protests within the coalfields in Northumberland and Durham. First, UAB offices were primarily placed in larger towns, and the relative isolation of villages must have hindered communication for coordinating action. Furthermore, with the absence of ribbon settlement, the topography did not provide a 'natural' course for marches and would have worked against more spontaneous activity. What exacerbated the situation was the limited presence of the NUWM within the coalfields. While new branches were formed in Spennymoor and South Bank (Durham) in April 1935, the NUWM failed to make further gains in these months.[97] For many, the DMA remained a vital source of leadership especially as the union had been involved in preparing the unemployed for the new regulations in the weeks leading up to the establishment of the UABs. The organisation of regional, county or even local marches was not, however, a priority of the union.[98]

The most decisive action taken by the DMA against the UABs occurred at an executive committee meeting held on 28 January. The committee announced that they were going to organise a conference of all lodge representatives to be held on 23 February to 'deal with the new Unemployment Insurance Act and Regulations'.[99] The demand for the conference was clearly strong; a new venue had to be found after the original choice with a capacity of 400 was deemed too small, and the scope of representatives was extended to include the North-East Federation of Trades Councils.[100] The conference formed the focus of activity for the DMA, even after the Standstill Act had been announced, and they sent individual letters and resolutions from lodges for the attention of the conference members. The meeting called for a 'united front' which for the DMA, like the executive committee of the SWMF, continued to exclude the Communist Party.

Although important in generating and expressing opposition, the united stance between the DMA, the Labour Party and other trade unions appeared to have achieved little. The official commitment at a regional level was not readily translated into united action at a local level.[101] One rare example of collaboration between the two organisations occurred at Boldon, north of Sunderland, on 3 February 1935. The men's section of the Boldon Labour Party and the local lodge organised a 'mass demonstration' that was attended by councillors, ex-Labour MPs and lodge officials.[102] In contrast to south Wales, individual lodges did not seek collaboration with the Communist Party or NUWM. Indeed, they were actively encouraged not do so as Mr Masheder's comments at the Sunderland all-in conference revealed.

On 22 January, a DMA circular to all lodges urged members not to pledge support for 'an organisation calling itself the "Birtley Unemployed Council"'. The executive committee stated that support from the body was unnecessary as information could be obtained from lodges. Furthermore, the DMA reminded members that 'the Labour Party has put up a strenuous fight against this Act, and it is our duty to support the Labour Party and our trade union movement, thus we will keep and preserve a united front and united movement, and we hope our Lodges will not give any support in any form whatever to this unofficial body'.[103] Another such circular was issued on 5 March warning members to 'refuse to deal' with the 'United Front Movement' which originated from Birtley.[104] The instructions to continue to adhere to DMA leadership resonated with the ideals of many of the unemployed within Durham who were not actively seeking to march against the UABs. While the trigger of drastic reactions was not apparent in the north-east, what was also crucial was the continued antipathy towards collective street action. The DMA did not offer leadership, but neither were many of the unemployed seeking it from more militant bodies like the NUWM. These factors were compounded by the absence of a broader cross-class and cross-community base of support for protest marches, and resolutions continued to be a prominent form of opposition.

On 5 February, at a public meeting in Crook, representatives were present from the Free Churches, Crook Urban Council, the Social Service Centre for the Unemployed and 'other public organisations'. The chair of Durham PAC, G. W. Bloomfield, county councillor J. Armstrong, Father Lamb and Rev. H. Fletcher addressed the meeting of more than 300 and passed a resolution against the UAB regulations and the means test.[105] As well as these specially convened meetings, the matter was also raised at monthly council meetings, principally at the end of January and beginning of February. Newcastle, Sunderland and Durham PACs, Morpeth guardians committee and councils at Newburn, Bishop Auckland and Auckland all passed resolutions of protest in their monthly meetings.[106] The resolutions against the means test show the extent of feeling against the new administration and active protest through written means. Newcastle PAC protested to the Ministry of Labour and appointed members to represent the city council at a national conference to be held at Glasgow on 27 February to discuss the regulations.[107] Sunderland PAC passed its resolution of protest after receiving a deputation from the local branch of the NUWM which requested that the PAC restore any reductions in allowances and that they provided men with relief who refused to attend training camps. The council also decided to send a member to the conference at Glasgow.[108] Labour Party councillors did hold a special meeting of the town council in this instance to discuss the regulations and passed a resolution of protest against the UABs.[109] Perhaps the most indicative comments of the nature of protest in the north-east came from the monthly meeting of Durham PAC.

Durham PAC had been at the forefront of condemnation of the means test in 1931 and 1932. Labour councillors refused to administer the test and continued to protest after commissioners replaced their work. The objection to the means test was stimulated by the concern for residents in County Durham as well as a response to calls from the unemployed. In January 1935, the means test once again dominated debates in the chamber as the unemployed turned to Labour councillors for support. Councillor Lavers at the PAC meeting commented that 'the unemployed of Durham had borne their sufferings as loyal citizens, but when it came to crushing the souls out of women and children they had a right to protest and say that those things should not continue'. A resolution condemning the UABs was sent to the Prime Minister, the Ministry of Labour, the Ministry of Health and the MPs for County Durham.[110] While G. W. Bloomfield noted that 'mass meetings and demonstrations against the Act were being organised in all parts', specific demonstrations in Durham and support of council members were not noted.[111] It was the 'loyalty' of the unemployed in Durham which was emphasised, and energies here, as elsewhere in the region, were focused upon the passing and sending of resolutions. Written opposition satisfied the desire for protest amongst the unemployed and their families.

The mass meetings that were organised and the conferences that were planned reveal a much broader level of discontent against the

Unemployment Act. While the peacefulness of the unemployed in the north-east was emphasised by various groups, the impression should not be taken that the unemployed were in any way apathetic to the changes made to the insurance scheme. Indeed, the *Northern Despatch* even ran a competition for the best answer to the question 'does the means test mean hardship?'[112] The continuation of means testing was a central issue in January and February 1935. J. S. Pearce, the UAB district officer for County Durham, later noted that there was 'agitation in the District against the Regulations' although it 'did not attain the violence experienced in some other parts of the country'.[113] Special correspondents within the region stressed the anger of the unemployed and their dependents throughout the first month of the UABs. In the middle of January, the *Daily Worker* reported how a 'storm of protest [is] growing amongst the wives of the unemployed' in South Shields who were alarmed at the intrusive investigations.[114] The *Daily Herald's* industrial correspondent at Gateshead declared that 'one need not be here long to be convinced how deep is the resentment. Nobody dares in public to defend the regulations, and I have no evidence that they do so in private'. Most illuminatingly, the correspondent noted how 'the situation is being discussed at trade union meetings called for quite other business. These are being better attended than for a long time past, and resolutions of strong protest against the means test are being carried'. The reporter also included the comments of two shopkeepers who complained of the effects of the new changes on their businesses. Both spoke out against the regulations although one noted that he was 'an old-fashioned Tory'.[115] Anger, discontent and opposition were all alive in 1935 in the north-east of England as elsewhere in the country. What makes the response of the unemployed different in comparison to south Wales, and indeed other regions, was that words did not so easily evolve into action.[116] Without an overarching agenda for protest marches, action was not exploited by the labour movement, and demonstrations remained isolated and sporadic with energies focused upon alternative means of protest. Although a wider community spoke out against the test, in the absence of large marches, such support could remain hidden.

By the beginning of February, while marches and demonstrations were gaining impetus in the north-east of England, elsewhere protest was reaching its zenith. Once more, attention focused on the dramatic events in south Wales and the activities of the labour movement. On Friday 1 February, a deputation from Wales of around fifty 'Trade Union, political Labour, and Co-operative representatives and ... representatives of the

National Labour Council' met with Oliver Stanley to discuss objections to the regulations and the UAB's administration of the means test.[117] The representatives mainly came from south Wales, although, interestingly, J. J. Lawson decided the night before the deputation that he should attend to represent England and Neil MacLean (Labour MP, Govan) to represent Scotland.[118] George Lansbury, the leader of the Labour Party, introduced the deputation and the main speakers who were a mixture of councillors and officials from the trade unions.[119] The speakers outlined their case and 'drew attention to the way in which the present Regulations were likely to break up homes, the inadequacy of the scales to meet the needs of life and the extreme hardship caused by the operation of the rent rule and the super cut. There was in addition a great deal of protest against the "inquisition" into homes'.[120] The Minister of Labour responded by stating that it had never been the government's intention to create unnecessary hardship and it had been planned for 'the [Unemployment] Act ... to operate for the benefit of the unemployed'.[121] The Minister agreed to raise the deputation's issues with the UAB and the House of Commons and ended by stating that he was 'personally impressed with the criticism and with the necessity for the review as a matter of urgency'.[122] In light of the events that were to follow, the Minister of Labour rather ironically thanked the deputation 'for the moderate way in which the case had been put forward'.[123] For, while the Minister promised to try and find a reduction or relaxation to the regulations, the unemployed in south Wales were not prepared to wait and the following day protest erupted across the region.

Press accounts of action on the weekend of 2 and 3 February give the impression that the vast majority of the population of south Wales had taken to the streets. The demonstrations on Sunday were deemed to be especially impressive, and as Hywel Francis and Dai Smith have eloquently described, 'it was as if...the whole coalfield had moved out of doors in a proud, defiant act of communal exposure distinguishing their continuing humanity from the blighted, ghost-towns around them'.[124] The estimated numbers marching were simply breathtaking; 15,000 assembled at Blackwood, 30,000 marched from across the Monmouthshire Valley to Pontypool, 30,000 demonstrated at Pontypridd, 40,000 at Aberdare and a further 55,000 congregated at Mountain Ash. The largest recorded demonstration took place in the Rhondda Valleys, and W. H. Mainwaring declared that he had attended a demonstration of 100,000 people. Mainwaring believed that the only people who were not marching were children and those in hospital. Sunday services were noted to have been suspended, and in Tredegar even the children marched as the

Sunday schools were closed. A united front was in evidence at many of these marches, and the breadth of opposition portrayed what a commitment to unity could achieve. The protests drew the attention of many major national publications.[125] Despite the large number of people on the streets, the day's events passed without incident.

The escalating mass of protest was beginning to have repercussions within government. As hundreds of thousands marched in south Wales, members of the central UAB and chief administrative officers in Scotland, Wales and the north of England were called to London to meet with Lord Rushcliffe. After all-day discussions, it was decided that members of the government should be sent across the country to investigate what was happening.[126] Oliver Stanley was scheduled on Tuesday to address the House of Commons on the unemployment assistance situation and speculation heightened as to what announcement he would make. The *Manchester Guardian*, the day before the proclamation was made, reported that 'the widespread explosion of anger against the new regulations and their administration has frightened the government'.[127] To compound the situation, on Monday afternoon events turned to violence in Merthyr, and unemployed marchers and the police clashed. One thousand women marched in a 'blinding snowstorm' to the Merthyr UAB office and on approaching the building were joined by a procession of unemployed men.[128] A deputation of women entered the building, and while inside, a group of men broke through a police cordon, smashed windows and forced their way into the offices. The police had difficulty in restraining the marchers, and the inside of the building was also damaged.[129] The actions of women more than the violence help to explain the interest in what was, as Neil Evans has noted, a 'minor' act of violence.[130] It added, however, to the impression of how easily protests could become more militant affairs and the potential danger of so many on the streets.

On 5 February, after a weekend of debates between the Cabinet and the central UAB, and mass action from the unemployed, Oliver Stanley announced a legal standstill of the Unemployment Act. The Standstill Act, as it became known, allowed transitional payment applicants to be assessed using both the new and old scales thereafter receiving whichever payments were higher. It was imposed indefinitely.[131] Benefit cuts were to be restored when reassessments were made on 14 February leaving applicants waiting at least a fortnight before their payments increased. Miller has argued that 'those who drew up this rule were still unaware of the difference a few shillings could make to the lives of the unemployed, who had no reserves to get them through the week of short pay'.[132] The unemployed acutely conscious of the difference continued to protest. The day after the announcement was made, rioting took place in Sheffield when the police allegedly baton-charged a crowd of 10,000 men and women.[133] The scale of violence led the government to promise an instant restoration of cuts there. Continued protesting elsewhere in the country, coupled with the decision by authorities to ignore the waiting period after the precedent set in Sheffield, led the government to restore cuts everywhere.[134]

Across Britain, the introduction of the Standstill Act was celebrated as a victory for the working class.[135] In south Wales, protestors believed it was their united action which had forced the government's hand.[136] Lewis Jones emphatically declared, 'it is a smashing victory for the united front and a smashing blow for the government. It is a result of mass action'.[137] Initially, the announcement gave the movement against the means test greater stimulus as it was believed that the complete withdrawal of the Act and the means test could be won. In the north-east, the announcement of the standstill gave encouragement and momentum to the protest movement. On Wednesday, 1,500 people marched to Gateshead, and a further 1,000 unemployed marched to the UAB offices at Blyth. The UAB officer at Blyth invited two members of a deputation, which had met with officers, to return in the evening to help reassess certain cases. Meetings and demonstrations were also reported at Houghton-le-Spring and Sunderland.[138] The workless in Jarrow began to participate more readily in demonstrations during the early weeks of February with crowds of up to 4,000 reported.[139] The visit of the Minister of Labour so soon after the introduction and temporary suspension of the regulations caused further action. On 8 February, protesting crowds greeted Oliver Stanley at Newcastle, and 500 people from Newcastle and Gateshead marched to the city hall. Despite a deputation being refused, some of the unemployed managed to enter the meeting, and as Stanley spoke, a group 'walked down the centre of the hall and, shouting at the top of their voices, declared that they protested on behalf of thousands of Newcastle unemployed'.[140] In the subsequent weeks, the unemployed in Blyth continued their protest, turning their attention to the local Conservative MP, Godfrey Nicholson. The *Blyth News* described scenes of 'uproar' following the march of an estimated 300 to a meeting of the local Women's Unionist Association where Nicholson was speaking. Not wishing to see the protests of militants celebrated, Nicholson wrote twice to the paper to question its portrayal of events and downplay the march of the unemployed.[141]

The Labour Party became much more active in organising the unemployed, and unity with the Communist Party was evident in some places.

In Blaydon, 500 unemployed gathered in the Empire Theatre and, given the recent concessions won, were encouraged to protest by Labour councillor J. Wilson. His views were furthered by county councillor Lawther who lamented the lack of action in Durham and declared that they could not simply wait for the next general election. A representative of the local Communist Party, Mr C. Wood, argued that unity within the labour movement, including the Communist Party, was needed.[142] Further Labour Party meetings were noted at Chester-le-Street, Birtley, the Durham Miners' Hall and West Auckland, and the DMA also passed a further resolution.[143] At the end of February, the DMA and Labour Party attempted to rouse the unemployed in the north-east to agitate against the means test at a specially convened conference of the DMA. Joseph Batey encouraged members to draw upon the recent successes: 'if ever there was the need for a clarion call to the people of Durham to wake up it was now'. His characterisation of the working class in Durham is telling:

> now that we have got a real grievance let us display some of the spirit of those who went before and not be afraid to demonstrate. Reforms can be gained only by agitation. If the men and women will not agitate we shall not secure the abolition of the Means Test or Part 2 of the Act. We should press for reforms that will lift the people out of the gutter and place them on to a decent standard of life.[144]

The Standstill Act encouraged action amongst the unemployed in the north-east. The NUWM, however, was quick to capitalise in the upsurge in protests, where the DMA and Labour Party were not. Beyond public meetings, local press reports of mass action in other parts of the country did not lead to calls for greater action amongst the unemployed.[145]

In south Wales, action remained focused on the planned one-day strike for 25 February, and marches continued to draw large numbers. The Communist Party and the NUWM in the region were also motivated by the apparent clear victory of class struggle and maintained their militant stance and leadership. In an open letter published by the Political Bureau of the Communist Party, events in south Wales were once more an exemplar of what could be achieved. The party called for a day of mass action throughout the country for the eve of the planned strike.[146] As action continued, the sympathy expressed by the wider public at the initial marches declined as it was questioned why so many of the unemployed were still protesting despite the apparent concessions. The very visible involvement of the Communist Party and the large number who had marched were not without repercussion and particularly because the police and Home Office felt that the party was responsible for the prolongation of collective action. It was the calling of the one-day strike, in possible breach of the Trade Disputes and Trade Union Act of 1927, which chiefly attracted the attention of the Home Office. Although the SWMF had been involved in the initial calling of a strike, it was the Communist Party that was blamed for the attempted industrial dispute. The south Wales coalfield had long been viewed as a militant region, and the Home Office's response to the planned strike belies the trepidation the government felt in clamping down on the illegal move. The Home Office finally decided that 'the danger of a prosecution in this particular case is that it may incite sympathy for the DW [Daily Worker] amongst (a) people with no communist beliefs who are disquieted by the effect of the new scales ... and (b) amongst the Trade Unionists who dislike the Trade Disputes Act of 1927'.[147]

Reluctant to act, the Home Office relied upon the *Daily Worker* and reports from Captain Lindsay to keep abreast of events. Lindsay's detailed accounts of Communist Party activity were gleaned from police spies based across south Wales. He reported that the desire for a strike had waned by the end of February and was only still advocated within the Rhondda Valleys. Lindsay portrayed the Rhondda Valleys with its 'concentration of the Communist Leaders' as a hotbed of radicalism where the party was gaining ground, attracting 'the support of many individual lodges of the South Wales Miners' Federation, local branches of other Trade Unions, Members of District Councils, certain members of the Clergy of the Church in Wales and Ministers of other religious denominations'.[148] While the extent of such support for the Communist Party may have been exaggerated, Lindsay was right to assume that support for the strike would collapse. Just days before the proposed one-day strike, the executive committee of the SWMF ruled against the action, arguing that energies should be focused on a General Strike throughout Wales to be held on 25 March. This second strike also failed at the final moment when the executive committee again ruled against such action.

On the day before the first strike should have taken place, planned demonstrations still went ahead. On Sunday 24 February, a 'national united front demonstration' took place in Hyde Park. Platform speakers included Hilda Browning and Sam Jennings from south Wales.[149] In the north-east, those areas with an active NUWM responded to the call for action. A 'mass meeting' was held in Blyth to demand the removal of the means test, and in Newcastle the newly formed women's section reported its part in the town's demonstration.[150] In south Wales, tens of thousands participated in individual street protests. The largest demonstrations took place in the Rhondda Valleys, Pontypool, Aberkenfig, Aberdare and Merthyr.[151] The following day, despite the strike being called off, shops did close in some areas of south Wales, and in Nantyglo children refused to go to school.[152] The police response to these protests was very different to those held just weeks previously. The Labour MP for Bedwellty Charles Edwards wrote to Harry Crookshank at the Home Office to complain about police heavy-handedness at Caerphilly. The members of the Abertridwr Lodge claimed that the march held at Caerphilly was 'conducted in an orderly manner' and permission for the route had been received. Importantly, they also noted the affiliation of the SWMF to the protest.[153] The Superintendent at Ystrad Mynach justified police action in breaking up the march at Caerphilly because although demonstrations had earlier been held 'which included all Public and Religious bodies', this particular march 'was organised by unattached undisciplined parties from the surrounding districts'.[154] However, it was the march at Blaina on the date of the second proposed strike that attracted particular attention.

The events of 24 March later became known as the 'Blaina Riots' following the police's depiction of what occurred. Contingents had marched from Blaina, Nantyglo, Abertillery and Brynmawr to meet at Blaina PAC for the purpose of sending a deputation to meet with council officials, although they had been informed a deputation would not be met. Seventy policemen were stationed in Blaina, and when contingents gathered in the town, violence broke out after the police charged the crowd.[155] The Chief Constable of Monmouthshire argued that the crowds 'were "begged" by the Police not to march to the Public Assistance Offices' and they were left with no choice but to baton charge the marchers.[156] However, it later emerged that the reason the PAC officers would not meet with the deputation was because they were not sitting on that day. The police only informed one contingent of this fact once the marchers had set off.[157] In the aftermath of the march, four men were charged with riotous assembly and were imprisoned for nine months and a further five were imprisoned for six months for unlawful assembly.[158] All were known Communists or NUWM members. Although outcry could have been predicted from the Blaina area, what is perhaps more remarkable is the wider breadth of opposition that came from right across Britain.

A memorandum prepared for the Home Secretary, for his review of the case, argued that 'when the Unemployment Assistance Regulations were suspended, the Nantyglo and Blaina unemployed claimed credit and preached the doctrine that by demonstrating anything could be secured. It became obvious to the Police that the demonstrators were depending on numbers to overawe resistance to their demands'.[159] There was no mention here of the united action and wider community support and involvement in the anti-means test demonstrations of January and February 1935, and instead, it was argued that '"Moscow" was a party to the original agitation', although 'here again, proof cannot be produced'.[160] The connection between alleged police brutality and the harsh sentencing of the men was all too clear to councillor Evans when he met months later with the Home Secretary: 'his point was that the Police emphasised that some of the men had belonged to a particular political party and he had never seen such a thing done on any previous occasion'.[161]

The treatment of the Blaina marchers and the government's attitude towards those who took to the streets drew criticism from across Britain; resolutions were sent to the government from bodies as diverse as Rutherglen Branch of the National Union of Railwaymen, an unemployed holiday camp at Clifton Hampden and Nantyglo Church Cricket Club.[162] Bodies from the north-east of England also associated themselves with the protest, revealing further areas of NUWM influence.[163] The constant barrage of written opposition led the government finally to shorten the sentences of the prosecuted men just days before Christmas. The government regretted that this act of clemency would probably be taken as the consequence of a letter written by the wives of those imprisoned.[164] The 'Blaina Riot' exposes quite dramatically how strained were the relations between the police and the unemployed in south Wales.[165] The unemployed who took to the streets continued to be demonised despite the peacefulness of the marches and the involvement of groups beyond the NUWM and the Communist Party. In south Wales, the hope that resulted from the government's concession meant that protest rumbled on into the summer months sometimes attracting large numbers despite police opposition. However, while there was a continuation of action, it was clear by the end of spring that the tempo for protest was slowing and the united front across trade unions, political parties and the wider community had unravelled.

By the end of March 1935, it was apparent that the government was not going to make any further concessions. Many of those who had faced large reductions found their benefit increased as the old scales became applicable. Such increases did not happen in every case, but the impression that this was occurring would have made the UABs less of a political issue and less urgent. Wide-scale protest therefore lost momentum although the means test remained an important issue within both regions despite the worsening industrial situation.[166] In Northumberland, for example, the Labour Party organised meetings and passed resolutions.[167] As the protest movement against unemployment declined, the militancy of working miners heightened. In October 1935, a series of stay-in strikes broke out in the south Wales coalfield. The strikes were part of the campaign against non-unionism, and Francis and Smith argue they emerged from the unemployment demonstrations which 'had created an atmosphere in which sudden action might be attempted on a wider front.'[168] Both the unemployed and the labour movement were well aware that the regulations were only temporarily suspended. However, with the loss of unity, those involved in organising demonstrations recognised that their protest would be largely impotent in forcing the hand of the government. Protest was therefore postponed to the reintroduction of the regulations the following year.

Through the establishment of the UAB, the National Government had hoped to finally remove the unemployment question from politics and wipe out abuse within the system. However, after just a month of the new scales and regulations becoming operational, the Minister of Labour relented to criticism and widespread protest, and the government temporarily suspended the new legislation. This embarrassed the government and the UAB to the extent that A. M. Carr-Saunders argued a year later that the Act had been 'the greatest fiasco in the whole history of social administration in this country'.[169] Wal Hannington believed that the government had been 'thoroughly discredited, its prestige down to zero'. Hannington, similar to many others on the Left, interpreted the Ministry of Labour's concession as the consequence of 'mass action'.[170] For the labour movement, it appeared as if the unemployed had finally won a victory in their battle against the National Government.[171]

The year 1935 was an important year in the history of the working class. The events in January and February were remarkable, and throughout Britain, hundreds of thousands of the unemployed took the streets, often in displays of united community action. At times, even a Popular Front appeared to be in evidence as divergent political parties, trade unions, movements of the unemployed, religious bodies and other community organisations stood united in the streets against a common threat. While at the highest organisational level trade unions and the Labour Party appeared inactive or distanced from what were viewed as the most radical groups, within the localities such matters were deemed irrelevant. Such a unity of action was most evident in south Wales where street protests were orchestrated on a massive scale. Indeed, the Conservative writer H. W. J. Edwards later argued that the means test in 1935 'aroused something of an insurrectionary spirit' in south Wales.[172] Events in south Wales revealed how the unemployed could successfully enter the political arena by taking to the streets, and the Communist Party's celebration of the movement against the means test in the region has continued in the historiography which has emphasised the role of south Wales in events. However, the united and mass action which occurred in south Wales does need a degree of qualification.

The mass marches in the region, although in part a spontaneous uprising of community, had a much longer history. The mobilisation of community during the General Strike and lockout, and the tradition of militant action in the face of an apparent threat to the working class, was significant in 1935. The changing leadership of the unemployed away from the 'traditional' sections of the labour movement, hinted at in the 1927 march to London, allowed the workless to be mobilised by divergent groups and not only by the SWMF or the Labour Party. However, what was imperative to the success of the massive protests was the campaign against the Unemployment Act from early 1933 and the existence of a movement against the means test from late 1931. The combination of these factors allowed in early 1935 for the mass mobilisation of the unemployed soon after cuts were made; the fervour of the movement and its centrality to public debate allowed other organisations within the community to become quickly involved. Although community was in action and unity was apparent, the existence of support for the unemployed should not be exaggerated within south Wales. Whether the street protests showed a united front of community or the United Front of the Communist Party, it was, essentially, a temporary mobilisation. Once the Standstill Act was announced, the widespread support for the unemployed in marches and demonstrations died away as soon as it had begun. Yet, it was significant nonetheless and conveyed both the unity of the labour movement within south Wales and its radicalism. For this reason, the events in south Wales should not be viewed as representative of the response of the unemployed elsewhere.

Only along the Tyne were street demonstrations apparent on any scale, and important comparisons can be drawn here with south Wales. The towns along Tyneside had a greater tradition of militant activity than elsewhere in the region. A movement against the means test, which included marches and demonstrations, had existed since the measure's implementation. Moreover, the topography of the Tyneside industrial belt allowed for marches across a wide geographical area in a similar way to the south Wales valleys. Elsewhere in the north-east region, the relative isolation of the population, a political culture which focused on a policy of coercion, and the continued minority support for the Communist Party and the NUWM ensured that the UABs would not be met with mass collective action. Although anger existed against the continuation of the means test, opposition was in the main expressed through resolutions, meetings and petitions and not street demonstrations. While in south Wales parallels were drawn with the response in 1926, in the north-east, such a return to militancy and community protest did not occur. Conversely, the consequences of the General Strike continued to dictate an aversion to extra-parliamentary collective action.

The response of the unemployed in both south Wales and the north-east of England demonstrates most pertinently how important it is to identify and examine different expressions of protest. Meetings and resolutions reveal the groundwork of opposition that could allow for the fruition of mass action. As Lewis Jones noted, the mass meetings in south Wales were 'the stepping stones for a mighty mobilisation of all workers'.[173] However, such expressions of opposition were protests in their own right and show how the unemployed made their stance in the north-east region.

For the working class and the labour movement, mass action in 1935 gave promise to the achievements of mobilising and marching in the streets, and these factors were to again surface the following year. The labour movement was all too aware in both regions that the Standstill was only a temporary reprieve until the regulations were again introduced in the summer of 1936. Furthermore, the UAB and its rigorous investigation remained despite the fact that the unemployed were entitled to receive the older and more generous scale of the PACs.

Notes

1 *Hansard*, HC (series 5) vol. 297, col. 47 (28 January 1935).

2 Allen Hutt, *The Post-War History of the British Working Class* (London, 1937), p. 264.

3 Frederic Miller, 'The British Unemployment Assistance Crisis of 1935', *Journal of Contemporary History*, 14 (1979), pp. 329–52.

4 The marches feature in practically all histories of the interwar period. For studies of south Wales and the north-east of England, see, *ibid.*; W. R. Garside, *The Durham Miners, 1919–1960* (London, 1971), p. 281; John Stevenson, 'The Making of Unemployment Policy, 1931–1935', in Michael Bentley and John Stevenson (eds), *High and Low Politics in Modern*

Britain (Oxford, 1983), pp. 204–5; Richard Croucher, *We Refuse to Starve in Silence: A History of the National Unemployed Workers' Movement, 1920–46* (London, 1987), pp. 167–71; W. R. Garside, *British Unemployment 1919–1939: A Study in Public Policy* (Cambridge, 1990), pp. 77–9; Hywel Francis and Dai Smith, *The Fed: A History of the South Wales Miners in the Twentieth Century* (Cardiff, 1998), pp. 253–62; Neil Evans, '"South Wales Has Been Roused as Never Before": Marching Against the Means Test, 1934–36', in David W. Howell and Kenneth O. Morgan (eds), *Crime, Protest and Police in Modern British Society: Essays in Memory of David J. V. Jones* (Cardiff, 1999), pp. 176–206; Matt Perry, *Bread and Work: The Experience of Unemployment, 1918–1939* (London, 2000), pp. 110–13; and Lewis Mates, 'Durham and South Wales Miners and the Spanish Civil War', *Twentieth Century British History*, 17: 3 (2006), pp. 378–9, 389.

5 Miller, 'The British Unemployment Assistance Crisis of 1935', pp. 329–52; Garside, *British Unemployment*, pp. 72–80.

6 NLW, Dr Thomas Jones CH Collection, *The Unemployment Assistance Scheme: A Short Guide to Regulations*, p. 20; Garside, *British Unemployment*, pp. 75–9; Miller, 'The British Unemployment Crisis of 1935', pp. 334–5.

7 TNA, AST 12/17, UAB Minutes of Meetings, 23 January 1935, p. 142.

8 Francis and Smith, *The Fed*, p. 253.

9 *Unemployment Bill (Brought from the Commons 15 May, 1934) Explanatory Memorandum on Clauses* (Cmd 4602), 1933–34, xxi, p. 809; *Report of the Unemployment Assistance Board for the Period Ended 31st December 1935* (Cmd 5177), 1935–36, xiii, p. 6; Miller, 'The British Unemployment Assistance Crisis of 1935', p. 333.

10 *Western Mail*, 12 March 1934, p. 14; *Free Press and Rhondda Leader*, 2 December 1933, p. 7; Michael Foot, *Aneurin Bevan: A Biography, Volume One, 1897–1945* (London, 1982), p. 161.

11 South Wales Miners' Library (hereafter, SWML), Swansea University, *The Royal Commission's Final Attack on the Unemployed: To Action Against More Starvation: An Examination of the Late Labour Government's Royal Commission of Unemployment's Final Proposal* (National Unemployed Workers' Movement, London, 1933), p. 2.

12 SCOLAR, Labour Party Archives Microfilm Collection, *Labour and the Unemployment Bill* (London, 1934); *Manchester Guardian*, 13 December 1934, p. 6.

13 *Labour and the Unemployment Bill.*

14 *The Unemployed Leader*, 3:1, May 1934, p. 6 and 3:3, July 1934, p. 4.

15 While Croucher argued that the NUWM discussed the changes made under the Unemployment Assistance Act from mid-1934, he does not note the significance of this. Similarly, although Neil Evans traces opposition from December 1934, and some longer-term activities of the NUWM, he does not outline the impact of this in building-up opposition and laying the

foundations for mass protests. Miller, 'The British Unemployment Crisis of 1935', pp. 335–8; Croucher, *We Refuse to Starve in Silence*, pp. 167–9; Evans, '"South Wales Has Been Roused as Never Before"', pp. 183–4.

16 DRO, Durham County Council PAC Minutes, 30 November 1933, pp. 317–21.

17 TWAS, Newcastle City PAC Minutes, 4 December 1933, p. 298.

18 DMOR, Durham Miners' Association Programme of Council Meeting to be Held on 27 January 1934, p. 2; DMA Minutes of Council Meeting, 27 January 1934, p. 2 and 29 January, p. 2.

19 DMA Minutes of Council Meeting, 29 January, p. 2.

20 TWAS, Colliery Ward, Sunderland, Minutes of the Women's Section of the Labour Party, 23 January 1934.

21 SWCC, MNA/NUM/3/3/43/4, Unemployed Lodges Misc., 1934–39, Letter from Mr W. G. Cooke (Secretary Penllwyngwent Lodge) to the General Secretary, 20 February 1934.

22 SWCC, MNA/NUM/3/1/1/25, SWMF, Minutes of Special Conference 20 January 1934.

23 *Free Press and Rhondda Leader*, 10 February 1934, p. 1.

24 SWCC, MNA/NUM/L/50/A/7, Maerdy Lodge Minute Books, 1934–38, Annual Meeting 22 December 1934; Public Meeting, 27 December 1934.

25 *Aberdare Leader*, 5 January 1935, p. 2.

26 *Report of the Unemployment Assistance Board, 1935*, p. 343.

27 These approximations are based on the number of those receiving transitional benefit in December 1935. The figures would have been higher for the beginning of the year, but there is no accurate record of such data. Given the industrial situation in both regions, the end-of-year figures provide a reasonable guide. *Ibid.*, p. 413.

28 The Unemployment Assistance Board began its work in the autumn of 1934. The Board was chaired by Lord Rushcliffe (Henry Betterton), who had been Minister of Labour until he took up this role, and was composed of a mixture of academics and civil servants with much public welfare and employment schemes experience between them. The other members were Sir Ernest J. Strohmenger (deputy chair), Professor H. M. Hallsworth, Thomas Jones, Violet Markham and Mr M. A. Reynard.

29 TNA, AST 12/16, Unemployment Assistance Board Minutes of Meetings, 9 October 1934, p. 57.

30 *Ibid.*

31 *Ibid.*, p. 53.

32 *Ibid.*, p. 56.

33 *Report of the Unemployment Assistance Board, 1935*, p. 572.

34 GAC, 'Some Notes on the Operation of the Scales of the Unemployment Assistance Board', 14 January 1935.

35 Miller, 'The British Unemployment Crisis of 1935', p. 338.

36 This point was made by county councillor Arthur Pearson at a demonstration in Pontypridd. *Rhondda Fach Gazette*, 2 February 1935, p. 2.

37 *Report of the Unemployment Assistance Board, 1935*, p. 520.
38 *Ibid.*, p. 571.
39 Durham PAC Minutes, 31 January 1935, p. 327.
40 *Manchester Guardian*, 25 January 1935, p. 11.
41 *Rhondda Fach Gazette*, 2 February 1935, p. 7.
42 *Ibid.*
43 It should be noted that the resolution was not passed unanimously, and while some members believed they should wait until more was known about the Act, Mr A. S. Fowler left the meeting in protest that the chamber should discuss the matter at all. *Aberdare Leader*, 12 January 1935, p. 4.
44 *Free Press and Rhondda Leader*, 26 January 1935, p. 1.
45 *Aberdare Leader*, 19 January 1935, p. 2 and 2 February 1935, pp. 1, 3.
46 *Daily Herald*, 29 January 1935, p. 1.
47 *Rhondda Fach Gazette*, 2 February 1935, p. 6.
48 *Aberdare Leader*, 19 January 1935, p. 2.
49 Evans, '"South Wales Has Been Roused as Never Before"', p. 184.
50 SWCC, SWMF Minutes of the Executive Council, 5 January 1935.
51 SCOLAR, Microfilm: Papers from the Communist Party of Great Britain Archives: Wal Hannington Papers, CP/IND/HANN/01/06, NUWM NAC Circular, 'Big Fight Against New Unemployment Assistance Scales Developing In South Wales', no date.
52 CP/IND/HANN/01/02, NUWM NAC Circular D24, 19 December 1934, Circular D27, 28 December 1934, Circular D28, 1 January 1935.
53 Reginald J. Barker, *Christ in the Valley of Unemployment* (Suffolk, 1936), pp. 31–44.
54 *Daily Worker*, 8 January 1935, p. 1.
55 From January 1930, the lodge was excluded from the SWMF because of its connection to the Communist Party. SWCC, MNA/NUM/L/50/A, Maerdy Lodge Minute Books, 19 January 1935 and 25 January 1935; Francis and Smith, *The Fed*, pp. 165–7.
56 Maerdy Lodge Minute Books, 10 January 1935.
57 TNA, HO 45/23590, Disturbances: Demonstrations Against Unemployment Legislation: Communist Incitement to Strike in South Wales Coalfields, 1927–35, Minutes, January 1935.
58 For example, on the weekend of 12 and 13 January, 1,500 marched to the UAB at Nantyglo and persuaded the officials to agree that a nourishment grant would not be taken into account when assessing need. *Daily Worker*, 16 January, 1935, p. 4.
59 *Free Press and Rhondda Leader*, 26 January 1935, p. 6; *Daily Worker*, 21 January 1935, p. 1.
60 *Free Press and Rhondda Leader*, 26 January 1935, p. 6.
61 The *Daily Herald* reported the march under the headline 'Valley Makes History'. *Daily Herald*, 21 January 1935, p. 11.
62 *Daily Worker*, 21 January 1935, p. 1.

63 *Free Press and Rhondda Leader*, 26 January 1935, p. 6.

64 *Daily Worker*, 22 January 1935, p. 3.

65 *Daily Worker*, 23, 25 and 29 January and 5 February 1935; *Free Press and Rhondda Leader*, 2 February 1935; *Aberdare Leader*, 2 February 1935; *Unemployed Leader Special*, 3:10, February, 1935. Such reported figures were susceptible to exaggeration, and the figure of 300,000 in particular deserves some explanation. On 5 February, the *Daily Worker* claimed that the *Manchester Guardian* had reported that 300,000 people had marched in south Wales. This report did not actually appear in the *Manchester Guardian*, and instead the paper recorded a number of individual marches whose figures do not add up to 300,000. It was, in fact, *The Times* which reported the figure stating 'it is estimated that 300,000 people attended indoor and outdoor meetings'. The figure of 300,000 has faced little dispute within secondary sources. In reality, attempting to record with any accuracy the number of people marching within south Wales would have been and is impossible. On Sunday, 3 February, action took place across the region, and it is probable that numbers marching did near 300,000. With all statistics relating to marches, what is perhaps more important than accuracy is the impressionistic value of just how many people were willing to participate in protest. *The Times*, 4 February 1935, p. 14.

66 Hutt, *The Post-War History of the British Working Class*, p. 264.

67 The protests in south Wales are mentioned in practically every addition of the *Daily Herald* between 21 January and 7 February, and they similarly dominated reports of action in the *Manchester Guardian*. *Daily Herald*, 21 January 1935–37 February 1935; *Manchester Guardian*, 7 January 1935–34 February 1935.

68 *Daily Worker*, 24 January 1935, p. 1.

69 *The Unemployed Leader*, 3:10, February 1935, p. 8.

70 GRO, Monmouthshire County Council PAC Minutes, 24 January 1935, p. 334.

71 *Aberdare Leader*, 2 February 1935, p. 1; *Rhondda Fach Gazette*, 2 February 1935, p. 4; *Free Press and Rhondda Leader*, 26 January 1935, p. 1.

72 *Free Press and Rhondda Leader*, 26 January 1935, p. 1.

73 *Aberdare Leader*, 26 January 1935, p. 4.

74 Francis and Smith, *The Fed*, pp. 257–8; Evans, '"South Wales Has Been Roused as Never Before"', p. 184.

75 *Manchester Guardian*, 25 January 1935, p. 11.

76 SWCC, MNA/NUM/L/20/A, Cambrian Lodge, Committee Meeting, 15 January 1935.

77 The NAC celebrated the creation of fifty-five new branches across Britain between 17 November 1934 and 8 February 1935. Branches were asked to use the protests as a way of drawing in new members. NUWM NAC Circular D49, 7 March 1935.

78 This again highlights how the valleys were an important arena of protest.

79 *Daily Worker*, 29 January 1935, p. 1.
80 The 'great emphasis on classic middle-class values' embodied during the hunger marches, as Matthias Reiss noted, was relevant also during these local marches. Matthias Reiss, 'Not All Were Apathetic: National Hunger Marches as Political Rituals in Interwar Britain', in Jörg Neuheiser and Michael Schaich (eds), *Political Rituals in Great Britain 1700–2000* (Augsburg, 2006), p. 117.
81 HO 45/23590, Disturbances, Demonstrations Against Unemployment Legislation, Communist Incitement to Strike in South Wales Coalfields, 1927–35, Minutes, January 1935.
82 This did occur, however, after the Standstill Act.
83 TNA, HO 144/20132, Correspondence between Will John and the Home Secretary, 21 March 1935.
84 *Daily Herald*, 30 January 1935, p. 4, 31 January 1935, pp. 1, 4 and 1 February 1935, p. 8.
85 *Daily Herald*, 30 January 1935, p. 4 and 31 January 1935, p. 4.
86 Wal Hannington, *Ten Lean Years: An Examination of the Record of the National Government in the Field of Unemployment* (London, 1940), p. 136.
87 *Manchester Guardian*, 17 January 1935, p. 11; *Daily Worker*, 18 January 1935, p. 1.
88 The paper did not note any demonstrations that had taken place. *Northern Echo*, 18 January 1935, p. 1.
89 *Daily Worker*, 1 February 1935, p. 3; *The Unemployed Leader*, 3:10 February, 1935, p. 6; Hannington, *Ten Lean Years*, p. 134.
90 *Daily Worker*, 5 February 1935, p. 3 and 7 February 1935, p. 2.
91 *Heslop's Local Advertiser and Monthly Record*, 15 February 1935, pp. 4–7.
92 *Daily Worker*, 1 February 1935, p. 3.
93 *Blaydon Courier*, 31 January 1935, p. 5 and 7 February 1935, p. 1.
94 For example, the *Daily Worker* noted how on 28 January the Sunderland branch of the Labour Party held a demonstration against Unemployment Act at West Park. *Manchester Guardian*, 30 January 1935, p. 9; *Daily Worker*, 2 February 1935, p. 7.
95 *Daily Worker*, 4 February 1935, p. 5.
96 *Ibid.*, 21 January 1935, p. 3.
97 CP/IND/HANN/01/04, *Headquarters Newsletter*, No. 1, c. April 1935.
98 This was true of the Northumberland Miners' Association which was involved in a dispute of 10,000 over the employment of non-union men. *Daily Express*, 14 January 1935, p. 19.
99 DMOR, Durham Miners' Association Executive Committee Minutes, 28 January 1935, p. 15.
100 *Daily Herald*, 4 February 1935, p. 8.
101 It is impossible to ascertain the situation at a local level because of the inaccessibility of individual lodge records. However, it can be generalised from the available sources that there was little active collaboration between the two.

102 *South Shields Gazette*, 4 February 1935, p. 3.
103 DMA Executive Committee Minutes, Circular, 22 January 1935.
104 DMA Executive Committee Minutes, Circular, 5 March 1935.
105 *Auckland Chronicle*, 8 February 1935, p. 9.
106 *Ibid*., pp. 7–8; *Blaydon Courier*, 9 February 1935, p. 8; *Stanley News and Durham County Advertiser*, 8 February 1935, p. 7.
107 Newcastle PAC Minutes, 4 February 1935, pp. 449–54.
108 TWAS, County Borough of Sunderland PAC Minutes, 4 February 1935, pp. 154–7.
109 *Daily Herald*, 30 January 1935, p. 4; *Daily Worker*, 7 February 1935, p. 2.
110 Durham PAC Minutes, 31 January 1935, p. 327; *Durham County Advertiser and Durham Chronicle*, 1 February 1935, p. 2.
111 *Northern Echo*, 1 February 1935, p. 3.
112 *Northern Despatch*, 2 February 1935, p. 1.
113 *Report of the Unemployment Assistance Board, 1935*, p. 465.
114 *Daily Worker*, 12 January 1935, p. 3.
115 *Daily Herald*, 4 February 1935, p. 8.
116 Andrew Richards has argued that 'sudden adverse economic fluctuations' do not always lead to protest and emphasises the importance of 'identity formation' in generating collective action. Andrew Richards, 'Mobilizing the Powerless: Collective Protest Action of the Unemployed in the Interwar Period', Working Paper 175, Juan March Institute (2002), p. 6.
117 AST 12/17, UAB Minutes of Meeting, 'Note of a Statement made on 1st February, 1935, by the Minister of Labour to a Deputation From Wales', 1 February 1935, p. 153.
118 *Northern Echo*, 1 February 1935, p. 1.
119 They were James Griffiths (Chair, SWMF), Alderman Sadler (Chair, Monmouthshire PAC), Mr Tooley (Transport and Gas Workers' Union), Alderwoman Rose Davies (Glamorgan County Council) and Walter Citrine (Secretary, TUC). 'Note of a Statement made on 1st February, 1935, by the Minister of Labour to a Deputation From Wales', p. 153.
120 *Ibid*.
121 *Ibid*., p. 154.
122 *Ibid*.
123 *Ibid*.
124 Francis and Smith, *The Fed*, p. 274.
125 *Rhondda Fach Gazette*, 9 February 1935, p. 6; *Aberdare Leader*, 9 February 1935, p. 8; *Manchester Guardian*, 4 February 1935, p. 9; *Daily Herald*, 4 February 1935, pp. 8, 11; *Daily Worker*, 4 February 1935, p. 1.
126 TNA, AST 12/18, Unemployment Assistance Board, Minutes of Meetings, 4–6 February 1935, pp. 2–4.
127 *Manchester Guardian*, 4 February 1935, p. 8.
128 NLW, Idris Cox Collection, Item no. 44, Rhondda Communist Party, *South Wales in the March of History: A Message to YOU from the Communist*

Party (Tonypandy, c.1937), p. 9. For a fictionalised account of this event see Lewis Jones, *We Live* (London, 1939), pp. 238–52.

129 *Manchester Guardian*, 5 February 1935, p. 11; *Daily Herald*, 5 February 1935, p. 9; *Daily Worker*, 5 February 1935, p. 1.

130 Evans, '"South Wales Has Been Roused as Never Before"', p. 185.

131 CAB 27/575, Cabinet Committee on the Regulations of the Unemployment Assistance Board, 6 February 1935, pp. 1–6; Miller, 'The British Unemployment Crisis of 1935', pp. 341–2; *Unemployment Assistance (Temporary Provisions). A Bill To make temporary provision for securing as nearly as may be that the allowance payable under Part II of the Unemployment Act, 1934, to persons who but for the operation of subsection (2) of section fifty-nine of that Act would at any time since the sixth day of January nineteen hundred and thirty-five have been entitled to transitional payments that would have been payable to them but for the operation of the said sub-section; to postpone the second appointed day for the purposes of the said Act; and for purposes connected with matters aforesaid*, 1934–35, iv, pp. 469–73.

132 Miller, 'The British Unemployment Crisis of 1935', p. 343.

133 *Daily Herald*, 7 February 1935, p. 1.

134 Hannington, *Ten Lean Years*, pp. 137–8.

135 The *Daily Herald* argued it was a 'memorable triumph for Labour's campaign'. *Daily Herald*, 6 February 1935, p. 1.

136 The Rhondda Communist Party later declared that 'South Wales showed the way to the rest of the country in commencing the agitation which forced the Government to withdraw the 1935 Regulations'. Rhondda Communist Party, *South Wales in the March of History*, p. 12.

137 *Daily Worker*, 7 February 1935, p. 1.

138 *Ibid.*, pp. 1–2.

139 *Ibid.*, 8, 11, 13, 18 and 27 February 1935.

140 *Northern Echo*, 9 February 1935, p. 1.

141 *Blyth News*, 18 February 1935, pp. 1, 3 and 21 February 1935, p. 3.

142 *Blaydon Courier*, 16 February 1935, p. 8.

143 *Auckland Chronicle*, 15 February 1935, p. 4, and 22 February 1935, pp. 3–4; DMA Executive Committee Meeting, 18 February 1935, pp. 27–9.

144 *Auckland Chronicle*, 1 March 1935, p. 6.

145 The largest demonstrations within south Wales were reported in the regional press. *Northern Echo*, 4 February 1935, p. 1, 5 February 1935, p. 1, and 7 February 1935, p. 1; *Northern Despatch*, 6 February 1935, p. 1; DMA Executive Committee Meeting, Circular, 5 March 1935.

146 *Daily Worker*, 9 February 1935, p. 1; NUWM NAC Circular D41, 'All Out on Feb. 24th: A Mighty Day of Demonstrating', 14 February 1935.

147 HO 45/23590, Agitation Against the Unemployment Act, 1934, Communist Activity, Minutes of Evidence, 30 January 1935 and 31 January 1935.

148 HO 45/23590, Correspondence between Captain Lindsay and Harry Crookshank, the Under Secretary of State, 21 February 1935.

149 CP/IND/HANN/01/12, Official Programme of the National United Front Demonstrations at Hyde Park, Sunday, 24 February 1935.
150 The women's section was formed as a consequence of the increased interest in the movement following the NUWM's campaign against Part II. *Blyth News*, 25 February 1935, p. 2; *Unemployed Leader*, 3:11, March 1935, p. 8.
151 *Daily Worker*, 25 February 1935, pp. 1, 4.
152 *Ibid.*, 26 February 1935, p. 1.
153 SWCC, MNA/NUM/3/3/43/4, Correspondence between W. Lewis, Secretary of the Abertridwr Lodge, and Oliver Harris, Secretary of the SWMF, 27 February 1935.
154 HO 144/20132, Correspondence between Charles Edwards and Captain Harry Crookshank, 9 April 1935, Correspondence between Captain Lindsay and the Superintendent at Ystrad Mynach, 17 April 1935.
155 Diane Preece, '"Defend the rights of the roads your fathers fought for": The Blaina Riot of 1935', *Llafur*, 10:2 (2009), pp. 73–100.
156 HO 144/20032, Correspondence, Chief Constable of Monmouthshire to C. D. C. Robinson (Home Office), 27 July, 1935.
157 HO 144/20032, Minutes of Deputation of Representatives from South Wales Meeting With the Home Secretary, Councillor Evans' Comments, 23 September 1935.
158 HO 144/20032, Resolutions and Protests Against Sentences.
159 HO 144/20032, Memorandum to the Home Secretary from C. D. C. Robinson, 12 August 1935.
160 HO 144/20032, C. D. C. Robinson from the Home Office, 6 August 1935.
161 HO 144/20032, Minutes of Deputation of Representatives from South Wales Meeting With the Home Secretary, Councillor Evans' Comments, 23 September 1935.
162 The NUWM issued a circular requesting that protests be held and resolutions passed. HO 144/20032, Correspondence between the Home Secretary and the National Union of Railwaymen, 22 July 1935, Unemployed Holiday Camp, Clifton Hampden, 21 July 1935, Nantyglo Church Cricket Club, 29 July 1935; NUWM NAC Circular D78, 1 August 1935.
163 HO 144/20032, Correspondence between the Home Secretary and J. Gibbons (on behalf of 'a meeting ... of Jarrow Workers'), 21 July 1935, Bishop Auckland NUWM, 15 August, 1935.
164 HO 144/20032, Correspondence from Mildred Abraham, 18 December 1935, Minutes of Evidence, 20 December 1935.
165 In May, an 'All-Monmouthshire Conference' was organised to discuss police action. *Unemployed Leader*, 3:13, May 1935, p. 5.
166 Will Lawther wrote a letter to Ernest Brown, the Minister of Labour, urging him to resign over the unemployment policy which he described as 'class legislation with a vengeance'. *Manchester Guardian*, 18 April 1935, p. 13.

167 *Auckland Chronicle* 11 March 1935, p. 1 and 14 March 1935, p. 4 and 21 March 1935, p. 5.
168 Francis and Smith, *The Fed*, p. 281.
169 A. M. Carr-Saunders, 'The Unemployment Assistance Board', *The Political Quarterly*, 7:4 (1936), p. 538.
170 Hannington, *Ten Lean Years*, pp. 139, 137.
171 Croucher, *We Refuse to Starve in Silence*, pp. 170–1.
172 H. W. J. Edwards, *The Good Patch* (London, 1938), p. 81.
173 Lewis Jones, *From Exchange and Parish to the PAC: For Decency and Destitution* (Central Marchers' Council, Tonypandy, n.d.), p. 16.

6

Towards the welfare state: class, community and collective action, 1936–41

> I have never seen the Tory members of the House of Commons so moved as when we were discussing the Bill to prevent the export of worn-out horses. Naturally we are all anxious to suppress cruelty to animals, and the scandal of the business ... but to see MPs who constantly refuse to abolish the Means Test ... almost weeping over the trade in horses was a strange sight. What is it that makes a man or woman, refuse to assist hungry children, and yet shed tears on animals?
>
> Emanuel Shinwell, Labour MP, Seaham Harbour, March 1937.[1]

> There are men of strong and independent character whose vitality has been so sapped by long employment and insecurity that to-day, when they are summoned to appear before a court of referees or U.A.B. investigators, they go in fear trembling – scared lest the last mean dregs be taken from them. I have seen men, when waiting to go before such investigators, trembling and on the verge of collapse. It is fear not so much for their own fate as that who are dependent on them.
>
> Wal Hannington, *The Problem of the Distressed Areas* (1937).[2]

Working-class novels like Walter Greenwood's *Love on the Dole* (1933), Walter Brierley's *Means-Test Man* (1935), Lewis Jones's *We Live* (1939) and, post-war, Gwyn Thomas's *Sorrow for Thy Sons* (1986) evoke a gritty realist image of depression-era Britain as a time of hardship and poverty.[3] These novels did as much to bolster the image of the 'Devil's decade' as *Vile Bodies* for the Jazz Age and 'Bright Young People'.[4] In *Love on the Dole*, and the other works, the means test features as either a plot device, shaping protagonists' experiences, or, as a background sub-narrative, an essential detail to contemporary life. In doing so, the novelists demonstrate why the means test became one of the best remembered features of the 1930s. It was the dramatic imagery of the novels, and later feature films, alongside what Matt Perry terms the 'lived experiences' of the decade which explain the prominence of the means test in popular memories of the interwar period.[5] While unemployment figures began to decline from 1935 as rearmament commenced, such improvements were not universal. Unemployment and the means test continued to affect large sections of the population and principally those living within the depressed areas. In the later 1930s, the image and legacy of the means test was secured and especially by the generation which lived within those areas which did not share in the recovery.

In June 1936, while the registered level of unemployment nationally at 13.5% showed an improved economic situation, in south Wales and the north-east of England, the recovery was less dramatic. Many Labour Exchanges reported well over a third or as many as a half of their work-force remained unemployed. In both regions, the long-term unemployed formed a hard core of those in the dole queue with 69% of all unemployed being means-tested in the north-east and 66% in south Wales.[6] National and regional trends hid those black spots such as Pontlottyn with 74.2% recorded as being unemployed. In some areas, Labour Exchange figures were combined to produce a lower average; this can be seen in the case of Jarrow and Hebburn.[7] Such adjustments aside, even on the eve of the Second World War unemployment still hovered between 10 and 20% in many areas of both regions and rose to over a third in others.[8] Added to the registered unemployed were those receiving public assistance and those unemployed who received neither. Unemployment was, therefore, part of the social landscape of south Wales and the north-east of England. The experiences of the long-term unemployed hardened by years without work undoubtedly contributed to the creation of the legacy of the means test; the Standstill Act had not lessened the impact of rigorous investigations. Within British society more broadly, the impact of the 'intractable million' unemployed could have only been ignored by the closed world of the wealthiest elite. In the popular press, in newsreels and in many other political and cultural mediums, unemployment and the means test were more than a novelist's backdrop.

Under the premierships of Stanley Baldwin (1935–37) and Neville Chamberlain (1937–40), the National Government continued to focus upon reforming the unemployment benefit system under the UAB. In late 1936, the revised regulations of the previous year were introduced, with cuts gradually implemented over an eighteen-month period. A rigorous means test examination remained, although the government ensured cuts were not as drastic and highlighted improvements in benefits for women and larger families.[9] The means test continued to affect the long-term unemployed, and the last stage of cuts arrived in the autumn of 1938. The test was finally abolished in May 1941 and was replaced with a personal (rather than household) investigation into need.

The decision to abolish the household means test occurred almost ten years after it had first been introduced, and the decision followed eighteen months of political wrangling over the measure. Whether the elderly should face a household means test before receiving a pension and whether wartime savings would be included in an investigation of means forced Ministers to consider a measure that had plagued the National Government for much of the 1930s. On 6 November 1940, the Prime Minister, after months of negotiation, announced that legislation would be introduced 'to remove causes for complaint against the household means test for Unemployed Assistance and Supplementary Pensions'.[10] Debate about the new legislation continued at the beginning of the following year: Labour MPs and Ernest Bevin, the Minister of Labour, were particularly vocal.[11] The following May saw the formal end of household investigations into means, and, as *The Times* noted, the event marked the advent of 'a new era of social help'.[12] In the end, the means test was abolished not as a consequence of mass protest and social unrest but after political discussion against the far more tumultuous backdrop of total war. Public opinion mattered much more in wartime. By abolishing the means test, the government sought to promote morale and appeal to Labour politicians and those who had endured the test's hardship.[13]

Rearmament, the rise of continental fascism, appeasement, the abdication crisis and the Spanish Civil War stimulated more column inches and parliamentary speeches after 1935, and the rise in the standard of living also lessened the preoccupation with the depression. Yet, within the rapidly changing social climate of the later 1930s, the negative view of the means test abided, provoking outcry and securing its place in popular legacies. For these reasons, the actions of the wartime government were mirrored in the social policy of post-1945 governments which only used a household means test tentatively for any form of benefit.[14] The impact of the means test in the closing years of the 1930s was intrinsic to its post-war legacy and influence. The rhetoric the means test generated and the findings of social investigators and politicians were likewise essential in the growing debates about welfare reform and the relationship between citizens and the state.

In assessing the reason why the means test became embedded in popular memories of the period and was key to working-class experience in south Wales and the north-east, the work of social investigators is crucial.

In the later 1930s, social investigators continued to be drawn to south Wales and the north-east of England.[15] The stagnation of industry provided a special case study for sociologists and political propaganda for left-wing intellectuals eager to publicise the human cost of capitalism's weaknesses. Eli Ginzberg, an American sociologist, travelled to south Wales for this very purpose.[16] As the economic revival began, focusing attention upon the depressed regions became all the more urgent as the sociologist Henry Mess noted.[17] It was such concerns that prompted the second set of industrial surveys and the Labour Party's own investigations into the depressed regions.[18] For Eli Ginzberg, the educationist and reformer John Newsom and Jarrow's Labour MP Ellen Wilkinson, the means test remained one of the chief complaints of the unemployed.[19] Wilkinson questioned 'why … is the Means Test so bitterly resented, that in an area like Jarrow a local speaker has only to hiss out the words to rouse any working-class audience to the same fury which they would have shown at the mention of the Poor Law in pre-war days?'[20] The contribution of social surveys to public and political debate about the means test, and unemployment more broadly, helps to explain why the government took special interest in those reports on unemployment over which they had influence.

George Orwell's *The Road to Wigan Pier* may stand as one of the best known social investigations of the period, but it is the Pilgrim Trust's *Men Without Work* which is most drawn upon by historians. The report funded by the Carnegie Trust aimed to compare the impact of unemployment across Britain.[21] While *Men Without Work* is, quite rightly, a key work for an examination of the lives and lifestyle of the unemployed, the government's hand behind the manuscript has been overlooked. With Thomas Jones serving as the first secretary of the Pilgrim Trust and a member of the UAB, a close relationship developed between the government and the report authors.[22] The final report of the Pilgrim Trust was not censored in any official sense, but passages relating to the means test were certainly reframed to avoid negative publicity for the government. For example, in the first draft of the report, a section was included on the impact of a household means test on families.[23] The findings of the effects of enforced financial support within homes went to the very heart of criticisms against the means test. The Trust authors concluded 'we have said above that we do not consider the sample taken to give adequate grounds for a full description of "Means Test Psychology". On the other hand, it does suggest that there are certain types of cases that cause what is perhaps a disproportionate amount of anxiety and resentment'.[24] Following correspondence between Wilfrid Eady and the report authors, the decision was reached to cut the section 'on the ground of it being too flimsy'.[25]

The initial conclusions the *Men Without Work* authors reached on how the means test could cause families to separate also caused disquiet. In the first draft of the manuscript, the Trust had argued that a generalisation from the figure of the eighteen homes where the authors had found families had separated would give an estimated number of 7,500 homes being broken up. W. Nevard noted that other such generalisations had been made elsewhere in the report and 'in view of these considerations it will, no doubt, be thought desirable that an officer of Administrative Division should read the report with an eye to the effect which its publication is likely to have on public opinion'.[26] The estimation was left out of the published report, and instead it was argued, in a footnote, that only eighteen cases had been found where the home had split but that 'we had come across several instances where leaving home was a "put up job"'.[27] The government's involvement in this report highlights the continued public interest in the means test and the sensitivity of the issue. While conclusions in *Men Without Work* were altered to suit governmental concerns for public opinion, in other social surveys reports proliferated of the disastrous effects of the means test on family life.

Claims about family separation were highly emotive, controversial and a difficult argument to disprove as deception was common. One of the major reasons for breaking the law and deceiving the means test man was to maintain the family unit while receiving larger transitional payments. Unemployed or wage-earning sons and daughters, in some instances, only pretended to leave the family home by securing an alternative address. *Disinherited Youth*, a report for the Carnegie Trust into the impact of youth unemployment, noted that although the practice was 'not so widespread as is sometimes assumed', some unemployed youths paid landladies around 2s. to 3s. for use of her address. A 'runner' informed applicants of their need to return to their official address when inspectors or investigators called. The authors found it 'most regrettable ... that such a state of affairs exist'.[28] Beatrice Wood from south Wales recalled in her autobiography how her family established such an arrangement. Wood's brother told officials he was living with a friend of the family when in fact he stayed at home. Wood argued that 'there was a lot of people doing it'. The main problem was 'that the Means Test Man would call when you least expected him', and so Wood and her family had to devise ways of hiding her brother in the pantry.[29]

Evidence of deception allowed the government to deny that home life was seriously affected, although it failed to bury the belief entirely. Indeed, the suggestion that government policy led to the break-up of families was damaging enough for it to commission its own enquiries into the issue. The Ministry of Labour issued a memorandum based on findings from the UAB in August 1935. Attempts to falsely secure extra funds were highlighted, and the UAB reminded the Ministry that the argument that families separated because of the 'administration of public assistance' had 'been made for at least 40 years' although 'there has never been much evidence in support of it'.[30] Despite the confidence in these assertions, UAB offices at a regional level were asked to monitor the situation. In south Wales and the north-east of England, the conclusions of UAB officers tallied with government accounts. J. S. Pearce, the Durham district officer, was keen to report that although the Board had found 250 cases of homes separating, these were not significant enough to cause alarm. How seriously officers took the belief of widespread collusion in such cases was revealed by the refusal to increase payments for those homes where officers believed they detected falsification.[31]

Despite these positive accounts from UAB officers, reports of family break-up continued to burgeon from left-wing parties, social investigators and intellectuals.[32] The perception of damaged family life was as important as the reality, and especially for memories of the means test.[33] Whether or not the means test led many homes to separate is highly debateable, yet few could deny that the means test was having negative repercussions for social harmony at the family hearth. While the desire for financial gain was stressed in official reports, in working-class households emotional rather than economic reasoning lay behind many attempts at collusion. Indeed, economically, the financial incentive was not particularly high: when the son or daughter's income was not included, transitional payments made up the difference. There were little economic benefits for such a high risk activity.[34] It was the disruption to 'normal' domestic hierarchies based on both work (formal and informal) and financial independence that explains why homes were reported to have separated in south Wales and the north-east, despite the strong attachment to family within working-class culture.[35] For those families that stayed together, and formed the majority of means test applicants, it was the psychological impact of the means test which was most damaging.[36] In the north-east and south Wales, the UAB's stricter assessment and the higher proportion of earning members in households undoubtedly contributed to the greater unease over this issue.

It was the compelled financial assistance of earning family members that gave rise to friction within households as John Newsom found to be the case for familial relations in Durham.[37] Tension existed not only between parents and children but also amongst siblings.[38] Eli Ginzberg commented that unemployed siblings in south Wales 'frequently feel great resentment toward their more fortunate brothers and sisters who are in employment. In part this resentment flows from a realization that even the cigarettes which they, the unemployed, smoke deprive the working member of the household of pleasure that he has earned'.[39] The increased tension in households was in no small part the consequence of the perceived attack on masculinity. It is worth stressing again how in both regions a masculinist culture was hegemonic and the hierarchy of a working-class household was structured along gender lines.[40] For many men, it was increasingly difficult to identify with the normative work-centred masculine identity. Social surveyors singled out both the older and younger worker for particular attention as they were affected by unemployment disproportionably.[41] For younger and older men, prolonged unemployment brought dramatic changes to the 'normal' life cycle pattern; older workers faced permanent joblessness as much as a decade before they should have, and younger workers may not have entered employment at all. The departure from these norms impacted negatively on men who attached pride, status and gendered identity to work.[42] While the inability to earn a wage in itself undermined the masculine sense of self, the means test exacerbated the situation through its enforced dependency.

The hierarchy of working-class households was transformed when fathers were forced to become dependent upon their children. The assertion of masculine identity was at best increasingly difficult and, at worst, an impossibility, especially when daughters became breadwinners. John Newsom recorded such feelings in his investigation:

> if unemployment be prolonged it means in a great many cases that a man's status in his own household is greatly undermined. He is no longer breadwinner; indeed, he may have to go cap in hand to his own children for money wherewith to buy baccy and cigarettes. When this happens the cup of bitterness is overflowing. On one occasion I was having tea with a family in which, although the two daughters were at work, the father had been unemployed for over a year. When his wife and I had been served he stretched out his hand to help himself, but was stopped by his wife with the exclamation 'Mary and Doris must chose first, after all they are the breadwinners'. Such a scene trivial though it may appear has its elements of tragedy.[43]

The loss of independence and therefore status could have a demoralising effect on male breadwinners. In a heartfelt description of the experience of unemployment, an unemployed miner from south Wales declared:

> people wonder why men commit crime and lose their balance when their applications for jobs have been refused time after time; they think that the unemployed are having a good time because they are idle. Yet here am I, who have become a pauper through having to depend upon my children for a living. I have always stood for independence, but now I have been compelled to lose mine through no fault of my own.[44]

The only way of restoring the hierarchy of a household and allowing a father to reassert his masculine identity was for some kind of financial independence to resume through full transitional payments.

While male breadwinners found their notions of masculinity undermined, the very construction of an adult masculine identity became much more difficult for unemployed youths. Without employment, the transition for youths from dependence to independence could not be made; in homes with working members, an unemployed person remained reliant on earning parents or became reliant on siblings. The authors of *Disinherited Youth* expressed much concern about the effects of the means test on notions of self-respect and masculinity: 'all the unpopular activities associated with the Means Test, the enquiries into family circumstances, the home visitations, the stripping of all privacy from life, are blows aimed at their pride'. The authors concluded that 'the possibility that the unemployment regulations may themselves be responsible for his living away from home, makes one doubt whether the Means Test, as presently operated, is in any real sense a saving to the State, if indeed it is not contributory cause of social and moral delinquency'.[45] Leaving the family home was one way in which younger men could attempt to gain independence. Young unemployed women who would have normally been expected to work before marriage must have faced a similar struggle to assert their independence; their predicament did, however, not raise nearly as much alarm.[46]

It was not only the lack of financial independence which stilted the progression to manhood. Other 'normal' paths in the life cycle were also greatly disrupted, and this was not only the case for unemployed young men. Working sons who supported families and young women who were courting found themselves unable to marry in the absence of the vital savings needed to secure a marital home. Hilda Ashby from Chopwell recalled how one of the first things she asked a potential sweetheart was 'are you working?' largely under pressure from her father.[47] Those who did marry on the dole were denounced in the media and stigmatised as was so grimly illustrated in *Love on the Dole*.[48] The National Government did not consider the wider impact of the means test upon all members of the household in this way. It led to young men and women leaving home at an earlier age, whether they were working or not, and contributed to an atmosphere not only of family disintegration but the breakdown of community life and even society.

The decision of whether or not the family home should separate was the consequence of hard emotional decisions and not a knee-jerk reaction to lowered benefits. In his memoir of the painful experience of long-term unemployment, Max Cohen recounted how he felt forced to leave his sister's home to avoid her husband supporting him: 'the Government, in some recondite way, regarded it as more eminently within the divine order of things if homes were broken up and dole-drawers starved in strange lodgings.'[49] Where families stayed together and children remained at home, the financial consequences of the means test clearly had a much deeper psychological significance for identity and gendered hierarchies. This was not the only way in which families were placed under increased pressure, and the very process of the means test investigation challenged the mental well-being of the family.

The means test man has become one of the most archetypal images of the 1930s. The establishment of the UABs saw the dreaded figure of the means test investigator become an unwelcome guest in working-class communities in south Wales and the north-east of England. Although many had long resented an inspector entering their homes, UAB officers were thought to have been more rigorous in their investigations and unlike PAC officials were not open to public pressure. This ensured that in both regions after 1935, the investigators became a much more prominent feature. In other areas of Britain, their notoriety had already been secured, and the means test man was the most complained about feature of the test after family breakdown. Anger levelled against investigators should not be viewed, in the majority of cases, as an attack upon individual persons and was a comment on the system more than anything else. Under both the PAC and the UAB administration, the investigators were sometimes, if not often, drawn from the ranks of the unemployed as men and women welcomed the prospect of employment despite what the job entailed.[50] However, this did little to dampen their impact, and opponents of the means test observed that the 'experience of dealing with the Board's Officers proves that however sympathetic an officer wishes to be, he is hemmed in by masses of Regulations, and his discretionary power is very limited'.[51] The investigators became the human face of the means test and its affront to self-respect. Personifying the means test's injustices, they were viewed with deep suspicion.[52] John Bell from the north-east recalled, 'the Gestapo wasn't in it. Some of these fellas had the same style as coming in: "Where's this?" and "What's that?" and you had to show them everything ... honest people made themselves liars because they were afraid of these fellas'.[53] The realisation that an investigation could lead to less money or even a disallowance ensured that the visits of inspectors were surrounded by anxiety and apprehension.

Walter Brierley's novel the *Means-Test Man* encapsulates the resentment of many unemployed households, which was strong enough to persist against any kind of official investigators entering homes for over a generation.[54] Fear of the investigators is a recurring theme and a point noted by Edward Warburton and Carl Butler in *Disallowed*, a record of their experiences as means test investigators.[55] The wife of an unemployed miner in Durham noted that one feature that was helping her family of eight survive were the eggs and meat that her father was able to get for her from a farm at which he worked. However, she expressed that 'we're always afraid that this will be found out and that the Means Test man will knock a shilling or two off my husband's money. Afraid that's the word, we're always afraid something's going to happen to reduce our little money'.[56] In south Wales, the Methodist minister Reginald Barker wrote how after the 1934 Unemployment Act, 'not all of these folks were able to deal with the investigator, and his coming struck fear into the hearts of the women; one fainted when she saw him coming'.[57] The fear of losing money undoubtedly played acutely on the minds of unemployed men. Will Oxley noted in some detail the effect of waiting to sign on:

> It was a revelation to see the crowds in the waiting-room who were to undergo the Means Test. Some would talk very valiantly about what they would say to the U.A.B. Board, some sat in sullen silence, some betrayed restlessness and fear in repeated journeys to the lavatory. One would talk very loquaciously in order to relieve the oppression of atmosphere and his own individual dread to an absolutely unresponsive neighbour, who was obviously preoccupied with the coming ordeal ... some would perspire although it was a raw cold day, literally steaming in fear ... And when they came out, there was the same difference to be observed, from those who were too broken for any attempt at pretence to others who sailed out with tremendous relief stamped on their faces, having safely passed the menace of the axe.[58]

One area in which an officer was allowed to use discretion was in the granting of one-off payments for 'special circumstances', such as the replacement of bedding and clothes. This Act became commonly known as the Pots and Pans Act, but again it was to be another source of contention and not least because of notions of respectability. On the one hand, people did not want investigators to enter bedrooms to assess whether payments were needed, and, on the other, the cleanliness and respectability of a home was thought to hide real need.[59] The Pilgrim Trust reported of one home in south Wales that 'they resent the intrusion of the UAB officer who is said to ask questions that do not concern him in the least. He may be suspicious because the house is so clean and the family so respectable'.[60] An investigation into unemployment in Abertillery argued that 'the respectability of a home is a bar to relief under this Clause'.[61] The misunderstanding on both sides that could develop served to harden anger against inspectors. The image of families selling their prized pianos, clothes and jewellery has persisted, despite its highly selective character.

While resentment against the UAB officials was noted by some, others felt that the monthly visits could foster familiarity and good relations. The government was keen to stress this positive aspect of the means test investigations, and UABs in south Wales and the north-east of England reported such feelings. The propaganda value of attempting to popularise the appeal of the Board needs consideration here, although social investigators also commented upon this.[62] While reporting on some negative aspects of the investigations, the authors of *Men Without Work* reported that the 'personal element in the administration of the Board is one of the most valuable features of it'.[63] Ellen Wilkinson and John Newsom also observed that the unemployed could see investigators 'as friends and counsellors in time of adversity'.[64] Whether good relations were built upon a genuine mutual respect or just a stoic acceptance of the investigators as part of the means test is uncertain. Undoubtedly, there were inspectors who were unnecessarily harsh in their treatment and manner, but it should not be concluded that all inspectors behaved in this way. Clearly, it was the wider effects of their visits – the fear and apprehension that were roused and the attack upon respectability – that were more threatening for households.

In both regions, the wives of the unemployed were found by practically all social investigators to have been suffering the most.[65] As mothers and wives, women were deemed responsible for maintaining positive familial relations. The husband's loss of breadwinner role placed women, in some circumstances, in a position of greater responsibility within a household. This was rarely empowering. Ginzberg noted that 'the woman suffered most ... from being thrust into the position of head of household, and, although the more sensitive tried hard to protect the morale of their men ... more and more women came to treat their husbands as their eldest children'.[66] The unemployed man with nothing to do with his time was thrust into the domestic, normatively female, world and this also contributed to increased tension. One investigation noted that 'in winter the fathers and sons are driven to the shelter of their homes, mooning and moping about. A nervous tension develops. Tempers get frayed, quarrels ensue, and harshness develops between husband and wife'.[67]

Mrs Pallas, the wife of an unemployed man from Sunderland, described how 'I've often said to my husband, "Don't you feel ashamed at bringing this amount to keep all these on?" And he'd say, "What can I do?" He'd work if he could get it. I'm not blaming my husband. I don't know who to blame, but I wonder who I should blame'.[68] Within such an atmosphere, men could assume a position of inferiority within the home, even assisting with what were seen as female chores.[69] In the 1930s, as Neil Penlington has argued, the experience of the means test, alongside long-term unemployment, did not overthrow traditional gendered hierarchies or reform the position of women.[70] It did, however, temporarily challenge established positions, especially masculine identity, and undoubtedly created tensions even for families which stayed together.

The struggle to maintain domestic harmony, under the most testing of circumstances, left women in a perilous position. Investigators did not, however, dwell on the psychological condition of women, as they did for unemployed men. Far greater efforts were given over to exploring how women managed household budgets and to monitoring female physical health. After many years with a husband and children out of work and on means-tested benefits, managing the household economy only became a greater challenge. E. Ll. Harry and J. R. E. Phillips from the University College of Wales, Aberystwyth, found that in unemployed households 'even the basic non-food requirements like housing, clothing, fuel and lighting and household equipment were inadequate to ensure a decent standard of living'.[71] The problem was more pronounced in the homes of the long-term unemployed.[72]Avram Taylor and Steven Thompson have shown how women in both regions could devise many strategies for balancing the weekly budget and the lengths to which they went to feed their families.[73] The desire to see the family fed led women to deny themselves a fair share and was one of the primary reasons for poor health of women in this period.[74]

The means test and transitional payments were widely believed to be responsible for a deterioration of health. As Charles Webster has argued, ‘there is very little contemporary evidence to suggest that benefit rates were regarded as adequate for subsistence, except under a very favourable combination of circumstances’.[75] G. D. H. and M. I. Cole felt the allowance given to transitional payment applicants to be inadequate and suggested that ‘in short, they are being starved, if not to death, at any rate into ill health’.[76] The Coles were not alone in such denunciations of the means test. Margery Spring Rice made the case explicitly in her study: ‘no unemployed married man with a family under the Assistance Board ... receives enough money to buy adequate food for himself, wife and children.’[77] Wal Hannington likewise argued that the unemployed were more susceptible to ill health. He believed that much of the hardship ‘can in large measure be traced to effects of the means test’.[78]

Accusations of intrusive investigations, family separation, increased mental anxiety and women driven to ill health all served to ensure that, for some, the means test would remain the most objectionable feature of long-term unemployment. What perhaps secured this was the allegation that the means test drove people to suicide. Hannington noted how reports often appeared in the press of ‘men and women driven to suicide through the operation of the means test and poverty’.[79] The *Daily Worker* also made a direct connection between the means test and suicide. In February 1935, the paper ran an article on ‘Welsh Lads Murdered By The Means Test’. Twenty-five-year-old Leslie Kent from the Rhondda Valleys had left home to avoid his parents supporting him. Leaving home ‘had played on his mind to such an extent that on Sunday night, while visiting his parents, he drank, it is alleged, Lysol and was discovered unconscious at the bottom of the garden by his father. Leslie was run to the Llwynypia Hospital where he died an hour later, a victim of the Means Test’.[80] Reports of suicide provoked by the test were also made by Fenner Brockway in the early 1930s.[81] That the means test was a key factor in the decision of a man or woman to take their life was the most emotive argument against the means test and cannot, of course, be quantified.[82] However, the impression certainly existed as the following drawing by the celebrated artist James Boswell confirms.

In south Wales and the north-east of England, the local press was littered with reports of suicide amongst the out of work. In the Rhondda Valleys, on two occasions during the 1930s, it was reported that there was an ‘epidemic’ of suicides. The comment was first made in April 1933, by the local coroner R. J. Rhys at an inquest. The *Porth Gazette*

Figure 6.1 James Boswell, *The Means Test*, 1934 (Boswell revisited the theme in *The Means Test 2*, 1934)

reporting on events argued that 'the economic conditions could be expected to induce many more'.[83] Three years later, a different local newspaper reported another 'epidemic of suicides in this district'.[84] In the north-east, Charles Graham recalled how a man was actually employed to fish suicide victims out of the Tyne after they had jumped off the Tyne Bridge.[85] Unemployed men and women when interviewed for social investigations expressed how the anguish of being unemployed could lead to suicide. They even talked openly of suicidal thoughts and feelings. In *Out of the Pit*, three separate instances about suicide, all referring to or by women, are recorded. One of the women stated, 'I read in our paper the other day of a man who did himself in after being out [of work] for a long time, he was afraid his money would be reduced because his son was working'. The woman noted how her neighbour regularly threatened to commit suicide and, although she doubted she would, she felt that 'it's not nice to live in an atmosphere where people talk that way'.[86] Even if a direct link cannot be made between suicide and the test, or even suicide and long-term unemployment, it contributed to a negative environment within communities.[87] Along with other key accusations placed against the test, it served to ensure that debates against the means test were kept alive and also hinted at the wider repercussions of the measure within communities.

While there were many accounts of how communities could mobilise to support one another and to protest together, historians should be careful of only viewing working-class communities in this positive way.[88] The effects of the means test within society showed how unity was not the only response to adversity. While there was a fear that investigators were 'out to catch people', they were aided most in discovering undeclared sources of income by information from other unemployed and working-class people. Some transitional applicants, in order to secure extra money, would fail to disclose income that had been earned in an *ad hoc* and informal way for fear that it would be included in the means test assessment.[89] However, as Eli Ginzberg noted, 'their efforts at secrecy ... were frequently frustrated, not so much by the vigilance of officials as by the envy of their neighbours. Every morning the Board received denunciatory letters about applicants who were hiding earnings'.[90] Edward Warburton, a means test investigator, confirmed such findings and described numerous instances of neighbours telling on one another in his semi-autobiographical novella.[91] Such evidence cropped up across the country, and George Orwell recounted how in the north-west of England there was 'much spying and tale-bearing' to the means test man.[92]

Volunteering information to UAB officials was an act of denunciation, and, as the important work by Fitzpatrick and Gellately reveals, denunciation by 'ordinary people' with an 'everyday grievance' played and plays a role in most societies.[93] The evidence of denunciation in south Wales and the north-east acts as a guard against romantic notions of working-class communities, and it is wrong to assume that in every case people informed as a response to a drastic situation. In south Wales and the north-east, the working class did not always display solidarity against those outside the community, and the existence of willing informants to the means test man could potentially fracture neighbourly networks. As David Vincent concluded, 'the new welfare system both consolidated and fractured the unity of the poor locality. Whilst households struggled to conceal their secrets, their neighbours secretly attempted to expose them'.[94] Community was too complex a configuration, however, for one factor to entirely undermine feelings of belonging beyond the household.

The seemingly unending mental pressure for the long-term unemployed and their families was not always expressed through sharp words and suicidal thoughts. People still wanted to fight against their position and to take a stand under the banner of community. This can be seen, for example, in the 'community' response to the stay-in strikes in south Wales in 1935.[95] Industrial relations and the Spanish Civil War, amongst other concerns, did not entirely dwarf protest against the means test although, by the end of the 1930s, its abolition was no longer the central objective of the labour movement. Trade unions and political parties as well as movements of the unemployed organised marches, demonstrations, conferences and meetings against the means test right up until the eve of the Second World War. The National Government also continued to be bombarded with resolutions denouncing the means test from south Wales and the north-east. The protest movement was certainly not as widespread as it had been, and it also suffered from an increasing lack of interest as unemployment declined. The existence of any recognisable form of organisation was in itself remarkable given the limited resources of the unemployed and as international events increasingly absorbed energies.

The last great upsurge in protest came in 1936 when the government reintroduced the UAB regulations.[96] Despite the levels of activity, historians have largely overlooked the protest that occurred in the summer months. While some have examined the response only once the regulations were in operation, many more have principally focused on the Jarrow Crusade and the NUWM hunger march.[97] If the Jarrow Crusade's significance has eclipsed other interwar protests, including even the national hunger marches, then this has been especially true of demonstrations in 1936 against the new regulations.[98] While the Jarrow Crusade captured the popular imagination, it was not this march or the hunger march that represented the final great mobilisation of the unemployed throughout Britain: the action against the regulations in the summer of 1936 led to protests and demonstrations throughout the country on a much broader scale.

With another election victory secured, the National Government under Stanley Baldwin felt confident in its handling the unemployment situation when the new regulations were announced. Given the scale of the response in 1935, the UAB and the Minister of Labour had taken pains in redrafting the new legislation to avoid any potential stimulus for action. Local investigations were carried out throughout Britain to gauge the impact of and potential response to the new regulations. Despite this careful reframing, and significant decline in transitional applicants, ministers still expected outcry in those areas which had been particularly militant in the previous year. Just two months before the new regulations were announced, the Minister of Labour stressed to the Cabinet committee that 'they were bound to encounter violent opposition in such areas as South Wales, and ... the Government must be prepared to meet it'.[99] The National Government was right to be concerned, and perhaps unsurprisingly, in light of events in early 1935, protest returned almost as soon as the regulations were announced on 9 July.[100] The *Daily Worker* reported just days after the announcement that 'from the derelict mining valleys of South Wales to the idle shipyards of Newcastle-upon-Tyne, and right over the border into Glasgow, the Labour movement has been into action against this new attack'.[101]

In 1936, protestors and the labour movement were able to draw upon a repertoire of protest from the previous year. Protestors in these months had a much greater sense of optimism about what their actions could achieve, and they looked for the complete withdrawal of the means test. The awareness of the temporary nature of the Standstill Act meant that the labour movement, like the government, had prepared for action long before the new regulations came into force. On 16 July, the National Council of Labour issued a manifesto calling upon the labour movement to 'oppose the new regulations' and to take inspiration from the government's response in the previous year.[102] In south Wales, the SWMF executive committee and individual lodges had been preparing for the new regulations since the beginning of the year.[103] In July, the attention of the media and the labour movement was focused on the region as protest yet again exploded on a scale unparalleled elsewhere. Although not as spectacular as the winter of 1935, a cross section of society was still present as the mass demonstrations began. Religious bodies voiced their opposition, and in the large demonstrations, ministers of religion, MPs, trade unionists, councillors, miners and traders were roused to joint action by Trades Councils and the Labour Party.[104] In a departure of previous years, the Communist Party played a much greater role at a regional level in united action as well as organising individual demonstrations. This was no doubt a reflection of the changed leadership of the SWMF under Arthur Horner.

On Saturday 18 July, an 'all-in' conference organised by the Council of Action for south Wales was held in Cardiff.[105] Around 1,000 delegates attended, including fourteen MPs, all trade unions, cooperative societies and councils, as well as the Communist Party and NUWM. The main demand that the conference issued was for the abolition of the means test. James Griffiths (Labour MP, Llanelli, and former president of the SWMF) presided over the meeting noting 'seventeen months ago we held a conference in this same hall. We then lit a flame which spread throughout the country ... Once again at this conference we aim to light a bigger flame, which will kindle the whole country, not only to abolish the Means Test, but to put an end to this National Government'.[106] The following day, the massive Sunday demonstrations got underway once more.[107] On 19 July, marches, meetings and demonstrations took place across south Wales, and these different expressions of protest were utilised to generate a mass movement. The unemployed and wider communities were mobilised, and resolutions of protest were passed at demonstrations across the region.[108] The action included a demonstration in Cathays Park in Cardiff against Stanley Baldwin who was visiting St Fagan's Castle.[109] On Monday, following a weekend of action, a deputation of Labour MPs, Arthur Horner and Mrs Pearce (representing women's organisations) met with the Minister of Labour to discuss the means test.[110]

These meetings and marches continued throughout the week, and on the following Sunday, the *Daily Worker* estimated that 200,000 people marched.[111] Huge demonstrations similar to 1935 were in evidence once again; 60,000 reportedly converged at Mountain Ash, and in the Rhondda Valleys an estimated 50,000–100,000 marched. Further demonstrations were noted to have taken place at Ebbw Vale, Pontypool and Ammanford.[112] The level of mobilisation in 1936 revealed the enduring significance of the campaign against the means test within the labour movement. Moreover, the recrudescence of collective action showed the commitment to street protests as a way of expressing opposition to the government. To confirm the well-established pattern of protest in south Wales, the unemployed were organised, determined and united in action. The protests drew the attention of the national press and were carefully monitored by the Home Office.

How seriously the government took the protests in south Wales was shown by the special meeting at the Home Office on 31 July convened to discuss the situation. It included representatives from the Ministries of Health and Labour, the War Office, MI5 and the Metropolitan Special Branch. The Chief Constables for Glamorgan, Monmouthshire and Cardiff gave evidence that formed the basis of the government's response. All in the meeting agreed that reductions should be introduced gradually and especially after the 'danger period' of November to February. Although the importance of local expertise had previously been dismissed, the Local Advisory Committees were now in place and had more power over the timing of reductions in benefit scales.[113] While confidence was expressed in the ability of the police to control protestors, the government was clearly uneasy about the number on the streets.[114] Although publicly the National Government betrayed little concern, the unemployed provoked more than a ministerial headache and commanded careful attention.

Government anxiety continued to focus on the unemployed in south Wales, and the early action in the area fed concern about escalating collective action. The only other 'places where there might also be some trouble' noted by the Minister of Labour were Glasgow, Hull, Barnsley and Sunderland. The preparations for the Jarrow Crusade were also discussed, but it was debated whether this march would even go ahead.[115] The concern of the Cabinet must have been spurred by the National Council of Labour urging the holding of local demonstrations on Sunday 26 July, and future national demonstrations.[116] Unemployed associations in the north-west of England and north Wales had already issued their plans to march on Manchester on Sunday.[117] However, while south Wales drew the greatest attention, action had also begun in Durham and Northumberland.

On 15 July, Sam Watson, unemployment officer of the DMA, issued a circular about the new scales and a copy of his interpretation of the regulations to all DMA lodges. Watson argued that the government sought to convince the unemployed that the regulations were a vast improvement on the preceding year, and he hoped his pamphlet would show that this was not the case.[118] As if aware that this was to be its last great stand against the means test, the DMA roused the region to action.[119] In 1936, words did not suffice for the protest of the DMA: it was decided that mass demonstrations should be held throughout County Durham on 16 August to express opposition against the continuation of means testing.[120] A circular urged 'all Lodges to associate themselves with the Demonstration in their area and render all possible help to make a success'.[121] The success of the demonstrations in the previous year in part explains the changed position of the DMA.[122] What was also important to the adoption of a more radical position was, as Lewis Mates has shown, the increasing 'degree of influence' of the Communist Party within the union.[123] In July, a delegate council agreed with the executive council's decision in favour of the Communist Party's affiliation to the Labour Party.[124] The DMA was undoubtedly offering the unemployed in Durham the most sustained leadership since 1933 and most militant action against the means test in the 1930s.[125]

In a further departure from familiar patterns of protest, greater efforts were made within the labour movement to coordinate action within and across the region. Like the DMA, the Labour Party was active in organising the demonstrations. Following meetings held in individual villages, on 8 August a 'mass demonstration' was organised at Crook which included marchers from 'all parts of the district'. Joseph Batey and Sam Watson spoke out against the means test.[126] Protest meetings were also held in Spennymoor, Blaydon, High Spen, Chopwell and Willington.[127] The Northumberland and Tyneside Federation of Labour Parties called for a conference of the Labour Party and all trades unions in conjunction with the North-Eastern Federation of Trades Councils on 1 August.[128] It was agreed to hold a mass demonstration against the means test in Newcastle on 30 August. In an unprecedented move, the DMA issued a circular to all of its lodges, advertising the demonstration and urging members to join in.[129] In the interim, the energies of the DMA remained focused on organising the mass demonstrations for mid-August. The week before, general secretary John E. Swan's circular urged 'Lodges to do all they can to induce their members with their wives to turn up in full force and associate themselves with this county protest'. He ended with the warning, 'if you are employed to-day – you may be unemployed to-morrow'.[130]

The power of the DMA to lead the unemployed was confirmed on 16 August when demonstrations took place across the county which surpassed the achievements of the 1933 action. Highlighting the break from the usual character of protest, Swan, addressing crowds at Birtley, declared, 'while Durham County had suffered more hardship than perhaps any other mining and industrial county in Britain, the people had maintained a quiet dignity of character which was most commendable.'[131] The following day, the executive committee placed on record their thanks to DMA members, other trade union organisations and political organisations. It celebrated the success of the marches and noted that a resolution passed at the demonstrations had been sent to the Prime Minister.[132] Will Lawther, committee secretary of the DMA, felt 'the demonstrations on Sunday proved beyond doubt that the people of Durham are wholeheartedly behind the demands put forward by the miners and that the miners have come to the conclusion that something drastic will have to be done in order to awaken the government from their stupor'.[133]

John E. Swan's call for wives to march and joint action with other sections of the labour movement showed the commitment of the DMA to unity for protest in 1936. Although the executive committee of the DMA continued to distance itself from association with the NUWM, at a local level collaboration was evident.[134] At the end of August in Chester-le-Street, a conference organised by the North-East District NUWM was attended by sixty-four delegates including fourteen DMA lodge representatives. Delegates also attended from men's and women's sections of the Labour Party, the Socialist League, co-operative guilds, the Ship Constructors' Union and the Shipwrights and Drillers' Union. DMA members were the most prominent speakers and made calls for a one-day stoppage against the new regulations.[135] This conference was a rare example of united regional opposition against the means test. While the miners' gala continued to attract the largest numbers marching, some 200,000 in 1936, other examples of protest convey how the government's response to the protests in the previous year had given both stimulus and perhaps legitimacy to action.

As action continued in August and September in Durham, so too the unemployed along Tyneside expressed discontent and prepared for action.[136] The greatest march from Tyneside was, however, the Jarrow Crusade. The Crusaders departed for London in October, and one of their central issues was the continuation of means testing.[137] As Matt Perry has noted in his recent work on the Jarrow Crusade, the march has come to represent and symbolise the protest of the unemployed in this period.[138] While the Labour MP Ellen Wilkinson may have headed the march, it was essentially non-political in that it was not affiliated to any particular party. Perry argues that the myth of the Crusade has obfuscated the complexity of the politics of the march which was not supported by the

Labour Party or other national institutions as in later years it was.[139] For Richard Croucher, it was a 'historical injustice' that 'it was the Jarrow Crusade that lived on as the symbol of unemployed action in the 1930s, as the officially approved motif of "peaceful protest"'. It was the 1936 hunger march, itself peaceful, which had a much greater contemporary impact and better represented the labour movement.[140]

In south Wales on 29 August, a further conference was held in Cardiff to discuss action against the means test. James Griffiths chaired and proposals were discussed for a one-day strike, a boycotting of Coronation celebrations and a refusal to work towards the rearmament programme. Arthur Horner's proposed resolution that the TUC should be asked to consider a one-day stoppage was adopted.[141] However, while there was growing support for industrial action in south Wales and in the north-east, the TUC at a meeting of its General Council in early September opposed such a motion. Sir Walter Citrine, the general secretary of the TUC, argued that the General Council did not believe that the government's hand should be forced through industrial action and that it was more important to 'rouse public opinion' through demonstrations and agitation. Although 'delegates from Durham and South Wales at once began to argue drastic industrial action was justified', Citrine reminded delegates that such action was now technically illegal. The General Council supported neither a proposed march to London nor a boycott of the Coronation celebrations.[142] Despite the lack of support from the TUC for another hunger march to London, Matthias Reiss has shown, in his study of the General Council's survey on attitudes to the hunger march, that within the Trades Councils there was 'widespread support for unemployed marches to London'.[143]

The 1936 national hunger march was advertised, like those of 1932 and 1934, as a national march against the means test and once again demonstrated the support across the country for the abolition of the test. The march planned to arrive in London just days before the new regulations came into effect, and the NUWM was adamant that their voices would be heard on this occasion. The proposal that marchers would lobby the King if the government would not meet a deputation spurred the Home Office to write to Buckingham Palace, and, as with the other hunger marchers, those involved were closely monitored by the police and MI5.[144] What made the hunger march different in 1936 was the presence of other national marchers in London, and the Jarrow Crusade, the National League of the Blind and a march of ex-servicemen from Scotland all arrived within days of one another. While all the marches were monitored, it was the hunger march which most interested the government who remained concerned about the activities of the Communist Party.

One hundred and fifty marchers left Newcastle on 12 October, and leading the contingents were the two recently elected Communist Party councillors Jim Ancrum and T. A. Richardson.[145] In south Wales, several demonstrations took place for the contingent of 504 hunger marchers. Captain Lindsay sent detailed records of the 249 men who marched from Glamorgan which provide a fascinating insight into the composition of the contingent. In addition to noting names, addresses and ages, Lindsay also detailed political affiliations, appearance and idiosyncrasies. The marchers, in the main, were unemployed and from within the coalfield. Revealing of the fluid nature of political affiliation in south Wales, the majority of the marchers were noted as being sympathetic to Labour, and not the Communist Party. These were not young radicals, and the average age was thirty-six; the youngest marcher was an eighteen-year-old unemployed youth from Skewen, and the oldest an unemployed sixty-four-year-old from Nantyffyllon. Twenty marchers were noted to be in employment, and this number included a town crier from Mountain Ash. While Lindsay warned that 'many of them' had criminal records, only thirty-eight had convictions and many for activities related to protest. Lindsay argued that 75% of the marchers were 'respectable persons', with the remainder described as Communists 'who would stop at nothing'.[146] Lewis Jones who led the contingent was claimed to be, like other marchers, an 'extremely dangerous agitator and revolutionary'.[147]

Lindsay need not have followed so closely the 'dangerous agitators' from south Wales, and the last hunger march largely passed without incident. Reminiscent of local marches, it was the class or status of those who marched which influenced the police response.[148] The Home Office argued that the march 'attracted less public notice than similar events in the past' and its reasoning for this was the start of the Spanish Civil War, the Battle of Cable Street and the Jarrow Crusade.[149] However, it is apparent that the Home Office may have downplayed events. A deputation did meet with the Minister of Labour on this occasion, and Croucher argues that important, although small, concessions were won.[150] The support from within the Labour Party and the lack of confrontation with the police certainly marked this march as invoking a quite different relationship between the marches and the government. There was some form of dialogue, although this should not be exaggerated.

The final demonstration of the hunger marchers in London took place the night before the introduction of the new regulations. The following day, on 16 November, 600,000 transitional applicants began to have their circumstances reinvestigated. In both regions, the end of the national march marked the end of widespread organisation against the means test and the new regulations. After all the build-up and mass action of the summer months, there was no widespread outcry once the regulations began operation. The marches and marchers had lost their momentum and did not garner wider public attention. While other national and international events were important in the decline of interest, what mattered more was the fact that massive benefit reductions were not occurring. The government had played its trump card and won: the prediction that gradual decreases would defuse the cause of protest was right, and it also lessened public sympathy. As the MP for Pontypridd, D. L. Davies had observed in the summer, 'if they dropped you from the top of the tree straight away the bump would be enormous.... But if they drop you from branch to branch for eighteen months, you may not feel the bump at the end'.[151]

King Edward VIII's visit to the region exemplified the decline of protest against the means test in south Wales. In November 1936, the largest crowds on the street were out to loyally cheer the King, not to protest against the means test. The concerns of the Home Office for the reception to the King must have appeared as scaremongering in hindsight, especially once Ernest Brown, the Minister of Labour, followed advice to stay away.[152] The King's visit proved incredibly popular despite previous calls to boycott Coronation celebrations. Thousands lined the streets to catch a glimpse of the glamorous young King just weeks before his abdication.[153] The King's infamous phrase that 'something must be done' after visiting Dowlais undoubtedly helped his popularity.[154] The anger of the working class did not focus upon the monarchy, and this was, perhaps, telling of a change in the wider climate of protest against the means test and unemployment. The most militant had left for Spain, while those in employment were distracted with their own battles. In the north-east too, a similar situation was apparent; both the return of the hunger marchers and the Jarrow Crusaders represented, in effect, the end of mass action against the means test in the region. The immediate move to protest through marches and demonstrations from July had had important consequences for the continuation of collective action. Protest was based upon anticipated effects of the regulations, and this – coupled with improvement in the economic situation – undermined the momentum of sustained mass protest by the time the regulations were introduced.

The protests in the autumn of 1936 achieved very little. Within government, the means test was not as sensitive an issue as it had been in

1935, it was not an election year, and events on the continent caused the government greater concern.[155] Furthermore, the revolt of a hundred MPs that something more should done by the government to assist those in the 'forgotten places' was met with agreement by ministers. While protest stunts could still grab headlines after this year, the movement against the means test did not capture the imagination of the public once again. It is difficult to conclude, however, how the protest against the means test simply ended. There were no further national hunger marches, and no further gatherings of hundreds of thousands, but the abolition of the means test as an objective continued in some quarters. As the case of south Wales and the north-east of England conveys, the effects of the means test continued to inflict suffering upon the unemployed, and for them, it remained a central issue. After 1936, patterns of protest in both regions reflected what had occurred in earlier years: while street demonstrations continued in south Wales, in the north-east dissatisfaction was more likely to be expressed through meetings and conferences.

In south Wales, protest against the means test continued right up until the start of the Second World War, and the unemployed remained willing to take to the streets to display their opposition. Indeed, another march to London was proposed for May 1937 after the SWMF had received correspondence from Wal Hannington. The march was organised by the NUWM, and the executive committee of the SWMF appointed Jack Davies from Llwynypia to represent the distressed area of south Wales and Mark Harcombe, from Trealaw, to represent the SWMF.[156] In the autumn of 1937, women's sections of the Labour Party played an active part in organising and participating in demonstrations against the means test.[157] The Labour Party in conjunction with the SWMF was also active in organising the large marches that took place in October 1938 against the final stage of the introduction of the 1936 regulations.[158] Local branches of the NUWM were likewise moved to action by these events. In the spring of 1938, the Dowlais branch of the NUWM was particularly energetic in organising demonstrations, deputations and meetings and even purchased a new banner for the planned processions.[159] While still playing a vital role in the leadership of the unemployed, it was, increasingly, the SWMF which was leading the battle against the test. For example, it was the Consultative Rhondda Committee of the SWMF which organised a demonstration of a reported 25,000 in Llwynypia in February against the means test.[160] By the later 1930s, the role of the Communist Party and the NUWM had dwindled.[161] The composition of the Communist Party in south Wales had been made up primarily of the unemployed, and the gradual return to work led to its membership declining.[162] Moreover, within the NUWM, leaders recognised the importance of the SWMF as an organising body. In June 1935, the NAC of the NUWM issued a circular calling for members to ignore Lewis Jones' suggestion to liquidate the regional branch in favour of coordinating through SWMF lodges and the Labour Party.[163] Jones was perceptive in his prediction of the future of the movement. In 1937, the NUWM agreed to calls from the SWMF to stop recruiting unemployed miners.[164] For those still active in the Communist Party and the NUWM, the Spanish Civil War became the major issue and not the abolition of the means test. Hywel Francis has noted how nearly a third of the volunteers for the International Brigade were NUWM members.[165] By the later 1930s, in south Wales the leadership of the unemployed had shifted to the Labour Party, as the affiliation of the hunger marchers in 1936 indicated.

In February 1938, the executive council of the SWMF called upon the Regional Council of Labour to organise a conference 'to deal with the means test'.[166] The subsequent conference of 672 delegates took place on 9 April 1938; trade unions, the Labour Party and Trades and Labour Councils were all invited.[167] The conference highlighted the returned Labour hegemony in the region over the unemployed. Arthur Horner, although president of the SWMF, was not invited to speak because he was a Communist Party member. The growing importance of Labour was mirrored by the SWMF's position. At a local level, the NUWM could struggle to achieve its previous unity. For example, the Dowlais branch of the NUWM struggled to secure involvement in the local demonstrations in the spring of 1938.[168]

Towns and valleys, especially within the coalfield, remained important arenas of protest as the demonstrations of 1938 show. On 6 February 1938, a march and mass demonstration took place in the Rhondda Valleys with contingents from both valleys converging in Ystrad. An advertisement for the march of the unemployed and employed carried the slogan 'DOWN with the Means Test, which robs the allowances of the Unemployed and attacks the wages of the Employed'.[169] In the same month, the miners' office in Bridgend, after an area meeting, decided to 'promote an intensive All-In Campaign, the object being to endeavour to get the Government to scrap the Means Test, and deal with increase in the cost of living'. A committee of eight was established and they were 'to ask Political, Social, and Religious bodies to meet and discuss what appropriate steps can be taken'. A provisional date for an all-in conference was set for 16 March 1938.[170] Although commitment to a united front may have decreased, there was still evidence of a dedication to all-in conferences and to the belief that 'unity is strength'.[171]

Of course such action, while important, was on a much smaller scale, and animosity towards continued action was apparent. On discussing the proposed resolution for the Regional Council of Labour's conference, Mr W. Hayes of the Mountain Ash Trades and Labour Council, a body previously supportive of anti-means test action, 'expressed his personal disgust' at the resolution, and the council decided not to discuss the matter further.[172] After seven years of debating and denouncing the means test, the interest of certain groups had subsided. Women from the Abertillery Labour Party women's section expressed in November 1937 that they would be glad when the means test campaign ended as the Communists were 'giving [a] few of the women a very difficult time'.[173] However, this was not the overwhelming case for the labour movement.

That the means test remained paramount for those undergoing the investigations was reflected in the SWMF's continued campaign at a time when it was facing some of its biggest battles for recognition and membership in all areas of the coalfield. Indeed, in April 1939, at the last SWMF annual conference before the Second World War, the means test remained an issue of debate. A resolution was passed calling for the Labour Party and the TUC to 'organize a nationwide movement to secure the abolition of the means test'.[174] The SWMF as a traditional leader of the working class in south Wales remained dedicated to ensuring that the suffering of the unemployed would not pass without protest. It continued to respond to demands for action into the war years. When the UABs refused extra relief for materials to blackout windows, the unemployed from Bridgend wrote to the SWMF to warn that 'if something is not done soon, the unemployed will have no alternative but to act in a manner that will certainly not reflect any credit upon this country'.[175] The continuation of marches, demonstrations and meetings – all of which kept the issue alive – was in no small part because of the efforts of the executive committee of the SWMF and individual lodges.

In comparison to the situation in south Wales, in the north-east examples of street protests, in line with earlier patterns, were far fewer. However, broad parallels can be drawn between the two regions. Support for the Communist Party declined within the major trade union, the DMA, and where pockets of activity for the Communist Party and the NUWM remained, the Spanish Civil War became the central cause. In the north-east, the changes were exaggerated; the DMA moved away from the Communist Party in late 1936, and support within the lodges did not remain.[176] Once more, activity took place in the most militant areas, and along the Tyne the unemployed were still willing to take to the streets. For example, when Ernest Brown, the Minister of Labour, visited Gateshead in October 1937, a demonstration was held after he refused to meet a deputation to discuss the means test.[177] Elsewhere in the north-east region, there were few examples of notable protest against the means test which involved a demonstration or march. In 1939, Ellen Wilkinson remarked that 'English men and women differ from French and Germans, and for that matter Scotch and Welsh, in that they hate going to the streets. Marching to a demonstration in some square or park of their town is about as much as the most enthusiastic among them can be persuaded to do'.[178] Clearly, she had the working class in the north-east in mind when writing these comments. As in previous years, however, the absence of street displays of action should not be taken to mean that opposition to the measure did not take place.

The DMA, which had led the way for demonstrations in 1936, remained involved in opposition although they did not organise further marches. In January 1938, the union was asked to represent the MFGB for a TUC deputation waiting on Ernest Brown. Sam Watson asked lodges for cases of individual hardship as it was felt that 'actual facts based on actual cases are the best weapons to use against the Means Test'.[179] For the DMA, protest once more concentrated on hard facts and written resolutions, and there are no examples of street protests organised by the union after 1936. The means test remained a key issue, and in August 1939 it was MPs from the north-east who led calls for the abolition of the means test. Although the Minister of Labour announced that transitional payment figures stood at their lowest at 462,474, the abolition of means testing was still argued for.[180] While opposition against the test continued, without the support of the DMA for marches, such forms of protest were absent in much of the north-east of England.

In the rest of Britain, protest against the means test was also sporadic. The NUWM with a dwindling membership and lack of public interest resorted to more elaborate forms of protest aimed at grabbing headlines including, infamously, tea at the Ritz.[181] Once the war began, the NUWM officially suspended its activities although the abolition of the means test was an issue kept alive in parliament. On 18 January 1940, during debates about the means test and wartime savings, James Griffiths asked the Minister of Labour Ernest Bevin 'would it not be a fine gesture to abolish the means test now?'[182] It was the use of the means test as part of the benefit system for the Old Age and Widows' Pensions Bill that really sparked debates. MPs saw an opportunity to eradicate means tests from the machinery of welfare once and for all.[183] Hugh Dalton argued in February 1940 that to introduce another means test would be 'an action which will tend to weaken, rather than strengthen, that morale.'[184] On 6 November 1940, Winston Churchill, the wartime Prime Minister, after months of debating the issue, announced in the House of Commons that a household means test was to be replaced with a personal test of need.[185] The announcement was greeted by a 'warm cheer' in the House amongst Labour MPs.[186] The long-term unemployed, the working class and the labour movement in south Wales and the north-east of England had finally had their calls answered for the abolition of a measure that had dominated family and community life since its inception in 1931. Whether to boost morale or in recognition of the mass protests and outcry of the previous decade, the abolition of a household means test removed one the most controversial pieces of interwar legislation. The part played in this process by Labour MPs, who were to take leading positions in the post-war Attlee Cabinet, highlights that the debates about means testing were not over.[187] The end of the means test came in the same year that *Love on the Dole* was released as a motion picture, a film which did much to secure the legacy of a measure already firmly rooted in popular consciousness.

While protest against the means test may have declined after 1936, the anger against it and the emotions it stirred did not. Although largely overlooked in the historiography, the protests of 1936 and, to a lesser extent, 1938 revealed the continued strength of the opposition from the unemployed. The marches and demonstrations of the summer of 1936 and the last hunger march embodied a largely united labour movement even if the wider community played a less important role. In many respects, these were class protests, and the presence of women marching confirmed that it was not only working-class men who were making a stand. The introduction of further cuts through the revised regulations sparked protests in 1936 and 1938, but it was the continuation of the effects of the means test which helps explain the readiness for collective action. While in Britain as a whole the number out of work had declined, the upswing of the economy certainly did not restore the depressed regions. Nevertheless, the organisation of the unemployed became much harder as more people returned to work. Protests could still, however, capture the public imagination, and this was pivotal to memories of the decade.

After 1935, the Communist Party and NUWM played a less important role in organising the unemployed as the trade unions and the Labour

Party assumed leadership over the campaign against the means test. In south Wales, Communism remained an important political force, but it was clearly Labour which was leading the way. In the north-east, outside of more militant pockets, the unemployed maintained its loyalty to the DMA, taking its lead for action here. South Wales and the north-east of England continued to differ in their stance, although parallels were often apparent in these years. Why patterns of protest differed will be the focus of the conclusion. In the later 1930s, as had been the case from the 1920s, the marches, letters and deputations of the unemployed were a vital form of dialogue with the government. How important public opinion and the voice of the workless were was demonstrated in the sensitivity and care the government took to introducing the new regulations. Whatever else politicians may have learnt about welfare and unemployment in this period, one message which stood out was that public opinion and the social impact of policy could not be ignored. As welfare was gradually centralised, a new era was to begin in the relationship between the state and those on the margins.

Notes

1 DRO, DX/1268, *The Socialist: The Official Organ of the Seaham Divisional Labour Party*, March 1937, p. 1.

2 Wal Hannington, *The Problem of the Distressed Areas* (London, 1937), p. 73.

3 Note *Sorrow for Thy Sons* was originally written in 1936.

4 Evelyn Waugh, *Vile Bodies* (London, 1981 edition; first published, 1930), p. 29.

5 Matt Perry, *Bread and Work: The Experience of Unemployment, 1918–1939* (London, 2000), p. 201.

6 Unemployment Assistance Act, 1934. *Return of the number of payments made at local offices of the Ministry of Labour in the week ended Friday, 26th June, 1936, by way of unemployment benefit under the Unemployment Insurance Act, 1935, and of unemployment allowances under the Unemployment Assistance Regulations, 1934, and the Unemployment Assistance (Temporary Provisions) Act, 1935* (Cmd 5240), 1935–36, xvii; *Local Unemployment Index, 1936*.

7 *Local Unemployment Index*, January 1936.

8 *Ibid.*, August 1939. In Britain, on average just over one worker in ten was unemployed. G. D. H. Cole, *The Intelligent Man's Guide to the Post-War World* (London, 1947), p. 41.

9 TNA, CAB 27/575, Cabinet Committee on the Regulation of the Unemployment Assistance Board Minutes, 21 October 1935, Appendix B, p. 11, 11 May 1936, pp. 2–18 and 15 June 1936, pp. 1–14.

10 *The Times*, 7 November 1940, p. 4.

11 This is especially true of Aneurin Bevan. Cole, *Intelligent Man's Guide to the Post-War World*, pp. 552–3; Michael Foot, *Aneurin Bevan: A Biography, Volume One, 1897–1945* (London, 1982), pp. 327–30; Derek Fraser, *The Evolution of the Welfare State: A History of Social Policy Since the Industrial Revolution* (Basingstoke, 2003), pp. 233–4.

12 It was argued that with the end of the measure 'goes the one great cause of contention in the Board's administration ... the household means test caused great resentment and not a little pain'. *The Times*, 31 May 1941, p. 5.

13 Cole, *Intelligent Man's Guide to the Post-War World*, pp. 552–3.

14 Alan Deacon, 'An End to the Means Test? Social Security and the Attlee Government', *Journal of Social Policy*, 11:3 (1982), pp. 289–306.

15 The most famous examples are Eli Ginzberg, *Grass on the Slag Heaps: The Story of the Welsh Miners* (London, 1942); John Newsom, *Out of the Pit: A Challenge to the Comfortable* (Oxford, 1936); Ellen Wilkinson, *The Town That Was Murdered: The Life Story of Jarrow* (London, 1939).

16 Ginzberg, *Grass on the Slag Heaps*, p. ix.

17 Henry A. Mess, 'Review: *Out of the Pit* by John Newsom', *The Economic Journal*, 47:186 (1937), pp. 358–9.

18 *The Industrial Position of the North-East Coast of England* (London, 1935); *The Second Industrial Survey of South Wales*, Vols 1–3 (Cardiff, 1937); Labour Party, *Durham and the North-East Coast: Report of the Labour Party's Commission of Enquiry into the Distressed Areas* (London, 1937); Labour Party, *South Wales: Report of the Labour Party's Commission of Enquiry into the Distressed Areas* (London, 1937).

19 Ginzberg, *Grass on the Slag Heaps*, pp. 32–3; Newsom, *Out of the Pit*, p. 48; Wilkinson, *The Town That Was Murdered*, pp. 217–18.

20 Wilkinson, *The Town That Was Murdered*, pp. 217–18.

21 The study focused on the Rhondda Valleys, Crook, Blackburn, Leicester, Deptford and Liverpool.

22 The authors were William Ebor, George Bell (Bishop of Chichester), A. D. Lindsay (Master of Balliol), Miss Iredale, Dr Thomas Jones, Sir Walter Moberly, Dr J. H. Oldham and Sir Edward Peacock.

23 The section was called 'Families where Unemployment Assistance is less than half the main income; other Means Test cases'.

24 TNA, AST 7/255, The Pilgrim Trust Unemployment Enquiry: Investigation into the causes of long-term unemployment and its effects. Supply of Information, letter from Wilfrid Eady to Miss Iredale, 22 November 1937.

25 AST 7/255, Correspondence between Miss Iredale and W. Eady, 25 November 1937 and 17 December 1937.

26 AST 7/255, minute sheet addressed to Mr Graham and signed by W. Nevard, dated 1 February 1935.

27 *Men Without Work: A Report Made to the Pilgrim Trust* (Cambridge, 1938), p. 148.

28 *Disinherited Youth: A Report on the 18+ Age Group Enquiry. Prepared for the Trustees of the Carnegie United Kingdom Trust* (Edinburgh, 1943), p. 55.

29 Beatrice Wood, 'Wednesday's Child', in Carol White and Sian Rhiannon Williams (eds), *Struggle or Starve: Women's Lives in the South Wales Valleys Between the Two World Wars* (Dinas Powys, 2002), pp. 126–7.

30 NLW, Papers of Dr Thomas Jones CH, Unemployment Assistance Board, Memorandum Giving Information Asked For by the Minister of Labour on 6th July 1935, dated 8 August 1935, pp. 29–30.

31 *Report of the Unemployment Assistance Board for the Period Ended 31 December 1935* (Cmd 5177), 1935–36, xiii, p. 470.

32 In south Wales, Idris Cox argued that 'no less than 40,000 working families have been broken up ... due to unemployment and the Means Test'. SWML, Idris Cox, *The People Can Save South Wales* (Communist Party of Great Britain, London, 1936), p. 8. See also, G. D. H. and M. I. Cole, *The Condition of Britain* (London, 1937), pp. 213, 216.

33 See, for example, Kenneth Maher, 'Caerphilly', in Nigel Gray (ed.), *The Worst of Times: An Oral History of the Great Depression in Britain* (Aldershot, 1985), p. 36; Charles Graham, 'Dead-End Jobs; "Dead Bodies"', in Keith Armstrong and Huw Beynon (eds), *Hello, Are You Working? Memories of the Thirties in the North East of England* (Newcastle, 1977), p. 27; Kate Nicholas, *The Social Effects of Unemployment on Teesside, 1919–39* (Manchester, 1986), p. 195.

34 Obviously, this situation was quite different when earning children only pretended to leave the household. In these cases, the financial incentive was much greater.

35 For evidence of a strong family spirit, see Ginzberg, *Grass on the Slag Heaps*, p. 86.

36 M. A. Crowther, 'Family Responsibility and State Responsibility in Britain Before the Welfare State', *The Historical Journal*, 25:1 (1982), pp. 142–3. Ellen Wilkinson said that in Jarrow the means test meant 'psychological damnation'. Wilkinson, *The Town That Was Murdered*, p. 220.

37 Newsom, *Out of the Pit*, p. 48.

38 For sibling tension, see Gwyn Thomas, *Sorrow for Thy Sons* (London, 1986).

39 The Pilgrim Trust noted how fathers were afraid to look as if they were spending 'an undue share of the family income' while unemployed. Ginzberg, *Grass on the Slag Heaps*, p. 34; *Men Without Work*, p. 148.

40 Chris Williams, *Capitalism, Community and Conflict: The South Wales Coalfield, 1898–1947* (Cardiff, 1998), p. 63; Valerie Gordon Hall, 'Contrasting Female Identities: Women in Coal Mining Communities in Northumberland, England, 1900–1939', *Journal of Women's History*, 13:2 (2001), pp. 109–10.

41 Both age groups were victims of a competitive labour market. Long-term unemployment was the greatest hindrance for a return to work: employers expressed anxiety over the effects of this on a person's character and the lack of training of young men. *Men Without Work*, p. 69.

42 *Disinherited Youth*, p. 29; *The Second Industrial Survey of South Wales*, p. 23.

43 Newsom, *Out of the Pit*, p. 46.

44 'Too Old at Forty – A South Wales Miner', in H. Beales and R. S. Lambert (eds), *Memoirs of the Unemployed* (London, 1934), p. 68.

45 *Disinherited Youth*, pp. 7, 56–7, 60, 69–70; see also A. J. Lush, *The Young Adult in South Wales* (Cardiff, 1941), p. 36.

46 Wilkinson gave the example of 'a sister, working as a skilled typist, made to keep a father and adult brothers, thus depriving her of the possibility of saving for old age, or getting clothes and nourishment needed for work'. However, generally, the continued dependency of women was not considered to have any particular effect on women especially as once married women in the two regions overwhelmingly became dependants. Moreover, although concern was expressed for those women leaving the area to become domestic servants, concerns related to social and moral decline were not associated with young women as they were for young men. Wilkinson, *The Town That Was Murdered*, p. 218.

47 Hilda Ashby, 'Wait till the banner comes home!', in Armstrong and Beynon, *Hello, Are You Working?*, p. 42.

48 Charles Graham, 'South Shields', in Gray, *The Worst of Times*, p. 109; Walter Greenwood, *Love on the Dole* (London, 1993 edition; first published 1935), pp. 221–4.

49 Max Cohen, *I was One of the Unemployed* (London, 1945), p. 97.

50 In south Wales, some investigators even requested maintaining their SWMF membership. SWCC, South Wales Miners' Federation, Minutes of Executive Council, 26 August 1932. See also, Edward Warburton and Carl Butler, *'Disallowed': The Tragedy of the Means Test* (London, 1935), pp. 1–2, 99.

51 NLW, Idris Cox Collection, *A Town on the Dole* (Published by the Brynmawr Communist Party, Abertillery, c.1937–39), p. 18.

52 Will Oxley, an unemployed ex-serviceman from the north-east, believed that the outcome of the means test investigation depended on the mood and temperament of the investigator. Oxley, 'Are You Working?', in Jack Common (ed.), *Seven Shifts* (London, 1938), p. 106.

53 John Bell, 'The Market', in Armstrong and Beynon, *Hello, Are You Working?*, p. 29.

54 Especially Chapter 5, Walter Brierley, *Means-Test Man* (Nottingham, 1983 edition; first published 1935). The memory also left an impression on Brierley's son. John Brierley, *In the Shadow of the Means Test Man: Memories of a Derbyshire Childhood* (Highedge Historical Society, 1995), p. 53.

55 Warburton and Butler, *Disallowed*, pp. 12–16, 26–7.

56 Newsom, *Out of the Pit*, p. 42.

57 Reginald J. Barker, *Christ in the Valley of Unemployment* (Suffolk, 1936), p. 31.
58 Oxley, 'Are You Working?', pp. 134–5.
59 The Communist *Rhondda Vanguard* noted that anger had been generated by 'the practice employed by Investigators of entering bedrooms to examine the condition of the bedclothes'. *Rhondda Vanguard*, No. 5, December 1935, p. 3.
60 *Men Without Work*, p. 185.
61 *A Town on the Dole*, p. 18.
62 Cabinet Committee on the Regulation of the Unemployment Assistance Board Minutes, 11 May 1936, p. 2. The Newcastle district officer, Arthur Sharp, noted letters of appreciation and verbal gratitude had been received on account of the good relations that existed. By the end of 1937, the Regional Officer for Wales, W. L. Addyman, was able to state with some confidence that relations between the Board and applicants were amicable: 'for a time the investigators were regarded as inquisitors who must be kept at arms length and to whom the scantiest information should be disclosed. Nowadays, however, in all but a small minority of cases investigators find little difficulty in securing all information which it is their duty to require'. *Report of the Unemployment Assistance Board, 1935*, p. 526; *Report of the Unemployment Assistance Board for the Period Ended 31 December 1937* (Cmd 5752), 1937–38, xiii, p. 239.
63 *Men Without Work*, p. 187.
64 Wilkinson argued the wives of the unemployed spoke positively of the kindness of some investigators. Wilkinson, *The Town That Was Murdered*, p. 218; Newsom, *Out of the Pit*, p. 76.
65 *Men Without Work*, p. 112; *A Town on the Dole*, pp. 2–3; Ginzberg, *Grass on the Slag Heaps*, p. 161; Newsom, *Out of the Pit*, pp. 22, 34, 42–3.
66 Ginzberg, *Grass on the Slag Heaps*, p. 161.
67 *A Town on the Dole*, p. 3.
68 Mrs Pallas, 'Time to Spare', in Felix Greene (ed.), *Time to Spare: What Unemployment Means by Eleven Unemployed* (London, 1935), p. 31.
69 Brierley, *Means Test Man*, p. 23.
70 Neil Penlington, 'Masculinity and Domesticity in 1930s South Wales: Did Unemployment Change the Domestic Division of Labour?', *Twentieth Century British History*, 21:3 (2010), p. 299.
71 E. Ll. Harry and J. R. E. Phillips, 'Expenditure of Unemployed and Employed Households: A Study of Yearly Budgets', *The Welsh Journal of Agriculture*, xiv (1938), p. 103.
72 *Ibid.*, p. 94.
73 Avram Taylor, '"You Never Told Your Mam": Women's Management of Household Finances and Credit During the Inter-war Period', *North East Labour History Society Bulletin*, 30 (1996), pp. 51–63; Steven Thompson,

Unemployment, Poverty and Health in Interwar South Wales (Cardiff, 2006), pp. 45–76.

74 Steven Thompson, 'Unemployment, Poverty and Women's Health in Interwar South Wales', in Pamela Michael and Charles Webster (eds), *Health and Society in Twentieth-Century Wales* (Cardiff, 2006), p. 102.

75 Charles Webster, 'Health, Welfare and Unemployment During the Depression', *Past and Present*, 109 (1985), p. 211.

76 Cole, *The Condition of Britain*, p. 218.

77 Margery Spring Rice, *Working-Class Wives: Their Health and Conditions* (London, 1939), p. 155.

78 Hannington, *The Problem of the Distressed Areas*, p. 62.

79 *Ibid.*, p. 70; Hannington also made this claim in *Ten Lean Years* where he provided evidence from coroners' reports in the press. Wal Hannington, *Ten Lean Years: An Examination of the Record of the National Government in the Field of Unemployment* (London, 1940), pp. 46–7.

80 Roberts, the second person the article writes about, died after he moved to London and continued to work despite being ill. It was argued that 'if it had not been for the means test he would probably have never left home'. *Daily Worker*, 12 February 1935, p. 1.

81 A. Fenner Brockway, *Hungry England* (London, 1932), p. 171.

82 David Vincent has argued that 'despite the tragedies highlighted by the NUWM, the suicide rate only rose slightly during the Depression'. David Vincent, *Poor Citizens: The State and the Poor in Twentieth Century Britain* (Harlow, 1991), p. 99.

83 *Porth Gazette*, 15 April 1933, p. 5, and 22 April 1933, p. 5.

84 Although there is no evidence to support the claim of an epidemic, the number of suicides in the Rhondda reached its highest point in the interwar years in 1936 and accounted for over a third of Glamorgan's total. *Rhondda Fach Gazette*, 18 July 1936, p. 6; Treorchy Library Local Studies Collection, Rhondda Urban District Council, *Annual Report of the Medical Officer of Health*, 1936; *Criminal Statistics, England and Wales*, 1936 (Cmd 5690), 1937–38, xxvii, p. 693.

85 The man was known locally as 'Dead Bodies'. Charles Graham, 'Dead-End Jobs; "Dead Bodies"', p. 25.

86 Newsom, *Out of the Pit*, pp. 42–3, 22, 34.

87 The debate on these issues continues. John Stevenson and Chris Cook have argued that 'although no conclusive answer was possible about the relationship between unemployment and suicide, it made a sufficiently strong impression on contemporaries to be regarded as a significant factor in the rising suicide rate'. John Stevenson and Chris Cook, *Britain in the Depression: Society and Politics 1929–39* (London, 1994), p. 97. See also, John Burnett, *Idle Hands: The Experience of Unemployment, 1790–1990* (London, 1984), pp. 233–4.

88 John Burnett, for example, has argued that there was 'resilience in communities' which were actually 'strengthened' by the experience of the depression. Burnett, *Idle Hands*, pp. 215, 235, 264.

89 Joe Hind, *A Shieldfield Childhood* (Newcastle-upon-Tyne, 1994), p. 45.

90 Ginzberg, *Grass on the Slag Heaps*, p. 45. The authors of *Disinherited Youth* reported similar evidence in their work. *Disinherited Youth*, pp. 70–1.

91 Warburton and Butler, *Disallowed*, p. 18.

92 Orwell stated that 'the favourite joke in Wigan was about a man who was refused relief on the ground that he "had a job carting firewood". He had been seen, it was said, carting firewood at night. He had to explain that he was not carting firewood but doing a moonlight flit. The "firewood" was his furniture'. George Orwell, *The Road to Wigan Pier* (London, 2001 edition; first published, 1937), p. 72.

93 The definition of denunciation here follows that of Sheila Fitzpatrick and Robert Gellately and includes almost all acts of telling upon someone from informing to the Gestapo to tax evasion. Sheila Fitzpatrick and Robert Gellately, 'Introduction to the Practices of Denunciation in Modern European History', in Sheila Fitzpatrick and Robert Gellately (eds), *Accusatory Practices: Denunciation in Modern European History, 1789–1989* (Chicago, 1997), pp. 1, 13–16.

94 David Vincent, *The Culture of Secrecy: Britain, 1832–1998* (Oxford, 1998), p. 153.

95 Hywel Francis and Dai Smith, *The Fed: A History of the South Wales Miners in the Twentieth Century* (Cardiff, 1998), pp. 283–4.

96 There were a number of demonstrations in 1938, but they were not as widespread as in 1936.

97 Croucher, *We Refuse to Starve in Silence*, pp. 179–82; Francis and Smith, *The Fed*, pp. 270–3; Neil Evans, '"South Wales Has Been Roused as Never Before": Marching Against the Means Test, 1934–36', in David W. Howell and Kenneth O. Morgan (eds), *Crime, Protest and Police in Modern British Society: Essays in Memory of David J. V. Jones* (Cardiff, 1999), pp. 197–9; Perry, *Bread and Work*, pp. 112–13.

98 Croucher, *We Refuse to Starve in Silence*, p. 182; Matt Perry, *The Jarrow Crusade: Protest and Legend* (Sunderland, 2005), pp. 1–20.

99 CAB 27/575, Cabinet Committee on the Regulations of the Unemployment Assistance Board, 11 May 1936, pp. 1–11.

100 The sense of expectation was heightened by a delay in announcing the new regulations. *Manchester Guardian*, 1 July 1936, p. 11.

101 *Daily Worker*, 13 July 1936, p. 1.

102 *Manchester Guardian*, 17 July 1936, p. 12.

103 The SWMF focused its energies on organising a questionnaire to explore levels of hardship. More radical lodges like Tillery Lodge called for militant action which did lead to some tension. SWCC, MNA/NUM/3/1/1/27, South

Wales Miners' Federation Minutes of Special Meeting, Cardiff, 14 January 1936; SWCC, MNA/NUM/3/4/42, Correspondence between D. J. Hawkins, Secretary of the Unemployed Lodge Pontycymmer, and Oliver Harris, General Secretary of the SWMF, 23 January 1936 and 27 January 1936; SWCC, MNA/NUM/3/3/43/4, Circular from Tillery Lodge to all Lodges of the SWMF, 4 January, 1936; MNA/NUM/3/3/43/3, Correspondence between Oliver Harris and United Unemployed Lodge Blaina, 27 January 1936, Ferndale Lodge, 15 February 1936, Caerphilly Lodge, 15 February 1936; MNA/NUM/3/3/43/3, Circular from Oliver Harris to all Lodges, 18 February 1936.

104 *Free Press and Rhondda Leader*, 18 July 1936, pp. 4, 8. In later months, Rhondda MPs W. H. Mainwaring and Will John wrote in the local Labour Party's journal that 'one of the most pleasing and outstanding features of the present agitation against the New Unemployment Regulations is the part played by the religious bodies in the Rhondda'. *The Rhondda Clarion (The Official Organ of the Rhondda Borough Labour Party)*, 12 October 1936, p. 3.

105 The left-wing press followed the build-up to the meeting with much interest. *Daily Herald*, 13 July 1936, p. 11; *Daily Worker*, 13 July 1936, p. 1.

106 *Daily Worker*, 20 July 1936, p. 1.

107 It should be noted that demonstrations were taking place in the week leading up to the conference. On Friday, 4,000 men, women and children marched to Nantyglo, and a 'huge demonstration' also took place at Abertillery which included Tillery Lodge, women's sections of the Labour Party, the Working Women's Guild and the NUWM. *Daily Worker*, 18 July 1936, p. 1 and 20 July 1936, p. 2.

108 *Daily Herald*, 20 July 1936, p. 11.

109 *Manchester Guardian*, 13 July 1936, p. 11.

110 *Ibid.*, 20 July 1936, p. 13; *The Times*, 21 July 1936, p. 9.

111 *Daily Worker*, 28 July 1936, p. 2.

112 *The Times* put the estimate of the number marching in the Rhondda at a more conservative 'several thousand'. *The Times*, 27 July 1936, p. 14; *Daily Herald*, 27 July 1936, p. 9; *Free Press and Rhondda Leader*, 1 August 1936, p. 1.

113 TNA, HLG 30/37, Minutes of Conference on Unemployment Assistance Regulations, Possible Disorder in South Wales, 31 July 1936, pp. 1–4; HLG 30/37, Report of Meeting Held to Discuss Possible Disorder in South Wales Following Establishment of the New Regulations, 31 July 1936, pp. 1–2.

114 The Minister of Labour stated, 'the forces concerned were excellent forces, with a good body of Superintendents, and although the Chief Constables of Glamorgan and Monmouth were themselves old and physically infirm there was not likely to be any lack of firmness and resolution in carrying out the duties which would devolve on the police in case of trouble'. *Ibid.*, p. 2.

115 *Ibid.*, p. 4.

116 *Manchester Guardian*, 23 July 1936, p. 3.

117 *Ibid.*
118 DMOR, DMA, Circular, 15 July 1936.
119 DMOR, DMA Minutes of Council Meeting, 11 July 1936, p. 2.
120 *Ibid.*, 27 July 1936, p. 2.
121 DMA, Circular, 28 July 1936.
122 *Daily Worker*, 15 July 1936, p. 1.
123 Representative of the increased popularity of Communism was the election of two Communist councillors in the region. Jim Ancrum (local leader for the NUWM) was elected in October 1935 to Felling Urban District Council, and T. A. Richardson was elected in August 1936 to Houghton-le-Spring Urban District Council. TNA, HO 144/20696, MI5, Progress Reports of the March to London, 22 October 1936; *Heslop's Local Advertiser*, 14 August 1936, p. 14; Lewis Mates, 'Durham and South Wales Miners and the Spanish Civil War', *Twentieth Century British History*, 17:3 (2006), p. 381.
124 *Daily Worker*, 14 July 1936, p. 2. Unity between the Labour and Communist parties was also in evidence at Chester-le-Street where a united front conference was organised. *Auckland Chronicle*, 30 July 1936, p. 2.
125 Mates has argued that 'there was a fine balance on the DMA executive between those sympathetic and antipathetic towards the Communist Party, and practical activity with the Communists was more difficult to achieve'. Mates, 'Durham and South Wales Miners and the Spanish Civil War', p. 381.
126 *Auckland Chronicle*, 23 July 1936, pp. 9–10.
127 *Ibid.*
128 *Daily Worker*, 13 July 1936, p. 1.
129 DMOR, DMA, Circular, 17 August 1936.
130 *Ibid.*
131 *Auckland Chronicle*, 20 August 1936, p. 16.
132 DMA, Minutes of Committee Meeting, 17 August 1936, p. 2.
133 *Auckland Chronicle*, 20 August 1936, p. 9.
134 Although communication took place between the DMA and the South Wales and Monmouthshire Unemployed Joint Council on the proposed hunger march to London in September, the suggestion raised by Follonsby Lodge, in the following month, that the DMA identify itself with the hunger march was considered 'off the board'. DMA, Minutes of Committee Meeting, 15 September 1936, p. 4; DMA, Programme of Council Meeting to be held on 17 October 1936, p. 3, Minutes of Council Meeting, 17 October 1936, p. 4.
135 *Daily Worker*, 25 August 1936, p. 2.
136 For example, on 17 October, the Newcastle and District Trades Council held a conference to consider the regulations and their effects.
137 Wilkinson argued that 'the march had struck the imagination of the people of Jarrow'. Wilkinson, *The Town That Was Murdered*, pp. 191–213.
138 Perry, *The Jarrow Crusade*, p. 7.
139 *Ibid.*, pp. 180–3.

140 Croucher, *We Refuse to Starve in Silence*, pp. 181–2.
141 *The Times*, 31 August 1936, p. 14.
142 *Ibid.*, 9 September 1936, pp. 7, 12.
143 Matthias Reiss, 'Circulars, Surveys and Support: Trades Councils and the Marches of 1936', *Labour History Review*, 73:1 (2008), p. 90.
144 TNA, HO 144/20696, Correspondence between Alexander Hardinge (Buckingham Palace) and A. S. Hutchinson (Home Office), 20 and 21 October 1936.
145 HO 144/20696, Correspondence between P. A. Newsam and the Home Office, including copy of the report from the Chief Constable of York, 22 October 1936.
146 HO 144/20696, Correspondence, Lionel Lindsay to the Under Secretary of State, 23 October 1936.
147 HO 144/20696, Report of the Hunger Marchers from South Wales, 23 October 1936, pp. 1–8.
148 Croucher, *We Refuse to Starve in Silence*, p. 179.
149 HO 144/20696, Home Office Report on the Hunger March 1936, 11 February 1937, p. 1.
150 Croucher, *We Refuse to Starve in Silence*, p. 181.
151 *Free Press and Rhondda Leader*, 18 July 1936, p. 8.
152 Lindsay wrote to the Home Office to warn that 'there is a section of the community which is very bitter against Mr Brown over the Means Test. It would be a terrible thing if someone booed Brown and His Majesty thought they were booing him wouldn't it?' TNA, HO 144/21066, Correspondence between Captain Lionel Lindsay and the Home Office, 10 November 1936; Correspondence between Roynon Baker, Superintendent Abertillery, and the Chief Constable of Monmouthshire Police, 6 November 1936.
153 *Daily Herald*, 16 November 1936, p. 1; GRO, Misc. Mss. 1259, Abertillery Urban District Council, *Abertillery: Visit of His Majesty King Edward VIII to Rhiw Park, Abertillery* (Abertillery Urban District Council, 1936).
154 Ted Rowlands, *'Something Must Be Done': South Wales v Whitehall, 1921–1951* (Merthyr Tydfil, 2000), p. 97–104.
155 Evans, '"South Wales Has Been Roused as Never Before"', pp. 197–8.
156 It appears that this march did not go ahead. SWCC, SWMF Correspondence, Unemployed Lodges and Unemployed Movement, 1933–38, letter from Wal Hannington to General Secretary Oliver Harris, not dated; letter from General Secretary to Wal Hannington dated 28 April 1937.
157 LHASC, LP/WPRG/37/704–36, Organiser's Reports, 13 September 1937 and 31 October 1937 and LP/WORG/37/319–344, Organiser's Report, Rhondda East and West, 18 October 1937.
158 NLW, Labour Party of Wales Collection, Executive Committee Minutes of the South Wales Regional Council of Labour, Annual Meeting Minutes, 11 June, 1938.

159 SWCC, MNC/PP/14/1, Arthur Lewis Jones Collection, National Unemployed Workers' Movement, Dowlais Branch Committee Minutes, 15 March 1938, 5 April 1938, 26 April 1938 and 19 May 1938.

160 *Daily Herald*, 1 February 1938, p. 11.

161 Communist Party membership in December 1936 in south Wales accounted for 7% of the total British membership figures. In 1935, it had accounted for 17.3%, and by January 1939, it had fallen to 5.7%. Andrew Thorpe, 'The Membership of the Communist Party of Great Britain, 1920–45', *Historical Journal*, 43 (2000), p. 790.

162 Chris Williams, *Capitalism, Community and Conflict: The South Wales Coalfield, 1898–1947* (Cardiff, 1998), p. 58.

163 SCOLAR, Microfilm: Papers from the Communist Party of Great Britain Archives: Wal Hannington Papers, CP/IND/HANN/01/06, NUWM NAC Circular, 5 July 1935.

164 Richard Flanagan, *'Parish-Fed Bastards': A History of the Politics of the Unemployed in Britain, 1884–1939* (London, 1991), p. 177.

165 Hywel Francis, *Miners Against Fascism: Wales and the Spanish Civil War* (London, 1984), p. 192.

166 SWCC, MNA/NUM/3/3/43/4, Unemployed Lodges Misc. 1934–39, Letter from Oliver Harris, General Secretary, to D. E. Thomas, Miners' Agent Area No. 5, 21 February 1938.

167 Executive Committee Minutes of the South Wales Regional Council of Labour, 22 February 1938, pp. 101–2, and 4 May 1938, p. 120.

168 A united platform was finally agreed upon which included speakers from the NUWM, SWMF and two vicars, councillor T. Evans, councillor Lewis Jones and Mrs McPhail to 'represent the Women of Dowlais and Penydarren'. National Unemployed Workers' Movement, Dowlais Branch Committee Minutes, 5 April 1938; GAC, GB0214 DXHV, S. O. Davies Papers, Minute Book of the Unemployed Miners' Branch Dowlais, 23 April 1938.

169 SWCC, MNA/NUM/3/8/19a, SWMF Circular, c. February 1938; *Rhondda Fach Gazette*, 12 February 1938, p. 3.

170 SWCC, MNA/NUM/3/3/43/4, Unemployed Lodges Misc., 1934–39, Letter from W. E. Hill, Secretary of Area No. 3 Miners' Office, Bridgend, to Oliver Harris, dated 17 February 1938.

171 MNA/NUM/3/8/19a, SWMF Circular, c. February 1938.

172 *Aberdare Leader*, 16 April 1938, p. 7.

173 LHASC, LP/WORG/37/408–444, Organiser's Report, Abertillery Constituency, 11 November 1936.

174 *The Times*, 14 April 1939, p. 11.

175 SWCC, MNA/NUM/3/3/43/4, Correspondence between D. R. Llewelyn, Secretary of the Garw Unemployed Lodge, and the General Secretary of the SWMF, 26 October 1939.

176 This did happen at an earlier point and the SWMF did maintain links with the Communist Party for much longer. Mates, 'Durham and South Wales Miners and the Spanish Civil War', pp. 381–2.
177 *The Times*, 11 October 1937, p. 20.
178 Wilkinson, *The Town That Was Murdered*, p. 196.
179 DMA Minutes, Circulars, Etc., January–June 1938, Letters to members of the DMA from Sam Watson, Unemployment Officer, dated 10 January 1938 and 26 January 1938; *Northern Echo*, 21 January 1938, p. 3.
180 MPs involved in the debate were R. J. Taylor (Morpeth), Mr Batey (Spennymoor) and Jack Lawson (Chester-le-Street). *The Times*, 4 August 1939, p. 6.
181 Croucher, *Unemployed Struggles*, pp. 190–91.
182 *Hansard,* HC (series 5) vol. 356, col. 195 (18 January 1940).
183 *Ibid*., vol. 357, cols 1209–309 (20 February 1940).
184 *Ibid.,* vol. 357, col. 1301 (20 February 1940).
185 *Ibid.,* vol. 365, col. 1343 (6 November 1940).
186 *Manchester Guardian*, 7 November 1940, p. 4.
187 Indeed, the NUWM did not see the reforms as a victory at all. *Unemployment, Labour and Social Services Bulletin*, 67, 24 February 1941, p. 1.

Conclusion

> South Wales is responsive to preaching of any kind, political preaching included, and here, if anywhere, a grievance becomes in a moment a battle-cry. Moreover, as the valleys are geographically bounded by the mountains, so those who live in them are bounded in outlook to their own concerns. They are not part of the world outside but belong to a world of their own, and a measure which has been taken for external reasons and which affects them adversely is in their thinking designed to crush them.
>
> *Men Without Work: A Report Made to the Pilgrim Trust* (1938).[1]

> The Durham miner who has been out of work for five years has not the perpetual sense of grievance, but rather – though he is actually poorer on the whole than the unemployed man in South Wales – a determination to make the best of things; to make his allotment or his poultry holding a life for himself, not an alternative to employment, but rather to keep himself fit for employment, to help at the family budget, and to retain active interests.
>
> *Men Without Work: A Report Made to the Pilgrim Trust* (1938).[2]

The separation of the short-term and long-term unemployed in 1931 represented a step backwards from both pre- and post-war welfare legislation which had been designed to protect insured workers from destitution.[3] The application of a household means test and its administration by the PACs carried with it the taint of the poor law: it was viewed by the unemployed in both south Wales and north-east England as an attack on working-class values and notions of respectability. Those used to regular employment and the attainment of financial assistance during periods of joblessness, either through the national insurance scheme or trade union and friendly society benefits, were horrified at the prospect of being viewed as destitute. Ideas of the deserving and undeserving poor were as important within working-class communities as they were to the government. Yet, while the means test may have represented a halt in the progress of welfare policies for the respectable worker, the repercussions of administration in the 1930s ultimately helped to transform welfare policies.

The record of PACs in south Wales and the north-east of England highlights the difficulties inherent in the local administration of central social and welfare policies.[4] Placing the responsibility for determining transitional payments in the hands of councillors left the administration of the means test open to the influence of local opinion and, ultimately, abuse. PAC officials could be directly lobbied through deputations, marches and correspondence and recognised that they risked electoral failure through implementing a deeply unpopular policy. The challenge to their administration came not only from the unemployed, since ratepayers, although not asking for clemency to be shown towards the out of work, spoke out against taxes that were levied to fund public assistance applicants. Providing generous transitional payments, therefore, allowed a PAC to both placate the unemployed and those who still paid taxes. In both regions, Labour-dominated PACs largely pursued this line until the Ministry of Labour forced officials to implement the means test more strictly. Although many PACs were threatened with replacement by governmental commissioners, it was only Durham PAC that refused to relent and administer the measure. This study has attempted to demonstrate the complexity of the events that led to PAC officials' decisions to defy the government: electoral propaganda, party policy and the personal connection to constituents were fundamental. It was the action of PACs like those in south Wales and the north-east of England that led the government to reorganise the administration of unemployment benefit through the UAB.

The response of the government in centralising the administration of the means test under the UAB marked a key change in welfare policy. As Derek Fraser has shown, during the war years, the activities of the UAB (renamed the National Assistance Board) were extended and 'thus anticipated post-war developments'.[5] This was undoubtedly one of the greatest impacts of the implementation of a household means test in the 1930s. Although many of the officials employed by the UAB were working class, had possibly experienced unemployment themselves and may have worked for the PACs, the centralised bureaucracy created a symbolic distance between the unemployed and the administrators of welfare. Officials of the UAB could not be influenced through direct action, as they did not have the power to increase rates of payments. Moreover, they did not face the threat of losing their position through nonelection.

After 1935, central welfare policy was always administered by centrally controlled bodies. Paul Bagguley has suggested that this had a longer-term significance for protest patterns, as the UAB's lack of susceptibility to local influence marked the decline of street protests to local administrative bodies.[6] By removing the power of administrating the means test from PACs, the government was both curbing the power of local authorities and the wider electorate. Change through extra-parliamentary protest effectively became redundant, and this was already demonstrated in the protests in 1936 in particular. For the unemployed, protest was a means of entering the political arena and a method of contributing to debate; the removal of a local focus for agitation had repercussions for the protests of the unemployed in later decades. The means test is also, therefore, revealing of the relationship between the unemployed and the state.

While the means test formed part of a wider programme of retrenchment, such benefit tests represented a hangover of middle-class Edwardian social ideals which, in contrast to working-class ideologies of welfare, maintained that state maintenance was not a right, but a privilege. Like the principles of the poor law, the means test of 1931 encouraged self-reliance or support *within* the household. At a time of a global financial crisis, ideas of state dependency were also framed within the context of a national emergency. The test was portrayed as the patriotic duty of the unemployed during a period of economic adversity. As transitional payments were funded from the Exchequer, the unemployed were asked to receive a reduced allowance to help the government economise. Asking ex-servicemen with disabilities to continue to do their bit for their country raises important issues about citizenship and obligation as well as notions of patriotism. The response of ex-servicemen and the British Legion through protest alongside the loyal cheers to the Royal family on tours of the depressed regions demonstrates the complexity of this issue. Indeed, how far patriotism could be used as a justification for benefit levels held particular resonance during the Second World War when UABs refused extra relief for materials to blackout windows.[7]

The creation of the UAB had repercussions beyond revolutionising the administration of unemployment benefit. Under the Unemployment Act, 1934, able-bodied public assistance came within the charge of the UAB, and certain elements of the poor law were changed as a consequence.[8] Moreover, the charge given to the body for all of the unemployed marked the gradual decline of the hierarchal distinction made amongst the out of work who required relief. While the distinction between the deserving and undeserving poor has persisted, since the creation of the welfare state, no form of governmental relief has carried with it the taint of destitution. It was the perceived attack upon notions of respectability that had generated the greatest outcry along with the claim that families separated. The arguments against the means test in this way reveal how the social signifiers of the respectable working class, although affected by unemployment, were no less important. The effects of the means test on gendered identity, and male identity especially, make this point most explicitly.

Working-class male identity has most often been portrayed as embodying a strong and powerful masculinity.[9] However, the impact of long-term unemployment and the means test demonstrated how the strength of masculine identity was dependent upon a particular socio-economic environment, within both family and community, which allowed for work, independence and the performance of the role of breadwinner. In the 1930s, therefore, it was a fragility of masculinity that most characterised the unemployed who, as younger workers, were unable to escape dependence or, in the case of older workers, found their independence and status removed. This is a point which remains underexplored within the historiography. The effect of the means test on masculine identity conveys how it was more than financial considerations that could lead to the break-up of the family home. A full transitional payment was also symbolic of a degree of independence within the household. Collusive desertion and children leaving home prematurely should also be seen as a way of reasserting masculinity and status within the family.

How masculine identity could be reasserted by the unemployed through means other than splitting the household remains to be explored; an examination of protest movements appears to be most important in this respect. Participation in politics and movements of the unemployed provided occupation for the long empty hours and gave men an opportunity to feel as if they were doing something positive rather than accepting their fate.[10] In south Wales and the north-east, the unemployed could march and demonstrate in their tens of thousands, and the function of these protests in allowing masculinity to be reasserted was one possible reason for the involvement of so many.

Although there was no credible difference in the effects of the means test within south Wales and the north-east of England and the administration of the measure was broadly comparable, the actions of the unemployed in the response to the means test differed considerably. While the unemployed in south Wales were mobilised throughout the period in dramatic displays of collective action, street protests were far less common in the north-east, and written resolutions of opposition formed a much more central role in the protest that occurred. The image of the working class in south Wales as militant and the working class in the north-east of England as acquiescent are well-established characterisations but do not, however, solely account for the differences in the response to the means test. Although events in the 1930s were not acted out in a historical isolation, the situation for many of those facing unemployment was unprecedented and unique. Just as the protest of the unemployed was not automatic, neither was the response of the labour movement. Why the unemployed responded so differently in south Wales and north-east was the consequence of a complex interplay between longer political and cultural trends and also the events of the previous decade.

Marching as an expression of protest was much more evident in those areas with a closer settlement pattern and with a tradition of industrial and political militancy. These factors suggest themselves as the two most important resources the unemployed could draw upon or utilise to mobilise for collective action. In south Wales and the north-east, protest occurred in those areas rapidly industrialised in the late nineteenth and early twentieth centuries and/or where settlements were closely connected. In south Wales, this accounted for much of the region and especially the industrial valleys, and in the north-east, protest was much more prevalent in the area around Sunderland, along Tyneside and the recently rapidly industrialised parts of Northumberland. The working class in these areas, where industrial action was more prevalent, were readily mobilised for collective action. In much of the Durham and Northumberland coalfields, which had a much longer tradition of industry and had pursued a trade union policy of cooperation and conciliation, such a radical and militant tradition did not exist. In these geographically isolated pit villages, street protests against the means test were not as common as elsewhere. Marching and demonstrating against the means test was more likely to occur where a tradition of collective action existed that could be called upon. This was especially true of the working class in south Wales, where from the 1910s until 1926 militant industrial politics characterised the coalfield. However, the case of south Wales also shows the importance of other factors in allowing for mass action against the means test; while the SWMF may have led the working class in their militant struggle against employers, they were not always so central to the battle against the means test.

Throughout this study, it has been emphasised how leadership for collective action was imperative for the successful mobilisation of the unemployed. Leadership gave protest coordination, longevity and unity across groups and geographical stretches. Who emerged as the leaders of the unemployed in an area or region, while dependent upon traditions of industrial relations and the political culture, also reveals the importance of shorter-term factors and the relationship between the labour movement and the unemployed. The end of the General Strike and lockout had dramatic and far-reaching consequences in both regions, although the repercussions had quite different outcomes for protest against the means test. While in many areas of the north-east of England loyalty to the trade unions remained unaffected by the General Strike, in south Wales leadership for action began to be sought elsewhere. The power of the rank and file in south Wales and the propensity of the workers to participate in collective action, amongst other dynamics, created the right conditions for alternative sources of leadership to emerge. While the SWMF remained an important source of support for many of the unemployed, it was not until 1934 that the executive committee established a clear policy towards its unemployed members.[11] Moreover, the executive committee did not always readily lead the unemployed in marches. This was also true of the Labour Party. Duncan Tanner has argued that 'as unemployment and its consequences escalated, the pressure to be "practical" grew.... Labour's desire to protect working-class communities meant rejecting some "militant" proposals for confronting capitalism'.[12] In the late 1920s and until the later 1930s, the Communist Party and the NUWM provided an alternative source of leadership that allowed for mass action against the means test.

The leadership of the NUWM with its emphasis on militant (although not violent) action ensured that numerous marches and demonstrations took place in areas where the movement gained popularity. This was true not only of south Wales but also the north-east where the prevalence of the NUWM in and around Tyneside, Sunderland and Blyth was demonstrated in the number of marches that took place. The NUWM worked tirelessly to mobilise the unemployed for local, regional and national marches against the means test.[13] The movement adopted the abolition of the means test as its chief cause, and although the national hunger marches are synonymous with its actions, the marches and deputations organised to PACs and UABs were vitally important within localities. They gave the unemployed an opportunity to lobby local officials directly, and this action could even influence scales of transitional payments.

Although important, the role of the NUWM and the Communist Party within the south Wales region should not be exaggerated. While they undoubtedly provided the unemployed with a leadership that allowed for constant action against the means test and gave a powerful voice to the plight of the out of work, the mainstream labour movement remained significant. Membership of the NUWM was fluid and did not represent a complete rejection of the SWMF or the Labour Party for many. Individual lodges of the SWMF and countless Labour Party councillors and MPs both led the unemployed for street protests and participated in other examples of collective action. It was the unity that could be achieved by the official labour movement and, at times, the Communist Party and the NUWM that made protest against the means test so dramatic in its scale.

The organisation of the SWMF across the coalfield allowed the unemployed to be mobilised across the whole region when a call for street protests against the means test was issued. The strength of the NUWM and the Communist Party in certain areas allowed for a unification of action between the SWMF and these groups. The affiliation of the SWMF with the Labour Party ensured further support, and when such a breadth of leadership and action was taking place, other community and political organisations could become involved. This unity of action, together with the prevalence of the issue of the means test in the working-class-dominated communities, helps to explain the scale of street protests in 1935. In south Wales, the desire for action from the unemployed coupled with the breadth of leadership and support from the regionally unified mainstream labour movement, as well as the NUWM and the Communist Party, explains the popularity of street protests as a response to the means test. What assisted the organisation of the unemployed in the region was the topography. The valleys of south Wales allowed for easier communication between villages, organisation across a wider area and provided an arena for protest.[14]

In much of the north-east, support for both the Labour Party and the trade unions, in particular the DMA, remained strong after the General Strike.[15] The loyalty to the union combined with an aversion to collective action after the lockout created a situation where the unemployed were not readily mobilised for protest. Policies of conciliation and cooperation continued to influence the politics of the unions, and they mediated grievances and protest against the means test between the unemployed and the government (local and national). Indeed, W. R. Garside has shown how the DMA 'acted as a liaison between its members and the U.A.B.'.[16] Furthermore, the DMA took an active interest in its unemployed members from an early date, and this undoubtedly contributed to the loyalty of its members.[17] Indeed, the most successful marches that were organised within the region, outside of the more militant areas and Tyneside especially, were led by the DMA. However, when the DMA did arrange such action, its county-based organisation and largely insular outlook prevented mobilisation on a regional level. More widespread action against the means test in the north-east was, therefore, prevented by an aversion of the trade unions to street protests, the lack of support for alternative leadership and the absence of a regionally organised labour movement. Even at a local level, there was little unity between the official labour movement and the NUWM or Communist Party. The relative isolation of pit villages undoubtedly hindered communication for marches and demonstrations and also removed a clear route for marches that could encapsulate a wide level of support. However, as has been emphasised throughout, the lower number of street protests in comparison to south Wales should not be taken as evidence that the unemployed in the north-east were either accepting of the means test or acquiescent.[18]

In articulating opposition in the north-east of England, other forms of protest, such as resolutions and petitions, were essential. An examination of these sources reveals how the unemployed expressed their opposition to the means test and the role of meetings, but not marches and demonstrations, in orchestrating these protests. Resolutions, petitions, meetings and letters acted both as a vital mode of protest and laid the foundations for the larger examples of collective action. These other expressions of protest created a constant bombardment of opposition against the government, and, as events in 1933–34 demonstrated, they could also act as a way of generating support for widespread demonstrations against the means test. Although an extremely prevalent source of opposition in the north-east, these other expressions of protest were utilised in south Wales and the comparative analysis demonstrates the need to look beyond street protests as the only expression of opposition. Part of the appeal of these other forms of opposition was the less radical connotations of this protest in comparison to demonstrating in the streets. The protests of the unemployed influenced the perception of the out of work, and this point was recognised by the unemployed and their leaders. Association with a particular expression of protest was favoured by those groups that wished to distance themselves from militancy and, chiefly, the label of Communist.

The comparison of protest movements against the means test in south Wales and the north-east of England suggests that place, political culture and tradition, working-class culture and values, and identity were imperative to the nature of opposition that emerged. While some broad themes can be drawn out that allow parallels to be ascertained between the two regions, it is an analysis of the formation of the labour movements and the nature of the political culture and communities that most help to explain the character of action against the means test. Only further regional comparisons, both within Britain and internationally, will reveal the importance of these factors/resources in other areas for the protests of the unemployed. Moreover, the reoccurrence of mass unemployment in the 1980s that was also regional in character and again affected the two regions that have been the focus of this study suggests that comparisons with other decades would also be relevant. Ben Pimlott addressed such issues in two articles in *The Political Quarterly* in the 1980s.[19] More broadly, the achievement of protest amongst a group with limited resources and an unstable identity underlines the continued need for understandings of how collective action could be formulated.[20] The extent of protest that occurred in both regions challenges the argument put forward by Stevenson and Cook that 'attempts to generate extra-parliamentary support by demonstrations and marches were largely ineffective'. The street protests that took place in south Wales and the north-east reveal that opposition was not confined to certain periods and that the wider labour movement, as well as the Communist Party and the NUWM, played an important role in leading the unemployed.[21] Those protests that appeared to encapsulate the entire community in the 1930s deserve greater attention. While this study has attempted to reveal the important place of women, and not only unemployed men, within these protests, a fuller exploration of the activities of women and children is needed.

Although certain factors created the right conditions for protest movements of the unemployed to emerge in the 1930s, one of the most important factors in explaining the level of action was the issue of the means test itself. The anger the household means test roused led the unemployed and their wider communities to want to demonstrate. The intervention of the investigations in what were believed to be private matters, the enforced dependency on family members, the fear of being caught out or denounced and the constant penny pinching led the means test to become a central and despised issue in working-class communities. It also ensured the test's place in popular memory.[22]

The claim that the means test caused families to separate and the suggestion that the means test investigator forced the unemployed to sell all of their possessions are two of the most recounted stories in oral testimonies.[23] While the extent to which homes separated in south Wales and the north-east of England is difficult to ascertain, the suggestion that personal artefacts needed to be sold before payments were made can be largely discredited. There is little evidence that means test investigators made the unemployed in either region sell pianos, furniture and bedding. Under the administration of the PACs, the issue would have locally provoked too much outcry to not have been mentioned in the press or council minutes, and this was not a policy of the UABs. Ross McKibbin has argued that 'the diabolical character of the means test, like that of the "means test man" and the insolence of the clerks, was almost certainly exaggerated in working-class memory'.[24] While there is certainly an element of truth in this, the fact that claims of the effects of the means test were, and are, exaggerated in south Wales and the north-east is testament to the dramatic and negative impact of the measure in both regions.

The means test was a central issue to the lives of the unemployed and working-class communities within both regions, and the effects of the measure went to the very heart of working-class values, as well as family and community life. Such an analysis does not, however, perpetuate the assumed 'myth' of the 1930s, and, as Matt Perry has noted, 'a selective reminiscence [was] rooted in ... real experience'.[25] It was the controversy of the application of a household means test to respectable working-class families and the connection made between the effects of the test and ill health, suicide, prostitution and family and community breakdown that ensured the test's place in popular memory. Exaggeration of this memory is, therefore, telling in itself of the impact of the means test. The means test made a great enough impression to have been remembered by adults who would have been children in the 1930s, and family stories, as well as the media, undoubtedly helped shape negative recollections of the household means test. However, it is also apparent that the test had such a grave impact that many working-class people in south Wales and the north-east of England did not want to forget the conditions they had lived through. Indeed, a Durham councillor proclaimed in 1933 that 'if the workers, and the women in particular, ever forgot the significance of the Means Test they ought to be compelled to suffer in the future for it'.[26] It was perhaps this desire to remember the test that ensured the endurance of a particular memory of the 1930s. The test was important within political culture in the post-1945 period and a household means test has not been introduced since for unemployment benefit.[27]Although not always directly referred to, the introduction of any form of means test for relief takes place within this context. The memory of the means test and the interwar depression remains powerful, politically and culturally.

Notes

1 *Men Without Work: A Report Made to the Pilgrim Trust* (Cambridge, 1938), p. 68.

2 *Ibid.*, p. 75.

3 David Vincent has argued that 'the force of the reaction' against the means test 'was derived precisely from the sense that the new species of home

visitor represented a reversal of the historical momentum'. David Vincent, *The Culture of Secrecy: Britain, 1832–1998* (Oxford, 1998), p. 153.

4 It should be noted that this was not the only area of local government administration that was changing in this period. R. Smith, 'The Reform of Local Government Finance, 1928–37: A Study of South Wales', *Welsh History Review*, 21:1 (2002), p. 153.

5 Derek Fraser, *The Evolution of the Welfare State: A History of Social Policy Since the Industrial Revolution* (Basingstoke, 2003), pp. 233–4.

6 Paul Bagguley, *From Protest to Acquiescence? Political Movements of the Unemployed* (London, 1991), pp. 38–44.

7 SWCC, MNA/NUM/3/3/43/4, Correspondence between D. R. Llewelyn (Secretary of the Garw Unemployed Lodge) to the General Secretary of the South Wales Miners' Federation, 26 October 1939.

8 Fraser, *The Evolution of the Welfare State*, p. 216.

9 Valerie Gordon Hall has argued that the classic views of a mining community portray a 'hypermasculine' culture. Valerie Gordon Hall, 'Contrasting Female Identities: Women in Coal Mining Communities in Northumberland, England, 1900–1939', *Journal of Women's History*, 13:2 (2001), p. 107.

10 Ellen Wilkinson said of marches like the Jarrow Crusade that they show 'if only something is being *done* about it ... somehow it helps to keep the spirit of men alive'. Ellen Wilkinson, *The Town That Was Murdered: The Life Story of Jarrow* (London, 1939), p. 196.

11 It was from this point that the membership to the SWMF began to stabilise and increase again. See Appendix 1.5; Hywel Francis and Dai Smith, *The Fed: A History of the South Wales Miners in the Twentieth Century* (Cardiff, 1998), p. 244.

12 Duncan Tanner, 'The Pattern of Labour Politics, 1918–1939', in Duncan Tanner, Chris Williams and Deian Hopkin (eds), *The Labour Party in Wales 1900–2000* (Cardiff, 2000), p. 132.

13 Richard Croucher, *We Refuse to Starve in Silence: A History of the National Unemployed Workers' Movement, 1920–46* (London, 1987), pp. 106–95.

14 Districts of the SWMF were in many cases organised on valley principles.

15 Membership to the DMA was much more stable than the SWMF throughout the 1930s. See Appendix 1.5.

16 W. R. Garside, *The Durham Miners, 1919–1960* (London, 1971), p. 281.

17 Unlike in the SWMF, an unemployment officer was appointed to deal specifically with the complaints of unemployed members. Sam Watson, who served in this position throughout the 1930s, produced innumerable pamphlets and memorandums detailing government policy and elucidating complex legislation. The DMA was often approached first when problems arose and the position of the unemployed was high on their agenda. DRO, D/DMA (Sam Watson) 45 (Box)/19; DMOR, DMA Minutes, Circulars, Etc., January–June 1938.

18 John Burnett has noted that 'disillusionment with the Labour Party and the trade union movement, neither of which seemed to offer much to the

unemployed, was often mistaken for apathy'. The case of the north-east of England underlines this analysis. John Burnett, *Idle Hands: The Experience of Unemployment, 1790–1990* (London, 1984), p. 257.

19 Pimlott drew comparisons between the experience of the unemployed in the 1930s in the north-east against the contemporary backdrop of rising unemployment. He conveyed how similar themes reoccurred in the causes, nature and experience of unemployment in the 1980s as well as the response of the unemployed. Ben Pimlott, 'The North East: Back to the 1930s?', *The Political Quarterly*, 52:1 (1981), pp. 51–63; Ben Pimlott, 'Unemployment and "the Unemployed" in North-East England', *The Political Quarterly*, 56:4 (1985), pp. 346–60.

20 Matthias Reiss, 'Not All Were Apathetic: National Hunger Marches as Political Rituals in Interwar Britain', in Jörg Neuheiser and Michael Schaich (eds), *Political Rituals in Great Britain 1700–2000* (Augsburg, 2006), p. 95.

21 John Stevenson and Chris Cook, *Britain in the Depression: Society and Politics 1929–39* (London, 1994), p. 291.

22 This was also true of other regions. Kate Nicholas argued in her oral history of Teesside that the reaction to the means test 'was so strong, and a point so often made by interviewees that it is worthy of separate consideration'. Kate Nicholas, *The Social Effects of Unemployment on Teesside, 1919–39* (Manchester, 1986), p. 195.

23 For example, Kenneth Maher, 'Caerphilly', in Nigel Gray (ed.), *The Worst of Times: An Oral History of the Great Depression in Britain* (Aldershot, 1985), p. 36; Joe Hind, *A Shieldfield Childhood* (Newcastle-upon-Tyne, 1994), p. 45; Ray Forsberg, *Means Test Kid: A Childhood in a Yorkshire Fishing Port during the 'Hungry Thirties'* (Hutton, 1985); and John Brierley, *In the Shadow of the Means Test Man: Memories of a Derbyshire Childhood* (Highedge Historical Society, 1995).

24 Ross McKibbin, *Classes and Cultures: England 1918–1951* (Oxford, 1998), p. 158.

25 Matt Perry, *Bread and Work: The Experience of Unemployment, 1918–1939* (London, 2000), p. 201.

26 Councillor W. Kelly, Durham Public Assistance Committee. *Northern Echo*, 6 February 1933, p. 8.

27 Deacon and Bradshaw have argued that the memory of the means test in the 1930s had a 'potent influence upon the politics of the 1940s'. Alan Deacon and Jonathan Bradshaw, *Reserved for the Poor: The Means Test in British Social Policy* (Oxford, 1983), p. 28.

Appendices

Appendix 1.1 Population of the ancient countries in south Wales and the north-east of England, 1801–1939

	County				
Year	*Glamorgan*	*Monmouthshire*	*Carmarthenshire*	*Durham*	*Northumberland*
1801	70,879	45,568	67,317	149,384	168,078
1811	85,067	62,105	77,217	165,293	183,269
1821	102,073	75,801	90,239	193,511	212,589
1831	126,612	98,126	100,740	239,256	236,959
1841	171,188	134,268	106,326	307,963	266,020
1851	231,849	157,418	110,632	390,997	303,568
1861	317,752	174,633	111,796	508,666	343,025
1871	397,859	195,448	115,710	685,089	386,646
1881	511,433	211,267	124,864	867,258	434,086
1891	687,218	258,133	130,566	1,016,562	506,030
1901	859,931	298,076	135,328	1,187,474	603,119
1911	1,120,910	395,719	160,406	1,369,860	696,893
1921	1,252,481	450,794	175,037	1,479,033	746,096
1931	1,225,717	434,958	179,100	1,486,175	756,782
1939	1,173,930	411,866	174,875	1,378,048	730,429

Source: *Census of England and Wales*, 1801–1939.

Appendix 1.2 Population of the ancient countries in south Wales and the north-east of England, 1801–1939

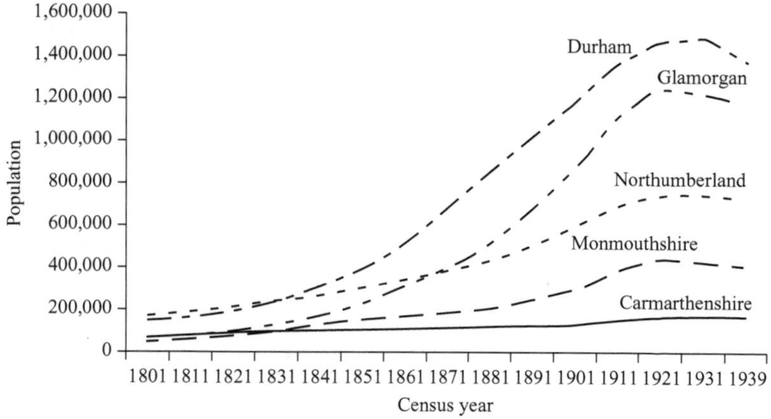

Source: *Census of England and Wales,* 1801–1939.

Appendix 1.3 County rates of net population change per 1,000 due to migration, 1851–1951

County	*1851–61*	*1861–71*	*1871–81*	*1881–91*	*1891–1901*	*1901–11*	*1911–31*	*1931–51*
Durham	+24	+104	+39	+10	–10	–22	–129	–101
Northumberland	–25	–28	–34	+32	+39	+24	–81	–32
Monmouthshire	–32	+35	–65	+59	–4	+199	–123	–111
Glamorgan	+133	+45	+144	+166	+54	+92	–131	–109

Source: D. Friedlander, and R. J. Roshier, 'A Study of Internal Migration in England and Wales: Part I', *Population Studies*, 19:3 (1966), p. 278.

Appendix 1.4 Total membership of the Durham Miners' Association and the South Wales Miners' Federation, 1919–39

	Durham Miners' Association		*South Wales Miners' Federation*	
Year	*Total membership*	*Percentage difference to previous year's figures*	*Total membership*	*Percentage difference to previous year's figures*
1919	148,834	–	185,044	–
1920	151,029	+1.5	197,668	+6.8
1921	151,253	+0.2	117,610	–40.5
1922	155,380	+2.7	87,080	–25.9
1923	158,339	+1.9	147,611	+69.5
1924	160,040	+1.1	148,469	+0.6
1925	155,773	–2.7	129,155	–13.0
1926	149,740	–3.9	136,250	+5.5
1927	137,853	–8.6	72,981	–46.4
1928	128,795	–7.9	59,858	–17.9
1929	132,081	+2.5	74,446	+24.4
1930	132,801	+0.5	75,480	+1.4
1931	127,976	–3.6	62,089	–17.7
1932	125,086	–2.3	64,138	+3.3
1933	122,824	–1.8	63,337	–1.2
1934	124,445	–1.3	76,949	+21.5
1935	124,613	+0.1	85,741	+11.4
1936	124,647	+0.03	88,379	+3.1
1937	127,157	+2.0	101,011	+14.3
1938	124,783	–1.9	103,322	+2.3
1939	122,031	–2.2	108,955	+5.5

Source: W. R. Garside, *The Durham Miners, 1919–1960* (London, 1971), p. 96; Chris Williams, *Capitalism, Community and Conflict: The South Wales Coalfield, 1898–1947* (Cardiff, 1998), p. 89.

Appendix 1.5 Total membership of the Durham Miners' Association and the South Wales Miners' Federation

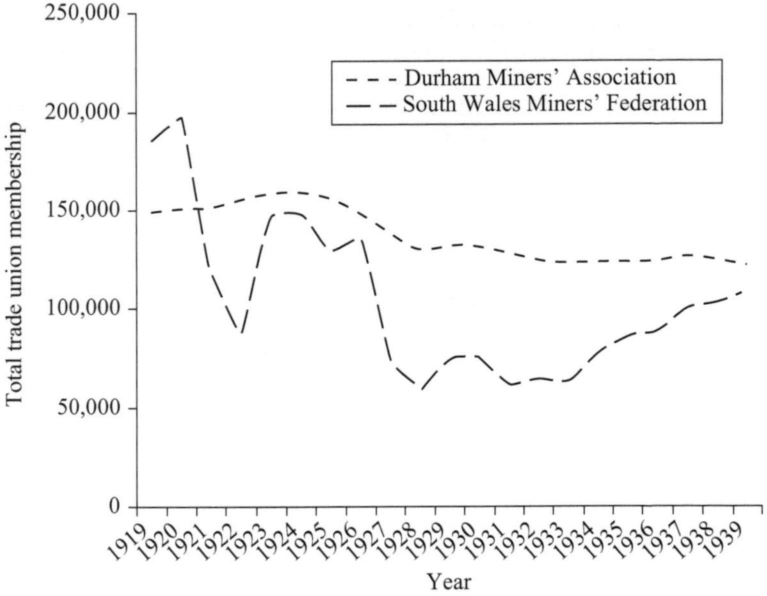

Source: W. R. Garside, *The Durham Miners, 1919–1960* (London, 1971), p. 96; Chris Williams, *Capitalism, Community and Conflict: The South Wales Coalfield, 1898–1947* (Cardiff, 1998), p. 89.

Bibliography

Manuscripts

Aberdare Library

W. W. Price Collection (LG5/4).

Durham Record Office, Durham

Chester-le-Street Urban District Council, Correspondence.
Durham County Council Public Assistance Committee Minutes.
Durham County Council, Standing Joint Committee Misc. Files.
Durham Miners' Association Minutes.
Miscellaneous Files including Letter to E. Edwards MP from Ramsay MacDonald dated August 1931.
Sam Watson Collection.

Durham Area Miners' Office, Redhills, Durham

Durham Miners' Association Executive Committee Minutes.
Durham Miners' Association, Programmes and Minutes of Council Meetings.
Durham Miners' Association, Minutes, Circulars, Etc.
Guide to the UAB Scales and Regulations: Issued by the Legal and Research Department of the NUWM (NUWM, London, c.1935).

Glamorgan Archives, Cardiff

Glamorgan County Council Public Assistance Committee Minutes.
Glamorgan County Council, Public Assistance Department Files.
Glamorgan County Council, Reports of the Public Assistance Officer.
Kenfig Hill Central Ward Labour Party, Secretary's Minute Book.
Maes-yr-Haf Settlement, Rhondda Valleys, Papers.
Rhondda Urban District Council Minutes.
Rose Davies Papers.
S. O. Davies Papers.

Gwent Record Office, Cwmbran

Abertillery: Visit of His Majesty King Edward VIII to Rhiw Park, Abertillery (Published by Abertillery Urban District Council, 1936).

Monmouthshire County Council Public Assistance Committee Minutes.

Labour History Archive and Study Centre, People's History Museum, Manchester

Labour Party Archive, Labour Party Additional Women's Officer Papers.

Labour Party Archive, Women's Officers' Papers.

Labour Women's Conferences, 1932–1940.

Northumberland Archives, Woodhorn Archives and Museum, Ashington

Wansbeck Divisional Labour Party Minutes.

National Library of Wales, Aberystwyth

Idris Cox Papers.

James Griffiths Papers.

Labour Party of Wales Collection, including the South Wales Regional Council of Labour Minutes.

Thomas Jones CH Papers.

SCOLAR, Cardiff University

Labour Party Archives Microfilm Collection.

Microfilm: Archives of the Trades Union Congress.

Microfilm: Papers from the Communist Party of Great Britain Archives: Wal Hannington Papers.

South Wales Coalfield Collection, Swansea University

Blaenavon Lodge Minutes.

Cambrian Lodge Minutes.

Ferndale Lodge Minutes, Correspondence and Handbills (MNA/NUM/L/33/45).

Maerdy Lodge Minutes.

Merthyr Vale Lodge Minutes.

Personal Papers, Arthur Lewis Jones, including National Unemployed Workers' Movement, Dowlais Branch Minutes (MNC/PP/14/1).

Personal Papers, Eddie Jones.

Personal Papers, J. S. Williams (Dowlais).

Records of the SWMF/NUM (South Wales Area) Correspondence, re Political Affairs, 1934–1941 (MNA/NUM/3/3/58).

Records of the SWMF/NUM (South Wales Area) Correspondence, Correspondence With Lodges Including Unemployed Lodges (MNA/NUM/3/3/43,30).

South Wales Miners' Federation, Minutes of Council Meetings, Annual and Special Conferences.

South Wales Miners' Federation Minutes of the Executive Council.

South Wales Miners' Library, Swansea University

Idris Cox, *The People Can Save South Wales* (Published by CPGB, London, 1936).

The Royal Commission's Final Attack on the Unemployed: To Action Against More Starvation: An Examination of the Late Labour Government's Royal Commission of Unemployment's Final Proposal (Published by the NUWM, London, 1933).

The National Archives, London

Records of the Unemployment Assistance Boards (AST)

AST 7/255-6 The Pilgrim Trust Unemployment Enquiry: Investigation Into the Causes of Long-Term Unemployment and its Effects. Supply of Information.

AST 7/8 Deputation of Members of Parliament From Distressed Areas, 1933.

AST 12/16–18 Unemployment Assistance Board Minutes.

Records of the Cabinet Office (CAB)

CAB/24/67 Cabinet Memorandum. Demobilisation and Unemployment.

CAB 27/497 Hunger Marches, 1932.

CAB 27/575-6 Cabinet Committee on Regulations of the Unemployment Assistance Board, Minutes and Memorandums.

Records of the Director of Public Prosecutions (DPP)

DPP 2/114, National March to London Against the Means Test Organised by the National Unemployed Workers' Movement.

Ministry of Health Files (HLG and MH)

HLG 30/37: Unemployment Assistance Board, Effect of the New Regulations in South Wales.

MH 58/309 Royal Tours and Visits: Visit of His Majesty King Edward VIII to South Wales, 1936–1937.

MH 79/334, Malnutrition Among the Unemployed, County Durham, Criticisms of the Health Services by Dr G. F. Walker and Dr W. G. Waugh.

Home Office Files (HO)

HO 45/23590 Disturbances: Demonstrations Against Unemployment Legislation: Communist Incitement to Strike in South Wales Coalfields 1927–1935.

HO 144/12143 Disturbances: Unemployed Miners' March to London in 1927. March of Unemployed to London in 1929. Hunger March to London in 1930.

HO 144/18187 Disturbances: National Unemployed Workers' Union to London in Protest Against the Means Test 1 November 1932 – 2 January 1933.

HO 144/19846 Disturbances: National Hunger Marches to London Communist Influence.

HO 144/20032 Disturbances: Blaina Rioters: Resolutions and Protests Against Sentences.

HO 144/20132 Disturbances: Industrial Unrest and Communist Activity in South Wales 1933–1936.

HO 144/20696-7 Disturbances: Hunger March 1936.

HO 144/21066 Royal Visit of King George VI [actually King Edward VIII] to South Wales in 1936 at a time of Industrial Unrest.

HO 144/22587 Disturbances: Demonstrations by Bristol Unemployed Workers 1932.

Records of the Metropolitan Police Office (MEPO)

MEPO 2/3071 National Hunger March to London, 1934. Police Arrangements and Reports of Demonstrations.

Papers of James Ramsay MacDonald (PRO 30/69)

PRO 30/69/442 Unemployment: Transitional Benefit and Means Test 1929–1935.

PRO 30/69/443 Unemployment: Scale of Allowance in force in Durham 1929–1935.

Tyne and Wear Archive Services, Newcastle

Boldon Urban District Unemployment File (UD/BO/27/46).

Borough of Jarrow Council Minutes 1930–1936.

Borough of Jarrow, Jarvis Committee Minutes (G/EMP2/4).

Colliery Ward, Sunderland, Minutes of the Women's Section of the Labour Party.

County Borough of Sunderland Council Minutes.

County Borough of Sunderland Public Assistance Committee Minutes.

Department of Employment Jarrow Papers (G/EMP2).

Newcastle City Council, Public Assistance Committee Minutes.

Records of the Transport and General Workers Union, 1882–1969.
Socialist League Gateshead Branch Executive Committee Minutes.

Treorchy Library Local Studies Collection

Rhondda Urban District Council, *Annual Report of the Medical Officer of Health*, 1931–1939.

Official publications (chronological order)

Reports of the Commission of Enquiry into Industrial Unrest: No. 1 Division, North-Eastern Area (Cmd 8662), 1917–18, xv.
Reports of the Commission of Enquiry into Industrial Unrest: No. 7 Division, Wales and Monmouthshire (Cmd 8668), 1917–18, xv.
Local Government Bill, 1928. Explanatory Memorandum on the Provisions of the Bill as Passed by the House of Commons (Cmd 3273), 1928–29, xv.
First Report of the Royal Commission on Unemployment Insurance (Cmd 3872), 1930–31, xvii.
Memorandum on the Measures Proposed by His Majesty's Government to Secure Reductions in National Expenditure (Cmd 3952), 1930–31, xviii.
National Economy Bill, 1931, 1930–31, iii.
Unemployment Insurance (National Economy) (No. 2) Order, 1931. Transitional Payments. Explanatory Memorandum (non-parl), HMSO, 1931.
Transitional Payments (Determination of Need) Bill, 1931–32, iii.
Transitional Payments Prolongation (Unemployed Persons) Act, 1932, 1931–32, iii.
Final Report of the Royal Commission on Unemployment Insurance (Cmd 4185), 1931–32, xiii.
Memorandum on the Financial Resolution to be Proposed Relative to Transitional Payments (Cmd 4042), 1931–32, xiv.
Transitional Payments (Determination of Need) Memorandum on Proposed Financial Resolution (Cmd 4190), 1931–32, xiv.
Report to the Minister of Labour by the Commissioners Appointed to Administer Transitional Payments in the County of Durham (Cmd 4339), 1932–33, xv.
Unemployment. A Bill. (As Amended in Committee on Recommital and on Report) To amend the Unemployment Insurance Acts, 1920 to 1933, and to make further provision for the training and assistance of persons who are capable of, and available for, work but have no work or only part-time or intermittent work; and for purposes connected with the matters aforesaid, 1933–34, iv.
Ministry of Labour, *Reports of Investigations into the Industrial Conditions in Certain Depressed Areas* (Cmd 4728), 1933–34, xiii.

Unemployment Bill (Brought from the Commons 15 May, 1934) Explanatory Memorandum on Clauses (Cmd 4602), 1933–34, xxi.

Unemployment Assistance (Temporary Provisions). A Bill To make temporary provision for securing as nearly as may be that the allowance payable under Part II of the Unemployment Act, 1934, to persons who but for the operation of subsection (2) of section fifty-nine of that Act would at any time since the sixth day of January nineteen hundred and thirty-five have been entitled to transitional payments that would have been payable to them but for the operation of the said sub-section; to postpone the second appointed day for the purposes of the said Act; and for purposes connected with matters aforesaid, 1934–35, iv.

Unemployment Assistance (Temporary Provisions) (No. 2) A Bill To make temporary provision for the financial adjustments necessary by reason of the second appointed day for the purposes of the Unemployment Act, 1934, have been postponed from the first day of March, nineteen hundred and thirty five; and to authorise the borrowing by public assistance authorities of sums required for the purpose of meeting expenditure incurred by them for the year ended on the thirty-first day of March, nineteen hundred and thirty-five, in excess of their estimates for that year, 1934–35, iv.

Unemployment Assistance Act, 1934. *Draft Unemployment Assistance (Determination of Need and Assessment of Needs) Regulations, 1934, dated December 11, 1934, made by the Minister of Labour under Sections 38 (3) and 52 (2) of the Unemployment Assistance Act, 1934*, 1934–35, xiv.

Unemployment Assistance Act, 1934. *Memorandum explanatory of the Draft Regulations made under Sections 38 (3) and 52 (2) of the Unemployment Assistance Act, 1934* (Cmd 4765), 1934–35, xiv.

Unemployment Assistance Act, 1934. *Memorandum on the Unemployment Assistance (Determination of Need and Assessment of Needs) Regulations, 1934* (Cmd 4791), 1934–35, xiv.

Unemployment Assistance (Temporary Provisions) (Extension). A Bill To Extend until a date not later than the thirty-first day of March nineteen hundred and thirty-six, the period in respect of which grants are to be paid to the local authorities out of moneys provided by Parliament under section one of the Unemployment Assistance (Temporary Provisions) (No. 2) Act, 1935, 1935–36, iv.

Report of the Unemployment Assistance Board for the Period Ended 31 December 1935 (Cmd 5177), 1935–36, xiii.

Unemployment Assistance Act, 1934. *Draft Unemployment Assistance Regulations, 1936* (Cmd 5228), 1935–36, xvii.

Unemployment Assistance Act, 1934. *Return of the number of payments made at local offices of the Ministry of Labour in the week ended Friday, 26th June, 1936, by way of unemployment benefit under the Unemployment Insurance Act,*

1935, and of unemployment allowances under the Unemployment Assistance Regulations, 1934, and the Unemployment Assistance (Temporary Provisions) Act, 1935 (Cmd 5240), 1935–36, xvii.

Unemployment Assistance Act, 1934. *Copy of Draft Unemployment Assistance (Determination of Need and Assessment of Needs) Regulations, 1936, dated July 8th, 1936, made by the Minister of Labour under Sections 38 (3) and 52 (2) of the Unemployment Assistance Act, 1934, together with an Explanatory Memorandum by the Unemployment Assistance Board* (Cmd 5229), 1935–36, xvii.

Unemployment Assistance (Temporary Provisions) Act, 1935. *Order made by the Minister of Labour under Section 1 (5) to terminate the operation of the Act*, 1935–36, xvii.

Report of the Unemployment Assistance Board for the Period Ended 31 December 1936 (Cmd 5526), 1936–37, xii.

UnemploymentAssistance(TemporaryProvisions)(Amendment)Memorandum by the Minister of Health and the Secretary of State for Scotland explaining the proposed Financial Resolution (Cmd 5322), 1936–37, xxi.

Report of the Unemployment Assistance Board for the Period Ended 31 December 1937 (Cmd 5752), 1937–38, xiii.

Criminal Statistics, England and Wales, 1936 (Cmd 5690), 1937–38, xxvii.

Unemployment Assistance Act, 1934. *Draft Unemployment Assistance (Winter Adjustment) Regulations, 1938, dated 2nd June, 1938, made by the Minister of Labour under sections 38 (3) and 52 (2) of the Unemployment Assistance Act, 1934*, 1937–38, xviii.

Report of the Unemployment Assistance Board for the Period Ended 31 December 1938 (Cmd 6021), 1938–39, xii.

Unemployment Insurance (Emergency Powers). A Bill To empower the Minister of Labour in case of war to modify or suspend the operation of any of the provisions of the Unemployment Insurance Acts, 1935 to 1939, and make provision with respect to any of the matters to which the said Acts relate, and for purposes connected with matters aforesaid, 1938–39, v.

Royal Commission on the Distribution of the Industrial Population (Cmd 6153), 1939–40, iv.

Newspapers

Dailies

Daily Herald
Daily Mirror
Daily Worker
Evening Chronicle

Manchester Guardian
Northern Despatch
Northern Echo
South Shields Daily Gazette
South Wales Evening Post
Sunday Sun
The Newcastle Journal
The Times
Western Mail

Weeklies

Aberdare Leader
Auckland Chronicle
Blaydon Courier
Blyth News and Ashington Post
Chester-le-Street Chronicle and District Advertiser
Durham County Advertiser and Durham Chronicle
Free Press and Rhondda Leader
Heslop's Local Advertiser
Merthyr Express
South Wales Weekly Argus
Stanley News and Durham Advertiser
The Observer
The Porth Gazette
The Rhondda Clarion (The Official Organ of the Rhondda Borough Labour Party)
The Rhondda Leader
The Rhondda Vanguard

Periodicals

Hansard
Local Unemployment Index
Seaham Harbour Labour News
The Economic Journal
The Geographical Journal
The Labour Woman
The Ministry of Labour Gazette
The Party Organiser
The Political Quarterly
The Socialist (The Official Organ of Seaham Divisional Labour Party)
The Unemployed Leader

The Unemployed Special
The Welsh Journal of Agriculture

Contemporary works

A Town on the Dole (Published by the Brynmawr Communist Party, Abertillery, c. 1937–39).

Administering Unemployment Insurance: Report of Trades Union Congress Deputation to the Minister of Labour (TUC General Council, London, 1929).

An Industrial Survey of the North East Coast Area (London, 1932).

Bakke, E. Wight, *The Unemployed Man: A Social Study* (London, 1935).

Barker, Reginald J., *Christ in the Valley of Unemployment* (Suffolk, 1936).

Beales, H. L. and R. S. Lambert (eds), *Memoirs of the Unemployed* (London, 1934).

Bevan, Aneurin, *Why Not Trust the Tories?* (London, 1944).

Beveridge, William H., *Full Employment in a Free Society* (London, 1944).

Bowley, A. L. and Margaret H. Hogg, *Has Poverty Diminished? A Sequel to 'Livelihood and Poverty'* (London, 1925).

Brierley, Walter, *Means-Test Man* (Nottingham, 1983 edition; first published, 1935).

Brockway, A. Fenner, *Hungry England* (London, 1932).

Brown, Maud, *Stop this Starvation of Mother and Child* (London, 1935).

Carr-Saunders, A. M., 'The Unemployment Assistance Board', *The Political Quarterly*, 7:4 (1936).

Carter, G. R., 'The Coal Strike in South Wales', *The Economic Journal*, 25:99 (1915), pp. 453–65.

Chegwidden, T. S. and G. Myrddin-Evans, *The Employment Exchange Service in Great Britain* (London, 1934).

Clarke, John J., *The Local Government of the United Kingdom (and the Irish Free State)* (Tenth edition, London, 1936).

Cohen, Max, *I Was One of the Unemployed* (London, 1945).

Cohen, Percy, *The British System of Social Insurance* (London, 1932).

—— *Unemployment Insurance and Assistance in Britain* (London, 1938).

Cole, G. D. H., *Out of Work: An Introduction to the Study of Unemployment* (London, 1923).

—— *The People's Front* (London, 1937).

—— *The Intelligent Man's Guide to the Post-War World* (London, 1947).

—— and M. I. Cole, *The Condition of Britain* (London, 1937).

Common, Jack (ed.), *Seven Shifts* (London, 1938).

Coombes, B. L., *These Poor Hands: The Autobiography of a Miner Working in South Wales* (Cardiff, 2002 edition; first published, 1939).

Cowen, Ned, *Of Mining Life and Aal Its Ways* (Place of publication unknown, 1973).

Crewdson, R. B., *Our Unemployment Problem* (London, 1923).

Davison, Ronald C., *British Unemployment Policy: The Modern Phase Since 1930* (London, 1938).

Daysh, George H. J., 'A Distressed Industrial Region – Tyneside', *Economic Geography*, 11:2 (1935), pp. 159–66.

—— and J. S. Symonds, *West Durham: A Study of a Problem Area in North Eastern England* (Oxford, 1953).

Dearnley, Irvine Herbert, *The 'Needs Test' for Unemployment Insurance Transitional Payments and Public Assistance* (London, 1931).

Disinherited Youth: A Report on the 18+ Age Group Enquiry. Prepared for the Trustees of the Carnegie United Kingdom Trust (Edinburgh, 1943).

Edwards, H. W. J., *The Good Patch* (London, 1938).

Elias, Sid, *Mass Murder: An Exposure of the Means Test* (London, 1932).

Evans, David, *Labour Strife in the South Wales Coalfield 1910–1911: A Historical and Critical Record of the Mid-Rhondda, Aberdare Valley and Other Strikes* (Cardiff, 1911).

Feis, Herbert, 'The Industrial Situation in Great Britain: From the Armistice to the Beginning of 1921', *The American Economic Review*, 11:2 (1921), pp. 252–67.

Fynes, Richard, *The Miners of Northumberland and Durham: A History of their Social and Political Progress* (Yorkshire, 1971 edition; first published 1873).

Ginzberg, Eli, *Grass on the Slag Heaps: The Story of the Welsh Miners* (London, 1942).

—— *A World Without Work* (New Jersey, 1991 edition; first published as *Grass on the Slag Heaps*, 1942).

Greene, Felix (ed.), *Time to Spare: What Unemployment Means by Eleven Unemployed* (London, 1935).

Greene, Lee S., 'State Policy in the British Depressed Areas: An Experiment in Regionalism', *Social Forces*, 18:3 (1940), pp. 337–50.

Greenwood, Walter, *Love on the Dole* (London, 1935).

—— *How the Other Man Lives* (London, 1939).

Hammil, Fred, *Out of Work: The Problem of the Unemployed* (Newcastle, 1894).

Hammond, J. L. and Barbara Hammond, *The Skilled Labourer, 1760–1832* (London, 1920).

Hannington, Wal, *The March of the Miners: How We Smashed the Opposition* (London, 1927).

—— *Unemployed Struggles 1919–1936: My Life and Struggles Amongst the Unemployed* (London, 1977 edition; first published, London, 1936).

—— *The Problem of the Distressed Areas* (London, 1937).

—— *A Short History of the Unemployed* (London, 1938).

—— *Ten Lean Years: An Examination of the Record of the National Government in the Field of Unemployment* (London, 1940).

Hardie, James Keir, *The Unemployed* (London, 1895).

Harry, E. Ll. and J. R. E. Phillips, 'Expenditure of Unemployed and Employed Households: A Study of Yearly Budgets', *The Welsh Journal of Agriculture*, xiv (1938).

Hutt, Allen, *The Condition of the Working Class in Britain* (London, 1933).

—— *The Post-War History of the British Working Class* (London, 1937).

International Labour Office, *Unemployment Enquiry: Remedies for Unemployment* (Geneva, 1922).

Jahoda, Marie, Paul F. Lazarfeld and Hans Zeisel, *Marienthal: The Sociography of an Unemployed Community* (English edition, London, 1972).

Jennings, Hilda, *Brynmawr: A Study of a Distressed Area* (London, 1934).

Jones, Gwyn, *Times Like These* (London, 1979 edition; first published, 1936).

Jones, Lewis, *From Exchange and Parish to the PAC: For Decency and Destitution* (Central Marchers' Council, Tonypandy, n.d.).

—— *We Live* (London, 1939).

Keynes, John Maynard, *The Economic Consequences of the Peace* (London, 1920).

Labour Party, *Smashing the Unemployed! The Meanness of the Means Test* (London, 1932).

—— *Durham and the North-East Coast: Report of the Labour Party's Commission of Enquiry into the Distressed Areas* (London, 1937).

—— *South Wales: Report of the Labour Party's Commission of Enquiry into the Distressed Areas* (London, 1937).

Lawson, Jack, *Who Goes Home? Broadcasts and Sketches* (London, 1945).

—— *A Man's Life* (London, 1951).

Lush, A. J., *The Young Adult in South Wales* (Cardiff, 1941).

MacDonald, J. Ramsay, *Syndicalism: A Critical Examination* (London, 1912).

Martin, Arthur J., *The Remedy for Unemployment* (London, 1895).

Massey, Philip, *Industrial South Wales: A Social and Political Survey* (London, 1940).

McKenzie, G. Grant, *County Council Guide England and Wales, Excluding London* (Labour Publications Department London, 1937).

Meara, Gwynne, *Juvenile Unemployment in South Wales* (Cardiff, 1936).

Men Without Work: A Report Made to the Pilgrim Trust (Cambridge, 1938).

Mess, Henry A., 'The Social Survey of Tyneside: An English Regional Survey', *The American Journal of Sociology*, 33:3 (1927), pp. 424–30.

—— 'Review: *Out of the Pit* by John Newsom', *The Economic Journal*, 47:186 (1937), pp. 358–9.

Moffett, Thomas, *A Canny Lad: The Early Life of Thomas Moffett An Autobiography* (Norfolk, 1998).

Monmouthshire Marchers' Council, *Monmouthshire Hunger March, of August 1933* (National Unemployed Workers' Movement, Monmouth, 1933).

Newsom, John, *Out of the Pit: A Challenge to the Comfortable* (Oxford, 1936).

Orwell, George, *The Road to Wigan Pier* (London, 2001 edition; first published, 1937).

Oxley, Will, 'Are You Working?', in Jack Common (ed.), *Seven Shifts* (London, 1938), pp. 105–44.

Paynter, Will, *My Generation* (London, 1972).

Priestley, J. B., *English Journey* (London, 1968 edition; first published, 1934).

Preliminary Report of the 18+ Age Group. Prepared for Presentation to the Trustees of the Carnegie United Kingdom Trust. November 1939 (Edinburgh, 1940).

Rees, J. Morgan, *Unemployment as an International Problem* (London, 1926).

Rhondda Communist Party, *South Wales in the March of History: A Message to YOU from the Communist Party* (Tonypandy, 1937).

Sharp, Thomas, *A Derelict Area: A Study of the South-West Durham Coalfield* (London, 1935).

Smailes, Arthur, 'Population Changes in the Colliery Districts of Northumberland and Durham', *The Geographical Journal*, 91:3 (1938), pp. 220–9.

Spring Rice, Margery, *Working-Class Wives: Their Health and Conditions* (London, 1939).

The Industrial Position of the North-East Coast of England. The Staff of the Economics Department of Armstrong College, Newcastle Upon Tyne (London, 1935).

The Second Industrial Survey of South Wales, Vol. 3 (Cardiff, 1937).

Warburton, Edward and Carl Butler, *'Disallowed': The Tragedy of the Means Test* (London, 1935).

Waugh, Evelyn, *Vile Bodies* (London, 1981 edition; first published, 1930).

Wilkinson, Ellen, *The Town That Was Murdered: The Life Story of Jarrow* (London, 1939).

Zweig, F., *Men in the Pits* (London, 1949).

Films and documentaries (chronological order)

Action Against the Means Test, Educational and Television Films Ltd (1935).

Rhondda, Educational and Television Films Ltd (1935).

Eastern Valley, Strand Film Company (1937).

To-Day We Live, Strand Film Company (1937).
Mam, Red Flannel Films (1988).
Dora's Story, Red Flannel Films (1993).

Secondary articles and essays

Alexander, Sally, 'Men's Fears and Women's Work: Responses to Unemployment in London Between the Wars', *Gender & History*, 12:2 (2000), pp. 401–25.

Armstrong, Craig, 'A Northern Community at War, 1939–1945: "Tyneside Can Take It!"', *Northern History*, 44:1 (2007), pp. 133–52.

Barker, Colin, 'What Is to Be Done? Contrasting Activists' Visions In Community Protest', in Colin Barker and Paul Kennedy (eds), *To Make Another World: Studies in Protest and Collective Action* (Aldershot, 1996), pp. 25–43.

Benson, John, 'The Thrift of English Coal-Miners, 1860–95', *The Economic History Review*, 31:3 (1978), pp. 410–18.

Berger, Stefan, 'Working-Class Culture and the Labour Movement in the South Wales and the Ruhr Coalfield, 1850–2000: A Comparison', *Llafur*, 8:2 (2001), pp. 5–40.

—— 'Comparative History', in Stefan Berger, Heiko Feldner and Kevin Passmore (eds), *Writing History: Theory and Practice* (London, 2003), pp. 161–79.

—— and Neil Evans, 'Two Faces of King Coal: The Impact of Historiographical Traditions of Comparative History in the Ruhr and South Wales', in Stefan Berger, Andy Croll and Norman LaPorte (eds), *Towards a Comparative History of Coalfield Societies* (London, 2005), pp. 29–42.

Bloch, Marc, 'Toward a Comparative History of European Societies', in Frederic C. Lane and Jelle C. Riemersma (eds), *Enterprise and Secular Change: Readings in Economic History* (London, 1953), pp. 494–521.

Boyns, Trevor, 'Growth in the Coal Industry: The Cases of Powell Duffryn and the Ocean Coal Company, 1864–1913', in Colin Baber and L. J. Williams (eds), *Modern South Wales: Essays in Economic History* (Cardiff, 1986), pp. 153–70.

Bruley, Sue, 'A Woman's Right to Work? The Role of Women in the Unemployed Movement Between the Wars', in Sybil Oldfield (ed.), *This Working-Day World: Women's Lives and Culture(s) in Britain 1914–1945* (London, 1994), pp. 40–53.

—— 'Women', in John McIlroy, Alan Campbell and Keith Gildart (eds), *Industrial Politics and the 1926 Mining Lockout: The Struggle for Dignity* (Cardiff, 2004), pp. 22–48.

—— 'The Politics of Food: Gender, Family, Community and Collective Feeding in South Wales in the General Strike and Miners' Lockout of 1926', *Twentieth Century British History*, 18:1 (2007), pp. 54–77.

Burge, Alun, 'Exorcising Demonologies? Coal Companies and Colliery Communities in South Wales', *Llafur*, 9:4 (2007), pp. 101–9.

Callcott, Maureen, 'Parliamentary Elections in County Durham Between the Wars: The Making of a Labour Stronghold', *North East Group for the Study of Labour History*, Bulletin 8 (1974), pp. 15–19.

Chandler, Andy, 'The Black Death on Wheels: Unemployment and Migration – The Experience of Inter-War South Wales', *Papers in Modern Welsh History*, 1 (1982), pp. 1–15.

Clarke, J. F., 'Engineering Workers on Tyneside', in Norman McCord (ed.), *Essays in Tyneside Labour History* (Newcastle, 1977), pp. 88–108.

—— 'Workers in the Tyneside Shipyards in the Nineteenth Century', in Norman McCord (ed.), *Essays in Tyneside Labour History* (Newcastle, 1977), pp. 109–31.

Colls, Robert, '"Oh Happy English Children!": Coal, Class and Education in the North-East', *Past and Present*, 73 (1976), pp. 75–99.

Coss, P. R., William Lamont and Neil Evans, 'British History: Past, Present - And Future?', *Past and Present*, 119 (1988), pp. 171–203.

Croll, Andy, 'Mabon's Day: The Rise and Fall of a Lib-Lab Holiday in the South Wales Coalfield, 1888–1898', *Labour History Review*, 72:1 (2007), pp. 49–68.

Crook, Rosemary, '"Tidy Women": Women in the Rhondda Between the Wars', *Oral History*, 10:2 (1982), pp. 40–6.

Croucher, Richard, '"Divisions in the Movement": The National Unemployed Workers' Movement and Its Rivals in Comparative Perspective', in Geoff Andrews, Nina Fishman and Kevin Morgan (eds), *Opening the Books: Essays on the Social and Cultural History of British Communism* (London, 1995), pp. 23–43.

—— 'Editorial: The History of Unemployed Movements', Special Issue on the History of Unemployed Movements, *Labour History Review*, 73:1 (2008), pp. 1–17.

Crowther, M. A., 'Family Responsibility and State Responsibility in Britain Before the Welfare State', *The Historical Journal*, 25:1 (1982), pp. 131–45.

Daunton, M. J., 'Miners' Houses: South Wales and the Great Northern Coalfield, 1880–1914', *International Review of Social History*, 25:2 (1980), pp. 143–75.

—— 'Down the Pit: Work in the Great Northern and South Wales Coalfields, 1870–1914', *The Economic History Review*, 34:4 (1981), pp. 578–97.

Davies, Sam, 'The Membership of the National Unemployed Workers' Movement, 1923–1938', *Labour History Review*, 57:1 (1992), pp. 29–36.

—— and Bob Morley, 'The Reactions of Municipal Voters in Yorkshire to the Second Labour Government, 1929–32', in Matthew Worley (ed.), *Labour's Grass Roots: Essays on the Activities of Local Labour Parties and Members, 1918–45* (Aldershot, 2005), pp. 124–46.

Deacon, Alan, 'An End to the Means Test? Social Security and the Attlee Government', *Journal of Social Policy*, 11:3 (1982), pp. 289–306.

—— 'Systems of Interwar Unemployment Relief', in Sean Glynn and Alan Booth (eds), *The Road to Full Employment* (London, 1987), pp. 31–42.

Deacon, Bernard and Moira Donald, 'In Search of Community History', *Family and Community History*, 7:1 (2004), pp. 13–18.

Digby, Anne, 'Changing Welfare Cultures in Region and State', *Twentieth Century British History*, 17:3 (2006), pp. 297–322.

Dowie, J. A., '1919–20 Is in Need of Attention', *Economic History Review*, 28:3 (1975), pp. 429–50.

Egan, David, '"A Cult of Their Own": Syndicalism and *The Miners' Next Step*', in Alan Campbell, Nina Fishman and David Howell (eds), *Miners, Unions and Politics 1910–47* (Aldershot, 1996), pp. 13–33.

Evans, Neil, 'Cardiff's Labour Tradition', *Llafur*, 4:2 (1985), pp. 77–90.

—— 'Two Paths to Economic Development: Wales and the North-East of England', in Pat Hudson (ed.), *Regions and Industries: A Perspective on the Industrial Revolution in Britain* (Cambridge, 1989), pp. 201–27.

—— 'Patterns of Protest and Regional Labour Implantation in South Wales and the North-East of England, 1780–1950', Regional Implantation of the Labour Movement in Britain and the Netherlands, Papers Presented to the Seventh British-Dutch Conference on Labour History, Groningen, *Tijdschrift voor sociale geschiedenis*, 2/3 (1992), pp. 212–30.

—— 'Across the Universe: Racial Violence and the Post-War Crisis in Imperial Britain, 1919–25', in Diane Frost (ed.), *Ethnic Labour and British Imperial Trade: A History of Ethnic Seafarers in the UK* (London, 1995), pp. 59–88.

—— '"As Rich as California ...": Opening and Closing the Frontier: Wales 1780–1870', in Gareth Elwyn Jones and Dai Smith (eds), *The People of Wales* (Llandysul, 1999), pp. 111–44.

—— '"South Wales Has Been Roused as Never Before": Marching Against the Means Test, 1934–36', in David W. Howell and Kenneth O. Morgan (eds), *Crime, Protest and Police in Modern British Society: Essays in Memory of David J. V. Jones* (Cardiff, 1999), pp. 176–206.

—— 'Life After Coal', *Agenda* (Autumn, 2004), pp. 83–4.

Ffrancon, Gwenno, 'Documenting the Depression in South Wales: *Today We Live* and *Eastern Valley*', *Welsh History Review*, 22:1 (2004), pp. 103–25.

Fitzpatrick, Sheila and Robert Gellately, 'Introduction to the Practices of Denunciation in Modern European History', in Sheila Fitzpatrick and

Robert Gellately (eds), *Accusatory Practices: Denunciation in Modern European History, 1789–1989* (Chicago, 1997), pp. 1–21.

Fredrickson, George M., 'Exceptionalism to Variability: Recent Developments in Cross-National Comparative History', *The Journal of American History*, 82:2 (1995), pp. 587–604.

Friedlander, D. and R. J. Roshier, 'A Study of Internal Migration in England and Wales: Part I', *Population Studies*, 19:3 (1966), pp. 239–79.

Gallie, Duncan, 'Social Consequences of Long-Term Unemployment in Britain', in Odile Benôit-Guilbot and Duncan Gallie (eds), *Long-Term Unemployment* (London, 1994), pp. 121–36.

Geary, Dick, 'The Myth of the Radical Miner', in Stefan Berger, Andy Croll and Norman LaPorte (eds), *Towards a Comparative History of Coalfield Societies* (Aldershot, 2005), pp. 43–64.

Glynn, Sean, 'The Scale and Nature of the Problem', in Sean Glynn and Alan Booth (eds), *The Road to Full Employment* (London, 1987), pp. 3–16.

Grace, R., 'Tyneside Housing in the Nineteenth Century', in Norman McCord (ed.), *Essays in Tyneside Labour History* (Newcastle, 1977), pp. 178–97.

Hall, Valerie Gordon, 'Contrasting Female Identities: Women in Coal Mining Communities in Northumberland, England, 1900–1939', *Journal of Women's History*, 13:2 (2001), pp. 107–31.

—— 'The Anatomy of Changing Consciousness: The Miners of Northumberland, 1898–1914', *Labour History Review*, 66:2 (2001), pp. 165–86.

Hannam, June, 'Women and Labour Politics', in Matthew Worley (ed.), *Foundations of the British Labour Party: Identities, Cultures and Perspectives, 1900–39* (Aldershot, 2009), pp. 171–92.

Heesom, A. J., and Brendan Duffy, 'Debate: Coal, Class and Education in the North-East', *Past and Present*, 90 (1981), pp. 136–41.

Hepburn, A. C., 'The Belfast Riots of 1935', *Social History*, 15:1 (1990), p. 76.

Howkins, Alan and John Saville, 'The Nineteen Thirties: A Revisionist History', *Socialist Register*, 16 (1979), pp. 89–100.

James, Leighton, 'Trade Union Development in the Ruhr and South Wales, 1890–1914', in Stefan Berger, Andy Croll and Norman LaPorte (eds), *Towards a Comparative History of Coalfield Societies* (Aldershot, 2005), pp. 253–66.

Johnson, Paul, 'Credit and Thrift and the British Working Class, 1870–1939', in Jay Winter (ed.), *The Working Class in Modern British History: Essays in Honour of Henry Pelling* (Cambridge, 1983), pp. 147–70.

Jones, Bill, 'Banqueting at a Moveable Feast: Wales 1870–1914', in Gareth Elwyn Jones and Dai Smith (eds), *The People of Wales* (Llandysul, 1999), pp. 145–78.

Jones, Dot, 'Counting the Cost of Coal: Women's Lives in the Rhondda 1881–1911', in Angela V. John (ed.), *Our Mothers' Land: Chapters in Welsh Women's History 1830–1939* (Cardiff, 1991), pp. 109–33.

Jones, Rosemary, 'Sociability, Solidarity, and Social Exclusion: Women's Activism in the South Wales Coalfield, ca. 1830–1939', in Jaclyn J. Gier and Laurie Mercier (eds), *Mining Women: Gender in the Development of a Global Industry, 1670 to 2005* (Hampshire, 2006), pp. 96–118.

Kerr, Clark and Abraham Siegel, 'The Interindustry Propensity to Strike – An International Comparison', in E. W. Evans and S. W. Creigh (eds), *Industrial Conflict in Britain* (London, 1977), pp. 233–53.

Laybourn, Keith, '"Waking up to the Fact that there are any Unemployed": Women, Unemployment and the Domestic Solution in Britain, 1918–1939', *History*, 88:292 (2003), pp. 606–23.

Levine-Clark, Marjorie, 'The Politics of Preference: Masculinity, Marital Status and Unemployment Relief in Post-First World War Britain', *Cultural and Social History*, 7:2 (2010), pp. 233–52.

Lewis, Richard, 'Political Culture and Ideology, 1900–1918', in Duncan Tanner, Chris Williams and Deian Hopkin (eds), *The Labour Party in Wales 1900–2000* (Cardiff, 2000), pp. 86–109.

Light, Julie, 'The 1917 Commission of Enquiry into Industrial Unrest – A Welsh Report', *Welsh History Review*, 21:4 (2003), pp. 704–28.

Lorenz, Chris, 'Comparative Historiography: Problems and Perspectives', *History and Theory*, 38:1 (1999), pp. 25–39.

Lynn, Pauline, 'The Influence of Class and Gender: Female Political Organisations in County Durham in the Interwar Years', *North East History*, 31 (1997), pp. 43–64.

MacDermott, T. P., 'Irish Workers on Tyneside in the 19th Century', in Norman McCord (ed.), *Essays in Tyneside Labour History* (Newcastle, 1977), pp. 154–77.

Mates, Lewis, 'A "Most Fruitful Period"? The North East District Communist Party and the Popular Front, 1935–9', *North East History*, 35 (2004), pp. 54–98.

—— 'Durham and South Wales Miners and the Spanish Civil War', *Twentieth Century British History*, 17:3 (2006), pp. 373–95.

McClelland, Keith, 'Masculinity and the "Representative Artisan" in Britain 1850–80', in Michael Roper and John Tosh (eds), *Manful Assertions: Masculinities in Britain since 1800* (London, 1991), pp. 74–91.

McCord, Norman, 'The Regional Identity of North-East England in the Nineteenth and Twentieth Centuries', in Edward Royle (ed.), *Issues of Regional Identity: In Honour of John Marshall* (Manchester, 1998), pp. 102–17.

McIlroy, John, 'South Wales', in John McIlroy, Alan Campbell and Keith Gildart (eds), *Industrial Politics and the 1926 Mining Lockout: The Struggle for Dignity* (Cardiff, 2004), pp. 139–56.

—— and Alan Campbell, 'Fighting the Legions of Hell', in John McIlroy, Alan Campbell and Keith Gildart (eds), *Industrial Politics and the 1926 Mining Lockout: The Struggle for Dignity* (Cardiff, 2004), pp. 49–106.

Miller, Frederic, 'The Unemployment Policy of the National Government, 1931–1936', *The Historical Journal*, 19:2 (1976), pp. 453–76

—— 'The British Unemployment Assistance Crisis of 1935', *Journal of Contemporary History*, 14 (1979), pp. 329–52.

Mills, Dennis, 'Defining Community: A Critical Review of "Community"', *Family and Community History*, 7:1 (2004), pp. 5–12.

Morgan, Jane, 'Police and Labour in the Age of Lindsay, 1910–1936', *Llafur*, 5:1 (1988), pp. 15–20.

Morgan, Kenneth O., 'Post-War Reconstruction in Wales, 1918 and 1945', in Jay Winter (ed.), *The Working Class in Modern British History: Essays in Honour of Henry Pelling* (Cambridge, 1983), pp. 82–98.

Morris, J. H. and L. J. Williams, 'The South Wales Sliding Scale', in W. E. Minchinton (ed.), *Industrial South Wales 1750–1914* (London, 1969), pp. 218–31.

Naylor, Barry E., 'Ramsay MacDonald and Seaham Labour Politics', *North-East Labour History Bulletin*, 15 (1981), pp. 4–39.

O'Leary, Paul, 'Networking Respectability: Class, Gender and Ethnicity among the Irish in South Wales, 1845–1914', *Immigrants and Minorities*, 23:2–3 (2005), pp. 255–75.

Olechnowicz, Andrzej, 'Unemployed Workers, "Enforced Leisure" and Education for "the Right use of Leisure" in Britain in the 1930s', *Labour History Review*, 70:1 (2005), pp. 27–52.

Pearce, Kit, 'Newcastle's Tyneside Flats 1850–1900: By-Law Housing or Cultural Phenomenon?', in Bill Lancaster (ed.), *Working Class Housing on Tyneside 1850–1939* (Whitley Bay, 1994), pp. 39–85.

Penlington, Neil, 'Masculinity and Domesticity in 1930s South Wales: Did Unemployment Change the Domestic Division of Labour?', *Twentieth Century British History*, 21:3 (2010), pp. 281–99.

Pimlott, Ben, 'The North East: Back to the 1930s?', *The Political Quarterly*, 52:1 (1981), pp. 51–63.

—— 'Unemployment and "the Unemployed" in North-East England', *The Political Quarterly*, 56:4 (1985), pp. 346–60.

Preece, Diane, '"Defend the rights of the roads your fathers fought for": The Blaina Riot of 1935', *Llafur*, 10:2 (2009), pp. 73–100.

Reiss, Matthias, 'Forgotten Pioneers of the National Protest March: The National League of the Blind's Marches to London, 1920 & 1936', *Labour History Review*, 70:2 (2005), pp. 133–65.

—— 'Not All Were Apathetic: National Hunger Marches as Political Rituals in Interwar Britain', in Jörg Neuheiser and Michael Schaich (eds), *Political Rituals in Great Britain 1700–2000* (Augsburg, 2006), pp. 93–121.

—— 'Introduction', in Matthias Reiss (ed.), *The Street as Stage: Protest Marches and Public Rallies Since the Nineteenth Century* (Oxford, 2007), pp. 1–21.

—— 'Marching on the Capital: National Protest Marches of the British Unemployed in the 1920s and 1930s', in Matthias Reiss (ed.), *The Street as Stage: Protest Marches and Public Rallies Since the Nineteenth Century* (Oxford, 2007), pp. 147–68.

—— 'Circulars, Surveys and Support: Trades Councils and the Marches of 1936', *Labour History Review*, 73:1 (2008), pp. 89–112.

—— and Matt Perry, 'Beyond Marienthal: Understanding Movements of the Unemployed', in Matthias Reiss and Matt Perry (eds), *Unemployment and Protest: New Perspectives on Two Centuries of Contention* (Oxford, 2011), pp. 3–37.

Rowe, D. J., 'The Population of Nineteenth Century Tyneside', in Norman McCord (ed.), *Essays in Tyneside Labour History* (Newcastle, 1977), pp. 1–24.

Royle, Edward, 'Introduction: Regions and Identities', in Edward Royle (ed.), *Issues of Regional Identity: In Honour of John Marshall* (Manchester, 1998), pp. 1–13.

Rucht, Dieter, 'On the Sociology of Protest Marches', in Matthias Reiss (ed.), *The Street as Stage: Protest Marches and Public Rallies Since the Nineteenth Century* (Oxford, 2007), pp. 49–57.

Sewell, William H., 'Marc Bloch and the Logic of Comparative History', *History and Theory*, 6 (1967), pp. 208–18.

Smith, David, 'Tonypandy 1910: Definitions of Community', *Past and Present*, 87 (1980), pp. 158–84.

Smith, R., 'The Reform of Local Government Finance, 1928–37: A Study of South Wales', *Welsh History Review*, 21:1 (2002), pp. 149–79.

Stead, Peter, 'The Voluntary Response to Mass Unemployment in South Wales', in Walter Minchinton (ed.), *Reactions to Social and Economic Change*, Exeter Papers in Economic History,12 (1979), pp. 97–117.

Stevenson, John, 'The Making of Unemployment Policy, 1931–1935', in Michael Bentley and John Stevenson (eds), *High and Low Politics in Modern Britain* (Oxford, 1983), pp. 182–213.

Supple, Barry, 'The State and Social Investigation in Britain Between The World Wars', in Michael J. Lacey and Mary O. Furner (eds), *The State and Social Investigation in Britain and the United States* (Cambridge, 1993), pp. 365–87.

Tanner, Duncan, 'The Labour Party and Electoral Politics in the Coalfield', in Alan Campbell, Nina Fishman and David Howell (eds), *Miners, Unions and Politics 1910–47* (Aldershot, 1996), pp. 59–92.

—— 'The Pattern of Labour Politics, 1918–1939', in Duncan Tanner, Chris Williams and Deian Hopkin (eds), *The Labour Party in Wales 1900–2000* (Cardiff, 2000), pp. 113–39.

Taylor, Andrew, 'So Many Cases But So Little Comparison: Problems of Comparing Mineworkers', in Stefan Berger, Andy Croll and Norman LaPorte (eds), *Towards a Comparative History of Coalfield Societies* (Aldershot, 2005), pp. 12–28.

—— 'Deadweight or Bedrock? The Mineworkers and Labour', in Matthew Worley (ed.), *Foundations of the British Labour Party: Identities, Cultures and Perspectives, 1900–39* (Aldershot, 2009), pp. 57–76.

Taylor, Avram, '"More Tick Than Big Ben": Working Class Credit on Tyneside in the Interwar Years', *North East Labour History Bulletin*, 26 (1992), pp. 48–86.

—— '"You Never Told Your Mam": Women's Management of Household Finances and Credit During the Inter-war Period', in *North East Labour History Society Bulletin*, 30 (1996), pp. 51–65.

Thompson, Steven, '"That Beautiful Summer of Severe Austerity": Health, Diet and the Working-Class Domestic Economy in South Wales in 1926', *Welsh History Review*, 21:3 (2003), pp. 552–74.

—— '"Conservative Bloom on Socialism's Compost Heap": Working-Class Home Ownership in South Wales, c. 1890–1939', in R. R. Davies and Geraint H. Jenkins (eds), *From Medieval to Modern Wales: Historical Essays in Honour of Kenneth O. Morgan and Ralph A. Griffiths* (Cardiff, 2004), pp. 246–63.

—— 'Unemployment, Poverty and Women's Health in Inter-war South Wales', in Pamela Michael and Charles Webster (eds), *Health and Society in Twentieth-Century Wales* (Cardiff, 2006), pp. 98–122.

Thorpe, Andrew, 'The Industrial Meaning of "Gradualism": The Labour Party and Industry, 1918–1931', *The Journal of British Studies*, 35:1 (1996), pp. 84–113.

—— 'The Membership of the Communist Party of Great Britain, 1920–45', *Historical Journal*, 43:3 (2000), pp. 777–800.

Tosh, John, 'Masculinities in an Industrializing Society: Britain, 1800–1914', *Journal of British Studies*, 44:2 (2005), pp. 330–42.

Turner, Graham, 'The Stronghold of Labour', in Martin Bulmer (ed.), *Mining and Social Change: Durham County in the Twentieth Century* (London, 1978), pp. 122–7.

Turner, Ian, 'A Spot of Bother', *North East Labour History*, 18 (1984), pp. 40–7.

Walton, J. K., 'Review of *North East England, 1850–1914*, Graeme J. Milne', Institute of Historical Research (Review no. 579), http://www.history.ac.uk/reviews/ paper/ walton2.html, date accessed 8 November 2007.

Ward, Stephanie, '"The Workers Are in the Mood to Fight the Act": Protest Against the Means Test, 1931–1935', in Matthias Reiss and Matt Perry (eds), *Unemployment and Protest: New Perspectives on Two Centuries of Contention* (Oxford, 2011), pp. 245–64.

Webster, Charles, 'Health, Welfare and Unemployment During the Depression', *Past and Present*, 109 (1985), pp. 204–30.

Whiteside, Noel, 'The Social Consequences of Interwar Unemployment', in Sean Glynn and Alan Booth (eds), *The Road to Full Employment* (London, 1987), pp. 17–42.

Williams, Chris, '"The Hope of the British Proletariat": The South Wales Miners, 1910–1947', in Alan Campbell, Nina Fishman and David Howell (eds), *Miners, Unions and Politics 1910–47* (Aldershot, 1996), pp. 121–44.

—— 'Labour and the Challenge of Local Government, 1919–1939', in Duncan Tanner, Chris Williams and Deian Hopkin (eds), *The Labour Party in Wales 1900–2000* (Cardiff, 2000), pp. 140–65.

Williams, John, '1890–1930: The Rise and Decline of the Welsh Economy', in John Williams, *Was Wales Industrialised? Essays in Modern Welsh History* (Llandysul, 1995), pp. 37–57.

—— 'The Climacteric of the 1890s', in John Williams, *Was Wales Industrialised? Essays in Modern Welsh History* (Llandysul, 1995), pp. 262–83.

—— 'The Coalowners', in John Williams, *Was Wales Industrialised? Essays in Modern Welsh History* (Llandysul, 1995), pp. 97–122

—— 'The Myth of Miners' Solidarity', in John Williams, *Was Wales Industrialised? Essays in Modern Welsh History* (Llandysul, 1995), pp. 310–33.

—— 'The Road to Tonypandy', in John Williams, *Was Wales Industrialised? Essays in Modern Welsh History* (Llandysul, 1995), pp. 214–37.

—— 'The Economic and Social Context', in Duncan Tanner, Chris Williams and Deian Hopkin (eds), *The Labour Party in Wales 1900–2000* (Cardiff, 2000), pp. 23–39.

Williams, Sian Rhiannon, 'The Bedwellty Board of Guardians and the Default Act of 1927', *Llafur*, 2:4 (1979), pp. 65–77.

Worley, Matthew, 'Left Turn: A Reassessment of the Communist Party of Great Britain in the Third Period, 1928–33', *Twentieth Century British History*, 11:4 (2000), pp. 353–78.

Secondary books

Allen, E., J. F. Clarke, N. McCord and D. J. Rowe, *The North-East Engineers' Strikes of 1871: The Nine Hours' League* (Newcastle-upon-Tyne, 1971).

Andrews, Geoff, Nina Fishman and Kevin Morgan (eds), *Opening the Books: Essays on the Social and Cultural History of British Communism* (London, 1995).

Armstrong, Keith and Huw Beynon (eds), *Hello, Are You Working? Memories of the Thirties in the North East of England* (Newcastle, 1977).

Bagguley, Paul, *From Protest to Acquiescence? Political Movements of the Unemployed* (London, 1991).

Barke, Mike, *Social Change in Benwell* (Benwell Community Development Project, Newcastle-upon-Tyne, 1977).

Barker, Colin and Paul Kennedy (eds), *To Make Another World: Studies in Protest and Collective Action* (Aldershot, 1996).

Barron, Hester, *The 1926 Miners' Lockout: Meanings of Community in the Durham Coalfield* (Oxford, 2010).

Baxendale, John and Chris Pawling, *Narrating the Thirties: A Decade in the Making, 1930 to the Present* (London, 1996).

Beddoe, Deirdre, *Out of the Shadows: A History of Women in Twentieth-Century Wales* (Cardiff, 2000).

Benôit-Guilbot, Odile and Duncan Gallie (eds), *Long-Term Unemployment* (London, 1994).

Benson, John, *Affluence and Authority: A Social History of Twentieth Century Britain* (London, 2005).

Berger, Stefan, Andy Croll and Norman LaPorte (eds), *Towards a Comparative History of Coalfield Societies* (Aldershot, 2005).

Beynon, Huw and Terry Austrin, *Masters and Servants: Class and Patronage in the Making of a Labour Organisation: The Durham Miners and the English Political Tradition* (London, 1994).

Breuilly, John (ed.), *Labour and Liberalism in Nineteenth-Century Europe: Essays in Comparative History* (Manchester, 1994).

Brierley, John, *In the Shadow of the Means Test Man: Memories of a Derbyshire Childhood* (Highedge Historical Society, 1995).

Bruley, Sue, *Women in Britain Since 1900* (Hampshire, 1999).

—— *The Men and Women of 1926: A Gender and Social History of the General Strike and Lockout in South Wales* (Cardiff, 2010).

Bulmer, Martin (ed.), *Mining and Social Change: Durham County in the Twentieth Century* (London, 1978).

Burnett, John, *Idle Hands: The Experience of Unemployment, 1790–1990* (London, 1984).

Campbell, Alan, Nina Fishman and David Howell (eds), *Miners, Unions and Politics 1910–47* (Aldershot, 1996).

Chandler, J. A., *Explaining Local Government: Local Government in Britain Since 1800* (Manchester, 2007).

Charlesworth, Andrew, David Gilbert, Adrian Randall, Humphrey Southall and Chris Wrigley, *An Atlas of Industrial Protest in Britain 1750–1990* (London, 1996).

Church, Roy and Quentin Outram, *Strikes and Solidarity: Coalfield Conflict in Britain 1889–1966* (Cambridge, 1998).

Cohen, Anthony P., *The Symbolic Construction of Community* (London, 1985).

Colls, Robert and Bill Lancaster (eds), *Newcastle upon Tyne: A Modern History* (Chichester, 2001).

—— and Bill Lancaster (eds), *Geordies: Roots of Regionalism* (Newcastle-upon-Tyne, 2005 edition).

Croucher, Richard, *We Refuse to Starve in Silence: A History of the National Unemployed Workers' Movement, 1920–46* (London, 1987).

Daunton, M. J., *Coal Metropolis: Cardiff 1870–1914* (Leicester, 1977).

Davies, John, *A History of Modern Wales* (London, 1994 edition).

Davies, R. R. and Geraint H. Jenkins (eds), *From Medieval to Modern Wales: Historical Essays in Honour of Kenneth O. Morgan and Ralph A. Griffiths* (Cardiff, 2004).

Deacon, Alan, *In Search of the Scrounger: The Administration of Unemployment Insurance in Britain 1920–1931* (London, 1976).

—— and Jonathan Bradshaw, *Reserved for the Poor: The Means Test in British Social Policy* (Oxford, 1983).

Douglass, David, *Pit Life in County Durham: Rank and File Movements and Workers' Control*, History Workshop Pamphlets, 6 (1972).

—— *The Miners of North Durham* (Socialist Union Pamphlet No. 3) (1975).

Emery, Norman, *The Coalminers of Durham* (Durham, 1992).

Evans, E. W., *Mabon: A Study in Trade Union Leadership* (Cardiff, 1959).

—— *The Miners of South Wales* (Cardiff, 1961).

Ferguson, Alex, *The Pineapple King of Jarrow and Other Stories* (North Shields, 2004).

Fitzpatrick, Sheila and Robert Gellately (eds), *Accusatory Practices: Denunciation in Modern European History, 1789–1989* (Chicago, 1997).

Flanagan, Richard, *'Parish-Fed Bastards': A History of the Politics of the Unemployed in Britain, 1884–1939* (London, 1991).

Foot, Michael, *Aneurin Bevan: A Biography, Volume One, 1897–1945* (London, 1982).

Forsberg, Ray, *Means Test Kid: A Childhood in a Yorkshire Fishing Port during the 'Hungry Thirties'* (Hutton, 1985).

Francis, Hywel, *Miners Against Fascism: Wales and the Spanish Civil War* (London, 1984).

—— and Dai Smith, *The Fed: A History of the South Wales Miners in the Twentieth Century* (Cardiff, 1998).

Fraser, Derek, *The Evolution of the Welfare State: A History of Social Policy Since the Industrial Revolution* (Basingstoke, 2003).

Gardiner, Juliet, *The Thirties: An Intimate History* (London, 2010).

Garside, W. R., *The Durham Miners, 1919–1960* (London, 1971).

—— *British Unemployment 1919–1939: A Study in Public Policy* (Cambridge, 1990).

Gazeley, Ian, *Poverty in Britain, 1900–1965* (London, 2003).

Gier, Jaclyn J. and Laurie Mercier (eds), *Mining Women: Gender in the Development of a Global Industry, 1670 to 2005* (Hampshire, 2006).

Gilbert, David, *Class, Community and Collective Action: Social Change in Two British Coalfields, 1850–1926* (Oxford, 1992).

Glynn, Sean and Alan Booth (eds), *The Road to Full Employment* (London, 1987).

Gray, Nigel (ed.), *The Worst of Times: An Oral History of the Great Depression in Britain* (Aldershot, 1985).

Herbert, Trevor and Gareth Elwyn Jones (eds), *Wales Between the Wars* (Cardiff, 1988).

Hind, Joe, *A Shieldfield Childhood* (Newcastle-upon-Tyne, 1994).

Hobsbawm, E. J., *Primitive Rebels* (Manchester, 1959).

Horner, Arthur, *Incorrigible Rebel* (London, 1960).

Isaac, Peter (ed.), *Newspapers in the Northeast: The 'Fourth Estate' at Work in Northumberland and Durham* (Richmond, 1999).

Jenkinson, Jacqueline, *Black 1919: Riot, Racism and Resistance in Imperial Britain* (Liverpool, 2009).

John, Angela V. (ed.), *Our Mothers' Land: Chapters in Welsh Women's History 1830–1939* (Cardiff, 1991).

Jones, Gareth Elwyn and Dai Smith (eds), *The People of Wales* (Llandysul, 1999).

Kelly, Stephen F., *Idle Hands Clenched Fists: The Depression in a Shipyard Town* (Nottingham, 1987).

Kingsford, Peter, *The Hunger Marchers in Britain 1920–1939* (London, 1982).

Lamont-Brown, Raymond, *Carnegie 'The Richest Man in the World'* (Stroud, 2005).

Lancaster, Bill (ed.), *Working Class Housing on Tyneside 1850–1939* (Whitley Bay, 1994).

Laybourn, Keith, *The Evolution of British Social Policy and the Welfare State* (Keele, 1995).

Lewis, Richard, *Leaders and Teachers: Adult Education and the Challenge of Labour in South Wales, 1906–1940* (Cardiff, 1993).

Macintyre, Stuart, *Little Moscows: Communism and Working-Class Militancy in Inter-war Britain* (London, 1980).

Mason, Anthony, 'The General Strike in the North East', *Occasional Papers in Economic and Social History 3* (Hull, 1970).

McCord, Norman (ed.), *Essays in Tyneside Labour History* (Newcastle, 1977).

—— *North East England: An Economic and Social History* (London, 1979).

McIlroy, John, Alan Campbell and Keith Gildart (eds), *Industrial Politics and the 1926 Mining Lockout: The Struggle for Dignity* (Cardiff, 2004).

McKibbin, Ross, *The Ideologies of Class: Social Relations in Britain, 1880–1950* (Oxford, 1991).

—— *Classes and Cultures: England 1918–1951* (Oxford, 1998)

Minchinton, W. E. (ed.), *Industrial South Wales 1750–1914* (London, 1969).

Moore, Bill, *All Out! The Dramatic Story of the Sheffield Demonstration Against Dole Cuts on February 6th 1935* (Sheffield, 1985).

Moore, Robert, *Pit-Men, Preachers and Politics: The Effects of Methodism in a Durham Mining Community* (Cambridge, 1974).

Morgan, Jane, *Conflict and Order: The Police and Labour Disputes in England and Wales 1900–1939* (Oxford, 1987).

Morgan, Kenneth O., *Rebirth of a Nation: A History of Modern Wales* (Oxford, 2002 edition).

Neuheiser, Jörg and Michael Schaich (eds), *Political Rituals in Great Britain 1700–2000* (Augsburg, 2006).

Nicholas, Kate, *The Social Effects of Unemployment on Teesside, 1919–39* (Manchester, 1986).

North Tyneside Community Development Project, *North Shields: Working Class Politics and Housing 1900–1977* (Newcastle-Upon-Tyne, 1978).

Oldfield, Sybil, *This Working-Day World: Women's Lives and Culture(s) in Britain 1914–1945* (London, 1994).

Overy, Richard, *The Morbid Age: Britain and the Crisis of Civilization, 1919–1939* (London, 2009).

Perry, Matt, *Bread and Work: The Experience of Unemployment, 1918–1939* (London, 2000).

—— *The Jarrow Crusade: Protest and Legend* (Sunderland, 2005).

—— *Prisoners of Want: The Experience and Protest of the Unemployed in France, 1921–45* (Aldershot, 2007).

Piven, Frances Fox and Richard A. Cloward, *Poor People's Movements: Why They Succeed, How They Fail* (New York, 1977).

Pugh, Martin, *We Danced All Night: A Social History of Britain Between the Wars* (London, 2008).

Purvis, June, *Women's History: Britain, 1850–1945. An Introduction* (London, 1995).

Reiss, Matthias (ed.), *The Street as Stage: Protest Marches and Public Rallies Since the Nineteenth Century* (Oxford, 2007).

—— and Matt Perry (eds), *Unemployment and Protest: New Perspectives on Two Centuries of Contention* (Oxford, 2011).

Richards, Andrew, 'Mobilizing the Powerless: Collective Protest Action of the Unemployed in the Interwar Period', Working Paper 175, Juan March Institute (2002).

Rowlands, Ted, *'Something Must Be Done': South Wales v Whitehall, 1921–1951* (Merthyr Tydfil, 2000).

Royle, Edward (ed.), *Issues of Regional Identity: In Honour of John Marshall* (Manchester, 1998).

Skinner, Jack, *Newcastle Memories: Childhood* (Norfolk, 1994).

Slater, Howard, *Working Class Novelists 1930–1950* (Working Press Association, London, 1994).

Smith, Dai, *Aneurin Bevan and the World of South Wales* (Cardiff, 1993).

Smith, David, *Lewis Jones* (Cardiff, 1982).

Stabler, Arthur, 'Ganning along the Scotswood Road: A Social History of the Scotwood Community from 1847 the Foundation of "Armstrong's Factory"'. *A Paper Read Before the British Association for the Advancement of Science, Annual Meeting, Lancaster, 1976.* (Author's copyright).

Stevenson, John and Chris Cook, *Britain in the Depression: Society and Politics 1929–39* (London, 1994).

Thomas, Gwyn, *Sorrow for Thy Sons* (London, 1986).

Thompson, Steven, *Unemployment, Poverty and Health in Interwar South Wales* (Cardiff, 2006).

Thorpe, Andrew, *The British General Election of 1931* (Oxford, 1991).

—— *A History of the British Labour Party* (London, 1997).

—— *The British Communist Party and Moscow, 1920–43* (Manchester, 2000).

Todd, Nigel, *In Excited Times: The People Against the Blackshirts* (Newcastle-upon-Tyne, 1995).

Vernon, James, *Hunger: A Modern History* (Cambridge, MA, 2007).

Vincent, David, *Poor Citizens: The State and the Poor in Twentieth Century Britain* (Harlow, 1991).

—— *The Culture of Secrecy: Britain, 1832–1998* (Oxford, 1998).

White, Carol and Sian Rhiannon Williams (eds), *Struggle or Starve: Women's Lives in the South Wales Valleys Between the Two World Wars* (Dinas Powys, 2002).

Whiteside, Noel, *Bad Times: Unemployment in British Social and Political History* (London, 1991).

Williams, Chris, *Democratic Rhondda: Politics and Society, 1885–1951* (Cardiff, 1996).

—— *Capitalism, Community and Conflict: The South Wales Coalfield, 1898–1947* (Cardiff, 1998).

Williams, John, *Digest of Welsh Historical Statistics Volume I* (Pontypool, 1985).

—— *Was Wales Industrialised? Essays in Modern Welsh History* (Llandysul, 1995).

Williamson, Bill, *Class, Culture and Community: A Biographical Study of Social Change in Mining* (London, 1982).

Williamson, Philip, *National Crisis and National Government: British Politics, the Economy and Empire, 1926–1932* (Cambridge, 1992).

Winter, Jay (ed.), *The Working Class in Modern British History: Essays in Honour of Henry Pelling* (Cambridge, 1983).

Worley, Matthew, *Class Against Class: the Communist Party in Britain Between the Wars* (London, 2002).

—— (ed.), *Labour's Grass Roots: Essays on the Activities of Local Labour Parties and Members, 1918–45* (Aldershot, 2005).

—— (ed.), *Foundations of the British Labour Party: Identities, Cultures and Perspectives, 1900–39* (Aldershot, 2009).

Unpublished theses

Ennis, Frank, *The Jarrow March of 1936: The Symbolic Expression of Protest* (MA thesis, University of Durham, 1982).

Rowlands, Bryn, *Class Against Class: Communists and the Labour Movement in the Ebbw Fach Valley, 1929–1935* (MA thesis, University of Glamorgan, 2007).

Thompson Steven, *A Social History of Health in Interwar South Wales* (Unpublished PhD thesis, Aberystwyth University, 2001).

Index